D1260597

Were slaves property or human beings under the law? In crafting answers to this question, Southern judges designed efficient laws that protected property rights and helped slavery to remain economically viable. But by preserving property rights, judges sheltered the persons embodied by that property – the slaves themselves. Slave law therefore had unintended consequences: It generated rules that judges could apply to free persons, precedents that became the foundation for laws designed to protect ordinary Americans.

The Bondsman's Burden is a compelling analysis of the common law of Southern slavery. It uses rigorous economic tools to inspect thousands of legal disputes heard in Southern antebellum courts, disputes involving servants, employees, accident victims, animals, and other chattel property, as well as slaves. The common law did not favor every individual slaveowner who brought a grievance to court, although it supported the institution of slavery.

The Bondsman's Burden

Cambridge Historical Studies in American Law and Society

Editors

Arthur McEvoy   *University of Wisconsin Law School*
Christopher Tomlins   *American Bar Foundation*

The Bondsman's Burden

An Economic Analysis of the Common Law of
Southern Slavery

Jenny Bourne Wahl

St. Olaf College

CAMBRIDGE
UNIVERSITY PRESS

PUBLISHED BY THE PRESS SYNDICATE OF THE UNIVERSITY OF CAMBRIDGE
The Pitt Building, Trumpington Street, Cambridge CB2 1RP, United Kingdom

CAMBRIDGE UNIVERSITY PRESS
The Edinburgh Building, Cambridge CB2 2RU, United Kingdom
40 West 20th Street, New York, NY 10011-4211, USA
10 Stamford Road, Oakleigh, Melbourne 3166, Australia

First published 1998

Printed in the United States of America

Typeset in New Baskerville

Library of Congress Cataloging-in-Publication Data
Wahl, Jenny Bourne.
The bondsman's burden: an economic analysis of the common law of
southern slavery / Jenny Bourne Wahl.
p.   cm. – (Cambridge historical studies in American law and society)
Includes bibliographical references and index.
ISBN 0-521-59238-0 (hb)
1. Slavery – Law and legislation – United States – History.
I. Title. II. Series.
KF4545.S5W34   1998
342.73'087 – dc21   97-14087
CIP

A catalog record for this book is available from the British Library.

ISBN 0 521 59238 0 hardback

The publisher wishes to acknowledge the generous assistance of St. Olaf
College toward the publication of this book.

For
Ned

Contents

Contents   ix

Acknowledgments

To The Glory Of God
And In Remembrance Of The Many Personal
Servants Buried Here Before 1865.
Faithful And Devoted In Life, Their Friends
And Masters Laid Them Near Them In Death,
With Affection And Gratitude.
Their Memory Remains, Though Their Wooden Markers,
Like The Way Of Life Of That Day,
Are Gone Forever.
— Marker at the Old Stone Chapel in Millwood, Virginia

Many thanks to those who commented on various parts of this book, including Lee Alston, Jon Bessler, Len Burman, Paul Finkelman, Farley Grubb, Naomi Lamoreaux, Pat Longan, Thomas Morris, Martha Paas, Mark Ramseyer, Melissa Raphan, Tom Rock, Ray Solomon, Rick Steckel, Jamil Zainaldin, workshop participants at the University of Chicago, University of Minnesota, Indiana University, University of Illinois, and Washington and Lee University, colleagues at St. Olaf and Carleton Colleges, and several anonymous referees. Special thanks to Bruce Dalgaard, Stan Engerman, Dave Emery, Mike Fitzgerald, David Galenson, Mike Hemesath, Art McEvoy, Judith Schafer, Loren Schweninger, Frank Smith, Christopher Tomlins, and Ned Wahl, who took time to read the entire manuscript. Ned Wahl was my faithful support and unerring critic. I am also grateful to my professors, who taught me the habits of mind necessary to collect and analyze a large data set. I thank Stephanie Sakson for superb editing, Lauretta Anderson and her student workers for copying assistance, Gail McCain for sharing her legal expertise, and Janice Murray for fixing many computer problems. I especially appreciate the kindness shown to our son Austin by his beloved companions, who helped me find the time for this work – Ann, Becky, Deb, Megan, Kate, Molly, Howie and Eileen, Bob and Nan, Kathryn. And a nod of thanks to the Mississippi State Senate, which decided to ratify the Thirteenth Amendment just as I finished my first draft in February 1995.

Three other people figured in my thoughts as I completed this book. Two are my great-great-grandfathers: John H. Thomas (Company B, 1st Regiment, Indiana Artillery), who enlisted at age sixteen on July 6, 1861, and was honorably discharged in Baton Rouge on May 13, 1864; and John McDaniel (Company H, 33rd Regiment, Indiana Volunteers), who enlisted April 1, 1862, and mustered out in Raleigh on April 12, 1865. John Thomas was wounded in the hip during the battle of Baton Rouge, playing dead until he nearly died of thirst. As he dragged himself toward a stream, two Confederates saw him and began to shoot. He jumped behind a hickory tree; family legend has it that the Rebel soldiers kept firing until they had peeled off all the bark, but they never came back to finish him off. He carried the bullet until the day he died. John McDaniel deserted in February 1863 to put in a crop of corn; he reenlisted elsewhere two months later after his original company lost so many men that it disbanded. He served honorably until war's end. A third ancestor John joins these two: John Bourne II, who died in 1720 at the age of thirty in Essex County, Virginia. In his will, he left three slaves: Jack, Frank, and Jenny. Their memory remains, though the way of life of that day is, thankfully, gone forever.

Chapter 1 is a revision of "American Slavery and the Path of the Law," *Social Science History* 20, no. 2 (Summer 1996): 281–316, reprinted with permission of Duke University Press; Chapter 2 is a revision of "The Jurisprudence of American Slave Sales," *Journal of Economic History* 56, no. 2 (March 1996): 143–169, reprinted with permission of Cambridge University Press; Chapter 4 is a revision of "The Bondsman's Burden: An Economic Analysis of the Jurisprudence of Slaves and Common Carriers," *Journal of Economic History* 53, no. 3 (September 1993): 495–526, reprinted with permission of Cambridge University Press; Chapter 7 is a revision of "Legal Constraints on Slave Masters: The Problem of Social Cost," *American Journal of Legal History* (January 1997), reprinted with permission of Temple University Press.

1

American Slavery and the Path of the Law

> It is true, slaves are property, and must, under our present institutions, be treated as such. But they are human beings, with like passions, sympathies, and affections with ourselves.
>
> – *Turner v. Johnson*, 7 Dana 435, 440 (Ky. 1838)

The common law of slavery, like all of the common law, was a bridge connecting past to future. The bridge arose from the Anglo-American practice of following precedent: Once a case was decided, judges typically had to decide similar cases in the same way. To construct slave law, judges drew upon prior cases concerning free persons, animals, and other property. The outcome was a set of economically efficient rules that served as structural support for the Southern way of life.[1]

In most contexts, efficiency means something good. Here, it was sinister: Efficient law preserved the market value of slaves and thus helped slavery flourish. But protecting property rights in slaves had other, unintended, consequences. In cases of personal injury, for example, antebellum courts tended to shield slaves more than free people. As a result, those who argued vigorously after the Civil War on behalf of ordinary consumers, workers, and victims of accidents or assaults sometimes turned to slave-law precedents for guidance.[2] The practice of *stare decisis* thus meant that slave law not only built upon earlier traditions but also paved the way for later law. In fact, slave cases did serve as precedents in many types of postbellum suits. In other conflicts, the connections to slave law were less direct, either because statutory rules supplanted the common law or because older cases tend to be cited less frequently.[3] Nonetheless, the judicial responses to injured livestock owners and, more notably, to free persons of the late nineteenth and early twentieth century resembled responses to antebellum slaveowners. Slave cases generated rules that eventually affected the lives not only of slaveowners and slaves, but also of Americans generally.

This work constitutes the first large-scale economic analysis of the common law of slavery. Over the past several decades, scholars have examined various narrow aspects of slave law, typically using as data a small set of leading cases, cases from a single state, or legislation.[4] In contrast to earlier studies, this one uses all of the nearly 11,000 published Southern appellate cases involving slaves.[5] These reported court cases serve as my data base: I use economic theory to help explain the development of slave law and of related laws governing livestock, servants, family members, and strangers.[6] The first chapter provides an overview of the economic analysis of law, then explores how and why slave law differed from other sorts of law. It ends with a note on methodology. Subsequent chapters emphasize particular areas of law, such as sales, employment, and tort law. Each chapter expands upon the differences between slave and nonslave law, then offers an empirical analysis of cases.

THE ECONOMIC ANALYSIS OF SLAVE LAW

[Y]ou can see the practical importance of the distinction between morality and law. A man who cares nothing for [a] . . . rule which is believed and practised by his neighbors is likely nevertheless to care a good deal to avoid being made to pay money, and will want to keep out of jail if he can.

– Oliver Wendell Holmes, Jr.[7]

Legal rules influence behavior. Because U.S. courts rely on precedent, liability and damages in a given lawsuit implicitly set prices for the future actions of similarly situated parties. Given the power of precedent, it is important to inquire whether the rules themselves tend to be economically efficient. As Robert Cooter and Daniel Rubinfeld have succinctly explained, legal disputes are resolved efficiently when costs of dispute resolution are minimized, legal liabilities go to parties who can bear them at least cost, and legal entitlements go to those who value them most.[8]

One can evaluate the efficiency of slave law by considering how well it met the criteria posed by Cooter and Rubinfeld. In what follows, I first discuss how courts assigned liability and damages in conflicts between slaveowners and others. I then turn to disputes in which slaveowners were accused of treating their own slaves too harshly – or too indulgently. I conclude that slave law tended to be efficient. Because legal rules encouraged people to settle their differences in the marketplace rather than the courtroom when doing so was cheap, slave law satisfied Cooter and Rubinfeld's first criterion. Because the legal rules governing the treatment of others' slaves typically allocated and measured losses just as litigants would have (had they done so themselves), slave law also met the second criterion. And because the courts assigned legal rights and responsibilities to slaveowners in ways that kept the social costs of slavery low and the social benefits high, slave law tended to fulfill the third criterion as well.[9]

To suggest that slave law was efficient is not to claim that judges intended to create efficient legal rules. Like anyone else, antebellum judges were motivated by a complex variety of factors. Ideology, prejudice, humanitarian impulses, responses to peer pressure: All of these and more helped form the opinions of Southern judges. Certainly, speculating as to the reasons why judges (and people generally) act as they do is a fascinating topic worthy of study, one that is touched upon throughout the book. But the economic analysis of law has a different emphasis: It focuses primarily on outcomes and incentives rather than on the underlying motives of judges. Here is an example. Masters often hired out their slaves for particular jobs.[10] If the slaves were hurt while doing something other than the agreed-upon tasks, judges typically required their employers to pay medical bills and damages to their masters. Some judges may have seen this as a matter of justice or fairness; others may have settled upon this practice as the best way to ensure that someone cared for the injured slaves. *Dicta* in various cases may (or may not) shed light on judges' intentions. But whatever the motivation of judges, economic analysis reveals something else as well. These rulings gave future hirers a message that, if any harm resulted from a breach of contract, hirers paid for the consequences. Hirers might still have found it profitable to break contracts, but they knew that the "price" of doing so included all relevant costs. Had judges decided otherwise, potential employers of slaves would have had greater incentives to exploit slaves and force them to do dangerous jobs and masters would therefore have been much less likely to hire out their slaves.

I must also emphasize that the concept of efficiency used here contemplates only the effects of law upon parties with legal standing. Throughout the book, I exclude the effects on slaves of alternative legal rules. "Efficient" damages in slave-injury cases, for example, encompassed only property loss, not the pain suffered by the hurt slaves themselves. Such disregard seems heartless. Yet to show that the law of slavery tended to be efficient *aside* from costs to slaves also shows how the law reinforced slavery. Understanding this connection is critical. As defined, efficient law furnished smoothly functioning slave markets, allowed slavery to survive alongside emerging means of modern technology and transportation, and harmonized the property concerns of masters with society's interest in public peace.

Enforcing Contracts: One's Word Is One's Bond

Southern masters profited by engaging in a variety of transactions that concerned their slaves. They hired out or sold slaves when work was slow at home; they sent their slaves to market or distant plantations aboard boats, trains, and stagecoaches; they insured slaves against accidents and disease; and they employed overseers to work with slaves. Many of these transactions involved oral or written contracts that specified the parties' rights and responsibilities. For example, slaveowners sometimes wrote contracts that restricted a hired slave's duties, banned certain forms of punishment used by overseers, or constrained the ability of slave buyers to re-sell slaves in the deep South. In similar fashion, insurance companies inserted clauses into policies to account for shipboard insurrections by slaves, whereas common-carrier owners who ferried slaves reserved the right to make side trips for profit. And slave sellers offered price discounts to those who would take on the risk of defective property.

Judicial regard for contracts agreed to by those trafficking in human flesh yielded efficient law.[11] Absent fraud, misrepresentation, and coercion, arrangements made ahead of time reflected what contractual parties thought was best for them. If one party failed to live up to his part of the deal and the other party suffered a loss, judges typically awarded damages for breach of contract based on prices established in the flourishing slave rental and sales markets. This practice led to efficient breaches: By consistently placing the cost of a broken contract on the breaching party, courts encouraged people to breach contracts only if expected benefits exceeded expected costs to all concerned. For example, if an employer agreed to use a slave for plowing but decided to increase his profits by sending the slave to raft lumber down a stream or blast the side of a hill, the employer paid for any resulting medical bills and lost services, even if the slave was careless. A seller who expressly warranted his slave as sound typically paid damages if the slave was defective, provided that the buyer had furnished adequate medical care and healthful living conditions. Damages equaled the difference in values of sound and unsound slaves. If a boatowner promised to carry slaves by one route but took another in hopes of bigger revenues, he paid damages equal to the slaves' market value if the slaves escaped. Such rulings gave future employers, sellers, and transporters of slaves incentives to honor contractual agreements – unless society gained more from a breach than it lost.

By supporting contractual agreements, judges also helped keep such transactions private and cheap, even easing the way for standardized forms of dealing. In particular, by using the market to determine damages, courts gave incentives to contractual partners to avoid litigation costs by means of liquidated-damage clauses – clauses specifying a sum of money the breaching party would pay to his contractual partner in the event of a breach – or initial pricing policies. If a slave buyer agreed to a bargain price in exchange for shouldering the risk of a slave's poor health or bad habits, for instance, courts refused to declare a breach of contract when a slave turned out sickly or unruly. These verdicts sent a clear message to future contractual parties that courts would not double-compensate those who garnered expected damages beforehand.

In sum, Southern courts came to efficient verdicts in slave cases when they deferred to private agreements. By leaving responsibilities where the parties had placed them, judges presumed that litigants had acted in their own best interests. A South Carolina judge put it well: "When men make contracts, and have fair opportunities of consulting their own prudence and judgment, there is no reason why they should not abide by them."[12] Those who abided by their agreements needed to fear nothing from courts; those who failed to stand by their word paid for any costs that resulted. Judges' verdicts in contract cases also encouraged people to resolve their differences in the relative tranquility of contract negotiation rather than in the adversarial atmosphere of litigation.

Assigning Liability in Contract and Tort Cases:
Courts Take a More Active Role

Although formal contracts governed some relationships between slaveowners and other parties, many interactions were far more casual – or even accidental – in nature. Slave sellers frequently touted the skills, health, or morals of their wares without offering express warranties. Slave-hiring and -overseeing contracts often proved sketchy or vague. Abolitionists and traders took slaves without permission, patrollers killed runaways, jailors neglected slave prisoners, homeowners shot slaves who were trespassing in henhouses and canefields, shopkeepers sold liquor to slaves, and common carriers posed a means of escape for slaves as well as a menace to life and limb. Some masters even complained that other people, especially doctors, had treated slaves too well.

When disputes arose under these circumstances, courts had the ticklish task of assigning responsibility for losses to plaintiff or defendant. Here I find that judges characteristically allotted losses to the party who could most cheaply have borne the risk of such losses, just as economically minded parties would have chosen to do.[13] Again, market prices formed the basis for damages. As a result, the common

law reinforced natural market tendencies, gave incentives to potential contractual parties to vocalize and formalize their true prefer-
ences, encouraged people to prevent accidents if doing so was
cost-effective, and helped reduce the joint costs of moral hazard and
adverse selection.[14] In particular, the verdicts in slave cases curtailed
two perverse incentives: people's incentives to overwork, over-
discipline, and undersupervise another's slaves if their actions might
go undetected, and slaveowners' incentives to foist off unruly, sickly,
careless, and escape-prone slaves on others.

What, exactly, were the sorts of rules that resulted? Courts often
placed liability on defendants who had failed to protect or care for a
slaveowner's property adequately. Immoral conduct toward female
slaves constituted grounds for dismissing an overseer, for example.
Placing explosives in the slaves' bunkhouse generated liability for an
employer defendant when a hired slave unsuspectingly went into the
quarters to search for a hat – blowing himself up in the process. Drinking oneself into a stupor with slaves as companions was no defense
against a lawsuit for damages when the slaves toppled into the river
and drowned. Trigger-happy homeowners and patrollers, and overworked sheriffs who let slave prisoners man the jailyard gates, found
themselves paying damages to unhappy plaintiffs who lost valuable
slaves to bullets or to the swampy underbrush that blanketed the
South. Criminal as well as civil suits sometimes ensued; in particular,
people who stole slaves, sold slaves liquor, fraternized with slaves, or
carried slaves to free states aboard public conveyances might face
fines and jail time. In circumstances like these, the defendant could
absorb the risk of loss at least cost because only he had control over
the actions leading to the injury. Making the defendant pay for a slave
who suffered or escaped because of the defendant's laxity (or deliberate actions) reduced moral hazard problems and encouraged
future potential defendants to care for others' property prudently, as
if it were their own.[15] Criminal penalties could further deter behavior that injured slaves or encouraged them to escape, especially when
defendants were too poor to pay civil damages.

But slaveowners did not always win in court. Judges refused to
award damages when solicitous defendants sent sick slaves home to
recuperate, unintentionally intensifying the slaves' illnesses. Doctors
who treated slaves in emergencies did not pay damages if slaves died.
And when a slave wearing a heavy ball and chain escaped from a boat
– in spite of close chaperoning by a crew member – his owner failed
to recover compensation. Judges gave relief as well to those who reasonably relied on slave sellers' (false) representations of their wares
as healthy, trustworthy, or specially skilled. To maintain control over
slaves, judges also granted some disciplinary authority to contractual

partners of slaveowners, to those officially charged with keeping the peace, and to citizens protecting their own homes, crops, and livestock. What is more, judges largely accounted for the unique capabilities of property that was also human. Slaves could lie, plot escapes, shirk duties, act carelessly, substitute for free laborers, and save their own lives. Although slaves were property, then, they might bear the paradoxical burden of behaving like reasonable persons. If slaves did not meet this standard, their owners were unlikely to recover damages when slaves were hurt.[16] As a Kentucky lawyer put it: "[Slaves] are to be regarded as reflecting, reasoning beings, and capable of using means for their own security and self-preservation."[17] These verdicts encouraged people to treat others' slaves compassionately, but not to overinvest in watching out for others' slaves or investigating a slave seller's veracity. They also preserved the integrity, in a twisted sense of the word, of slave markets. Had judges ruled otherwise, adverse selection problems could have arisen. People would have had perverse incentives to hire out, transport, sell, and otherwise dispatch slaves who were "lemons" – particularly feckless or foolhardy slaves, slaves likely to decamp, and slaves with concealed disabilities, diseases, or defects. As a result, Southerners would have lost the benefits of "good Samaritans," paid more to transport slaves, and shopped in hiring and sales markets loaded with "lemons."[18]

These examples show that the common law of slavery tended to be allocatively efficient, even when judges had to go beyond mere contract enforcement. In assigning liability in one such case, a Maryland opinion used language that particularly reflected economic principles: "If one or the other must suffer, ought not the loss to fall on him who could most conveniently have prevented it?"[19] But allocative efficiency is not enough to label slave law efficient. When parties can cheaply transact, allocating liability through the courts is an inefficient way to spread losses. Rather than settling matters privately and cheaply, people might lean on the legal system and waste society's resources. In fact, the rulings in slave cases steered people toward the marketplace. Judges did not award damages to masters who knew or should have known the hazards of tasks that slaves were hired to perform. Likewise, courts did not grant damage awards to slave buyers when the slaves had obvious defects at the time of sale. These practices encouraged slaveowners to build risk premiums into requested wages and slave buyers to ask for price discounts, thus self-insuring against loss. By the same token, employer defendants had incentives to make inexpensive contracts with slaveowners. Failing to obtain a master's consent before employing his slave usually was enough to make an employer defendant liable for any slave injury or escape, rather than facing the lesser negligence standard applied in consensual-hiring cases. Southern courts therefore tended to administer slave law efficiently, as well as allocate risks efficiently when the parties themselves could not do so cheaply.

Slave–Master Relations: Legal Rules Tended to Reduce Social Costs

Slaveowners worried about the injuries others might inflict upon their slaves; so too did others fear the mischief perpetrated by mistreated or indulged slaves. Although masters enjoyed great freedom in dealings with their slaves, they had to live under rules designed to protect all of Southern society. Consequently, slaveowners sometimes appeared as defendants before Southern judges in matters involving their own property. Judges refused to interfere with the master–slave relationship if other free persons benefited from a slaveowner's actions, but they penalized masters who treated slaves in ways that might harm surrounding Southerners. In short, courts attempted to make slaveowners account for many external costs (and sometimes benefits) associated with their behavior. By doing so, the Southern judiciary placated those who might otherwise have opposed slavery.

Slaveowners proffered small kindnesses and rewards to their slaves: These provided a cheap means of motivation or appeasement. Southern planters commonly bestowed trifling Christmas gifts on slaves and gave prizes to those who picked the most cotton. Plantation owners flattered some slaves by making them managers or deputies; of course, by doing so, they also profitably exploited slaves' human intelligence. The verdicts in slave cases encouraged slaveowners to continue these practices, which in turn helped solidify the South's system of subordination. At the same time, courts granted slaveowners substantial authority in disciplining their slaves. This practice had social benefits: Masters who policed their own slaves saved the public from doing so. By refusing to interfere with many forms of punishment, courts also enhanced slaves' obedience to their owners. Here again, legal rules reinforced the fetters of slavery.

Yet the law limited masters. Why? Because slaves given too much pleasure or power forgot their place in society, while neglected and abused slaves stole from others, escaped, or plotted revenge on free Southerners. Property ownership to antebellum Americans typically meant dominion over all aspects of the property – control, enjoyment of income, right of disposal, and so forth. But to preserve the status of slaves as a form of property, private control gave way to some public regulation. People could be kind or harsh to their slaves only in ways that would not offend or injure their neighbors. Accordingly, masters could beat their slaves but could not withhold food. People could host parties to distract slaves from daily burdens or to keep slaves busily making quilts or foodstuffs, but they usually could not give slaves drums, horns, or guns. Slaveowners could trust slaves to convey and receive certain goods, but they could not ask slaves to whip white trespassers. By putting restrictions on masters' ability to brutalize, pamper, and empower their slaves, Southern judges therefore made slaveowners internalize at least some costs they might otherwise have imposed on free society. As a result, Southerners could more easily accept and support slavery, knowing that the legal system looked out for the interests of free citizens generally, not just the interests of a particular slaveowner.

SLAVE LAW: HOW AND WHY IT DIFFERED

To call slave law "efficient" entails adopting the view that the costs of legal rules to those affected most – the slaves – simply did not matter.[20] Even if one can swallow something so noxious, the economic analysis of law runs the risk of lacking historical perspective. The common law of slavery, whether it concerned the sale, hiring, transport, or injury of a slave, looks more like modern-day commercial, employment, tort, and family law than nineteenth-century law. In what follows, I first compare slave law with other antebellum law, then view these comparisons against a backdrop of earlier social and legal changes. Next, I analyze differences in law from an economic viewpoint and show how slave law influenced various areas of postbellum law.

A Comparison of Contemporaneous Slave and Nonslave Law

Slave cases shared common elements with antebellum lawsuits involving other forms of property. Judges in the North and the South respected express agreements no matter what the object of sale, for example. And buyers could not win damages for any items – including slaves – that were clearly defective at the time of sale. Overseers, employers, and mortgagees had affirmative duties to care for others' property, slave or otherwise. So did common-carrier owners and operators, public officials, and ordinary citizens. In slave cases, as in other types of disputes, traditional theories of sovereign immunity made people reluctant to require governments to pay for damage to private property, preferring instead to hold government employees personally responsible. Furthermore, damage calculations in slave cases closely resembled those in livestock cases. In both types of cases, the index of damages was designed to make an owner whole: Damages for a killed slave or animal typically equaled the property's market value. For temporarily injured chattels, damages amounted to the value of the forgone market hire. A permanently disabled slave or animal garnered for his master the diminution of his market value.

Yet slave cases appeared far more frequently and manifested more subtle reasoning than lawsuits over other chattels. Slave sales generated closer judicial scrutiny of sales contracts, bills of sale, and buyer behavior, for example. In addition, whereas nineteenth-century courts tended to apply the doctrine of *caveat emptor* to nonslave sales that lacked express agreements, Southern courts resolved disputes in slave sales by looking at prices, representations made by sellers, and knowledge that sellers and buyers had or should have had. Judges also generally required sellers to disclose known flaws in slaves and considered various types of remedies more carefully in slave-sale cases. Cases other than sale transactions also reveal differences in law. Courts sheltered slaves more than other types of property from abuse and kidnapping. In the rare instances when nineteenth-century Southern municipalities faced liability, the injured property was a slave. Although slaveowners never benefited from the strict liability rules on railroads that livestock and commodity owners often enjoyed, they eventually succeeded in making railroad companies liable for injuries to slaves under the "last-clear-chance" doctrine. In a nutshell, this doctrine considers the person who has the last clear chance of avoiding an accident solely responsible for its consequences, notwithstanding the negligent acts of the victim or a third party. Slaveowner plaintiffs recovered damages under the last-clear-chance doctrine – usually because engineers failed to warn slaves off the tracks – in several cases heard in the late 1850s and early 1860s.

The divergence between slave law and the contemporaneous law governing free persons is even more striking than the differences in the legal treatment of property. By comparison with injured free employees, passengers, trespassers, and assault victims, slaveowners established and collected damages relatively easily when their slaves were injured or killed. Although slaves, like free persons, bore a legal duty to behave like reasonable persons, their masters stood a good chance of winning compensation under this standard. The opposite was true for injured free plaintiffs in the nineteenth century. In workplace disputes, for example, judges either dismissed charges brought by free laborers or accepted one of several employer defenses: contributory negligence by the worker, assumption of risk by the worker, or negligence by a fellow worker (the "fellow-servant rule"). Transporters of free passengers likewise avoided liability in many cases, arguing that victims had carelessly contributed to their injuries –

often by sticking arms out windows or jumping off moving vehicles that failed to make scheduled stops. And ordinary nineteenth-century accident victims found damages for personal injuries hard to collect, especially from railroad companies. Courts even denied compensation for children hurt while playing on the tracks, holding that the children had acted unreasonably. Similarly, assault victims seldom collected damage awards from their assailants. Free persons found the law governing fatalities even grimmer than the law regarding injuries. Erasing a claim upon the accidental death of the victim was an important means of cutting off civil suits in the 1800s. Early settlers fared better in this respect than their nineteenth-century counterparts. When a free person was killed, colonial courts had occasionally compensated the decedent's family as a byproduct of a criminal proceeding. In the first years of the American republic, relatives of an accident victim sometimes sought damages in court and, more successfully, from the legislature.[21] When railroads began to expand, however, American courts generally adopted the reasoning in the 1808 English case of *Baker v. Bolton*.[22] Under *Baker*, a tort died with the victim. The first post-*Baker* American case that actually denied a cause of action for a free person's death was from 1848 Massachusetts: *Carey v. Berkshire R.R.*[23] *Carey* and other cases signaled a departure from British legal trends: *Carey* was decided the year after the passage of Britain's Fatal Accidents' Act (Lord Campbell's Act, 9 & 10 Vict. 93), which for the first time allowed legal recovery of damages by the family of a British man killed by the negligence of another. American courts instead followed the *Carey* precedent in cases involving free victims at least to the end of the nineteenth century.

Even the law governing a slaveholder's treatment of his or her own slaves departed from the law regarding the treatment of one's servants, livestock, and family members, despite parallels in social status. Indeed, the kinship between owner and slave resembled that between master and servant, man and beast, husband and wife, parent and child. A Georgia slave viewed it this way: "I belong to them and they belong to me."[24] One might similarly expect the laws protecting slaves from their masters' ire to resemble bars against corporal punishment of servants, sanctions against cruelty to animals, and prohibitions against domestic abuse. Not so: Adult American laborers gained freedom from virtually all forms of physical abuse by their employers early in the nineteenth century, while slaves enjoyed only limited legal protection. Yet the law shielded slaves from some brutal treatment by their masters, more than it protected livestock, wives, or children during the same time period.

The Nineteenth Century: Changes in Society Called
Forth Changes in Law

A brief history of the social changes in early America helps put the differences in antebellum law into context. Although British common law during the eighteenth century had emphasized the protection of property owners, consumers, and masters of indentured servants, the focus of American law had to adjust to new patterns in demography, technology, and political and social thought soon after the Revolution. Various areas of law underwent adjustment. Growth in population density led to more conflict over the use of property. Citizens of the nineteenth century, unlike those of earlier times, increasingly had to confront the fact that quiet enjoyment of one's property might well interfere with another person's quiet enjoyment of his property. Morton Horwitz offered an illustration: The construction of dams and mills around 1800 gave rise to some of the earliest, most acrimonious disputes over the use of property and the external effects resulting from certain uses.[25] To resolve these tensions, judges had to adapt old rules of property and design new ones. Likewise, the rise of private corporations, the development of modern insurance, and the shift toward mass production and factory-made goods led to a need for fresh principles and practices in commercial law of the 1800s.[26] Not only did the nineteenth century herald significant changes in property and commercial relations, it also ushered in a new set of conflicts and accidents associated with industry and transportation. The advent of modern machinery strained the applicability of the scattered writs and doctrines that had sufficed for accident law in preindustrial societies. (One dispute questioned the propriety of putting hired slaves to work on the first circular saw in the city of Columbia, South Carolina, for example.) As in other sorts of cases, American judges had to extend ancient common-law rules and formulate new ones regarding the rights and duties of potential injurers and potential victims. The eminent Justice Oliver Wendell Holmes, Jr., put it this way: "Our law of torts comes from the old days of isolated, ungeneralized wrongs, assaults, slanders, and the like. . . . But the torts with which our courts are kept busy today are mainly the incidents of certain well known businesses. They are injuries to person or property by railroads, factories, and the like."[27] Political and social ideology, along with changes in demography and technology, also refocused the law. Indentured servitude began to look uncomfortably like slavery to early Americans, particularly to those who resented the incursions of slaveowners into free states and territories. People felt a mounting sense of unease with earlier practices of whipping and beating unrelated adult servants and employees, although they continued to view corporal punishment of children and other family members as the prerogative of the household head.

How did the common law – aside from slave cases – reflect these changes? Early-nineteenth-century judges began to move away from strict liability toward a negligence standard that considered the degree of carelessness associated with a defendant's actions. Fairly quickly, moreover, they moved even further to embrace legal rules that seemed to promote economic expansion, mobilization of capital, and a "release of energy," to use the terminology of legal scholar J. Willard Hurst. In commercial transactions, for example, courts paid attention to manufacturers' and merchants' demands for standardized, foreseeable costs and tended to shy away from placing liability on sellers of consumer goods. The doctrine of *caveat emptor* for sales replaced the sound-price rule (which presumed that any item sold at full price was sound) by the early 1800s and remained strong through the early twentieth century. What is more, nineteenth-century laws and policies seemed to place small importance on ensuring the safety of free workers or of citizens generally, even as industrial machines and trains created horrible new accidents.[28] But in the years following the American Revolution, free laborers succeeded in one area: They redefined themselves as the juridical equals of their employers. Consequently, by the 1820s employers could no longer legally beat or abuse their employees (at least adult employees); the law instead granted employers considerable economic control. The principal means of persuasion was this: If a worker did not complete all agreed-upon services, his or her employer could legally withhold all wages. The first separate American treatise on the law of masters and servants (published in 1877) explained why: "This doctrine is predicated upon a sound public policy, and in the interest of the industrial interests of the country. If servants could be permitted to leave their employers at will [with simply] a deduction from the wages earned . . . contracts for service would be of little value, and the rights of employers would be constantly at the mercy of employees."[29] In contrast to the new disciplinary laws for unrelated adult employees, the laws of husband–wife and parent–child relations stagnated. Adult males remained in their position as lawful heads of household, with a panoply of powers akin to those of a ruler of a miniature state.

The shifts in the law governing altercations over property other than slaves, commercial disputes, and corporal punishment, the new doctrines favoring industrial employers and mechanized transportation, and the continuing official disregard for the safety of those at home correspond roughly to the surges of economic growth following the turn of the nineteenth century.[30] At first glance, then, these legal developments appear to have given rise to improved economic conditions without using valuable legal resources. The substitution of wage penalties for corporal punishment brought more employment matters into the marketplace. Certainly, the doctrine of *caveat emptor* for commodity sales, the powerful legal defenses granted to employers and railroads in accident cases, and the refusal to interfere in family matters made the task of administering law easy. Provided that people could cheaply contract around any laws that were allocatively inefficient, the new legal regime accommodated well the needs of the new century.

Yet could people contract around these laws? In some instances, yes. When buyers could ascertain flaws in commodities as easily as sellers, for example, price adjustments and warranties could neutralize the effect of the *caveat emptor* doctrine. Similarly, wage premiums could compensate for job risks to laborers or explicit employment contracts could override employer defenses, if workers and bosses could cheaply agree to such measures. And possible victims of domestic abuse might have kept their abusers in check with threats of retribution from other family members. Transactions costs, however, could have rendered these adjustment mechanisms ineffective. Under conditions of high transactions costs, nineteenth-century law potentially placed the burden of growth on those whose political voice was slight and whose losses were not fully measured. Some scholars have subscribed to the theory that nineteenth-century law subsidized certain industries at the expense of those with less economic power.[31] Others have pointed out that the growth in measured income masked declining life expectancy, deteriorating diets, increasingly long and boring work hours, and the disappearance of privacy.[32] Douglass North described the first seventy years of the American republic as an era marked by high economic growth but qualified the description: "[T]he benefits that were internalized and the costs that were externalized were consistent with a high rate of growth *as measured by national income accounts* [emphasis added]."[33]

Commercial, employment, tort, and family law all governed situations of potentially large transactions costs. Take sales transactions, for instance. The markets created by mass production and nineteenth-century commercial law made the ultimate consumer insignificant. Individuals who could be injured or disappointed by commodities – even livestock – likely would not have joined forces to override the *caveat emptor* doctrine, even if doing so would have benefited them as a whole. In markets where commodities were not easy to inspect, then, *caveat emptor* was an allocatively inefficient rule. Likewise, if workers could not fully contract around employer defenses, nineteenth-century employment law may also have been allocatively inefficient. What about the law for accident victims? By their nature, those potentially involved in accidents face high transactions costs. Antebellum citizens could not easily have contracted around rules that consistently excused railroad companies from liability, even when a simple warning could have prevented a calamity. Much of the antebellum law governing free victims of train accidents (other than passengers, perhaps) thus seems allocatively inefficient. And courts' reluctance to aid those who suffered neglect or cruelty at the hands of their loved ones failed to acknowledge situations in which no one else would come to the rescue. Nor did this disregard account for the inability of women and children to extricate themselves from abusive relationships. In the boisterous, expanding, capital-hungry economy of early America, then, ordinary consumers, laborers, and victims of railroad mishaps and domestic abuse seemed to count for little. Even the developments in law regarding the treatment of servants reflected a change in the view of appropriate coercive mechanisms, rather than a liberalization in attitudes toward the rights of wage workers. Antebellum courts still sat squarely in the camp of property owners, but bodily punishment was out and economic duress was in.

Using Economics to Help Explain the Divergence Between Slave Law and Nonslave Law

Slave law differed from other antebellum law in part because the litigants were not small-time consumers, employees, or victims of accidents or domestic abuse, whose losses might not figure into the grand sweep of nineteenth-century American economic growth. Instead, litigants were slaveowners, whose concerns could not be dismissed lightly. Although economic progress mattered to Southerners, so did slavery. Slaves contributed significantly to Southern wealth and the Southern way of life. Some Southerners even referred to slavery as the "cornerstone" of the Confederacy.[34] Moreover, because a slave might have represented a substantial chunk of one's assets, litigation was worth the cost to many a slaveowner plaintiff when litigation over lesser-valued property or an ill-defined value of life was not.[35] Compared with other antebellum disputes, then, arguments over slaves led to more litigation, more detailed legal rules, and more attention paid to all disgruntled parties.

Whereas the size and ascertainability of slaves' value tilted the scales of justice toward slaveowner plaintiffs, the all-too-human volition of slaves weighted the balance the other way. Because slaves were human, they could more readily avoid accidents – and mischief – than animals or inert goods. Laws that uniformly compensated the owners of livestock harmed in accidents or injured while trespassing, and laws that granted damages for commodities lost aboard common carriers were therefore inappropriate for slaveowners. Yet applying nineteenth-century laws that brushed aside losses to human victims would have ignored the substantial property value embodied by slaves. By striking a compromise between contemporaneous livestock and free-victim accident law, for instance, Southern judges came up with solutions in slave-accident cases that preceded modern-day personal-injury law as well as discouraged perverse behavior by slave-owners (like placing dead slaves on railroad tracks). Such compromises permeated slave law. A comparison of trespassing cases yielded the following: Owners of livestock usually won damages for trespassing animals killed by spring guns or enraged homeowners; slaveowners sometimes won damages for slaves injured in similar circumstances; petty thieves were lucky to escape with their lives, much less with any civil damages. In similar fashion, although masters typically failed to prevail in cases where hired slaves could have reasonably avoided danger, they more frequently recovered damages from employers for on-the-job injuries than did nineteenth-century free laborers. Likewise, the law regarding the transport of slave passengers combined the laws for commodities and for free passengers. And the laws regarding the accountability of masters for the actions of their slaves, like other laws, had to grapple with the twofold nature of slaves. Like servants, slaves were intelligent. Like beasts, slaves were fully owned by someone else. As a result, slave law in this area partook of the contemporaneous laws for servants and animals.

The humanity of slaves, as well as vesting them with volition, made their attributes harder to evaluate upon inspection. As in other types of cases, the law of slave sales therefore is more complex than the rest of nineteenth-century commercial law. Sellers typically knew more about their wares than buyers, but the gap in information was larger and the likelihood of adverse selection greater in slave cases. Placing more responsibility on slave merchants than on other antebellum vendors reflected this greater divergence in knowledge between seller and buyer. Buyers' lack of information may offer another reason for legally protecting them. Owned slaves could substitute for free laborers. Yet unlike employers of free persons, slaveowners could not fire unsatisfactory workers. Instead, the laws that protected slave buyers from adverse selection at the point of sale stood in the place of the laws favoring nineteenth-century employers of free persons.[36]

Just as adverse selection problems afflicted slave sale markets, so too did moral hazard problems plague slave rental markets. Whereas free persons had direct work and contractual relations with their employers, slaves worked under terms designed by others. Free workers could have judged for themselves whether their treatment squared with their expectations and, arguably, could have walked out or insisted on different conditions or pay. Not so for slaves. Certainly masters and their slaves had some common interests – neither wanted slaves to suffer physical injury, for example. Masters did use hiring contracts to address concerns about employers' treatment of slaves. But because masters were absent from the workplace itself and slaves had little say over immediate work conditions, unregulated slave rental markets would have been ripe for negligent, exploitative, or abusive employers. In short, certain moral hazard problems existed in the slave hiring market – as in markets for other hired chattels – that were not present in the free labor market. The circumstances surrounding employment of slaves naturally called for a more active judiciary than did employment of free people.

Like other areas of law, the differences in legal rules governing cruelty toward one's slaves, servants, animals, and family members hinged upon slaves' dual nature as persons and as property. Although slaves substituted for free employees in producing marketable goods and services, the tools of the market could not make slaves behave as their masters wished. But Southern society could not consign slaves solely to the rule of their owners, as it did for animals. The external economic effects of leaving slaves to the mercy of their masters might simply be too great. As the 1821 South Carolina case of *Smith v. McCall* reminds us, cruelty often begets cruelty: "The character of a slave depends so much upon the treatment he receives." And as the Kentucky case of *Jarman v. Patterson* pointed out, mistreating one's slaves could have had relatively high external costs because "to the power of locomotion, [slaves] add the design and contrivance of human intellect, and of course are more capable than other animals to injure and annoy society."[37] Depriving or abusing one's slave could very well have endangered one's neighbors. To nineteenth-century judges, however, interfering with the rights of husbands and fathers created more harm than good. Unlike market matters, household matters were thought best left to the household head.

Slave Law as an Important Influence upon Other Areas of Law

The more complex calculations undertaken in slave cases resemble those that arose decades later in other lawsuits. Consumer-protection law lagged farthest behind. Legal protection of consumers other than slave buyers is really a tale of the twentieth century: The Uniform Sales Act of 1906 and, much later, the Uniform Commercial Code finally robbed *caveat emptor* of its potency. Both pieces of legislation contained provisions that resemble protections earlier afforded slave-owners by the common law.

Employment law underwent changes earlier than consumer-

protection law, but several issues remained open well past Recon-
struction. Most American industrial-relations policies arose long after
the Civil War.[38] The fellow-servant rule and other employer defenses
worked successfully for decades after slavery was abolished, subsiding
in some state courtrooms during the late 1800s but vanishing only
when twentieth-century legislators overrode them. Other areas of
employment law also shifted after the Civil War. For example, unlike
antebellum employers of free persons, today's employers (much like
slaveowners) face responsibility for many acts of their underlings.
Strikingly, slave cases served as precedents in various employment
cases of the late 1800s and early 1900s. Postbellum courts gradually
began to adopt liability rules that assigned risks to employers, much
as antebellum courts had done in slave hiring cases. What is more,
modern workers' compensation laws represent a balancing of risks to
employer and employee, just as earlier slave law had balanced risks
to hirer and slaveowner. Workers' compensation statutes may have
partly replaced market mechanisms. But these laws may also have
been part of a larger pattern that placed the state as the appropriate
regulator of employment relations, as well as the staunch protector
of property rights. Ironically, the antebellum South's concern for the
capital interests of slaveowners did not carry over to a rapid adoption
of workers' compensation statutes: The South trailed the North considerably. In 1948, Mississippi was the last state to pass such statutes.[39]

The law for accident victims also evolved in the postbellum era.[40]
Railroads faced increasing regulation and statutory liability after the
Civil War. Yet although free victims of nineteenth-century train accidents had some statutory consideration, they still were unlikely to
obtain damages in court. As Charles Francis Adams once dryly
observed, the idea of any duty a railroad company owed the public
was lost sight of between 1866 and 1873.[41] Plaintiffs injured in train
accidents finally began to turn to slave cases to support their arguments for compensation.[42] Significantly, the last-clear-chance rule did
not gain a foothold in cases involving free victims until the twentieth
century. Nor did American courts and legislatures begin to consider
seriously when and how to compensate the families of those who were
killed in train wrecks – or any other sort of accident – until the late
nineteenth and early twentieth century.[43] Even today, calculating the
value of human life is a controversial issue.[44]

The reach of slave law went beyond these three large areas. By the
1930s, even trespassers injured by homeowners looked to slave cases
as precedents. The late nineteenth and early twentieth century also
saw erosions in governmental immunity for damages caused by public
officials and the enactment of protective laws for wives and children.
These developments, like those in commercial, employment, and tort

law, looked much like the earlier rules established in disputes over slaves. Slave cases, whether they served as legal precedents or simply provided testing grounds for new doctrines, helped blaze the path of American law.

A NOTE ON METHODOLOGY

The analysis of text is not typically the bailiwick of economists. Even economic historians tend to collect quantitative data to use in regressions, frequency tables, graphs, and charts. Court cases provide a far different source of data. Each lawsuit is unique, and judges are supposed to decide cases based only on the narrow set of facts in front of them.[45] Patterns nonetheless emerge. Anglo-American courts rely on precedent, so common threads run through the common law. But because lawyers comb through many cases to craft arguments favoring their clients, judges must still decide what precedents pertain to the dispute at hand. Distinguished legal scholar Edward Levi put it this way: "[I]t cannot be said that the legal process is the application of known rules to diverse facts. Yet it is a system of rules; the rules are discovered in the process of determining similarity or difference."[46] To extract the legal rules surrounding nineteenth-century disputes, then, I assembled all the Southern appellate slave cases published in official court reporters, and the parallel cases for livestock, servants, passengers, accident victims, employees, criminals, and the like.[47] Although Helen Catterall's *Judicial Cases Concerning American Slavery and the Negro* is an invaluable resource, it does not cite all the slave cases. Moreover, Catterall's cryptic notes often reveal little about the nature of the lawsuits. I therefore went through each appellate court reporter by hand and read each case, using Catterall and the *American Digest, Century Edition* as cross-checking devices.[48] Table 1 shows the number of reporters by state, separating out the postbellum volumes.[49]

The distribution of cases across states over time provides one intriguing set of patterns. Southern judges heard nearly 80 percent of slave cases in the four decades before the commencement of the Civil War. Half of all cases come from North Carolina, Louisiana, Alabama, or South Carolina. These four states also reported more than half of the cases during the two decades immediately before the Civil War, although the proportions heard in North Carolina and Alabama rose while the proportion heard in South Carolina fell. (By 1845, all fifteen slave states had been admitted to the Union, with the latest entries being Arkansas in 1836 and Texas and Florida in 1845.) In postwar years, North Carolina, Louisiana, and Alabama still faced numerous slave cases, but the three states with the most cases were

Table 1. *Number of case reporters by state*

	Prewar and war[a]	Postwar to 1875[b]	Total
Alabama	57	15	72
Arkansas	24	6	30
Delaware	8	2	10
District of Columbia	9	3	12
Florida	11	3	14
Georgia	40	20	60
Kentucky	62	14	76
Louisiana	67	10	77
Maryland	64	15	79
Mississippi	41	12	53
Missouri	36	22	58
North Carolina	68	13	81
South Carolina	90	11	101
Tennessee	43	28	71
Texas	26	17	43
Virginia	61	10	71
U.S[c]	61	28	89
Federal[d]			28
Total	768	229	1,025[e]

[a]These numbers do not include colonial or territorial reporters; they do include reporters that spanned war and postwar years.
[b]I used the 1875 cutoff date only for slave cases. The *American Digest* pointed me to nonslave cases heard after that year.
[c]This category represents reporters for the U.S. Supreme Court.
[d]This category represents federal district and appellate court reporters. Cases recorded in these reporters are arranged alphabetically rather than by year.
[e]The row total is 997, which excludes the 28 federal reporters.

Georgia, Tennessee, and Kentucky. These six states – North Carolina, Louisiana, Alabama, Georgia, Kentucky, and Tennessee – accounted for nearly two-thirds of slave cases heard after the Civil War. Table 2 reports the distribution of slave cases by state and time period.[50]

A second interesting breakdown of the data is the dispersion of cases across states by type of dispute. Obtaining this information took considerable effort because antebellum court records little resemble modern-day legal documents. Slaveowners typically brought actions for unintentional injuries in trover or trespass on the case. Intentional injuries generated a trespass action. Other arcane causes of action and references to various obsolete writs sprinkle the pages of antebellum court reporters.[51] To add to the confusion, most states had

Table 2. *Distribution of slave cases by state and time period*

	Pre-1800	1801–10	1811–20	1821–30	1831–40	1841–50	1851–60	War	Postwar	Total
Alabama	—	—	1	30	130	453	516	81	65	1,276
Arkansas	—	—	—	—	5	61	121	27	22	236
Delaware	4	5	0	1	32	31	23	4	5	105
District of Columbia	0	61	39	67	92	8	2	4	1	274
Florida	—	—	—	—	—	16	47	12	13	88
Georgia	0	9	1	2	14	85	322	56	101	590
Kentucky	1	44	91	183	195	176	143	48	78	959
Louisiana	—	—	92	188	247	423	405	22	66	1,443
Maryland	45	23	30	35	49	63	81	14	15	355
Mississippi	—	—	3	12	41	177	272	3	41	549
Missouri	—	—	—	36	60	79	145	24	17	361
North Carolina	59	43	100	127	220	407	539	48	68	1,611
South Carolina	50	53	124	157	262	288	243	10	36	1,223
Tennessee	0	11	25	20	126	308	130	12	96	728
Texas	—	—	—	—	—	42	199	24	45	310
Virginia	60	54	86	78	118	114	90	9	46	655
U.S.[a]	6	19	5	22	22	36	30	0	28	168
Federal[b]	2	11	8	6	4	6	13	0	8	58
Total	227	333	605	964	1,617	2,773	3,321	398	751	10,989

Note. The data encompass all slave cases heard in the District of Columbia and in each state where slaves were held at the time of the Civil War. Pre-statehood and post-1875 cases are not included.

[a]This category represents U.S. Supreme Court cases heard for the slave states and the District of Columbia.

[b]This category represents federal district and appellate court cases heard in the slave states. The federal reporters record some District of Columbia cases, but I include these cases only in the row for "District of Columbia."

separate courts for matters of law and matters of equity.[52] A plaintiff
might have had a legitimate cause of action, but bringing it to a
chancery court instead of a law court (or the reverse) dealt a death-
blow to his or her case. After successfully deciphering the underlying
reasons for each lawsuit, I classified cases into several different types,
including hiring cases, sale cases, cases with common-carrier defendants, debt and mortgage cases, will contests, cases regarding slaves'
rights to freedom, cases concerning other rights of slaves and free
blacks, cases dealing with the rights of husbands and wives, disputes
over rightful ownership of slaves, criminal cases with slaves as defendants, and cases concerning masters' and others' treatment of slaves.
I developed the typology as I went along, initially placing cases into
one or more of twenty-three categories, keeping handwritten notes
on each case, and eventually gathering cases into broader categories.
About 40 percent of the lawsuits involved the inevitable squabbles
over inheritance or debts; the next largest type in most states was sale
cases. Table 3 combines these classes of cases into six categories:
hiring cases, sale cases, cases with common-carrier defendants, transfer cases other than sale cases, cases involving the rights of black
persons, and other cases. Most slave cases involving wills, mortgages,
and gifts rested solely on the property aspects of slaves, whereas
criminal-slave cases and civil rights cases revolved principally around
the human nature of those in bondage. Because others have written
extensively on these topics, I focus in this book on cases that address
both property and personal attributes of slaves.

How good are published appellate cases as a data source? Certainly
they have drawbacks. Using appellate cases to trace the path of American common law naturally neglects cases heard in trial courts but not
appealed, lawsuits that ended in settlements, and minor disputes not
worth the cost of litigation. As in today's world, antebellum appellate
courts heard only a minuscule proportion of cases filed.[53] And
because antebellum cases were published at the whim of the individual compiling the records, the various reporters may not contain comprehensive listings of cases heard. Published reports also omit the
details of lawyers' briefs and other parts of the underlying record.

Yet although they have shortcomings, published appellate cases
shed considerable light on American law.[54] Appellate verdicts bind
the courts below them, serve as precedent within the jurisdiction, and
persuade (although they do not bind) judges in other jurisdictions.
Published appellate decisions also provide lucid and accessible guidance to law-abiding citizens and their advising counsels so that they
can conform their conduct to the law. Published appellate cases,
moreover, are the core materials of legal education and the legal
process. To persuade judges, antebellum lawyers, like those of today,

Table 3. *Distribution of slave cases by state and type of dispute*

	Hire[a]	Sale	Common-carrier[b]	Transfer[c]	Blacks' rights[d]	Other[e]	Total
Alabama	97	171	13	633	174	188	1,276
Arkansas	11	54	1	95	30	45	236
Delaware	0	1	5	16	66	17	105
District of Columbia	5	16	10	13	183	47	274
Florida	7	13	3	35	15	15	88
Georgia	36	89	22	225	67	151	590
Kentucky	43	157	17	461	174	107	959
Louisiana	27	453	47	423	285	208	1,443
Maryland	4	34	6	152	126	33	355
Mississippi	13	98	1	244	44	149	549
Missouri	27	42	14	131	100	47	361
N. Carolina	73	204	14	828	243	249	1,611
S. Carolina	42	182	25	526	160	288	1,223
Tennessee	39	138	6	293	140	112	728
Texas	41	39	2	108	55	65	310
Virginia	17	97	1	306	151	83	655
U.S.[f]	1	15	2	52	48	50	168
Federal[g]	3	2	3	10	13	27	58
Total	486	1,805	192	4,551	2,074	1,881	10,989

Note: The data encompass all slave cases heard in the District of Columbia and each state where slaves were held at the time of the Civil War. Pre-statehood and post-1875 cases are not included.
[a]This category excludes common-carrier hirers.
[b]This category includes cases in which the common-carrier defendant hired the slave.
[c]Transfer cases involve debts, gifts, bequests, mortgages, and other transfers of slaves, excluding sales.
[d]This category includes cases regarding slaves' and free blacks' civil rights and criminal actions brought against slaves and free blacks.
[e]Other cases include criminal actions brought against slaveowners and other free persons who allegedly mistreated slaves, some equity cases, and miscellaneous other cases.
[f]This category represents U.S. Supreme Court cases heard for the slave states and the District of Columbia.
[g]This category represents federal district and appellate court cases heard in the slave states. The federal reporters record some District of Columbia cases, but I include these cases only in the row for "District of Columbia."

used appellate cases to prepare briefs and oral arguments.[55] The language of appellate cases also serves as a useful sort of legislative history for a time when the proceedings that yielded statutes were not well documented. And although Southern legislation codified many rules surrounding the treatment of slaves, court cases – particularly readable printed cases – offer a clearer picture of the day-to-day regulation of relationships in a slave society.[56] The *dicta* in these opinions especially can enhance our understanding of the underlying economic, social, rhetorical, and political concerns of the South.

CONCLUSION

There is some soul of goodness in things evil,
Would men observingly distill it out.
                          – William Shakespeare, *Henry V*

Slavery darkens the history of a people that values life, liberty, and the pursuit of happiness. François-René de Chateaubriand's 1791 diary entry offers one traveler's poignant first impression of America: "I gave my silk handkerchief to the little African girl: it was a slave who welcomed me to the soil of liberty."[57] My survey of all the Southern appellate court cases involving slaves shows that judges came to verdicts that tended to facilitate the operation of slave sale, hire, and transport markets, reduce the external costs of slavery, and balance the varied interests of Southern citizens. Like the politics, social customs, and religious practices of the region, the common law of the South strengthened the shackles of slavery.

The findings of this research therefore have important implications for our view of the antebellum South. Economists, historians, and other scholars have argued for years about whether slavery was essentially an economic institution.[58] Although the evidence presented here does not resolve that issue, it nonetheless shows that the law of slavery played a vital role in shaping the everyday life of those who took part in the South's economy. Slave cases also reveal that Southern judges were attuned to economic consequences and helped keep slavery economically viable. They show as well the zeal with which many courts defended slavery – a zeal matching that of other Southern institutions and underscoring the motivations behind secession.[59]

Antebellum cases also open a window on the world of slaves. The sheer number of cases involving sales, bequests, gifts, deeds, mortgages, and hires of slaves tells how easily the average slave's life was disrupted. The dry recitation of facts reveals the uncertainty, meanness, and despair in the lives of many slaves. When one slave was sold to a man he despised, he calmly went to his quarters, slit his throat, returned to the yard and bled to death in front of a horrified gathering. More than one captured fugitive, heavily shackled, dove into deep water to certain death rather than return to the master's fields. Lawsuits betray as well the frustration slaves must have felt in answering to others, especially to those less able than the slaves themselves – one slave was shot to death by an overseer who could not comprehend the slave's fluent French; another bit off his thuggish overseer's ear. And *dicta* couched in carefully compassionate tones sometimes cloaked profit-making motives – courts that approved the joint sale of mothers and children by administrators of estates commented on the humanity of the practice, even as they extolled the greater prices thus generated. Yet the genuine fondness of masters for their slaves appears as well. One woman wept at her uncle's estate sale as she frantically raised her bid – far beyond market price – for a slave she had grown up with. (The duplicitous auctioneer, knowing of the attachment, had slyly placed a plant in the audience to escalate the bidding.) Lawsuits also show that the property value of slaves helped protect them – more so than free persons, in many contexts – from personal injury. In a sense, the apologists for slavery were right: Slaves fared better than free persons in some circumstances because someone powerful had a stake in their well-being.

Court cases also reveal that slave law served as an important influence on the development of American law generally. A close reading of slave cases and the principles they generated therefore helps us understand the evolution of modern law. Various doctrines now commonly applied in commercial, employment, and accident cases appeared initially in slave cases. The slave's double identity provides one key to understanding these timing differences. His human nature complicated the assessment of liability in slave cases relative to other antebellum property disputes. Yet in comparison with cases involving free persons, the slave's marketability simplified damage calculations. Even an Alabama mob that murdered a slave knew the financial consequences – they passed the hat to collect money for the slave's owner after doing the bloody deed. Awarding damages or applying criminal sanctions in property matters was considerably less controversial than granting compensation for losses in the quality or length of human life, especially in a society that treasured capital investment. In slave cases, then, plaintiff and defendant alike could make strong arguments. In contrast, only after the Civil War did liability rules in non-slave cases begin to change. In part, this may have reflected changes in technology, production, and distribution that led to greater information asymmetries and strained the adjustment capabilities of markets. But the law also began to account for certain social costs suffered by small-time consumers, workers, and ordinary citizens, especially as industrial, railroad, and product-related accidents increased. Changing the law did not necessarily get rid of the burden, as Justice Holmes once observed, but it did change the mode of bearing it.[60] Both judges and legislators began to place more responsibility on employers, railroads, and manufacturers of consumer goods. Slave cases were, in fact, used as legal precedents in many lawsuits heard after the Civil War. And although slave anticruelty laws fell far short of the protective laws for antebellum employees, the official measures shielding slaves from their masters nonetheless foreshadow the legal sanctions against domestic abuse. In Shakespeare's parlance, the evil laws that reinforced slavery contained some soul of goodness.

2

The Law of Sales
Slaves, Animals, and Commodities

In the village of Sharpsburg, Maryland, scarcely a mile from the site
of the 1862 Union victory that served as catalyst for the Emancipation Proclamation, rests a small stone. It is unremarkable save for its
inscription: "From 1800 to 1865 This Stone Was Used as a Slave
Auction Block. It has been a famous landmark at this original location for over 150 years." As these words testify, slave sales were com-
monplace in the antebellum – and even Civil War – South.[1] Like all
commercial transactions, slave sales spawned litigation. Indeed, disputes surrounding the sales of slaves constitute one-sixth of all appellate slave cases. Judges drew on general legal principles, including
those concerning the sale of animals, to settle such disputes. Yet the
humanness of the property sold – and its value to the Southern
economy – complicated the determination of liability and the types
of remedies used by judges, as well as the terms of the sale contracts
themselves.

In what follows, I first hypothesize as to why the law of slave sales
differed from that of other commodities, particularly livestock. I then
apply economic analysis to three sets of cases: those in which specific
covenants such as warranties gave rise to the dispute; those in which
judges determined liability based on parties' representations and
knowledge rather than on express stipulations; and those in which
people other than owners had sold the slaves. I find that slave sales
law developed in a way that minimized the cost and uncertainty of
trafficking in human flesh and, thus, strengthened the institution of
slavery. I also suggest that, in some cases, divergent legal rules
reflected disparate market characteristics. At times, however, the
value of slaves and the power of their masters led to sales law that was
efficient relative to the law governing sales of other items.

HISTORICAL CONTEXT AND THE LAW OF
SLAVE SALES

Slave sales law carefully balanced the rights and responsibilities of
buyers and sellers. As such, it resembles commercial law of the early

27

twentieth century more than that of the antebellum era, which subscribed to the doctrine of *caveat emptor*.[2] In some instances, different
rules fit different market conditions. The simple *caveat emptor* doctrine was well suited to the face-to-face trades of easily inspected goods
that occurred in many antebellum commodity markets. By contrast,
Southerners conducted many slave sales through traders even in the
early years of the republic, which made a rule of *caveat emptor* less
workable.[3] Placing more responsibility on slave merchants than on
other types of sellers also reflected the greater divergence in knowledge between seller and buyer. Sellers of all stripes are typically more
familiar with the merchandise than buyers.[4] Compared with the
quality of relatively fungible agricultural and manufactured goods,
however, the qualities of human beings were difficult to discern by
would-be buyers. Obtaining information about purchases therefore
cost slave buyers more than other buyers. At the same time, slave
sellers could gain such information more cheaply than, say, livestock
sellers. Because slaves could talk, their owners knew more about the
slaves' well-being than owners of beasts knew about their property.[5]
These information gaps caused the law of slave sales to differ from
the contemporaneous law of livestock sales – its closest relative – in
key respects.

The informational disadvantages of slave buyers suggest an additional reason for the relatively greater protection afforded them by
the courts. The rules that shielded slave buyers from adverse selection took the place of protections enjoyed by employers of free
persons. In the antebellum free labor market, employers could adjust
pay and work conditions and fire unsatisfactory subordinates at will.
Slaveowners dealt with a much different labor force. Even buyers who
conducted inspections at the time of sale probably knew little about
slaves' work capabilities for weeks or even months. If a bought slave
was not as skilled or productive as a buyer had good reason to believe,
the buyer did not have the option of lowering wages or discharging
the slave. A slave buyer with no legal recourse might have tried to
foist off such a slave onto another unsuspecting purchaser, but the
end result would have been lower overall prices and a faltering sale
market.[6]

Caveat emptor did not suit the slave sale market, then. Nor, however,
did it fit all nonslave sales. For some commodities and some markets,
caveat emptor was allocatively inefficient: It placed risks on buyers when
sellers could have borne them more cheaply. Why, then, did courts
accept the doctrine here but not in slave cases? The sheer market
value of slaves suggests an answer. This value enhanced the likelihood
of litigation and the importance of well-tailored rules to govern sales
transactions. Plaintiff and defendant were more evenly matched in

slave cases as well: Buyers and sellers alike figured prominently in most Southern states and could make strong arguments in the court-room. As a result, slave buyers tended to enjoy more legal protection than buyers of other commodities. These legal rules were allocatively efficient. Admittedly, slave sales law may have cost more to adminis-ter initially than *caveat emptor*. But it soon created implicit warranties of merchantability, duties to disclose flaws, and incentives to offer explicit warranties, all of which tended to lead to law that was effi-cient overall. Such devices did not arise in commercial law generally until much later.

One other element distinguishes slave sale cases from other cases: Unlike other marketable items, slaves were humans. The all-too-human slave posed particularly knotty concerns for antebellum judges. A slave could kill himself in anguish upon separation from his family, go free at the whim of the sovereign, or form strong personal attachments within his master's household. Judges therefore pon-dered contractual interpretations more when slaves were on the auction block; they also acknowledged that damages might prove an inadequate remedy, particularly for family slaves.

CASES IN WHICH PEOPLE MADE EXPRESS AGREEMENTS

Southern judges respected express agreements made by buyers and sellers of slaves. By leaving risks where parties had placed them and fixing damages by reference to market prices, legal rules helped settle expectations and contribute to orderliness in slave-sale markets. The first section below shows that sellers typically paid damages for unful-filled promises, provided buyers lived up to their end of the bargain. But sellers avoided liability when buyers took price discounts in exchange for explicitly acquiring the risk of defective property, as the second section discusses. Compared with the law for livestock sales, slave law exhibited more complexity and tended to place greater responsibility on sellers.

Warranties

Sellers of slaves frequently offered warranties of a slave's title, sound-ness, or specific characteristic. Then as now, warranties cheaply com-municated to buyers that sellers would take financial responsibility for defective products. As a result, buyers paid higher prices for war-ranted slaves.[7] In turn, a seller who expressly warranted his slave as sound typically paid damages if the slave was defective.

What sellers knew about their wares did not matter in slave warranty cases. Even sellers unaware of their slaves' unsoundness had to pay up.[8] In one intriguing North Carolina case heard in 1852, a slave was warranted to have no defect in his eyes. When he turned out to be nearsighted, the court decided the warranty had been breached. Justice Thomas Ruffin dissented, saying, "It is known that there are more myopic persons, among the educated and refined classes . . . and many more among white[s]" but that nearsighted whites were not thought of as defective. Yet a slave was different, as the majority opinion recognized, because the slaveowner bore the loss of the slave's circumscribed abilities to perform tasks or, alternatively, had to pay for spectacles. Of course, to recover in a warranty case, the plaintiff actually had to prove that the property purchased was unsound; he could not simply speculate that the slave was prone to unsoundness. In an 1850 Georgia case, for instance, the court refused to adjudge the children of tubercular Sofa as unsound, in part because they were apparently born before Sofa fell ill.[9]

Certainly sellers who knew their slaves were defective had to deliver on warranties. In the illustrative 1824 North Carolina case of *Ayres v. Parks*, buyer David Ayres insisted upon a warranty of soundness for slave Peggy that stated she was "sound, healthy and clear of disease, . . . and warranted and defended from all manner of claims whatsoever." Peggy had frequent nosebleeds. The seller initially refused to sign the bill of sale unless the bleeding was excepted, but Ayres would not buy Peggy unwarranted because he wanted to resell her farther south. The defendant eventually acceded to Ayres's wishes, saying that the price was "very large . . . greater than she could ever get again." When Peggy died from a severe nosebleed shortly after the sale, the court supported purchaser Ayres's action for breach of warranty.[10]

In a case that pairs nicely with *Ayres*, seller Slatter refused to warrant his slave's health unless he received an extra $200. Buyer White agreed to take the slave without a warranty and with a clause in the sale contract stating that "White . . . runs the risk of her health." The slave died soon after the sale; White sued for damages. In 1850, a Louisiana court decided in Slatter's favor. This case was not simply a no-warranty one: The buyer specifically agreed to shoulder financial responsibility for the slave's health, and the court respected the arrangement.[11]

Vendors who gave warranties of soundness did not have to pay damages for slaves that, after the sale, suffered at the hands of their buyers or lacked necessary medical attention. Buyers could more cheaply have foreseen and guarded against these circumstances, so judges' rulings circumvented moral hazard problems and discouraged buyers from behaving perversely. In the 1842 Arkansas case of *Pyeatt v. Spencer*, for example, Pyeatt warranted his slave Sophia as sound. Buyer Spencer claimed Sophia was insane because she talked to herself and ran away; the jury awarded damages. An appellate court reversed and awarded a new trial, however, because Spencer had whipped Sophia severely shortly after buying her, salted her wounds, and staked her to the ground naked. This court attributed Sophia's actions to her grief at being separated from her children and to Spencer's monstrous behavior, not to madness. Buyers who subjected warranted slaves to an unhealthy environment, even without intentional cruelty, did not prevail in court when slaves died. Two cases heard the same year as *Pyeatt* illustrate this. In one, a Kentucky slave died from tuberculosis after transferral from the country to a large, crowded hotel. In the other, a Louisiana slave succumbed after exposure to measles en route to his new master's house. In neither case did courts award damages for breach of warranty. Nor did an 1851 court when another newly purchased Louisiana slave died after working in a cholera-laden pork warehouse.[12]

Far more slave than livestock warranty cases were heard in Southern courts in the first six decades of the nineteenth century (at least at the appellate level). This is not surprising, because slaves were more valuable. Courts also interpreted contractual language more broadly and more consistently when slaves were sold than when beasts were. The greater value of slaves, along with larger information gaps between slave buyers and sellers, explains the greater responsibility of slave sellers. The phrases "sound and healthy," "stout and healthy," and "young, likely, and healthy" all created warranties of soundness in slaves.[13] In contrast, affirming that a horse was sound did not typically generate a warranty for sellers – Southern or Northern – unless the word "warranty" was used.[14] Other differences in slave and livestock law likewise show the greater burden borne by slave sellers. Agents who offered warranties on behalf of slaveowners bound the owners. But a seller's statement to the agent of a buyer that he warranted a horse as sound was insufficient to sustain an action.[15] And temporary injuries or curable diseases did not violate general warranties of soundness for livestock, but they might for slaves.[16]

Slave warranty cases also posed more complicated questions than livestock cases, and the nature of the chattel sold influenced the degree of scrutiny judges devoted to particular disputes. Determining what features constituted the soundness of a slave was considerably more difficult than doing the same for a cow or horse, for example. In slave cases, judges had to decide whether warranties covered mental capabilities; not so in livestock cases. An 1833 Alabama court included soundness of mind in a warranty of soundness of a person, saying that the word "person" was used to distinguish rational from irrational creatures and therefore referred especially to the mind. The North Carolina Supreme Court decided in 1843 that a general warranty of soundness encompassed the quality of a slave's mind, where the inability "to comprehend the ordinary labors of a slave, and perform them" meant a slave was of unsound mind. According to an 1849 Georgia court, "healthy slave" covered the slave's physical – but not mental – capacities. Interestingly, a warranty of soundness did not include any guarantee of a slave's "moral qualities." *Dicta* in an 1821 South Carolina case explain why: "The character of a slave depends so much upon the treatment he receives, the opportunities he has to commit crimes, and the temptation to which he is exposed. . . . A vice which would render him worthless in one situation, would scarcely impair his value in another. A habit that would render him useless to one man, would scarcely be considered a blot upon his character in the hands of another."[17] Drunkenness in a slave, for instance, did not necessarily constitute a breach of a warranty of soundness.[18] Buyers and sellers could, of course, agree to a specific warranty for a slave's good character. And acknowledged moral qualities could increase a slave's value.[19]

Damage calculations also reveal the more sophisticated reasoning in slave cases on the part of judges and litigants. In both slave and livestock cases, a defective chattel that had been expressly warranted would yield damages equaling the difference between a sound and an unsound chattel.[20] Yet in slave cases, courts adopted much more complicated formulas, considering the forgone use of the purchase money, the value of the slave's services, the expected life span of the slave, the place of purchase, and so forth. In an 1831 Maryland case, the court even consulted life tables specific to the "African" race.[21] Certain damage calculations demonstrate judges' special scrutiny of slave cases. One example involved the 1835 Missouri case of warranted slave Dinah, who had died after purchaser Soper tortured her. Unbeknownst to the parties, Dinah apparently had suffered from some slight disease at the time of the sale. During a postmortem examination, a doctor discovered the disease. A court instructed that, if Dinah's death had resulted from Soper's cruelty, seller Breckinridge should pay damages only for the impairment to Dinah's value caused by the disease. In a similar 1849 Alabama case, warranted slave Major was shot in the arm. In the course of amputating the arm, the surgeon discovered a defect in Major's lungs. Major's lung affliction, according to doctors, hastened his death. The court determined that the damages due to the warranty breach should pertain only to the lung ailment itself (about $50 worth), not the additional complications resulting from the wound.[22] In an 1861 Arkansas case, the court did not order money damages for defective warranted slaves but rather permitted traders to maintain a trade-in policy. The policy operated as a means of economizing on the traders' cash flow. By respecting this practice, the judiciary enabled the traders to operate more cheaply.[23]

The paucity of antebellum cases involving warranted livestock makes it difficult to evaluate how Southern appellate courts determined standards of proof, liability of ignorant sellers, and responsibilities of buyers. Civil War Northern and postbellum Southern livestock cases suggest, however, that livestock law grew to resemble the slave law of earlier years. In an 1861 Wisconsin case, a buyer could not simply speculate that warranted livestock was defective; like slave buyers, he had to offer convincing proof.[24] Postbellum sellers of livestock had to make good on their warranties even when unaware of defects, just as slave sellers had.[25] And the Wisconsin buyer of a horse, like the Arkansas buyer of slave Sophia, could not win damages for breach of warranty in 1862 because he likely caused the aberrant behavior of his recently purchased chattel.[26]

Price Discounts and Locality Restrictions

In addition to warranties, other specific clauses appeared in slave-sale contracts. Family or sentimental ties among slaves led some sellers to discount prices if buyers agreed to keep slaves in the neighborhood.[27] Sold slaves could then stay near friends, parents, children, or partners. If buyers violated such clauses, courts awarded damages, taking into account the profit-making opportunities of selling slaves further South. A Kentucky court upheld a restrictive covenant in one such case heard in 1838, fervently appealing to the obligations due to slaves as human beings. Despite this rhetoric, the court sided with seller Turner on economic grounds as well. Slave Edmond was sold for $300 to $500 below market price because buyer Johnson had agreed to keep Edmond in Warren County near his wife. This arrangement was intended to keep Edmond's wife happy and productive. Johnson broke his word and instead sold Edmond to a state farther south.[28]

Why not simply require unscrupulous buyers to return slaves in these sorts of cases? Such a remedy might seem to have offered a greater deterrent than damages – and to have prevented costly litigation between future buyers and sellers of slaves. One explanation has to do with procedure: Nineteenth-century courts of law did not have the ability to grant such "equitable" remedies. Yet buyers could have complained to courts of equity instead. They typically did not, for a simple reason: Slaves sold south were often impossible to trace, particularly when sold by an itinerant trader. Any remedy other than money damages would have left unhappy sellers with no real remedy.

An 1849 Kentucky inheritance case shows clearly how plaintiffs could lose without recourse to a damage remedy. Here, a master named a particular slave in his will, leaving the slave as a specific bequest. Just before the master died, the slave was beaten to death. The heir to the slave petitioned the court to award him the slave's monetary value; the court refused, on the grounds that money was not the same as the specific slave. The plaintiff ended up with nothing.[29]

The damage awards granted in no-resale cases in fact offered considerable deterrence, because they tended to focus on the gain to the seller rather than the loss to the buyer. Virginia vendor Brent sold slave Nelson for $475 instead of Nelson's estimated local-market value of $700 when buyer Richards agreed not to sell Nelson without giving Brent first refusal at the same price (of $475). Instead, Richards sold Nelson to a trader for $1,000. A trial court awarded Brent $225; in 1846, an appellate court increased the damage award to $525. In legal terms, the appellate court required Richards to disgorge his total profits. Arguably, the value of the first-refusal clause to Brent was the original damage award of $225. By upping the award to include the additional gains from the second sale, the court diminished the incentive of potential defendants to cheat.[30]

CASES IN WHICH PEOPLE LACKED EXPRESS AGREEMENTS

In cases where slave buyers and sellers did not make their agreements clear, judges tended to assign liability to the party who could have most cheaply foreseen and protected himself against the risk of loss. These rules stand in marked contrast to the *caveat emptor* doctrine commonly applied in commodity sales. The relative costs to seller and buyer of acquiring information about the condition of a particular slave (or of slaves generally) figured significantly in many dispute resolutions. The first section below examines disputes in which neither party knew of a defect; the second section discusses the liability of sellers for their representations; and the third takes up disclosure issues and the responsibility of buyers to inform themselves. The final section considers special hazards associated with sold slaves: suicide, insanity, and emancipation. Because verdicts paralleled what contractual parties would have chosen for themselves, the common law mimicked the market and gave incentives to potential slave buyers and sellers to formalize their arrangements.

Buyers and Sellers Unaware of Defects in Sold Slaves

Slave sellers knew (or should have known) relatively more than buyers about the property they purveyed. Judges tended to place liability on sellers in cases where buyer and seller claimed to know nothing about a slave's infirmity or vice; this rule reflected the seller's cheaper access to information about his slave. To illustrate: a Kentucky court in the 1822 case of *Hanks v. McKee* said the existence of a disease "must be a matter best known by the one who possesses and employs the subject of the disease."[31]

South Carolina was most pro-buyer, subscribing to the sound-price doctrine: Any slave sold at full price was presumed sound. If the buyer could not observe (and was not told of) a defect, but had paid the price of a sound slave and could prove the defect had existed at the time of the sale, the buyer was entitled to damages.[32] In an 1840 case, for example, a South Carolina court awarded damages under the sound-price doctrine for slave Philander who died from a lung ailment. The buyer had been informed of Philander's recent fall from a house and his subsequent shortness of breath but paid full price for the slave.[33] But another plaintiff could not rescind a sale on the grounds that his newly bought slave had spread venereal disease because he did not prove the slave was diseased when he bought her. And if a South Carolina buyer paid a discounted price for a slave, he needed an express warranty to obtain relief for a defect unless he could prove deceit or fraud.[34]

Louisiana slave buyers enjoyed extensive statutory protection. A sold slave who later manifested an incurable disease or vice – such as an "addiction to running away" – could generate a "redhibitory" action. If successful, slave buyers who brought such actions obtained a rescission of the sale. (Redhibitia is a concept in Roman law refer- ring to the process of canceling a sale because, at the time of the sale, the merchandise had hidden flaws.)[35] The Act of 2 January 1834 pre- sumed against the seller if a defect showed up within three days for Louisiana slaves and within fifteen days for slaves who had been in the state for less than eight months. Louisiana judges generally con- sidered running away as evidence of a redhibitory vice: Under the 1834 Act, slaves who fled within sixty days of sale were presumed flawed at the time of sale. Still, Louisiana judges, like those elsewhere, gave careful consideration to buyer behavior and expectations. Unusually harsh treatment by a buyer could block a rescission. And in the 1844 case of *Fazende v. Hagan*, ten-year-old Ben was sold by defendant Hagan, then ran back to Hagan's slave yard. Ben was not considered to be vice-ridden, only young and scared. (Fazende retrieved Ben; Ben then threw himself into the river to drown.) About the same time, a Louisiana court determined that the buyer of a Kentucky slave should have expected the slave to flee because Louisianians generally treated slaves much more harshly than Kentuckians.[36]

Certain states protected sellers somewhat more than South

Carolina and Louisiana because many state residents not only bought slaves but also sold slaves to traders, often for export out of state.[37] Traders were in the business of buying and selling slaves, so they typically could have evaluated the attributes and worth of a slave more cheaply than the ordinary buyer – and perhaps more than the ordinary person selling to traders. As a result, buyers who were also traders enjoyed relatively less legal protection. For example, Virginia slave trader Wilson had to pay the agreed-upon price of $700 to Shackleford for a woman and her three children in 1826, even though the woman had dropsy that became evident soon after the sale. Wilson resold the family in South Carolina for $475, paid this sum to Shackleford, and persuaded a trial court to prohibit Shackleford from seizing an additional $225 worth of Wilson's property. The issue at appeal was whether Shackleford knew about the dropsy at the time of the sale. He did not and had offered no warranty, so Wilson ended up paying the full $700 for the slave family.[38]

Slave buyers in all states tended to have more protection than buyers of livestock. For instance, a fair price typically implied a general warranty of title to a slave. This was not true for livestock. And litigation costs relative to the value of property exchanged also mattered. An Arkansas court explained why the sound-price rule should not be used for animals, for example: "[T]he immorality of [the present] rule is counterbalanced by the tendency to vexatious litigation which would be encouraged by the [sound-price doctrine]. The common law requires vigilance and prudence on the part of the purchaser. . . ."[39]

Sellers' Representations

Antebellum Southern courts held slave sellers to their representations but tended to view statements about livestock quality as puffing; these legal rules reflected the greater asymmetry in information between buyers and sellers in slave markets. If a slave buyer reasonably relied on a vendor's representations about his wares, the seller paid damages or faced rescission of the sale if the sold slave did not measure up. Had judges ruled otherwise, people would have had perverse incentives to sell lemons, but to represent them as trustworthy and healthy.[40]

One might argue that holding slave sellers responsible only for express warranties would have been a superior legal rule. Then courts would not have had to infer warranties, and sellers who wanted higher prices for higher-quality slaves could simply have offered express warranties. Although this argument seems persuasive, I suggest that the law as administered was efficient. Why? Courts inferred warranties only in limited circumstances – not when flaws were obvious to buyers, nor when buyers relied on the statements of the slaves themselves, nor when buyers ill-treated their new slaves. Moreover, many people who bought and sold slaves were illiterate and had to rely on oral communication. If so, express written warranties were of little use and express oral warranties would have been hard to prove. But witnesses could likely attest to the nature of representations relied upon by the buyer. Often, the representations closely resembled express warranties, except that sellers may have omitted the word "warranty."

Touting the skills, health, or trustworthiness of slaves bound sellers, for example. In one case, a slave described as a good "washer, ironer, and cook" did not, in fact, possess these qualities. Because skilled female domestics fetched a 20 percent price premium, the plaintiff understandably won damages of $170. Likewise, sickly slaves represented as healthy yielded damages or rescission. Runaways represented as otherwise gave rise to similar remedies. Prices clearly indicate why plaintiffs won damages in such cases: Runaways and the physically impaired sold for discounts of up to 65 percent.[41]

Because the reproductive potential of female slaves affected their prices, buyers misled about slaves' fecundity brought their complaints to court. In the 1859 Georgia dispute of *Hardin v. Brown*, Hardin bought slave Eliza, who was said to be pregnant. The slave died and was buried; Hardin exhumed her seventeen days later so that he might avoid paying for Eliza if she in fact had not been pregnant. (Hardin ended up having to pay for Eliza because he dug up and inspected the corpse hastily during a stormy night. The court determined that Hardin did not give enough evidence of the slave's barrenness. If he had, the court likely would have awarded damages or rescinded the sale.) The facts in *Hardin* recall those in an 1887 Michigan case famous to first-year law students – *Sherwood v. Walker*. In *Sherwood*, the buyer bought a cow that was thought barren. The cow was in fact pregnant. The court let the seller rescind the sale on the grounds of mutual mistake. Interestingly, an antebellum Kentucky case involving a cow generated a result opposite to *dicta* in *Hardin* (and contrasting with *Sherwood* as well). Here, the seller represented a cow as a "good breeder." These words did not create a warranty, according to the court – which refused to rescind the sale when the cow was found barren.[42] Similarly, advertising one's stallion or jack as a "good foal-getter" was not typically considered a warranty. (Kentucky, a state noted for horse-breeding, made some exceptions to this rule.)[43]

Sellers often included a slave's age as part of the terms of sale. A slave's productivity corresponded to his age; prices reflected this relationship.[44] Courts usually held sellers to these representations in slave cases – and less so in livestock cases – because judges thought slaves' true ages were hard to pinpoint. Louisiana plaintiffs and their witnesses said that slaves over the age of thirty tended to look five to fifteen years younger. South Carolina blacks were said to wear their age better in slavery than in any other condition.[45] Slaves, of course, often did not know their ages – as one anonymous slave reported, "When I come here, colored people didn't have their ages. The boss man had it."[46] Small inaccuracies did not yield liability for the seller. For example, courts found for the sellers in cases where the sold slaves were said to be aged twenty-five and twenty-two, respectively, but were truly aged twenty-nine and twenty-six. But Kentucky courts understandably ordered rescissions in two other cases. In one case, vendor McCann claimed that slave Hannah – who was forty years old with nine or ten children – was age twenty-nine with three children. In the other dispute, a seller represented his slave's age as twenty-five instead of her true age of forty. In a similar Tennessee lawsuit, a trial court decided a slave's age was not warranted, even though the seller represented the slave as thirty-five years old instead of her true age, forty-five years old. Both parties allegedly knew the slave's correct age. But an appellate court reversed and remanded the case, saying the seller should be accountable for his representation.[47]

In some cases, courts also held sellers to their representations about animals' ages. A Georgia seller who represented a horse as fourteen years old was determined to have warranted that the horse was no older than age fourteen. But in an 1850 Tennessee case, the seller warranted a horse as sound and stated that the horse was age nine, when in fact the horse was age twenty. The court decided that the revelation did not sustain the charge that the horse's soundness was misrepresented. Similarly, in 1851 New Hampshire, a horse advertised as "six years old, . . . warrant[ed] sound and kind," was not warranted as to age.[48]

The Civil War made for intriguing cases involving sellers' representations. The federal Draft Act of 1863 exempted any drafted man from service if he furnished a substitute or paid $300. Kentucky slave Henry was bought to be a substitute in the Union army. Henry (absent at the time of the sale) was represented as suitable for this purpose, but he was actually underweight, underage, and too short. Although a jury determined that the buyer had to pay the $700 note given for Henry, an appellate court reversed and remanded the case, instructing that the sale included an implied warranty – essentially one of fitness for the particular purpose of soldiering. (By spending $700 on Henry rather than paying $300 to the government, the buyer may have revealed his expectation that slavery would continue after

Henry's military stint expired – or that courts would not enforce the note.)[49] In another Civil War–era case, seller Hawkins had sold slave Pete to buyer Brown for $1,000 in 1858. Because Pete had run away before, Hawkins agreed to refund $500 if Pete did so again. Pete did run – in 1864, along with innumerable other slaves. The court determined that Pete's escape was not due to a passion for running away, but rather to the chaos of wartime. Hawkins did not have to refund the money.[50] (When sellers did have to pay damages for warranted runaway slaves, the calculation resembled that for unhealthy slaves – damages equaled the difference between the values of stay-at-homes and runaways.)[51]

Reliance on a seller's representations about a slave's human character protected the buyer only to a certain extent. Deliberate misrepresentations by sellers certainly created liability. Slave Anthony was said to be honest and industrious, but was actually a lazy liar. Although a trial court rejected evidence of the slave's character, an Alabama appellate court reversed and remanded the case in 1833 for evaluation of the damages the buyer had sustained by relying on the seller's misstatements. But judges also expected buyers to exercise a good influence on slaves, refusing to award damages for bought slaves who later exhibited poor morals or character. In an 1839 South Carolina case, slave Charles was represented as honest, sober, honorable, and not given to running away. The purchaser complained he had been deceived, yet he had to pay full price for Charles because "[o]ccasional flights of a slave . . . would not constitute any material moral defect . . . occasional thefts among tolerably good slaves may be expected . . . such habits were easy of correction by prudent masters. . . . Like master, like man . . . in drunkenness, impudence, and idleness."[52]

These examples show that a seller's representations about a slave's physical attributes and skills bound him, although statements about morals and character might not. Judges' rulings in such cases helped prevent adverse selection and moral hazard problems in slave-sale transactions. Responsibility for his own representations did not, however, carry over to statements made by the seller's slave. Courts considered admitting evidence of a slave's remarks only if a slave had spoken to a doctor about his current condition, or if impartial other people had made supporting comments. Why? Slaves might have wished to stay with their masters or, alternatively, to find new ones. An 1822 Kentucky court noted: "[T]here is a strong indisposition in such creatures to be sold, and . . . to avoid a sale, they may frequently feign sickness, or magnify any particular complaint with which they are affected. . . ." An 1855 Alabama court countered: "[I]t would be an easy matter to prove slaves unsound by their declarations of unsoundness, oftentimes feigned as an excuse to avoid labor, or to procure a change in masters."[53]

Sellers' Disclosure of Flaws and Buyers' Knowledge of Defects

As well as being responsible for their own representations, slave sellers had a duty to disclose flaws. As Richard Posner has noted, disclosure of an item's attributes is most important, economically speaking, when the item sold is valuable and its characteristics costly for the consumer to discover.[54] Both prerequisites held true in slave sales. If a seller knew (or should have known) that a slave had a hidden defect, the seller was liable for damages if he deliberately concealed the flaw or did not inform the buyer about it.[55] Courts also protected the viability of long-distance sales, saying that sellers had to describe their slaves truthfully when buyers lived too far away to inspect them.[56]

Yet judges did not let slave buyers use ignorance as an excuse. A South Carolina court declared in an 1837 case where the buyer knew of the slave's exposure to measles, "Both may be innocent parties, but let the loss fall on him who voluntarily encountered all the responsibility."[57] If a buyer knew or should have known about a slave's defect, judges would not award damages. These rules encouraged slave buyers to incorporate their knowledge into the prices they paid, effectively insuring themselves against later calamities and thus staying out of court.

Warranties of soundness did not, for instance, cover obvious defects in slaves or animals, although they included defects not discernible by the unskilled eye. As an example, an Alabama buyer knew about a slave's tendency to have fits. The court therefore did not interpret the clause "sound at this time" to mean "always sound." Nor did an express warranty of soundness pertain to a slave's crooked arm in the 1860 South Carolina case of *Scarborough v. Reynolds*. The rule was more complicated than first appears, however, and its interpretation is rich with economic overtones. The essence of *Scarborough* was this: The buyer could see the crookedness of the arm, which "did not affect [the slave] in labor; she could hoe and chop with an axe as well as women generally can." So South Carolina, one of the most buyer-protective states, refused to award damages to buyers who received no economic injury. But an Arkansas appellate court, subscribing to the same "obvious-defect" rule in *Jordan v. Foster*, awarded buyer Jordan damages under breach of warranty for eight-year-old slave Hannah, who also had a crooked arm. Why the different result? Although Hannah's crooked arm was obvious, her true defect – a creeping paralysis that medical experts testified would eventually incapacitate Hannah – was not.[58] Animal law looked much the same.[59]

Chief Justice Johnson colorfully explained this in *Jordan*, saying that a warranty of soundness was not breached when a horse lacked a tail or ear because the buyer knew a part was missing and could presumably calculate the effect on productivity. But a horse blind in one eye might trigger a breach of warranty, because this defect might not be obvious to the typical horse buyer.

Just as obvious defects precluded recovery of damages, courts did not grant relief to slave buyers told of defects. Knowledge conferred responsibility. A South Carolina buyer openly accepted the risks associated with a sickly looking slave at the time of sale and therefore could not recover damages in 1812 when the slave died. In an 1831 case, the seller informed the buyer of a slave's venereal disease; the buyer had to pay even though the slave died from the affliction. In a poignant 1840 case, a free man of color gave his note for $500 to buy his obviously sick wife, even though she would have been worth only $300 sound. He had to pay, although his wife died soon after the sale. In an 1848 Mississippi case, Dr. Otts had to pay for a scrofulous twelve-year-old that he had bought and nursed with great care. The doctor wanted to return the slave to seller Alderson in exchange for the purchase price plus nursing expenses. The court denied Ott's claim, saying that "the purchaser . . . must charge his loss to a presumptuous reliance on his own judgment, and his improvidence in failing to obtain a warranty against defects. . . ." In a South Carolina case heard at about the same time, plaintiff Gist had purchased slave Linder, knowing that Linder frequently ate dirt. Gist had refused to allow mention of this in his receipt because he had wanted to resell the slave without revealing this knowledge. Linder died from complications arising from dirt-eating; Gist recovered nothing. The opinion stated: "The purchaser . . . bought with his eyes open, and with avowed willingness to run all the risks of his bargain."[60]

Buyers who should have known of a slave's illness or injury could not garner damages, either. Consequently, buyers had incentives to adjust prices at the time of purchase rather than relying on courts to compensate them later. Several cases offer illustrations. Although a South Carolina jury granted damages for a slave who died from lockjaw after injuring his foot, an appellate court granted the seller a new trial in 1840 because the wound was clearly visible at the time of sale and had been examined by the plaintiff's physician. In a similar, contemporaneous Tennessee case, infant slave Wesley bore the marks of spinal disease when sold. Although a jury awarded the buyer damages, an appellate court granted a new trial. A Louisiana slave's visibly swollen knee at auction prevented the buyer from rescinding the sale later. In an 1856 North Carolina case, the seller refused to warrant slave Lewis in any way. Lewis was noticeably sick at

the time of the sale, and a neighbor informed the buyer that Lewis
suffered from spells in the head and religious mania. The buyer
nevertheless paid full price of $850 for the slave, then brought suit.
A trial court decided for the buyer, but an appellate court reversed
and awarded a new trial, saying the plaintiff should have asked for an
express warranty or refused to buy Lewis. In an 1860 South Carolina
case, a different slave Lewis was loudly proclaimed not to be warranted as "sound in any way" at an estate sale; Lewis died eighteen
days after the sale, and his purchaser had to pay.[61]

Special Hazards: Suicide, Insanity, and Emancipation

Buyers had to exercise caution in property transactions generally, but
courts also expected slave buyers to account for the special perils
associated with human property. Cases in which sold slaves killed
themselves vividly illustrate this expectation. If a slave committed
suicide at or around the time of sale, who bore the loss? Generally,
the buyer did – courts considered suicide a hazard of sale the buyer
should have contemplated. Sometimes slaves even gave notice to
potential new masters: When the cruelest slave master in the county
bid at an auction for Delicia Patterson, she shouted: "Judge Miller!
Don't you bid for me. . . . I will take a knife and cut my own throat
from ear to ear before I would be owned by you."[62] Buyers paid for
dead slaves in *Bunch v. Smith* and *Walker v. Hays*, for example.[63] In the
1851 *Bunch* case, slave Bob slashed his throat in front of the buyer,
the seller, and a group of other people. The buyer retrieved his money
from Bob's stunned seller minutes after the suicide, but Justice
O'Neall reinstated the sale and ruled that the buyer should bear the
loss of Bob's death. In *Walker*, heard nine years later, slave Agnes
drowned herself and her child Virginia after being sold. The buyer
claimed that Agnes must have been insane, but the court determined
she was not, only despondent over the sale.[64]

Insanity in a sold slave in fact gave rise to many disputes. The merits
of the plaintiff's case usually rested on his ability to evaluate the slave's
condition: If a buyer could easily have determined that a slave was
insane, courts would not hold a seller liable. Louisiana buyer Chambliss had ample opportunity to inspect insane slave Riley, for instance.
A court refused to award damages in 1857, deciding Chambliss
should have seen that Riley had no sense. But sellers were liable in
such cases if the slave's insanity was not obvious to the buyer. In some
instances, the buyer could not cheaply inspect the slave. Seller Bontz
forbade buyer Grant to talk to slave Celia because the slave "might
run away" if she knew about the sale, for example. (In truth, Celia
was an idiot and Bontz did not want Grant to discover this fact. When

Grant found that Celia was mentally disabled, he put the slave in jail while trying to get his money back; she died. A D.C. court awarded Grant damages in 1819 equal to Celia's price plus costs.) Nor could buyers always determine the slave's mental capabilities as readily as sellers could. In 1825, a South Carolina court judge argued that the idiocy of a slave might elude the vigilance of a buyer, although it "can not escape the knowledge of the owner." In a note of caution on the matter, an 1840 Louisiana opinion stated: "It is very difficult . . . to fix a standard of intellect by which slaves are to be judged. . . ."[65] In 1851, Dr. Samuel Cartwright attempted to shed light on this issue in his "Report on the Diseases and Physical Peculiarities of the Negro Race." He described two mental illnesses unique to bondsmen: *drapetomania* (manifested by slaves who continually tried to escape), and *dysaesthesia Aethiopis* (exhibited by slaves who neglected or refused work).[66] To the modern ear, both sound like perfectly reasonable responses to enslavement.

A slave could suffer mental illness and die by his own hand; he could also go free at the hands of others. Courts expected slave buyers to acknowledge that the government might someday free their human property. When property worth billions of dollars disappeared with emancipation, frantic slave buyers attempted to shift their losses to sellers. Yet nearly all courts recognized sales made before war's end, refusing to adopt plaintiffs' arguments that warranties of title or "slave for life" had been breached.[67] A Virginia slave buyer had to pay a bond dated October 1863 in the amount of $13,110, for example. Why? "[T]he purchaser acquired all he contracted for, but his enjoyment was not commensurate with his expectations. . . . The [plaintiff] . . . assumed all the risks attending the acquisition of this species of property in the then existing condition of the country." Similarly, an Alabama court enforced a note given for slaves on February 1, 1864 – the day President Lincoln issued his order to draft 500,000 men for three years or the duration of the war. The court recognized the uncertain value of slave property during the Civil War but noted that people could still lawfully buy and sell this contingent interest. In its opinion, the court said that the Emancipation Proclamation (effective January 1, 1863) might have affected slaves' values but not their transferability. An Arkansas court recognized that defendant Dorris probably did not intend to pay $3,000 for a slave bought on August 29, 1863. After all, the Confederacy had only recently suffered serious setbacks at Gettysburg and Vicksburg, and the fall of Little Rock was a mere fortnight away. Dorris in fact may have been trying to evade a stamp tax by paying cash. Yet the court refused to relieve Dorris of his obligation when the slave was freed.[68]

By making purchasers pay for slaves later emancipated, judges avoided double-compensating buyers who had (or should have) adjusted prices for the probability of emancipation. Judges also adhered to the standard practice of refusing to undo voluntary agreements. This practice is no different from one that requires buyers of a futures contract for grain, say, to pay the price agreed upon, even if the bottom drops out of the grain market. By settling expectations that agreements are enforceable, judges keep matters out of court when circumstances change. As one Arkansas judge wrote in 1867: "We are not unmindful of the hardship and ruinous loss which have very often arisen out of circumstances connected with the late war, by which individuals, in consequence of acts not their own, have been made to suffer, but can not on account of such hardship, depart from well established principles of law; to do so would open a wide and disastrous field of litigation."[69]

SALES OF SLAVES BY THOSE OTHER THAN OWNERS: THE IMPORTANCE OF BEING HUMAN

Slave sale cases often reveal the underlying human essence of the property sold. The disputes discussed thus far demonstrate Southern judges' recognition of a slave's ability to talk, reason, behave willfully, fall under the influence of others, lose his mind, and gain freedom by governmental actions. Judges also knew well the importance of sentimental and family ties, and they respected contractual clauses designed to keep sold slaves in the neighborhood. But sales of slaves by those other than their owners also generated disputes that bore directly upon the human nature of slaves. In these cases, judges had to grapple with the emotional ties between slave mothers and their children (reviewed in the first section below), and between slaves and their owners (discussed in the second section). As in other cases, economic considerations figured into the rulings that resulted.

Ties Between Slave Mothers and Their Children: Should Economics or Humanity Prevail?

Many states encouraged keeping slave mothers and their young children together. Although judges might wax eloquent about this humane custom, their words disclose the economic benefits that could arise. (One court even acknowledged in 1832 that "there was little that legal decisions can do to enforce humanity: this must depend on public opinion.") In an 1819 will contest, a South Carolina court called it sound policy, as well as humane, to bequeath and sell mothers and children together. Why? Because these practices generated "an additional and powerful hold on [the slaves'] feelings and security for their good conduct." The court suggested particularly that executors who allocated slaves of equal value across heirs would maximize economic benefits by keeping slave families together.[70]

Whether courts advocated selling slave mothers and children together in fact depended upon economic consequences. Courts rarely interfered in cases where people sold slaves directly, because prices reflected the value placed on keeping families together.[71] If an agent sold slaves, however, judges might inquire as to whether the agent had fulfilled his fiduciary duty. An 1811 Kentucky court determined that a sheriff had acted for the economic benefit of a creditor in selling mother and child together, for example: "If the child had been sold separately from its mother, it is pretty certain that its value would have been greatly diminished . . . if the mother had been first sold . . . her value might have been lessened in the estimation of purchasers. . . ." But an 1830 North Carolina court made clear that an executor had to sell family slaves separately if doing so fetched a higher price for the estate, "for [the executor] is not to indulge his charities at the expense of others."[72]

Ties Between Slaves and Masters: The Use of Equitable Remedies

> Slaves are a peculiar species of property. They have moral qualities, and confidence and attachment grow up between master and servant; the value of which cannot be estimated by a jury.
>
> – *Allen v. Freeland*, 3 Rand. 170, 176 (Va. 1825)

Southerners acknowledged that slaves and masters formed strong attachments. This gave plaintiffs a reason to argue that money damages awarded in a court of law could not fully compensate for the loss of favorite slaves. In the restricted-locality and no-resale cases discussed previously, the discounted price at least reflected the value of the clause to the seller. But if a favorite slave were sold or seized unlawfully, without his owner's consent, the sale price might not accurately mirror the value of a slave to his master. In these sorts of disputes, judges agreed with plaintiffs that equitable relief was appropriate, saying there was "a value in this species of property, arising from circumstances [such as the length of time in possession] independent of their mere pecuniary value in the market. . . ." An 1819 North Carolina appellate court expressed this sentiment most eloquently: "With respect to other chattel property, justice may be done at law by damages for nonperformance, and therefore equity will not interpose: But for a faithful or family slave, endeared by a long course of service or early association, no damages can compensate; for there is no standard by which the price of affection can be adjusted, and no scale to graduate the feelings of the heart."[73]

What alternative remedies did plaintiffs pursue in such cases? Suppose the owner of a life estate in a slave sold the slave. The remainderman – the person entitled to the slave after the death of the life-estate owner – might ask an equity court to require the return of the specific slave, rather than seek damages in a court of law for the slave's cash equivalent. Or suppose a creditor seized and sold a slave, mistakenly thinking that a debt remained outstanding. The debtor could argue that he must have his seized slave back because money equaling the slave's market value would not make him whole. As another example, suppose a creditor seized slaves of an innocent person (a wife or minor, for example) to satisfy the debts of a third party (a husband or guardian, for instance). The hapless slaveowner almost certainly would approach an equity court to protest his or her loss. When judges compelled the return of a slave sold (or seized) unlawfully or mistakenly, this equitable remedy essentially reflected the extra value of a slave to his fond owner over and above market price – what economists call consumer surplus. When consumer surplus was large, damages based on a market price for a fungible commodity would have been too small to compensate grieving owners and true damages too difficult to compute. By using equitable remedies in these cases to acknowledge the links forged between master and slave, Southern judges protected property interests and strengthened the shackles of slavery.[74]

Other types of cases reflect judges' understanding of the consumer-surplus value inherent in family slaves. In an early Virginia case, for example, a female slave had been living with the plaintiff for many years. The slave was legally owned by another person, John Robinson. When Robinson died, his heirs put the slave up for sale. The plaintiff bid frantically to buy her back. The auctioneer had planted a confederate in the audience to escalate the slave's price far past her true market value. The judge in the case determined that the plaintiff need only pay the slave's market value, not the bid-up price. Interestingly, an 1891 case alluded to the consumer-surplus value of family pets. Here, Texas plaintiffs brought suit for malicious poisoning of five dogs. Their evidence of the dogs' special value and usefulness was enough to sustain a damage verdict, even though the court said that the animals had no particular market value. (One dog reportedly notified his owners of the arrival of all visitors, using different signals for men, women, and children.)[75]

Judges used equitable remedies only for household slaves at first; some states eventually applied these remedies for other slaves as well. South Carolina offers an illustrative history. South Carolina courts advocated equitable remedies for domestic servants in *Sarter v. Gordon* and for "family" slaves in *Horry v. Glover*. A few years later, *Young v. Burton* opened the doors of equity courts to cases concerning any specific slave.[76] Chancellor Johnson noted in *Young* that the use of equitable remedies in his state was inevitable, because early-nineteenth-century South Carolina law judges typically instructed the jury to find damages exceeding disputed slaves' values. These instructions virtually compelled the return of specific slaves. Several Southern equity courts eventually granted hearings for disputes regarding nearly all types of slaves. Virginia was the extreme case, determining finally that equity courts could hear disputes over any slave.[77] Mississippi, Alabama, North Carolina, Tennessee, and Missouri approved of equitable remedies in many instances as well.[78] Kentucky, Arkansas, and Georgia were less likely to institute equitable remedies, particularly for merchandise slaves.[79] In spite of Georgia's more conservative use of equitable remedies, Georgia Justice Joseph Lumpkin went furthest in lauding the bonds that tied together master and slave: "Those who are acquainted with this institution, know, that the master and slave form one family, or social compact.... And not withstanding a distinguished statesman at the North has predicted that in case of war, the South could become the Flanders of America, ... history ... falsifies this opinion. No subordinate class in the world entertain the same strength of attachment toward their superiors. And this feeling is to a great extent reciprocated. The very strength and security of the South consists in the loyalty of our [N]egro population to their owners."[80] Lumpkin lived just long enough to rue his words; he died June 4, 1867.

CONCLUSION

Appellate judges typically came to verdicts in slave-sale cases that facilitated the smooth operation of the domestic slave trade and, thus, the institution of slavery itself. Court cases also demonstrate that this body of law exceeded other commercial law in sophistication. Although slave law resembled the law for livestock in some respects, slave sale contracts exhibited more complexity, their interpretation required more subtlety, and the remedies for their breach were more comprehensive.

In part, product and market differences explain these disparities in law. Slaves possessed the complex nature of a human being, which led to relatively large information asymmetries between buyer and seller. The capabilities of slaves also made them substitutes for free employees. Yet people who unwittingly bought inferior slaves could not easily dispose of them – unlike antebellum employers, who could fire unsatisfactory workers at will. The possibility of adverse selection thus shadowed slave sale markets, resulting in more complicated legal rules than those governing the sale markets for livestock or fungible commodities. But factors other than slaves' humanness mattered. The large value of slave property increased the probability of litigation and the importance of settled law; it also generated a more even match of power between plaintiff and defendant than in other antebellum commercial cases. Consequently, in some instances slave sales law tended to manifest efficient rules before other areas of commercial law did.

3

The Law of Hiring and Employment
Slaves, Animals, and Free Persons

Slave hiring was common in the South.[1] Slaves' mobility and intelligence helped them adapt to different jobs, locations, and supervisors, so masters could benefit from hiring out slaves when work was slow at home. Yet these same attributes tempted people to exploit hired slaves when unexpected needs or profit opportunities arose. And slaves, being only human, were sometimes careless and disobedient. Consequently, clashes between slave employers and masters often landed in Southern courts.[2] In keeping with the twofold nature of slaves as property and as humans, antebellum judges drew upon principles established in two broad areas of law to design rules governing slave hiring: the law of hired chattels (especially animals) and the law of employers and employees. The result was a set of rules that enhanced the operation of slave-hiring markets.

But slave-hiring law not only reflected other areas of law, it also served as an important influence. Slave-hiring cases provided precedents for many lawsuits involving livestock or free workers. In other instances, Southern judges developed reasoning in slave cases that later appeared in other types of employment disputes. What follows is, first, an overview of the similarities and differences in laws. Next, the analysis turns to cases in which employers and property owners fixed the terms of their agreements. The chapter ends with a discussion of disputes where courts played a more active role in determining the intentions of parties involved in an employment relationship.

Perhaps the most important finding is this: Although slaves and free workers both faced legal duties to behave like "reasonable persons," slaveowners recovered damages for injuries far more often than free workers. I offer two explanations for this finding. Moral hazard problems associated with slave rental meant that wage premiums could not control for job risks as well as they did in free labor markets. Slave-hiring markets therefore required more legal intervention to function effectively. In addition, the capital concerns of slave masters figured more prominently in antebellum courtrooms than did the interests of mere laborers, just as capital interests prevailed in antebellum society generally. As one consequence of disparate laws, hired slaves encountered better working conditions than did many free employees.

THE UNIQUENESS OF SLAVE-HIRING LAW:
AN OVERVIEW

In choosing workers, antebellum Southern employers faced two labor forces – slave and free – and two sets of laws. Hiring a slave often generated the same rights and responsibilities as hiring a work animal like a horse or a mule. Accordingly, courts applied some common principles to hiring disputes over slaves and over animals. But slave cases appeared more often and required more subtle reasoning than animal cases, because hired slaves substituted for free employees. Like free workers and unlike beasts, hired slaves had legal duties to behave like reasonable persons. Despite seemingly similar behavioral standards, slaveowners collected damage awards in antebellum labor disputes far more often than free employees. In fact, free workers (and their representatives) throughout the nineteenth century rarely won lawsuits for on-the-job injuries. Why the dissimilar laws? Two reasons seem plausible: differences in the potential use of market mechanisms for risk shifting and differences in the political power of capital and labor.

The apparent lack of legal recourse for antebellum free workers did not necessarily imply a lack of compensation for job risks. For example, Peter Way found that dangerous jobs in antebellum canal construction paid higher wages.[3] Stanley Lebergott reported that antebellum miners and workers in iron and steel manufacturing earned more than farm and common laborers, domestics, and textile workers.[4] Some antebellum employers kept injured free workers on the payroll and set up funds to pay medical bills, although these practices were voluntary rather than part of enforceable contracts. In their work on postbellum labor markets, Price Fishback and Shawn Kantor revealed evidence of wage premiums for dangerous work and noted that some labor disputes ended in settlements rather than court-awarded damages.[5] Empirical evidence suggests, therefore, that free workers in the nineteenth century received at least partial compensation for the risks of jobs.

The salient question, however, is whether free workers earned more than slaves in comparable jobs to compensate for the different liability rules. Much of the evidence points to an affirmative answer. Antebellum employers continued to use both types of labor, despite complaints by free workers.[6] This fact alone leads to the logical inference that compensating differentials existed. The scant data available indicate that total outlays for slave labor – excluding expected litigation costs and including rent paid to masters, overwork costs, and expenses for clothing, food, and shelter – fell short of the wages paid to free workers.[7] In some instances, the harmonizing factor may have been productivity rather than wages. Slave workers earned the same hourly rate for overwork as free workers in comparable jobs. However, slaves may have been more reliable (they were a captive labor force, after all) and more productive.[8] Productivity differences therefore could have counterbalanced divergent liability rules and led to comparable earnings for slaves and free workers.

If free workers used the market to shift risk, why did slaveowners resort to courts? In part, because market devices may not have served the slave-hiring market as effectively. Free workers and their employers had a direct relationship; slaves and their hirers did not. By its nature, the slave-hiring arrangement had three parties: slaveowner, slave hireling, and employer. Slave masters, like free workers, requested higher payments for dangerous jobs. Unlike free workers, however, masters were not on the spot to protect their interests. And although slaves likely were as interested in saving their own necks as their masters were in avoiding property damages, they could not resist employers as readily as free workers.[9] The tripartite structure of slave-hiring arrangements generated moral hazard problems that were absent in free-worker cases. As a vehicle for shifting risk, then, the market probably adapted better for free employees.

I suggest that another factor came into play, however: the economic and political power of capital interests. Slaveowners, like enterprising industrialists, laid claim to highly valuable capital assets. Wage workers did not. Whereas a slave's worth – at least to his owner – was readily calculated, the value of a free person remains a controversial subject today. Accordingly, bringing a claim for an ill-defined value of life simply might not have been worth it for individual workers, even if they were not fully compensated for job risks. And through much of the nineteenth century, laborers found collective action costly or even illegal to undertake.[10] Those who did venture into court were likely to encounter the same legal attitude as an 1881 South Carolina employee plaintiff who had lost her eye in a loom accident. Here, the court said the plaintiff should not win damages because "[t]o hold an employer as insurer . . . would be a death-blow to some of the most important enterprises upon which the material progress of the country depends. . . . It would . . . destroy capital."[11] Had the unfortunate woman been a slave, her master might successfully have argued that the defendant should pay up because the job was riskier than the slaveowner could have reasonably expected.

The relative lack of power held by laborers meant something else, too: Despite the existence of compensating differentials, the weight of empirical evidence tends to show that workers did not fully succeed in shifting risks to employers. Although Richard Epstein reported that English colliers explicitly contracted around legal rules in order to shift risks to employers, Richard Posner did not find the same for American workers.[12] Fishback and Kantor's work suggested that workers received only partial compensation for the risks of accidents and no compensation for occupational illnesses. Hazards not easily foreseen by workers caused particular problems. Although employees could have quit jobs upon discovering unanticipated dangers, court cases show that they did so at the peril of losing back wages.[13] Back wages were potentially substantial in jobs that paid retroactively and at long intervals.[14] What is more, workers might have uncovered risks only after suffering injuries. One might suppose that, although these injured workers lost out, future workers would have demanded wage premiums. Yet court cases show that judges presumed workers to have legally "assumed" risks that had little to do with their job duties or work surroundings. Such risks would have been difficult even for future workers to foresee and build into wage requests. What of the post-accident payments made to workers? Christopher Tomlins confirmed that, by the time industrial accidents were relatively common, any employer handouts to hurt workers were in fact mere pittances.[15]

One other point deserves mention. Even if the average free worker had been compensated by wage premiums for adverse liability rules, antebellum life and disability insurance markets probably did not function well enough to permit individuals to protect themselves fully against job risks.[16] Consequently, workers who did not get hurt likely ended up richer than their productivity justified, whereas injured workers never accumulated sufficient wage premiums to pay for their losses.[17]

COURT ENFORCEMENT OF EMPLOYMENT CONTRACTS

Owners and employers of slaves sometimes stipulated contractual terms in advance. In the event of litigation, employers who complied with these stipulations faced no liability, but those who breached contracts bore the resulting losses.[18] The first two sections below offer details of slave cases in which slaveowner plaintiffs won damages for lost services when employers violated specific covenants or put slaves to work at jobs or locations other than those specified in contracts. Employer defendants prevailed in court, on the other hand, when they had fulfilled their contractual obligations. These rulings reassured future contractual parties that courts would respect voluntary agreements. Consequently, the judiciary encouraged cheaply made, market-based transactions that reflected the parties' joint desires.

Similar verdicts appeared in postbellum livestock-hiring cases, supported at times by the verdicts in slave cases. The final section describes some of these cases.

Special Covenants Between Employers and Slaveowners

Courts sometimes had to determine whether a slave employer violated a specific contractual clause. If so, the defendant paid damages to the slaveowner when his slave fled or was injured. In an 1808 Maryland case, for example, a slave was hired as a cook on a boat that was sold halfway through the voyage. The captain put the slave aboard another boat for the return trip; this boat was blown off course and the slave escaped. Because the employer had explicitly assumed the risks of supervision, the plaintiff recovered the slave's market value. A Kentucky court similarly awarded damages in 1830 when a boat captain failed to see a hired slave safely home to his master after promising to do so, and the slave escaped. And in an 1852 Arkansas case, the employer paid for a runaway slave because the hiring contract contained a special covenant promising the slave's safe return. The employer voluntarily took the risk that he would return the slave; he was (or should have been) compensated for the risk he bore under this clause by a wage reduction. As the court said, "[t]his covenant . . . may have materially influenced [the owner] in making the hire upon the terms agreed upon. . . . These terms, onerous or not, were voluntarily assumed by the employer." Plaintiff slaveowners recovered damages as well in a pair of North Carolina cases heard in the 1850s. In one, the parties had agreed that a white overseer would always supervise hired slave Alfred. When Alfred died, no overseer was present. Master Knox recovered damages for Alfred's value. The parties in another dispute had agreed to a clause stating that the employer was responsible for all injuries caused by a female slave's drinking. The slave committed suicide while intoxicated, so the defendant had to pay damages equal to her value. In an 1857 South Carolina case, an employer had to pay $600 to a slaveowner for breaking his promise to teach hired slaves carpentry and caulking skills. Such skills would have added approximately $300 each to the values of slaves Woden and Abbott. Instead, as the court put it: "The slaves were four years older, with habits of obstinacy increased by indulgence. . . ."[19]

Duties and Job Location

Slaveowners often specified the duties that hired slaves were to perform and the places they were to work. Naturally, slaveowners could not win lawsuits against employers who followed orders. Louisiana master Andrus could not recover damages in 1840 when he sent slave Henry to work as a hired ostler, for instance. Henry perished while driving a wagon and team, but such duties were part of Henry's job. Similarly, when Alabama and Kentucky slaves employed in sawmills died while working at typical tasks, their owners were not reimbursed for the slaves' values. In an 1861 Texas dispute, a slave had died while cleaning out a well. Here, an appellate court remanded the case, asking the trial court to determine whether the ordinary duties of a ranch hand included such tasks.[20]

If a slave was put to work in a job or location other than that for which he was hired, however, his employer paid for losses. In particular, judges inferred that slaveowners would not have hired their slaves to work in capacities more dangerous than the ones specified – at least not at the agreed-upon wages. Likewise, employers faced liability if they assigned slaves to tasks or work areas expressly prohibited. These legal rules held even if slaves were disobedient, suicidal, drunk, or careless. Such practices tended to produce only efficient breaches, because they assigned the costs of going outside a contract to the party that potentially benefited from doing so. Note, however, the key element in such cases: The employer breached the contract. As discussed later, courts typically granted no damages for injuries resulting from a slave's negligence rather than from a contract breach by the employer.

Slaveowners considered some jobs simply too dangerous for slaves. Historian James Oakes told of a Virginia slaveholder who hired Irish workers to drain swamps and use explosives because he considered his slaves too valuable for such hazardous work.[21] An 1847 Tennessee lawsuit bears this out. Slave Jordan had been hired for general and common service to a man named Condon, who subhired Jordan to Mr. Ensley. Ensley made the slave blast rock to help construct a road. Jordan lost an eye and injured his hand. His owner recovered $250 for the reduction in Jordan's value. In a Virginia case heard sixteen years later, slave Jefferson was hired explicitly not to work near dynamite. After a shower of blasted rock blinded Jefferson as he toiled alongside a railroad bed, employer Harvey had to pay damages equal to the loss in Jefferson's value.[22]

Hazards other than blasting cropped up in slave-hiring cases. For example, people generally viewed water work as fraught with danger and deserving of higher wages than land work. Those who hired slaves for jobs on land faced liability and damages, then, if the slaves were injured while working on water. In an illustrative 1826 South Carolina dispute, slave Edmond had been hired expressly not to work in deep water. Edmond, his employer Freshly, and several other men were drinking and floating down the river when they reached the rapids. Freshly ordered everyone to jump out but to save the tools; Edmond immediately drowned. At trial, Edmond's owner won damages – of one cent. An appellate court remanded the case, saying that damages should have equaled the slave's value of $1,000. In an 1853 Alabama case, slave King was hired as a livery-stable hand. Without the knowledge of King's owner, the employer subhired King to raft lumber. Even though King took the lumber to a different river crossing than his subemployer had ordered, King's owner recovered damages when the slave fell in and drowned. The owner of Georgia slave London likewise won damages the same year. London drowned while clearing obstructions from the path of the boat *Sam Jones*. Hired slaves did not customarily perform this hazardous job; London did so for half an hour under the eyes of the boat's captain. In a similar 1856 Florida case, the owner of slave Peter also prevailed in court. Peter, hired to work in a mill, drowned while trying to fish out a log clogged in the mill wheel. Although his employers claimed that everyone employed slaves in the most profitable capacity, the court disagreed in this case because the employers knew Peter could not swim and had rescued him once before. Testimony also indicated that hired slave mill hands did not typically retrieve logs.[23]

Other injuries caused by misuse of hired slaves also yielded damage awards for slaveowners in cases heard in the late 1850s and early 1860s. A Texas plaintiff recovered damages for a slave who ruptured his abdomen doing a job outside his contractual duties. In another dispute, a Tennessee slaveowner had specified that his slave not work on railroads, mills, rivers, or boats, or in water or mud. The slave was put to work digging a mill race, standing in mud for hours. He died from exposure and disease contracted on the job; his owner won damages for the slave's value. Kentucky slave Edmund died when the iron ore pit in which he was working collapsed. *Dicta* indicate that the employer was liable if Edmund had been expressly hired to work only in the forge, even if the slave had voluntarily entered the pit or deliberately killed himself. An 1853 Louisiana lawsuit apparently even influenced state statutes. Slave Jesse was scalded to death in a boiler explosion on a vessel owned by the Brilliant Steamboat Company. Because Jesse's owner had consented only to his working on a specific boat – not the one with the defective boiler – she recovered damages equal to Jesse's market value. After this case was decided, Louisiana enacted a law stating that boiler explosions constituted *prima facie* evidence of negligence by the captains and owners of steamboats. As a result, Alice Porée automatically recovered damages

under the civil code for her slave, killed by the dramatic boiler explosion on the steamboat *Louisiana* while he was working aboard another
vessel.[24]

Besides specifying job duties and other employment conditions,
slaveowners sometimes requested that hired slaves work only in a
certain county. As in other breach-of-contract cases, employers who
took a slave out of a contractually specified county had to pay for any
injuries that occurred. Although hiring contracts rarely stated why
slaveowners made such restrictions, the facts of various lawsuits
suggest plausible reasons. Among these are differences across counties in the level of public health, in the amount of water work, and in
opportunities for slave escapes. North Carolina slave Jacob was to
work only in Currituck County, for example, not on the water. His
employer sent Jacob to another county to work in a shingle swamp;
Jacob died from disease. A jury found for the plaintiff, but the trial
judge overruled the jury. An appellate court reinstated the jury
verdict in 1854. Two years later, the same court came to a similar
holding when hired slave Jack died from bad health after working in
a shingle swamp in Bertie County; Jack was not supposed to have
worked outside Gates County. A jury awarded damages in 1855 when
Virginia slaves hired to work on a railroad in Amelia County were
taken to Chesterfield County, where they died of pneumonia. The
same year, a Tennessee court even came to the legal presumption
that, if owner and employer lived in the same county, a hired slave
would work in that county unless the parties specified otherwise. Slave
Martin died after he was removed from the county – all the way to
Alabama. Although a jury found for the employer defendant, an
appellate court ordered a new trial and advised that the plaintiff
should receive compensation for Martin's value.[25]

Because wages, duties, and job locale were closely linked, wage data
gave courts clues as to the type and location of jobs for which a slave
had been hired.[26] When Virginia slave Monroe drowned on a trip
down the Ohio River, his owner sued for Monroe's value and won.
The 1837 verdict rested in part on evidence that slaves hired in Wood
County (Virginia) for voyages on the Ohio and Mississippi rivers
received higher wages than those hired for fieldwork on a nearby
farm; Monroe's wages were in line with the latter. Why were wages
higher for river trips? "[It is] partly owing to the great risque and
danger which are considered to attend the employment . . . and
partly to there being a greater demand for slave labor [in this employ-
ment]." In deciding what evidence to admit, the court said: "The
object in this case was to ascertain whether, at the time of hiring, the
parties contemplated any extraordinary risks; and the fact that a difference in the amount of hire was generally made when slaves were

to be employed out of the county, in certain purposes attended with greater hazards, seems . . . relevant . . . testimony."[27]

Postbellum Livestock Cases: Mirrors of Slave Cases

Animal hiring cases heard after the Civil War reflected principles similar to those in slave cases and often used slave cases as precedents. Many lawsuits centered around the uses to which animals had been put. In an 1868 Louisiana dispute, the owner of wagons and teams worth $2,310 hired his property out for a specific hauling task. The employer completed the task, then sent the teams out on a second errand; the horses ran away. The owner recovered damages for the entire value of his property. Missouri offers a pair of suits (heard in 1886 and 1891) involving mules. In one, an employer was liable for damages when the animals were hurt, because he had substituted another driver for the one chosen by the mules' owner. In the other, an employer paid for a killed mule. Here, even though the mule owner's driver was in charge, the animal had been worked alongside a scraper in an unauthorized way. In an 1899 Alabama case, a hired horse contracted blood poisoning from a wound caused by a protruding cornstalk. As in other cases, the jury had to determine whether the employer had been using the horse in a way other than specified. A 1907 Georgia case relied upon a slave case to deny damages to the owner of two mules that, while working at approved tasks, were killed by a falling tree. A 1941 case from the same state illustrates the obverse rule, citing slave cases to support a finding for the plaintiff when his mare was used for an unsanctioned purpose. The animal was intended for work only on the defendant's farm, but it died after being struck on a highway. Slave law even influenced Northern courts. An 1885 Wisconsin case cited numerous slave cases to justify awarding damages to the owner of horses hired to haul logs. The horses instead were put to hauling hay over ice; they fell through and drowned.[28]

Injured hired animals taken beyond an agreed-upon distance generated damages for their owners, just as injured slaves had in earlier cases. For instance, although a Georgia judge instructed the jury to find for the employer defendant, an appellate court reversed and remanded the case in 1891 on such grounds. The appellate opinion said that the extra distance may have fatigued the animal, causing it to stumble and suffer injury. The court used several slave cases to support its position. Even borrowers of horses could face liability for injuries if they took the animals beyond an agreed-upon destination.[29]

Some postbellum Southern livestock cases dealt with the liability of employers who kept beasts beyond the time specified in the hiring contract, at times relying upon slave cases for guidance. These employers paid damages for any injury that occurred. A North Carolina employer promised to return a spirited mare the same night it was hired, for example, or he would pay the horse's owner the value of the mare ($250). The horse was returned days later, injured and distressed. The owner sold the mare for $150 and sued the employer for damages. In 1876, he recovered $100 – the mare's value less the resale price.[30]

COURT-ASSIGNED LIABILITY IN EMPLOYMENT CASES

When slaveowners and employers did not plan for a contingency, judges generally placed liability on the party who could have most cheaply foreseen or prevented the loss. Employers were not to be imprudent or cruel in their treatment of slaves, nor were they to employ slaves without masters' permission. Yet judges were mindful of the possibility that slaveowners might mislead employers, and they crafted rules that accounted for adverse selection as well as moral hazard problems. Postbellum livestock cases contained similar verdicts, often using slave cases as precedents.

In contrast, legal rules governing nineteenth-century free labor markets were more one-sided. Employees of the 1800s rarely succeeded in proving their employers were negligent. If they did succeed, employers usually avoided paying damages by using one of three defenses: contributory negligence, assumption of risk, or the fellow-servant rule.[31] An 1877 treatise on master–servant law further noted that employers could always exonerate themselves simply by giving express notice of the risks of service, or by saying that defects in machines and negligence of fellow servants would not create liability.[32] Only toward the end of the nineteenth century did courts begin to pay more heed to the merits of employee complaints, in some instances relying upon the opinions in slave cases to resolve disputes.

The first section below focuses on the standards of care set for employers: Those hiring slaves were expected to be "prudent," as were those renting animals in the years after the Civil War. By comparison, although the letter of the law required employers of free persons to provide safe working conditions, the law as practiced gave few incentives for employer safety until close to century's end. The second and third sections discuss the defenses that employers could raise and contrast their application in slave and free-worker cases. Here as well, hirers of slaves faced far more legal responsibilities than employers of free persons.

Standards of Care for Employers

Employers of Slaves: Bound to a Prudent-Person Standard. Southern courts typically held negligent employers of slaves liable for injuries. Such a standard is inherently economic in nature: It gives people incentives to prevent accidents only when doing so costs less than the accident itself is expected to cost.[33] In a 1798 Maryland case, for example, employer Clagett had sent hired slaves home by boat, unattended, on a Saturday. When the slaves drowned, Clagett could not excuse himself with evidence that the master had told his slaves to return Saturday no matter whether their job was completed. A Missouri sheriff seized a boat to pay damages in 1844 when a hired slave cook fell through a hole in the boat's kitchen floor and drowned. About the same time, Missouri employer Christy was initially held liable for damages of $600 when he failed to warn hired slave South of the dangers of a nearby sandpit. Falling sand crushed South to death. A South Carolina slaveowner won damages in 1846 when neither hired slave Jack nor a boat captain could save Jack from drowning. Why? "The censurable part of the captain's conduct was in getting drunk himself, and suffering Jack to get drunk, thereby voluntarily bringing about a state of things not only to increase the hazard of the employment, but to prevent the means of relief."[34]

A series of cases heard in the 1850s show that carelessness cost other slave employers as well. An Alabama boat owner was liable for the loss of hired slave June, who jumped overboard after an unexpected night collision. The court reasoned that the defendant's negligence, due to his inexperience at steering the boat, caused June's drowning. The confusion of the moment, said the opinion, made June lose his life even as he attempted to save it. In a Tennessee dispute, railroad defendants could not excuse their own negligence when a train ran over a drunken hired slave, even though the engineer claimed he thought the slave was a sack of clothing. A Florida slaveowner recovered slave Esop's value from his employer because Esop died from untreated pneumonia. In a North Carolina case, *Biles v. Holmes*, Holmes hired slave Green to work in a gold mine. When Green was in a pit, several iron drills fell on his head and fractured his skull. A jury found for defendant Holmes, but Justice Pearson ordered a new trial, saying that the court, not the jury, needed to determine what constituted ordinary care. He also (guardedly) ruled that testimony by slaves as to how they felt could be admitted as evidence of injury, just like dog barks or hog squeals: "The only advantage of this . . . evidence, when furnished by brutes, . . . is that [slaves] having intelligence, may possibly have a motive for dissimulation."

And in the truly bizarre 1870 North Carolina dispute of *Allison v. R.R.*, an employer had stored an open powder keg under the hired slaves' bunks. An unsuspecting slave, who had gone into the bunkhouse with a torch to look for his hat, died when the keg exploded. The employer paid for the slave's value.[35]

Careful employers avoided liability when hired slaves suffered injuries. In contrast to the preceding cases, *dicta* in an 1861 North Carolina opinion suggested that a railroad company should not have to pay for the loss of Haden's slave Dick. Dick was sick and anxious to return home; the railroad company sent him. The bumpy journey aggravated Dick's typhoid fever, killing him. Haden sued for Dick's market value. A trial court ruled for the plaintiff, but an appellate court reversed and ordered a new trial, saying that any prudent employer would have sent Dick to be cared for at home by his attentive family. An 1838 Kentucky appellate court had reasoned similarly. Slave Philip had secreted himself aboard his employer's train. The conductor discovered Philip but did not make him disembark. Philip later jumped from the train, crushed his leg, and died. Although a trial court found for the plaintiff, an appellate court reversed and remanded the case. The appellate opinion said that, once Philip had been found, keeping him on the train for the return trip was better for both master and employer than forcing Philip off to face the dangers of walking home.[36]

Employers could be guilty of cruel as well as negligent conduct toward hired slaves. Because employers typically operated out of the master's sight, judges had to tread carefully in deciding exactly what sort of power employers possessed. To elicit work, employers needed enough authority to direct and discipline slaves, but slaveowners naturally feared the possibility of overly harsh supervisors. Court cases reveal the balance that Southern judges struck. One Georgia employer was cleared of liability in 1855 when he employed slave-catcher Hamblin to use the customary dogs to hunt for an escaped slave. The frightened slave plunged into a nearby creek and drowned. In a case heard the same year, an Alabama employer who (in the court's opinion) justly punished slave Sam for going to visit his wife without permission, was not liable when Sam died from the whipping. In contrast, Tennessee slaveowner Baynham recovered damages when employer Lunsford made Baynham's slave drive a wagon on a cold wet day, nearly naked. The court admonished Lunsford, saying: "Putting aside all consideration of what was due to the slave himself as a rational being . . . looking only to the legal rights of the owner. . . . The necessary protection of the rights of the master . . . demands that employer of the slave should be taught to understand that more is required of him than to exact from the slave the greatest amount of service, with the least degree of attention to his comfort, health, or even life." In a North Carolina case heard about the same time, hired slave Jacob drowned when forced to work in a fishery on a stormy day. His owner recovered damages. In 1821, a Kentucky court had even admitted evidence about the "general moral character" of an employer to determine whether a slave had been handled cruelly.[37]

Although courts tolerated some cruelty from employers of slaves, hirers who deliberately hurt slaves were responsible for civil damages. In an 1858 Texas dispute, employer Callihan had ordered slave Humphrey to hand over a pistol. As Humphrey did so, Callihan killed him. Humphrey's owner recovered damages. The same year, Alabama employer Goodson brutally punished slave Simon, reducing Simon's market value by $300. Although slaveowner Hall had accepted the full hire for Simon's term, he could still recover the diminution in the slave's value. Tennessee slaveowner Mrs. James hired out her slave Bill to Champ, the owner of the local public house. Carper, Champ's guest, accused Bill of stealing his pocketbook. Although the slave protested his innocence, Carper and Champ beat Bill severely. A vagrant white man later confessed to taking Carper's purse. An appellate court determined in 1857 that Mrs. James was entitled to recover damages from the two defendants. One of the strangest of all these cases comes from 1827 Missouri. Here, the hiring contract required the employer either to return slave Fanny on time or purchase her outright. After the employer killed Fanny, he had to fulfill his promise to pay for her, even though he had won an acquittal on a murder charge.[38]

Employers were also civilly responsible when their overseers treated hired slaves cruelly. In an 1853 Kentucky case, for example, Lee's overseer beat a pregnant hired slave. She later had a miscarriage and died. Lee had to pay damages. So did the defendant in a North Carolina case heard at about the same time. Here, slave Willie claimed he was sick. Infuriated, his employer's overseer (Massey) beat Willie, denting his skull and paralyzing him. The employer was responsible for Massey's actions. Such responsibilities did not extend past the employer's agent: A Virginia employer was not liable, for instance, when the overseer of a subemployer killed a hired slave.[39]

Despite civil sanctions against slave-hirer abuse, criminal penalties rarely arose. A Virginia court made clear that only excess punishment by employers was indictable. A North Carolina court agreed, saying that battery of a slave by a stranger might be criminal, but battery by an employer was not: "The end [of slavery] is the profit of the master, his security and the public safety. . . . The power of the master [including a temporary master] must be absolute, to render the submission of the slave perfect."[40] This was not true in some states, however: Tennessee slaveowners could punish their own slaves, for example, but employers and strangers could not punish the slaves of others.[41]

Interestingly enough, some courts expected employers to look out for slaves' morals as well as their physical well-being. An 1822 D.C. court ordered an employer to pay wages for a slave imprisoned for theft ten days after the hiring term started, even though the employer was not involved with the crime. According to an 1843 Alabama court, a slaveowner was entitled to take his slave back before the end of the hiring term and to receive a credit after he discovered that the employer had used the slave to steal property. Employing the slave in such a way, said the court, "was not only impairing his morals and thereby his value to his owner, but was also putting his life in peril."[42]

These cases show that courts typically instructed employers to care for chattel property as if it were their own. Such a standard encouraged the efficient use of resources. Yet establishing the degree of an employer's care was often difficult. Suppose a hired slave fell ill. Had the employer neglected the slave, or was the slave sickly to begin with? When judges could not ascertain the timing and cause of a slave's illness, they generally split liability – requiring employers to pay wages and medical bills for an idle sick slave, but abating wages if the slave died without clear employer negligence.[43] (Similar rules held for mortgaged slaves.)[44] One court explained why employers had legal duties toward sick slaves: "[I]f [the employer] be . . . not bound to employ a physician when necessary, and be entitled to an abatement proportioned to the time the slave is sick, then he can have no incentive to treat the slave humanely, except the mere feeling of humanity, which we have too much reason to believe in many instances of this sort are too weak to stimulate to active virtue."[45] Abating the hire for slaves who died without fault of the employer, on the other hand, recognized the incentive owners had to hire out slaves who looked healthy but were actually quite sick. When judges could not pinpoint fault, they subscribed to rules that simultaneously discouraged employers from ill-treating slaves and slaveowners from cheating employers.

In only three cases, employers paid the entire hire rate for slaves who died midway through the hiring term; here, judges focused on the problem of moral hazard without considering the possibility of adverse selection. Two cases were later overruled; the third was actually a sale case. The best-known case, *Lennerd v. Boynton*, was heard in Georgia in 1852. Here, Justice Joseph Lumpkin acknowledged employers' incentives to neglect slaves but failed to consider owners' superior knowledge of slaves' health: "The uncertainty of the [N]egro's life was equally well known to both Boynton and Lennard, when the contract for the hire was entered into between them. . . .

Apart from the principle involved, motives of public policy forbid a rescission of this contract. Humanity to this dependent and subordinated class of our population requires, that we should remove from the employer . . . all temptation to neglect them in sickness, or to expose them to situations of unusual peril and jeopardy." In a case heard one year later, Lumpkin further noted that *Lennard* gave weight to the rule that employers pay medical bills. If employers paid wages for dead slaves as well as medical bills for live ones, they would have an extra incentive to take good care of hired slaves. Again, Lumpkin failed to recognize the informational advantage of owners. *Lennard* was eventually overruled by the Georgia legislature. These statutes, written by Thomas R.R. Cobb, resembled the common-law rules adopted in other Southern states.[46] The opinion in the 1827 Kentucky case of *Harrison v. Murrell* foreshadowed the *Lennard* one, saying that the uncertainty of a slave's life was equally well known to both parties. In a third case, an employer paid full hire because an Alabama court considered a hire to be a temporary sale and buyers generally bore the loss of service.[47]

As in slave injury cases, two factors were at issue in slave escape cases: the employer's greater ability to keep a slave from running away and the slaveowner's superior knowledge of his slave's propensity to flee. Employers thus paid wages for runaways and had duties to pursue them. Unless employers had shown clear negligence in watching over their charges, however, they did not reimburse owners for the value of runaways.[48] Nor did they have to return slaves who escaped, unless the hiring contract contained a special clause promising re-delivery.[49] By adhering to these rules, courts discouraged owners from hiring out slaves prone to absconding. They also gave employers an incentive to prevent slaves from escaping, but not at exorbitant cost. Employers did not have to fetter slaves, for example, as courts recognized the price of such a strong measure: "[A]ppellees were not prevented from delivering the slave by an act of God, or the incursions of an alien enemy, but by the act of the slave himself [running away] . . . by an event over which it was impossible for them to have any control . . . unless they had caused the slave to be watched day and night, or had exercised a rigor and cruelty by keeping him constantly in chains; and it would be absurd to suppose [the parties] intended to bind themselves to observe such extraordinary diligence."[50]

The legal rules discussed thus far show that certain rights and responsibilities belonged to employers and slaveowners when a contract linked the two parties. But people sometimes employed slaves without their masters' permission. When disputes arose in this circumstance, courts generally sided with injured slaveowners. Because

hiring contracts cost little to make, this assignment of liability encouraged parties to engage in market transactions when doing so was
cheap. To illustrate: People who employed slaves without a master's
consent paid for slaves' injuries, regardless of fault. A series of cases
heard in courts across the antebellum South reveal this legal rule. In
an 1811 North Carolina case, an employer paid damages when he
subhired the slave without the owner's knowledge, then returned the
slave badly injured. In an 1836 Louisiana case, runaway slave Stephen
worked on a steamboat without his master's consent; Stephen jumped
overboard and drowned when he spotted his master in pursuit. The
boat's owners paid damages. A Louisiana case heard three years later
involved the drowning of a thirteen-year-old slave. A boat's cook put
the slave to work without permission from his owner. When the slave
slipped, fell overboard, and drowned, the master of the boat had to
pay damages. Kentucky slave Berry drowned when a man hired him
to ride a horse into deep water without his master's approval. When
Berry struggled, his employer threw him a life preserver – to no avail.
In 1851, a court found the man liable to Berry's owner. In an 1855
Georgia case, slave Wesley went to mill corn. When he arrived, the
waterwheel was broken, so Wesley helped pry it up. A lever hit the
slave and killed him. The owner of the mill (who had seen the slave
at work) was liable for Wesley's value. A Missouri slave transported by
boat from Kentucky to St. Louis was employed without his owner's
consent. When he drowned, the boat was seized in 1856 to raise
money for damages. In Alabama, Rachel Jones hired out her slave
Orange to Lowry. Lowry's son, thinking that Orange belonged to his
father, sent the slave to neighbor Fort's to help raise a gin house.
Some timber fell on Orange, killing him. A court determined in 1860
that, although local custom entailed helping neighbors out, custom
could not be imported into hiring contracts. *Dicta* indicated that both
Lowry and Fort could be liable for the death of Orange.[51]

As in injury cases, judges' rulings in escape cases encouraged slave
employers to use the market: slaves employed without their masters'
permission generated damage awards when they escaped. Courts
carefully calibrated damages as well. A Louisiana court did not allow
recovery of the full value of a slave employed by a boat owner without
permission (and returned promptly) while the boat was docked, for
example.[52] Ruling otherwise would have double-compensated the
slaveowner – he would have had his slave and the money, too.

Employers of Animals: A Postbellum Standard of Prudence. Southern
courts applied a prudent-person standard to employers of animals,
just as they did to employers of slaves.[53] Plaintiff owners typically
recovered damages if they could show evidence of ill-use or neglect

of a hired animal, especially in the late 1800s. Without such evidence, employers (and borrowers) faced no liability.[54] Employers were allowed, for example, to carry the typical amount of baggage on a horse.[55] But a North Carolina jury determined in 1875 that a prudent man would not have ridden a hired horse 33 miles in seven and one-half hours on a hot day. (The horse died of heat stroke.) In a Missouri dispute, the defendant returned a hired horse only to find the stable doors locked. He tied up the horse outside and left; the horse disappeared. The defendant won at trial on a directed verdict, but an appellate court reversed and remanded the case in 1889, saying that the jury should have considered the surrounding circumstances, the character of the property, and the likelihood of theft.[56] As in slave cases, deliberately cruel employers – such as those who drove horses that were noticeably ill – paid damages.[57]

Those who cared for someone else's animals – providing pasture-land, primarily – had duties to guard against malnourishment, illness, wounds, and escape, just as employers did. One Missouri defendant was liable for injuries inflicted on an animal by another horse in his pasture, for instance, because the latter was known to be vicious. And a Louisiana defendant was liable for the loss of cattle who escaped through ramshackle fences, even though the cattle owner may have known about the disrepair.[58]

Interestingly, the rules governing payment of wages may have differed in slave and animal cases. Non-negligent employers paid wages for sick slaves. In contrast, a South Carolina employer did not pay the hire for a sick beast because the plaintiff could not prove that the employer's abuse or neglect had caused the illness.[59] This difference likely reflects the political and economic power of slaveowners relative to owners of livestock, at least in South Carolina.

Employers of Free Persons: Minimal Safety Standards in the Nineteenth Century. In comparison with slaveowners and livestock owners, free workers of the nineteenth century enjoyed less protection from what modern observers might consider unsafe working conditions.[60] (To the extent legal rules protecting slaves led to better workplace safety, of course, free workers may have benefited indirectly if employers hired both free and slave workers.) In at least some instances, employers seemed almost unbelievably – or cruelly – negligent. In an 1892 Arkansas case, an employee lost his fingers in the knives of a planing machine. To oil the machine, he had to lie underneath it and hold up a bowl of oil, tilted near the knives. He failed to recover damages. A Missouri household servant was ordered to climb into a loft and retrieve pigeons using a too-short ladder. She fell and broke her hip but recovered no damages in a case brought in 1895. In the 1894

Alabama case of *R.R. v. Banks*, a railroad company was not found negligent for having a bridge so low that brakemen had to stoop to go
under it, even though the cost of raising the bridge was minimal.

Other courts took a more balanced approach, basing verdicts upon
the relative costs and benefits of preventing accidents. Twenty years
before *Banks*, a Georgia court had come to the opposite result under
similar facts. So did a Kentucky court in a case heard a year after
Banks. In a different Kentucky case (heard in 1890), a worker's family
could not recover under a statute for willful neglect because the man
was killed by a defective trestle that, to all accounts, seemed perfectly
sound.[61]

In many cases, plaintiffs who successfully established the negligence (or cruelty) of a nineteenth-century employer had vested interests comparable to those of slaveowners: They were parents of the
injured workers. A Missouri employer paid $1,000 in 1879 to the
father of a child employee whose hand was severed by a brick
machine, for example. The court said that the machine should have
had a sideguard. A Texas mother recovered statutory damages in
1882 for the death of her conductor son because the conductor previously on duty had known (or should have known) about a defective
brake and failed to warn the victim. One appalling Northern case
heard in 1885 involved a young and inexperienced girl whose first
period began at the home of her employer. The wife of the employer
told the girl that menstruation was dangerous and could cause insanity and death; the best and only known remedy, she claimed, was hard
and unremitting work. The frightened child worked so much beyond
her strength that she became permanently crippled and disabled. A
trial court granted the defendant's demurrer in a suit for damages of
$1,000 brought by the girl's father, but an appellate court overturned
the demurrer.[62]

Adult workers who won lawsuits that charged their employers with
negligence sometimes used slave cases to buttress their arguments.
Over two decades after the Civil War ended, Missouri courts for the
first time held defendants responsible for falling items that injured
employees – just as in slave case *Biles v. Holmes* – but only if the
employer had known about the problem or failed to cover mining
cars as required by statute.[63] In 1907, a North Carolina court relied
on slave case *Allison v. R.R.* to require employers to furnish safe
appliances and careful workers. Other courts of the early 1900s used
Allison to justify awarding damages to plaintiffs injured by warehoused
dynamite. In *Bush v. R.R.*, for instance, a Washington plaintiff won
damages of $1,200 for injuries he sustained while riding his
employer's train. Sparks from the engine ignited dynamite stored in
the caboose, causing an explosion that severely burned the plaintiff.[64]

The Fellow-Servant Defense

What if an employer was not directly negligent, but a careless co-worker caused an accident? Slaveowners typically won compensation for injuries to hired slaves under these circumstances, but injured free workers were out of luck. Employers of free workers simply pointed fingers at the fellow workers, who rarely had the means to pay any damages. *Brodeur v. Valley Falls Co.*, heard in 1889, illustrates one use of this "fellow-servant" defense. Here, the court determined that a company was not liable for the death of an employee struck by a barrel thrown from the fourth floor by an unidentified fellow worker.[65] The Georgia case of *Walker v. Spullock* provides another apt example of creative judicial reasoning, even where legislators had constricted the fellow-servant defense. Plaintiff Walker brought an action against the Western and Atlantic Railroad for the death of her husband under the Georgia statute of March 5, 1856, which granted damages to the families of persons killed through the negligence of fellow employees of railroad companies. Because the railroad was owned by the state, however, the court reasoned that it was not a "company" included in the statute and refused to allow damages on the grounds that the state could not be sued.[66]

Unlike employers of free laborers, employers of slaves paid damages for slaves injured by co-workers.[67] Because slaves could not negotiate wages, report fellow workers, testify in court, or quit jobs, most courts rejected the fellow-servant defense in slave cases even as they embraced it in disputes involving free workers. It is true that slaves had little power over their working conditions or co-workers. Yet along with North Carolina's Chief Justice Thomas Ruffin, I disagree with the majority of judges on this asymmetric treatment. Ruffin held that this distinction between slaves and free persons might have been sound if the slave had recovered damages. But the slaveowner brought the lawsuit and he, even more easily than a free laborer, could instead have adjusted the terms of the employment contract. If the fellow-servant rule was appropriate when a free man was injured, so was it when a slave was injured: In both circumstances, the plaintiff was theoretically free to negotiate contractual rights and duties.[68]

A larger question is this: Was the fellow-servant rule appropriate? Probably not, at least not after the industrial revolution and the dawning of the factory age. Although easily administered, the rule did not recognize the employer's probable comparative advantage in making the industrial workplace safe and the transactions costs workers may have faced in bargaining with their bosses and fellow laborers.[69] By rejecting the fellow-servant rule for slaves, Southern courts crafted law that probably should have applied to many free workers of the day. Postbellum Southern courts in fact appealed to slave cases to limit the application of the fellow-servant defense.

Georgia's case law provides a pertinent illustration. Antebellum Georgia courts rejected the fellow-servant defense in the slave case of *Scudder v. Woodbridge*, but approved it in a case involving injuries to a free minor employee, *Shields v. Yonge*.[70] About the time of the Civil War, however, Georgia courts (among others) began to limit the use of the fellow-servant rule in railroad cases where the plaintiff could not have influenced his fellow employees. In these cases the courts analogized the plaintiffs' situation to that of the hapless slave in *Scudder*.[71] Despite this development, employees who had agreed to accept the risks of their co-workers' actions remained uncompensated by the courts, regardless of how little influence they had had at the time of their injuries. In one such case heard in 1874, brakeman Macon Strong was thrown from the train after a badly soldered coupling broke. Strong died an agonizing death: the train ripped off his face as it dragged the man for several yards. His widow sued for $10,000. A jury awarded her $500, but an appellate court reversed the verdict because the company showed a contract that Strong had signed, excusing the company from any damages occurring through a fellow worker's negligence.[72] Although the evidence indicated that Strong probably considered these terms to apply to the men he worked with daily, the court decided that anyone ever employed by the company – including the unknown welder – was Strong's fellow worker. Still, in the same year as Strong's case, a Georgia court acknowledged that the fellow-servant rule might not succeed as a defense if the employer had provided dangerous machinery.[73] By the close of the nineteenth century, Georgia courts had overturned *Shields*, determining that the fellow-servant defense did not apply in cases of child workers. In one case, the opinion cited *Scudder* and said: "But has the Legislature been less careful of the rights of parents and less mindful of the safety of these little factory operatives [than of the rights of slaveowners and the safety of slaves]? . . . We think it is liable to no such reproach."[74] The ruling reflected the atmosphere of the 1880s rather than the 1853 legislation to which the opinion referred, however. The Act of 1853 provided only the flimsiest support for repealing the fellow-servant defense: The law merely regulated work hours and corporal punishment of minor employees.

Developments in employment law of the 1900s were rooted in slave-hiring cases as well. Under early-twentieth-century common law, the fellow-servant rule often failed as a defense if a superior servant had been grossly negligent or if a fellow servant had committed a reckless or malicious act to further the master's business. Slave law in fact foreshadowed this: In the 1853 Alabama case of *Walker v. Bolling,* a boat owner was responsible for the loss of slave Isaac when the ship's boilers exploded because the boat's engineer had been grossly negligent.[75] A series of postbellum cases used *Walker* as a precedent.[76] Other postbellum cases similarly relied upon slave cases in prescribing that employers must furnish careful, responsible co-workers and supervisors.[77] In the early twentieth century, state legislators finally overrode the fellow-servant rule, perhaps because they recognized that the industrial workplace was a far cry from small craftsmen's shops and that factory workers – like slaves – had much less control over accidents than their craftsmen predecessors.

Assumption-of-Risk and Contributory-Negligence Defenses

Besides the fellow-servant defense, other sorts of employer defenses succeeded more often in antebellum free-worker cases than in slave cases. For example, judges considered free workers to have assumed nearly any risk that led to an on-the-job injury. But under the law, slaveowners assumed only the risks that they knew about or could reasonably have anticipated. Arguably, one such risk was the potential carelessness of slaves. Indeed, slaveowners recovered damages only if their injured hired slaves had acted like reasonable persons. Put bluntly, hired slaves bore a legal burden in spite of their lack of legal standing. Still, such contributory-negligence defenses worked better if the injured employee was a free person. Nineteenth-century courts held free workers – including children – to an almost "super-reasonable-person" standard of care.[78]

Courts Carefully Evaluated Which Risks Slaveowners Had Assumed. Wage evidence helped judges ascertain the type of job for which a slave had been hired, as earlier-mentioned cases have shown. But even if an employer had paid a wage premium for a slave, the premium might not have encompassed certain risks. Courts carefully evaluated which risks masters had contemplated. This close scrutiny warded off moral hazard problems: Judges looked out for the financial interests of slaveowners who could not easily monitor the behavior of employers.[79] In an 1836 Virginia case, for example, Randolph employed Hill's slave to work in a coal pit, paying a substantial wage premium. Although Randolph took sufficient precautions to ascertain whether foul air permeated the pit, he was found liable for the value of Hill's slave, who suffocated. The majority opinion reasoned that the defendant was at fault because he relied on a single bucket to extract a dozen persons from the pit. A Louisiana court noted in a case heard the same year that people employing a slave in a dangerous occupation would not escape liability if owner and slave were unaware of the risks involved. Two decades later, Texas courts came to similar conclusions. Slaveowner Ashe received $5 more monthly because Ashe had hired out his slave Henry to work on a boat that frequently went beyond the sandbar lying across the harbor's mouth. When Henry drowned, however, a court determined that his death had resulted from the boat's lack of a pilot rather than from the risks associated with open water. (Henry worked as an ordinary boat hand, but had to sound the bar when the boat's pilot was inexplicably absent.) The wage premium Ashe received did not compensate him for the risk that had caused Henry's death, so the boat owners paid damages equaling Henry's estimated market value. In a different Texas dispute, employer Buchannon moved slave Biddy from DeWitt County to Old Caney County to pick cotton in the swamps. Biddy died. Master Pridgen sued for Biddy's value but failed to persuade a jury of the merits of his suit. An appellate court reversed and remanded the case, however. Because Old Caney was notoriously unhealthy, the court determined that Biddy's move was more hazardous than the parties could possibly have contemplated at the contract wage.[80]

Courts did not hesitate, however, to relieve an employer of liability when a slaveowner knew about a risk. Knowledge of the risk meant assumption of the risk. When owners could easily have insured against a risk by demanding higher wages, courts would not double-compensate them with damage awards. These rulings sent masters a message to anticipate potential losses and not to waste judges' time. Alabama slaveowner Taylor recovered no damages in 1836 when his slave fell into a boat's flywheel and died, for instance. Taylor had hired out his slave to the boat owner, knowing the flywheel was exposed. In an 1839 Tennessee sawmill case, hired slave Isaac was forbidden to work on water – but his owner knew that the mill sat on the opposite side of the river from Isaac's quarters. When Isaac fell in and drowned while crossing from home to work, his owner could not recover damages. The Louisiana courts similarly denied damages for slaves killed when their owners had permitted the slave to hire themselves out in specific capacities: selling milk, gathering wood, or towing boats.[81]

Expectations and customs mattered in assumption-of-risk cases. In an 1850 Alabama dispute, a hired slave boat hand drowned nearly one hundred miles outside the posted route and a jury awarded his owner damages. But an appellate court recognized that boats often made side trips for profits, probably with the knowledge of the slaveowner. The case was remanded so a jury could determine the customs existing at the time of the hire. By comparison, a South Carolina court found a railroad company liable in a seemingly similar 1846 case. Here, however, the owner had specified the work area for his slave Wesley and a train conductor knew that Wesley had traveled beyond these bounds. Tragically, Wesley jumped off the train to his death. Owners of runaways, like owners of injured slaves, could not recover damages from employers when they might reasonably have anticipated the likelihood of loss. The Missouri owner of blond, blue-eyed, light-skinned slave David could not automatically recover damages in 1847 when David fled, because any reasonable owner knew the risks of hiring out a white slave, particularly on a boat. As the court stated, the slaveowner was aware of the ease of escape and "must be presumed to contract with reference to it. He insures his slave, or indemnifies himself for the increased risk by increased wages." A Kentucky court heard evidence in the 1856 case of *Meekin v. Thomas* about the consequences of compensating slaveowners who had (or should have) contemplated the risks of hire in advance: "[I]t is always understood that the employer pays greater wages for slaves in consequence of the owner running that risk [of slave escapes]. . . . [I]t is not the custom of boats hiring slaves on board to iron or confine them when they enter a free port. If that should become common, the practice of hiring slaves on steamboats would be at an end." In this case, slave Lewis had been employed as a fireman. He escaped in Cincinnati. Although a trial court found for the plaintiff, an appellate court reversed and remanded the case. In contrast to the *Meekin* court, a Louisiana appellate court facing similar facts in 1860 sympathized instead with the slaveowner. Yet the Louisiana case differed because the plaintiff reasonably expected his slave would never reach a free port. Although the boat carrying the hired slave was bound for Cincinnati, Louisiana vessels customarily left slaves in Louisville or Covington under the protection of the slave state of Kentucky. Because the captain did not do so, the slave escaped; his owner recovered damages for the slave's value.[82]

Courts Applied a "Reasonable Person" Standard to Hired Slaves. Accidents occur, not only because jobs have risks, but also because humans make mistakes. If a hired slave was hurt or killed through the slave's own carelessness, the loss fell on the slave's owner as long as the employer had complied with the contract. Placing responsibility on slaveowners for losses resulting from the careless acts of hired slaves protected against adverse selection problems. Because a slaveowner knew – or should have known – his own slave's character better than an employer did, the owner could more cheaply bear this risk of loss. An 1852 Texas court heard these arguments when a slave hired in a steam mill caught himself in the machinery. "[The] . . . bailor knew

the character and disposition of his [N]egro . . . , which the employers did not know. . . . A slave is a rational being, capable, in ordinary
cases, at least, of taking care of himself." In an Arkansas case heard
about the same time, a slave hired for milling fell into the millstream
and drowned when he was off-duty. His owner failed to recover
damages. So did Florida slaveowner Nash when his slave Jackson contracted lockjaw after a train wheel ran over his foot. Here, both
contributory-negligence and assumption-of-risk defenses succeeded.
Jackson was a fireman on the train; his wages reflected a premium for
the risks accompanying that job. Although a trial court awarded
damages, an appellate court reversed and granted a new trial in 1868
because the accident was "entirely owing to the carelessness of
Jackson himself." Nash bore the cost of his slave's negligence, just as
he was paid for the risks of the job: "[Jackson] was hired by his master
to labor in an occupation which is at all times attended with danger,
and there was exacted a higher rate of wages on account of this
danger."[83]

The North Carolina Supreme Court followed similar reasoning in
a series of cases heard in the 1850s. In the 1857 case of *Couch v. Jones,*
slave Calvin carelessly got too close to a dynamite blast; his owner had
no claim when Calvin was hurt. Two years later, the court also refused
to hold employer Smith liable for hired slave Edmund's injuries when
Edmund, given a pass by Smith to travel by train to Wilmington for
his job, got drunk and turned up badly hurt near the tracks. Justice
Pearson reasoned that attributing negligence to Smith for giving the
pass would have encouraged him to confine Edmund, making
Edmund virtually useless as a hired slave. As a result, Smith never
would have employed Edmund in the first place. In the same year,
slaveowner Washington recovered nothing when his slaves deserted
their employer, ventured out in a blinding snowstorm, and suffered
frostbite. The court saw no reason to consider slaves differently than
anyone else injured through personal carelessness, because "slaves
have the same natural reason and instinct to self-preservation and
escape from bodily suffering and damages." Another North Carolina
slaveowner failed to recover damages because his "boy's life was lost
by his own folly or imprudence." In this case, slave Davy, who could
not swim, blithely rode someone else's blind horse into deep water
and drowned. The court also denied slaveowner Heathcock damages.
Heathcock's ten-year-old slave was hired to drive a horse around a
shaft of Pennington's gold mine. The slave fell into the mine and
died. Chief Justice Ruffin ruled for the defendant in *Heathcock v. Pennington,* reasoning that "a slave, being a moral and intelligent being,
is usually as capable of self preservation as other persons. [I]f an

owner let his slave for a particular purpose . . . the owner must have foreseen those risks and provided for them in the hire. . . . No-one could suppose, that the boy, knowing the place and its dangers, would incur the risk of stumbling into the shaft by not keeping wide awake. It was his misfortune to resemble the soldier sleeping at his post, who pays the penalty by being surprised and put to death."[84] Justice Pearson expressed dissatisfaction with this decision in a dissent to *Couch v. Jones*, questioning whether Pennington had taken too much risk by making a young slave work during a cold night. He also opined that the overseer in *Couch* was guilty of gross neglect for blasting after dark, especially because slave Calvin was known to have disobeyed orders before. Yet Pearson did not evaluate whether the slaveowners in these cases knew of their slaves' behavior or job conditions. Ruffin, writing for the majority, clearly thought the owners had (or should have had) this knowledge and should have provided for these risks in requested wages.

An 1848 South Carolina court even expected hired slaves to adapt to innovative machinery. In this case, the slave John Howell had worked as a house carpenter. His employer, the proud owner of the first circular saw in Columbia, put Howell to work on it. The slave cut off three fingers, injured a fourth, and later died from his wounds. Howell's owner recovered nothing. In determining whether the employer had appropriately employed the slave, the court in a divided opinion said yes, adding: "[W]hen the superstitious dread of steam shall have yielded to experience of its great utility and familiarity of its use, no master workman . . . will carry on a trade without [it]."[85]

Thoughtful slaves, like careless ones, sometimes paid with their lives; their owners paid with their purses. Kentucky slave Edmund drowned when he stepped into deep water to save a fellow slave after both had freed a boat from a sand bar. An 1847 court said Edmund had made his own choice to attempt the rescue, so his employer was not responsible for the injury. Naturally, an employer would prefer that a prudent slave try to save another slave's life if the employer might be at risk for the latter's loss. Here, both slaves were apparently considered imprudent in doing a contracted-for job, so the employer likely would have – and should have – faced no liability for the loss of either. The grounds for refusing to award damages in an 1853 South Carolina case are not as well founded. Hired slave Andrew tried to help the defendant's elderly slave when the latter's raft broke apart. Andrew disappeared, apparently having drowned; his owner received nothing. In this case, the court based its holding only on Andrew's volition, not his prudence: "The slave being a moral agent, and having volition, adventured from the impulses of his nature in an effort to protect his master's interest, during his absence, and without his knowledge or consent."[86]

Free Workers of the Nineteenth Century: "Super Reasonable" Persons Who Assumed Nearly All Risks. Nineteenth-century employees assumed the risks of an arguably negligent employer or co-worker, as discussed earlier. But they assumed other risks as well. In the eyes of antebellum judges, in fact, free persons assumed virtually every risk that led to injuries at work. Employers made persuasive arguments in some cases. In one example, no damages were awarded to an Arkansas mother whose son was killed in a train wreck. The accident occurred when the train skidded off a switch rail that was slightly lower than the other rails. An 1887 court determined that the difference in rail heights was widely known to be necessary for the operation of trains, so the man had accepted the risk that resulted in his death when he accepted the job.

More typically, assumption-of-risk defenses persuaded nineteenth-century judges but seem less than warranted by the facts of the case. A Georgia employer escaped liability in 1877 for injuries caused by a defective, dangerous machine that the employee allegedly used of his own accord. A Maryland father could not recover damages in 1892 for the death of his son, who perished in a smoke- and gas-filled tunnel. According to the court, the son must have known of the risks when he accepted the job. In a similar 1893 Alabama case, a workman died from breathing escaped gas, but his family recovered nothing because the court determined the company was not negligent – and the worker should have known of this hazard. In 1892, Virginia and Kentucky courts also concluded that free employees killed or injured in dynamite blasts had assumed the risk. Even an employee who expressed doubts about whether the blast was finished – but whose boss forced him to go back into the blasting area – could not recover damages when a cap exploded. Nor could an employee who failed to escape a blast when the defendant's cars blocked the only exit, because the employee allegedly knew of the cars' presence.[87] In these cases, one doubts that the plaintiffs had been compensated by wage premiums to undertake the risks that led to their injuries.[88]

Contributory-negligence arguments also convinced judges in many cases. In evaluating the possibility that workers contributed to their injuries, courts often held free laborers to a far higher standard than they imposed on slaves. In one case, a Texas jury awarded a railroad worker $10,000 when he fell from a handcar on some broken track and fractured his spine. The award was reversed in 1893, on the reasonable grounds that the worker was supposed to supervise the repair of the track. But in an 1895 Georgia case, an engineer who broke his arm when he jumped to avoid a collision with another train could not recover jury-awarded damages of $1,250, because the engineer supposedly had started his journey a few minutes late. Lost body parts failed to convince judges of the merits of a plaintiff's case. In an 1892 Texas lawsuit, an employee smashed his hand as he tried to couple cars in a railroad yard (at the order of his supervisor) and had several fingers amputated. The jury verdict of $3,000 was reversed. Similarly, a South Carolina appellate court reversed a jury verdict of $2,000 for an employee who lost her eye. A Missouri plaintiff recovered no damages for a lost leg.[89]

Defendants even won when the victim's actions, however careless or reckless, had little to do with the accident itself. For example, because a watchman had boarded an engine against the posted rules of the railroad company, his employer bore no liability for the man's death when he was pinned in the engine after a wreck and drowned. Testimony indicated that employees frequently violated such rules, sometimes at the employer's request. Still, an 1889 Virginia appellate court set aside a jury verdict of $8,000. About the same time, the heirs of an Arkansas trainman – who fell to his death from a bridge that was under repair, unbeknownst to the decedent – could not recover the damages of $9,600 initially awarded, either, because the man allegedly ran the train at a speed slightly higher than usual.[90]

Even children were held to lofty standards of care in the nineteenth-century South. In one horrible 1889 Missouri case, a young boy used a freight elevator because he wanted a drink; the only water available was on the top level of his employer's building. The elevator operator sat in the basement and could not see the elevator from his perch. When the boy was just about to get off the elevator, the operator suddenly reversed the machine, then sent it back up again, crushing the boy in the shaft. His father could not recover damages, because the boy allegedly knew where the operator sat and knew he was supposed to use the stairs. In an 1896 Louisiana case, a fourteen-year-old boy hired to punch holes in tin was killed when he adjusted a motorized belt and fell into an open machine. His father failed to recover damages.[91]

By the twentieth century, some of these employer defenses failed, particularly when plaintiffs used slave cases as supports. The plaintiff in the 1911 North Carolina case of *Haynie v. Power Co.* cited *dicta* in a slave case to reinforce his arguments, for example.[92] Here, the plaintiff was the father of a thirteen-year-old boy killed in the machinery of his employer's engine room. The father produced evidence that the boy was supposed to be carrying water on the other side of the river. Although a trial court nonsuited the plaintiff, an appellate court granted a new trial, saying that parents could specify contractual duties for their children just as slaveowners had done for slaves. According to the *Haynie* court, if employers used children in ways other than those specified in the contract, their parents were entitled to damages, just as slaveowners had received damages for ill-used slaves. Other twentieth-century courts relied on the slave case of *R.R. v. Jones* to invalidate certain hiring contracts that assigned all risks of employment to the employee; these courts ruled that employers could not contract out of gross negligence.[93] No more could employers resort to the tactics like the one revealed by an 1890 South Carolina case. There, a conductor had hit his head on a projecting roof in February 1887. He died in November; his wife sued and received a jury award of $6,974. An appellate court reversed, however, because the man – who, to all accounts was suffering from a severe and disorienting head injury – had agreed in writing on August 8 to take $390 in exchange for releasing the company from future claims.[94] Eventually, of course, workers' compensation statutes took the place of litigation over the negligence of the parties to employment contracts.[95]

CONCLUSION

In crafting the law of slave hiring, Southern judges took seriously the challenge put forth by Sir William Jones in his classic statement on bailments: "Nor must it ever be forgotten, that [these] contracts are among the principal springs and wheels of civil society; that, if a want of mutual confidence, or any other cause, were to weaken them or obstruct their motion, the whole machine would instantly be disordered or broken to pieces."[96] Antebellum judges protected the Southern way of life in part by paying particular attention to the workings of slave rental markets. Indeed, the law of slave hiring, like that of slave sales, showed sophistication far beyond the law governing the bailment of cheaper chattels like livestock. Similar principles applied in some instances, but judges considered slave cases much more frequently and more carefully than animal cases. Most animal cases in fact arose after the Civil War; many of these relied on slave cases as precedents. But hired slaves shared characteristics with free workers as well: They possessed human intelligence, volition, and a superior ability to avoid danger. The law also reflected this. Like free employees, slaves had a duty to look out for themselves – to be "reasonable persons." Still, judges distinguished hireling slaves in important ways: Masters established liability and won damages more frequently for injuries to hired slaves than did free persons hurt on the job. Judges nearly always rejected the fellow-servant rule in slave cases; they less frequently presumed that a slaveowner had assumed job risks; and they scrutinized contributory-negligence arguments more closely when the possibly negligent victim was valuable property owned by the plaintiff. And damage claims for slaves, unlike damage claims for personal injuries, did not die with the victim.

Why did these differences in law occur and how did they affect the well-being of workers? One explanation lies in the efficacy of market mechanisms to shift risks. Because free workers had direct relationships with their employers, they could more easily use wage premiums as a risk-shifting device. But political power probably affected the law as well. The evidence suggests that wage premiums, coupled with the workings of antebellum insurance markets, did not fully compensate workers for job risks. Injured workers were unable to make up the difference in the courtroom. Injured slaves were another matter entirely. Although costs to slaves – like costs to ordinary laborers – counted for little in antebellum society, the capital interests of powerful slaveowners mattered considerably. To protect slaveowners, courts had to protect slaves. Consequently, the same legal structure that kept hired slaves in bondage also made them less vulnerable than free workers to the negligence of their employers. Parallel developments in the law for free persons came much later, at times relying upon slave cases to provide legal precedents.

4

The Law Regarding Common Carriers
Slaves, Animals, Commodities, and Free Persons

Freedom of movement was a hallmark of the young American republic. Slaveowners, like other citizens, could use the burgeoning network of public transportation to their advantage: They profited if they could easily shift slaves from place to place. But common carriers, with all their conveniences, posed perils for the slaveowner. Trains, boats, and stagecoaches caused grievous injuries to slaves as well as offered a convenient means of escape. Faced with these threats to the Southern lifestyle, slaveowners naturally wanted to protect their substantial property interest in other humans. Owners and backers of railroads, stagecoach lines, and shipping concerns were equally intent on preserving capital investments as they extended modern means of transportation throughout the nation. Judges settling disputes between these propertyholders had to reflect on the slave's characteristics as they considered the interests of plaintiff and defendant. At the same time, judges had the unenviable task of applying law generated in a largely rural, agrarian society to controversies involving highly destructive machines wrought by the industrial revolution.

This chapter focuses first on the differences among laws for slaves, commodities, and free persons. It then turns to an analysis of the legal rules governing the carriage of goods and passengers, law regarding train accidents, and rules concerning slave escapes from common carriers. The law established by cases where slaves were injured or killed by common carriers sat squarely between contemporaneous law for free persons and for commodities (especially livestock). Common-carrier defendants answered for nearly all damages to inert commodities, many injuries to slaves, some injuries to free passengers, and virtually no injuries to other free persons. As in some sales and hiring cases, slave accident law was efficient relative to the law for free persons. And just as the law gave employers incentives to treat slaves well relative to free workers, so too did it encourage common-carrier owners and operators to watch out more for slaves than for free persons. In fact, certain doctrines commonly applied in today's personal-injury cases arose first in slave cases, where considerable property value was involved. The value of slaves also generated duties to prevent slave escapes from common carriers. Yet where judges had discretion, their verdicts in escape cases reflected a balance of social costs and benefits.

A BRIEF COMPARISON OF LAWS GOVERNING COMMON CARRIERS

Slaves, like other chattels, constituted valuable cargo aboard common carriers. Unlike inanimate goods, however, slaves could escape from danger. Unlike livestock, slaves possessed human intelligence. But cargo they nonetheless were – unlike free passengers, slaves embodied large and easily calculated property values. Consequently, when judges had to determine liability in slave-transport cases, they struck a balance between the laws governing goods and passengers. Like antebellum free passengers, slaves had to meet a standard of care when they rode aboard common carriers. Owners of careless or reckless slaves typically bore losses when these slaves were hurt. But just as in hiring and sales cases, slaveowners more often recovered damages when slaves were injured because slave property values were large and readily ascertained. Although antebellum legal rules governing the transport of commodities, livestock, and slaves usually allocated risks efficiently, the law for free passengers often failed to do so until the onset of the Civil War. Passenger plaintiffs after the war, like employees, borrowed from slave cases to buttress their arguments.

Not only were slaves sometimes hurt when they traveled aboard common carriers, they also suffered serious wounds or death in accidental collisions. Train accidents in particular figured prominently in nineteenth-century tort cases. With 35,085 miles of track spanning the nation in 1865, railroads shaped America's antebellum law as well as her landscape.[1] The evolution of this law in the South especially evokes the struggle between the old order and the new – between entrenched slave society and the emerging importance of modern transportation. Although some states held railroad companies strictly liable for injuries to livestock, judges flatly refused to do the same for injuries to slaves. In fact, early court opinions favored transportation interests in railroad mishaps involving any person, slave or free. Over time, Southern courts modified liability rules: Common-carrier defendants that had failed to offer slaves a "last clear chance" to avoid an accident ended up paying damages to slaveowners. As used, this rule had the twin virtues of allocative and administrative efficiency: It assigned risks to those who could most cheaply bear them and it cost little to carry out. Yet the "last-clear-chance rule" did not apply to free victims until this century. This is a key example of slave law as a laboratory for the development of modern personal-injury law.

Besides suffering property losses when slaves died or were injured by common carriers, masters lost valuable property when slaves escaped. Southern courts often had to assign responsibility in escape cases; in early cases, they held common-carrier defendants to a negligence standard. For the most part, these verdicts reflected careful evaluation of incentives and costs. By the late 1840s and early 1850s, however, Southern legislators and judges had begun to implement a higher standard of care to prevent slave escapes. In some states, this standard approached the rule of strict liability – which places blame even on careful injurers – that was applied when inanimate objects were lost. These laws, designed to insulate the South and its way of life, mirrored the mounting tensions that culminated in the shots fired at Fort Sumter.

THE LAW GOVERNING DAMAGES TO GOODS AND PERSONS TRAVELING ABOARD COMMON CARRIERS

Responsibilities of Common Carriers for Transported Slaves

[Slaves] have volition, and are endowed with reason and feelings, and cannot be safely stored away like a bale of goods. . . .

　　– *Scruggs v. Davis*, 3 Head 664, 665 (Tn. 1859)

When judges had to interpret contractual responsibilities in slave-transport cases, they generally assigned liability to the party who could have borne the loss at least cost, much as they did in slave-hiring cases. Failure to stock adequate rescue equipment was enough to make boat owners pay for slaves blown overboard, for example. In one such case heard in 1860, the defendant had to pay a slaveowner damages in a civil suit even though the court had determined the defendant's negligence from his violation of a criminal statute requiring boat owners to carry rescue yawls.[2]

An intriguing 1856 Louisiana case involving the actions of a common carrier actually had an insurance company as the defendant. Here, the plaintiffs had insured their slaves against drowning by shipwreck or stranding. When the slave ship foundered, the crew threw goods (rather than slaves) overboard. The plaintiffs paid part of the general average contribution for the lost goods, then sought to retrieve it from the insurance company under a standard clause in the policy. The company refused to pay, arguing that the special clause concerning drowning overrode the contribution clause. A court disagreed and approved the claim, saying the jettison was proper. Otherwise, the slaves would have been lost. Insurers as well as insured therefore profited from the crew's actions. As the opinion said: "The insurers . . . were directly benefited by the sacrifice, which was made to avert a loss for which they would otherwise have been liable." In essence, the ruling approved the destruction of lesser-valued property to protect greater-valued property.[3]

Yet slaveowners did not always win in slave-transport cases. Courts were mindful of whether a ship owner or operator acted in a slave-owner's best interests. Crew from the *Washington* tried to rescue slaves aboard a burning boat, for instance, only to have the panicked slaves fall overboard and drown. The *Washington*'s owner was not held liable in 1829 for the loss of the slaves.[4] Had the court come to the opposite result, future potential rescuers would have left slaves in similar situations to certain death. Although the owner of these slaves lost out, then, slaveowners generally benefited from the verdict.

Slaveowners did not prevail in court in other situations, either, such as when they could have protected against a risk more cheaply than defendants. No damages were awarded in 1859 for a Tennessee slave who committed suicide by jumping overboard while traveling with his master, for example. Because the boat's owner and captain reasonably expected the master to care for his own slave, they were not liable for the slave's loss. The slave was a captured runaway; he had told the ship's clerk he would rather die than return home. The clerk informed the slave's owner, who breezily said not to worry – thereby assuming the risk of loss.[5]

As in hiring cases, judges weighed the ability of slaves to take care of themselves. Courts refused to award damages to several owners of slaves who drowned, either through fecklessness or by acting without orders. In the 1827 South Carolina case of *Clark v. McDonald*, for example, a female slave died in the hold of a ship that had grounded on an oyster bed during the night and filled slowly with water. Because slaves "possesse[d] the power of locomotion," the court determined that any reasonable slave would have attempted to climb up to the deck.[6] It is not clear why the slave did not try to escape. Fear, ignorance, or unconsciousness might have played a part. The plaintiff recovered at trial, but an appellate court awarded a new trial, with *dicta* directing the trial court to excuse the captain. The slave was not chained. In fact, if she had been, the captain *would* have been held liable for her drowning (as he would have been for the loss of water-logged inanimate goods). Exonerating the captain, therefore, set appropriate incentives: Those carrying slaves would watch over them but not expose slaves to easily preventable injury, and slaveowners would not transport careless or ignorant slaves.

Courts reasoned that slaves had been negligent in other cases as well and refused to award damages to their owners. In a South Carolina case heard twenty-four years after *Clark*, slave Richard had climbed onto a lighter attached to a boat rather than the boat itself; a mulatto employed by the ship owners went duck-hunting and accidentally shot Richard. The court did not grant damages to Richard's master. About the same time, another South Carolina slave apparently drowned when he tried to swim across a river where a toll bridge had partly washed away. The bridge was clearly marked as unsafe. Although a bystander also verbally warned the man not to cross, the slave dove in and never reappeared. His owner recovered nothing. Nor, in 1861, did a Louisiana slaveowner when his slave Baptiste carelessly fell overboard and disappeared.[7] These verdicts placed the burden on slaves, and thus their masters, to avoid danger when they could easily do so.

The verdicts in slave-carrier cases gave people incentives to engage in market transactions as well. People who transported slaves without first gaining permission from the slaveowner were usually responsible for slaves' injuries, just as independent hirers paid damages under similar circumstances. In an 1850 Georgia case, for example, slave Jacob broke his leg when he jumped off a moving train. Although the company was not found negligent in causing the accident, it paid damages because Jacob was not carrying a permit that specifically stated the time and place of his travel. An important element in the case was the fact that the company had taken money for Jacob's fare. If Jacob had been rescued from distress, the railroad would have been liable only for gross neglect (as in the *Washington* case discussed previously).[8]

Responsibilities of Common Carriers to Shippers of Commodities and to Free Passengers

Antebellum common-carrier owners generally faced liability for the loss of inert commodities on board, unless the loss came about through an act of God or a public enemy. These rules recognized the advantages that carriers had in assessing and avoiding risks of damage to the goods entrusted to their care. A Louisiana boat owner was liable in 1856 for damages to a carpet caused by the bursting of casks containing chloride of lime, for example. Ten years later, so were the owners of a Georgia railroad whose employees left cotton in an open car upon a sidetrack within ten feet of operating steam engines. As one might expect, the cotton caught fire.[9]

Lively discussions naturally arose as to what constituted acts of God. Lightning, storms, perils of sea, earthquakes, and inundation might be considered as such, but rising water and currents that upset wagons or boats in streams were not.[10] Hitting snags or rocks did not excuse boat owners from liability for lost property.[11] Defendants who placed cotton within fifteen feet of a campfire on a calm night paid for losses in 1847 when a wind blew up and caused the cotton to burn, as did defendants who lost goods in the Chicago fire of 1871 – which arguably was ignited by a cow, not God.[12] And an 1858 Pennsylvania court in *Goldey v. R. Corp.* refused to believe a railroad company's claim of "unavoidable accident" when its cars hurtled off the track after running over a man. The man was a drover attending cattle on the train; he fell off while clinging to the side of the train because the company provided nowhere to stand. (The case concerned damage to carried goods, not the death of the drover.) In these cases, defendants could not hide behind the "act-of-God" exception for liability. And even if defendants could not prevent a God-sent accident, they had a duty to mitigate losses. Employees of a steamboat line were expected to air out barrels of furs when a storm soaked the goods, for example.[13]

The nature of the "public enemy" also created controversy in the Southern states. In Civil War Tennessee, the enemy was the Federal forces, so the Southern Express Company was not liable when troops led by Union Major-General George Stoneman attacked the Lynchburg depot and carried off stored household goods. Missouri also considered the Federal army a public enemy. But in Civil War Kentucky, Confederate cavalrymen under Brigadier-General John Hunt Morgan were considered public enemies when they stole a package containing $2,279. Kentucky common carriers were therefore excused from liability for damages inflicted by Confederate soldiers. In contrast, a North Carolina common carrier recognized the authority of the Confederate government. Consequently, the carrier's lawyers could not establish that a Confederate marshal's destruction of whiskey was the act of a public enemy. In an odd case, Tennessee did not consider the Southern army a public enemy, but its courts still refused to hold a railroad company liable for whiskey blown up by Confederate soldiers as the Union army approached. (This court first held that the company was no longer a common carrier once it was captured by the Confederate army. In a re-hearing, the court continued to state that the Confederates were not a public enemy, but it requested an evaluation of whether proper notice had been served to the owner of the whiskey.)[14]

Common-carrier defendants paid for most damages to inanimate objects on board due to their comparative advantage in insuring against losses. They faced less liability for livestock because animals could inflict wounds on themselves or others.[15] Owners more likely knew the characteristics of their animals, so this legal rule guarded against adverse selection. Had courts held otherwise, owners of vicious animals would have been tempted to ship the beasts in hopes that the creatures would destroy themselves, then to blame the carrier. Despite their lesser accountability for livestock, carriers paid damages when they could have more easily prevented losses, just as in slave and commodity cases. Common carriers had to furnish safe cars and reasonable facilities for loading and unloading beasts, for example, and they were responsible for unreasonable delays that caused animals to lose weight en route.[16] And when a horse carried in a Tennessee steamboat disappeared in midstream, the boat owner was held *prima facie* negligent in an 1847 lawsuit.[17] But legal rules also recognized that people could contract around widely known risks. Railroads could avoid liability by offering lower rates to livestock owners in exchange for exemption from losses due to overheating and fire, for instance.[18]

What about common-carrier duties toward passengers? Although antebellum passengers received damages less frequently than did commodity owners, they won victories in court more often than employees did. In a Delaware case heard the year before *Goldey*, for example, a drover similarly hanging on the side of the train lost his eyes when they melted in a blast of scalding steam. He recovered $13,000 because the court deemed him a passenger instead of an employee, despite the fact that the train carried no regular passengers.[19] Still, passengers found damages hard to win. In some cases, the rulings are reminiscent of those in commodity-sale cases – judges presumed that passengers bought a service with all possible accompanying risks attached. But just as the *caveat emptor* doctrine inefficiently allocated risks when sold goods were not easily inspected, the verdicts denying damages to injured passengers sometimes seem similarly lopsided. When a Georgia train ran off a worn piece of track in 1863, an injured plaintiff could not recover compensation. An 1866 court reasoned that, because iron was difficult to obtain during the war, people had to realize that train travel was dangerous. In the same year, a Missouri court decided that a railroad company was not liable for injuries to passengers when a train plunged into a river after the U.S. army burned a bridge – because the accident resulted from the act of a public enemy. Although a Georgia widow won $7,775 at trial when her husband was killed while standing on a train's rear platform, an appellate court reversed the verdict in 1869. Why? Because the platform carried a small sign requesting passengers not to stand there. Even though the train was extremely crowded and the conductor had seen the victim outside, the court determined that the man was responsible for his own injuries.[20] Nineteenth-century passengers who stuck arms out train windows typically failed to receive damages – including a Kentucky passenger, whose arm was crushed when two trains rubbed lengthwise against each other.[21] Georgia and Louisiana plaintiffs who jumped off moving trains could not recover damages if they were injured, even when trains failed to make scheduled stops. Even a Mississippi plaintiff too sick to disembark quickly could not win damages in 1869 when the train started up as he was stepping off.[22]

About the time of the Civil War, some passenger plaintiffs began to prevail in court, just as slaveowners previously had. South Carolina considered the possibility of allowing damages in 1855 when both parties were determined negligent but the common-carrier defendant was more negligent. By 1860, Virginia railroads had a duty to keep track clear for passengers' safety. In an 1872 Tennessee case, a passenger could recover damages if he showed that the train operator was negligent. A Texas passenger recovered damages in 1893 for an injury received when he got off a train that unexpectedly lurched forward. Yet a Nebraska passenger injured under similar circumstances failed to win compensation in a lawsuit brought the same year. Both cases relied on a slave case for authority.[23] And carriers in several states were liable for injuries to passengers in the 1880s and 1890s if animals strayed onto tracks in areas where the company was obliged to erect a fence, or if bushes obscured the view of the engineer.[24] Today's common carriers tend to face yet greater liability for injuries to passengers, sometimes even paying damages for emotional distress suffered in near-collisions.[25]

THE LAW OF TRAIN ACCIDENTS

Slave and Livestock Cases: Duties of Plaintiff and Defendant

Although many slaves suffered or died from injuries received while working as hired hands or traveling as passengers on common carriers, numerous others simply fell victim to accidents. William Goodell cited a particularly gruesome advertisement from the 1838 Natchez *Free Trader*, offering a Negro's head found by a railroad track for use as evidence by his owner against the railroad company, provided the slaveowner paid for the ad.[26] In accident cases, slaveowner plaintiff and common-carrier defendant were strangers, not contractual partners.

Some slaveowners argued that railroads should face strict liability for accidental injuries to slaves, just as they typically did for injuries to livestock in states where the practice was to fence out others' animals rather than to fence in one's own. English common law made livestock owners responsible for damages inflicted by their cattle and horses, but the American colonies adopted policies that required landowners to fence animals out.[27] As the new republic matured, some states (mostly in New England and the Mid-Atlantic) began to place greater duties on animal owners to fence and control their stock. Kentucky's common law placed a duty on livestock owners to keep cows, horses, and swine from straying onto railroad tracks, particularly if the owner had lost livestock in train accidents before. But fencing out remained the norm in much of the South. Animals were fenced out on the sparsely populated frontier and in states where animals outnumbered people – for instance, South Carolina, Missouri, Georgia, Texas, and Alabama. Georgia required engineers to inform the railroad about all livestock killed or else the landowner received five cents per mile of track on his property for every train passing through. Alabama even had a statute that granted double damages for injured animals if the defendant had an inadequate or damaged fence. Still, even in fencing-out states, livestock owners did not always prevail. For example, South Carolina held that railroads were usually responsible for killed cattle but not for killed dogs. And a South Carolina court logically denied damages in 1851 for a cow that had strayed into a railroad yard, because "[i]ngress and egress, for the purposes contemplated, must be permitted. . . ." Courts would not enforce a strict liability rule if parties had made advance arrangements to the contrary, either. One 1861 Georgia case concerned two mules killed by a train when they broke through a hole in the fence surrounding the tracks. Ordinarily, the railroad company would have been liable. But the defendant's lawyer produced a contract that stated his client would pay all expenses for a fence if the plaintiff built the fence and kept it in good repair. As a result of his own neglect, the plaintiff had to bear the loss of the mules.[28]

Despite their entreaties, slaveowners never benefited from the strict liability rules on railroads that some livestock owners enjoyed. In determining the liability of railroads for injured slaves, a Maryland court held that the state's Act of 1846 excluded slaves from the definition of "stock" for which owners were compensated if a train injured the stock. The court decided that "[N]egroes were intentionally omitted [from a long list of protected animals], because of their greater capacity to avoid such dangers than stock." A Georgia court included slaves under the state's Act of 1847 protecting "livestock and other property," yet it carefully added that only negligent companies were at fault. A strict liability rule would "deny to the public the incalculable benefits of Railroads. . . ."[29]

Rejecting a strict liability rule for injuries to persons made economic sense. Getting people off the tracks cost less than forcing trains to stop, run behind schedule, and use extra fuel to restoke engines. Although people used rails as a thoroughfare because cleared ground in a railroad right-of-way meant easier walking, they were smart enough to move to safety when a train passed; not so with inanimate objects or animals. A North Carolina appellate court put it this way in 1857: "In the care which is to be taken of a slave, he is to be considered an intelligent being, with a strong instinct of self-preservation, and capable of using the proper means for keeping out of, or escaping from, scenes of danger."[30] Unlike other forms of transportation, moreover, trains could not veer away from an accident; they could only stop. And until the invention of the air brake in 1868, engineers could not halt trains in any short distance.[31]

What liability rule did Southern judges choose in train accidents involving slaves, then? Not only did they rule out strict liability, but early verdicts favored railroads even if they arguably were negligent. In particular, courts denied damages in cases where engineers had not seen slaves because their view was obstructed. In the 1842 South Carolina case of *Felder v. R.R.*, a train ran over a slave concealed by tall grass growing over the tracks. The plaintiff argued unsuccessfully that the railroad should have kept the grass cut. In a case heard twelve years later, a bolt through the train's cowcatcher struck slave Ned's head, killing him. Ned was lying beside the tracks on bare ground, but the engineer could not see Ned in time to stop or give warning because a fence partially blocked the trainman's view. Again, the plaintiff contended that the railroad had a duty to keep the track clear so as not to hinder the engineer's field of vision. In both cases, courts refused to award damages. In the nascent days of railroads, courts did not even require engineers to warn of a train's approach. Cases from the 1840s illustrate this. Two North Carolina slaves were crushed to death while sleeping near a tunnel. The engineer saw them, did not stop, but supposed the slaves would get off the tracks because they had both the "instinct of self-preservation" and "the power of locomotion." Yet he did not blow his warning whistle. No damages were awarded. Nor was compensation granted for an apparently drunken Louisiana slave injured by a train, although again the engineer failed to sound a whistle. In another Louisiana incident from the same year, the defendant's train sped across a crowded street and the engineer neglected to blow the whistle at the crossing. Slave-owner Lessups could not recover damages for his slave, mules, and cart, all of which were demolished.[32]

These rulings that cleared railroads of all liability in accidents involving slaves were no more efficient than the rejected standard of strict liability. Although simple to administer, a no-liability rule failed to allocate risks appropriately in a situation where parties faced high transactions costs. Whereas a victim might more easily have avoided an accident until immediately before it occurred, the alert injurer might have prevented the disaster more cheaply at the last minute – simply by blowing a whistle or ringing a bell. It seems curious that people on or near railroad tracks would not hear a train approaching. But evidence indicates that, despite the clatter of an approaching train, people do not necessarily recognize the danger.[33]

Why did judges rule as they did in these early cases? The cheapness of administering a no-liability rule must have been attractive initially, when few accidents occurred. But the answer may also lie in the *dicta* of two nonslave antebellum disputes. One is from 1839 Kentucky: "The onward spirit of the age must, to a reasonable extent, have its way. The law is made for the times, and will be made or modified by them. . . . And, therefore, railroad and locomotive steam cars – the offspring, as they will also be the parents, of progressive improvement – should not, in themselves be considered as nuisances, although, in ages that are gone, they might have been held so." The other opinion comes from 1852 New York: "Lives are sometimes destroyed by an omnibus, a carman's cart, a stage or a steamboat, but so long as they are not imminently dangerous they cannot be prohibited. We cannot enjoy our private rights nor can we avail ourselves of the many advantages resulting from modern discoveries, without encountering some risk to our lives, or our property, or to some extent endangering the lives or injuring the property of others." The South, like the rest of the nation, gauged progress partly by the great thrust of steel rails through the countryside. A Georgia court went so far as to say, "Our State is, unquestionably, mainly indebted to railroads, for the proud pre-eminence which she occupies in the Union."[34] Many thought that assigning losses to railroads could hurt emerging entrepreneurs and stunt economic growth. States' partnerships with antebellum enterprises, particularly railroads, canals, and roads, could hardly have failed to influence the judiciary.[35]

As railroads expanded and trains claimed more lives, however, judges developed new doctrines, applying them first in slave – or occasionally livestock – cases. Southern courts began to refine their rulings to make engineers blow a whistle whenever something lay visible on the tracks. A North Carolina appellate court said in 1858, for example, that engineers had to sound a warning for cattle.[36] By the end of the antebellum period, many courts had adopted this "last-clear-chance" doctrine – which places responsibility on the injurer to warn of an impending accident – to justify granting damages to slaveowners. The engineer's failure to blow a warning whistle was an essential part of the slaveowner plaintiffs' reasoning in several lawsuits heard between 1858 and 1862. In the 1858 case of *R.R. v. McElmurry*, the court said that, if an engineer did not check speed and blow the whistle at a crossing, the railroad was *prima facie* negligent. This left the door open for railroad liability, but the court also said that, if the slave woman in this case was grossly negligent, her owner could not recover damages. Several other slaveowner plaintiffs were more successful in their quests for compensation. Georgia slave Cicero was killed when a train backed up across a highway without giving a signal, after it had crossed normally. Another Georgia slave was hurt when the train started too quickly out of the station without giving a warning. In one Tennessee case, the engineer neither stopped nor blew the whistle, although he saw something lying on the tracks. The "something" was a hired slave, who was killed. A court in another Tennessee case (*R.R. v. St. John*) acknowledged that railroads were the "most grand and useful improvement of the age," but they also had a duty to avoid accidents because they "enjoy almost a monopoly in the business of common carriers." In these cases, slaveowners recovered damages for injured slaves because no alarms were sounded.[37]

The last-clear-chance doctrine not only clarified the law and benefited slaveowners, it did not impose heavy costs on railroad companies.[38] Trains probably suffered fewer derailments if warned slaves got off the track.[39] More important, even with the last-clear-chance doctrine in place, only negligent defendants paid damages. In an 1853 Georgia case, for instance, a slave had apparently been sitting on a crosstie. The engineer blew the whistle at twenty paces (although he had seen the man at several hundred yards), but the slave did not move and was killed. The court determined the engineer was not at fault for believing that the victim would have speedily jumped aside. A South Carolina court in 1859 also excused the defendant from liability for running over a slave lying on the tracks in mid-afternoon. The engineer had blown the whistle, yelled, braked, and reversed, although he could not stop in time to avoid killing the slave. In an 1863 Georgia case, a railroad company was not held liable for a slave killed around midnight on a neighborhood footpath across the tracks. Because the slave was not visible at night, the court said that he should have been more careful. But the opinion in the 1861 case of *Poole v. R.R.* offers the most striking illustration of the doctrine working in favor of the defense. Poole's slave Guilford was struck and killed as he was walking on the rails in the North Carolina countryside. The engineer could perhaps have stopped when he first saw Guilford but assumed that the man would hear the train and leave the tracks. When Guilford did not, the engineer blew the whistle continuously until he unavoidably hit the slave. Why did Guilford remain on the tracks? He was a deaf-mute. The court held that the engineer, not knowing the slave was deaf, took all reasonable precautions. Eerily enough, *dicta* in the earlier North Carolina case of *Herring v. R.R.* foreshadowed *Poole*: "If a deaf-mute . . . be unfortunately run over, it would certainly not be negligence, unless . . . the engineer knew the man and was aware of his infirmity."[40]

By permitting railroads to exonerate themselves and their employees if a whistle had been sounded before a slave was hit by a train, Southern courts also curbed perverse behavior by slaveowners. The *Herring* court recognized certain incentives: "If the cars are to be stopped, whenever a man is seen . . . on the road . . . a knowledge of this impunity would be an inducement to obstruct the highway and render it impossible for the company to discharge [its] duty to the public, as common carriers." But preventing other perversities was more important. Owners might have been tempted to tie recalcitrant and defective slaves to the tracks to save selling costs if railroads could not have used warnings to mitigate damages. Even more to the point, masters might have recovered inflated damages for such slaves. If only the owner knew that his dead slave had been disobedient or disabled, he could have won the greater value of a submissive or robust slave from the railroad company. If the slave were sold instead, his owner would have had to accept relatively less money or, as Chapter 2 shows, run the risk of a lawsuit that awarded the buyer damages or rescinded the sale. The defense in *Felder v. R.R.* made perhaps the best argument for exonerating a railroad when the engineer blew a warning whistle.[41] Without the defense of the last-clear-chance rule, said the railroad's lawyers, owners might place dead slaves on tracks in the hopes of shifting their loss to the train company. In *Felder*, circumstances certainly suggested foul play: The slave's head and shoulders lay uncomfortably on the rail even before he was mangled.

Free Accident Victims: Little Recourse Against Common-Carrier Defendants

In contrast to slaveowner plaintiffs, free victims of common-carrier accidents – like free employees and passengers – found damages difficult to recover throughout the nineteenth century. Significantly, the last-clear-chance rule did not explicitly work to the advantage of free victims until this century.[42] (Applying the last-clear-chance rule in slave cases may have benefited some free potential accident victims, of course, just as liability rules in slave-hiring cases may have improved safety for all workers. Without knowing whether a person lying on the tracks was a slave or not, engineers would have taken precautions regardless of the person's status.) In many instances, courts cited slave cases as precedents to justify granting damages to the victim or the victim's family.[43]

Until the later 1800s, persons hit by trains could not win damages under the common law unless they could show that a railroad

employee had been willfully negligent.[44] Courts even denied compensation for children killed while playing on the tracks, saying the
children acted unreasonably.[45] In one gruesome 1868 Maryland case,
a widow recovered damages for the death of her husband, but not
because the engineer had negligently hit him – rather, because the
company had been negligent after the accident. After a train struck
the man, the engineer and the brakeman put what appeared to be a
corpse into a nearby warehouse. When they returned the next day,
they saw that the "corpse" had crawled across the floor of the building and died while reaching for the door. Not surprisingly, some
courts denied damages because the victims had probably committed
suicide. In an 1883 Virginia case, for example, the decedent had been
walking along the tracks, then lay down as the train drew near. (Evidence showed that the man had known the train schedule and could
have taken another road directly home.) When the engineer blew the
whistle, the man raised up, reclined on his elbow and faced the train,
then stretched himself out with his head toward the engine. Although
the engineer tried to stop, the man was crushed.[46]

Free accident victims had some statutory consideration but were
still unlikely to obtain damages in court. Tennessee and Georgia,
among the first states to apply a last-clear-chance rule to protect
slaves, acted much later on behalf of free victims of railroad accidents.
Tennessee statutes required the overseers of public roads to place
warning signs at railroad crossings and gave duties to engineers to
keep a constant, vigilant lookout for obstacles and to blow an alarm
if they spotted someone on the tracks. As in slave cases, engineers and
their employers were absolved of liability if they could prove that they
had complied with these duties.[47] Yet even if trains had no headlights
and blew no whistles, Tennessee victims' wives might not win damages
if the husbands were reputed to have been drunkards. Some of these
postbellum opinions came close to saying that the victims' relatives
should have paid the railroad for taking the men off their hands.[48]
Tennessee's statutes even perversely worked against the plaintiffs in
two postbellum cases. In one, authorities had failed to put up the
proper sign at a crossing, so the engineer essentially had no duty to
warn the plaintiff of danger. In the other, the plaintiff was hurt at an
"undesignated" crossing and the statute put no duty on engineers to
sound warnings at such crossings.[49] By the beginning of the twentieth century, however, Tennessee courts were citing the slave case *R.R.
v. St. John* to support the award of damages to plaintiffs injured on
railroad tracks.[50] Still, a Tennessee court in 1915 reversed the
damages of $1,000 awarded to a widow whose husband had been
killed along a curve in the track. The court determined that a lookout
had a duty to look ahead, not across the arc of a curve (which in this

case was occupied by an oncoming train). The court also decided that trains did not necessarily have to slacken speed on curves, because doing so would injure the general public by retarding the business of transportation. A railroad defendant also prevailed in a case heard ten years later. Here, a man walking between tracks near a manufacturing district was sucked beneath the train after the engine had passed him. The court noted that the Tennessee statute awarding damages did not apply to those employed near tracks; otherwise, railroads would have had to abandon timetables. The judges thought that, for similar reasons, this victim – though not an employee – should not recover damages.[51]

Georgia's law was as mixed as Tennessee's. Georgia statutes required engineers to sound warnings when they passed certain stakes alongside the tracks, typically located near crossings.[52] If the plaintiff had been warned, he or she could not recover damages for injuries.[53] By the mid-1880s, however, inadequate warnings could generate damages. In one 1897 case, the opinion fulminated: "[The whistles] must have rung in the victim's ears . . . more like shouts of victory than notes of warning. They were in time to announce his death, but not to aid in preserving his life." A twentieth-century Georgia court cited the Tennessee slave case *St. John* to support a damage award. Here, a drunken man was injured while crossing a footpath. The train had accelerated to make up for lost time just before hitting the man.[54] But plaintiffs who had crossed the tracks at a dangerous place or ducked underneath cars could not recover damages.[55] In an 1897 case, the railroad was excused simply because the train had been going at a lawful speed.[56] In three postbellum Georgia cases the tracks alone were deemed sufficient warning to the victims to deny them damages.[57] Georgia courts also decided that the state's midcentury statutes might allow damages for killed husbands and children but not for killed wives.[58]

As railroads spread throughout the postbellum South, other states eventually passed laws regarding the victims of train accidents. Missouri and Kentucky authorized compensation under limited circumstances.[59] After the Civil War, Kentucky courts used the slave case of *R.R. v. Yandell* to support awarding damages in cases where the defendant could have prevented the accident by using ordinary care to discover a helpless plaintiff, even if the plaintiff had also been negligent.[60] Many states similarly used the Alabama slave case *Cook v. Parham* to justify awarding damages to plaintiffs who had attempted to escape danger.[61] Yet a Missouri court in 1917 made clear that trains did not have to stop at every shadow. In one heartwrenching Louisiana case, a father sued for $15,000 for the death of his three-year-old daughter. An appellate court allowed him damages because the brakeman was not at his post at the time of the accident – but only of $250. The court determined that punitive damages could not survive to the child's representative. In applying Louisiana law, a federal court also decided that railroads had the right to a free track and that trespassers therefore assumed all risks. The court refused to award damages to a man whose foot was crushed as he attempted to jump off the tracks.[62] Maryland courts, like those elsewhere, eventually determined that engineers had a duty to blow whistles and put on brakes if they saw someone ahead.[63] But plaintiffs who had crossed the tracks in a dangerous area or ridden the cars in an allegedly risky way could not recover damages.[64] In 1890, a North Carolina court cited slave cases and used the last-clear-chance doctrine to support awarding damages to a possibly drunken victim lying insensible upon the tracks, yet four years later the court denied damages to a similar victim, despite a furious dissent that said: "Population is increasing, and likewise the speed . . . of trains. It will be more and more impossible to keep people off the track as the country settles up. . . . Commerce requires the free use of the track by these deadly machines, but the hand upon the throttle must be steady, and a lookout for danger well kept." By 1923, North Carolina courts had accepted the last-clear-chance doctrine. In *Moore v. Ry. Co.*, the court relied on the Tennessee slave case *St. John* and said the defendant could not speculate that the accident would have occurred even if a signal had been sounded. Here, the victim had been standing in the railroad yard, absorbed in checking over a list of cars. With no warning from the oncoming train, the man was run over and killed. His family recovered damages from the railroad company.[65]

THE LAW GOVERNING SLAVE ESCAPES FROM COMMON CARRIERS

Common carriers frightened slaveowners, for they provided an easy means of escape for slaves. But holding common-carrier defendants responsible for all escaped slaves would have hampered the movement across the country of other persons and goods, as well as obedient slaves. In a few slave-escape cases, the courts could look to contractual terms for guidance; the first section below reviews these. In most cases, however, judges had to assign liability. Certainly, common-carrier defendants who aided and abetted the illegal transport of slaves faced civil damages. When the master of a steamboat helped a Louisiana debtor move slaves to Texas in 1844, for example, the shipmaster was accountable to the creditor for $13,330, the value of the outstanding debt.[66]

Yet many slaves escaped via common carriers, not as passengers or invited guests, but simply as bold impostors of free blacks or as scared stowaways. During much of the antebellum period, only negligent common-carrier defendants paid damages for escaped slaves in these cases, even when courts had to apply statutes. As tensions grew between North and South, however, common carriers began to face a heightened standard of care. Soon after Congress failed to pass the Wilmot Proviso, common-carrier owners and operators in many Southern states found themselves paying for any slave that escaped on their conveyances.[67] The second and third sections below trace these developments.

Courts Respected Contractual Arrangements in Slave-Transport Cases

As in other disputes, courts looked to contractual obligations in slave-transport cases. Transported slaves sometimes had particular means of travel, routes, or destinations prescribed by their owners; naturally, plaintiffs could not recover if defendants had complied with the terms of the contract. In 1817, a ship captain did not have to pay for the loss of slaves who escaped in Liverpool, for example, because their master had agreed that the city was one of four acceptable ports-of-call. But slaves conveyed by unapproved routes or in an unapproved manner yielded damages for their owners if they escaped. A Louisiana ship was supposed to travel to New Orleans but went to a different destination, for instance. When a slave on board successfully escaped, the defendant was liable for the slave's value under an 1837 verdict. In a Missouri case heard four years later, master Chilton had booked passage on Lepper's boat for his family and slaves with Lepper's repeated assurances that the boat would leave Cincinnati that evening. The vessel did not depart until the next day; one of Chilton's slaves escaped under cover of darkness. Chilton paid dearly to retrieve the slave, then sued Lepper for reimbursement. Chilton won his suit.[68]

A Negligence Standard Before Midcentury

From early days, state legislatures (particularly in border states and states with navigable interstate waterways) constrained the judiciary in administering the law regarding slave escapes.[69] Owners and operators of common carriers were jointly and severally liable for escaped slaves under Maryland's Act of 1715. By 1787, North Carolina forbade slaves from being aboard ships after sunset. Under an 1804 statute, Virginia punished ship masters by fine and imprisonment if slaves on board went out of state. North Carolina's Acts of 1825 and 1833 prescribed the death sentence for those who concealed slaves on ships. North Carolina in 1830 quarantined vessels for thirty days if free blacks were on board.[70] In 1840, North Carolina and Louisiana imposed substantial fines for transporting a slave out of state. (Other Louisiana statutes had been passed in 1816 and 1835.) By laws passed in the 1830s and '40s, Missouri common-carrier owners could be sued for statutory damages when slaves escaped.[71] Georgia (1841) and Louisiana (1839, 1843) required bonds from shipowners to indemnify them against possible stowaway slaves.

Many statutes required common-carrier operators to see written permission from slaveowners before letting slaves board.[72] Maryland required this in its Act of 1838, as did North Carolina in 1840. Kentucky passed numerous statutes about slaves escaping by boat, the earliest in 1824. Its Act of 1837 prohibited slaves from boarding stagecoaches or trains without permission from their masters, else the common-carrier owner faced having to pay a $100 fine, double the value of the slave, and costs of retrieving the slave. Tennessee's Act of 1833 imposed a $2 to $200 fine and three to six months in prison for owners of boats and stagecoaches who carried slaves without written or verbal permission from their masters. Virginia's Act of 1836 instituted a $100 fine for those who transported slaves without permission, half of which went to the plaintiff and half to the literary fund. Virginia passed additional laws for ferries and bridges in 1839. Louisiana had specific laws that governed the transport of blacks aboard steamboats. Free blacks had to show their freedom papers; slaves had to produce evidence of their owners' consent.[73]

Stowaways typically generated damages for their masters – and sometimes fines – under these statutes. This gave common-carrier owners and operators the incentive to police their vehicles. Because people could secure their own conveyances more cheaply than outside slaveowners could, such a rule was efficient. A Maryland appellate court, for example, interpreted an 1838 statute "prevent[ing] the transportation of people of color upon a railroad or in steam boats" as including cases in which owners or operators did not know a black person was on board; New Jersey, Delaware, and Alabama courts held likewise.[74] A federal statute passed the same year said that slave escapes on steamboats indicated negligence unless the boat owners could show otherwise.[75] An 1840 Louisiana statute even stated that, if a slave was found on board, the captain presumably knew of his presence and was therefore subject to a fine.[76] A rare exception was the early case of *McCall v. Eve*. Here, the master of a vessel was not liable under Virginia's Act of 1792 for unknowingly carrying a slave out of the commonwealth. Even in this 1804 case, Judge Fitzhugh dissented: "[T]he act of assembly should be construed literally [because] slaves constitute a large proportion of our property, disposed to escape from our possession; and a disposition having been discovered in captains of vessels to aid them in their attempts, it was found necessary to impose severe penalties."[77]

Aside from stowaway cases, Southern courts initially gave common-carrier defendants the benefit of the doubt. Through the first few decades of the nineteenth century, for example, courts tended to excuse common carriers from liability when slaves displayed authentic-looking papers or a white person boarded with the slave. In the 1840s, stagecoach owners were not accountable for escaped slaves who had shown seemingly valid documents.[78] Nor was a Louisiana ship captain in 1832 because the slave's apparent owner accompanied him. In a later Louisiana case, a court would not let a slaveowner recover the depreciation in the value of slaves who had escaped using false documents but later returned. Why? Because the court determined the slaves must have already been vice-ridden when they arranged for forged papers. An 1835 D.C. court initially held a railroad liable when slaves had gotten on without papers, even though their tickets had been bought in advance by a white woman. The court ordered a re-hearing, though, after it discovered that the ticket purchaser was the plaintiff's sister. *Dicta* indicate that an 1850 Kentucky court – in applying a penal statute – would not require a ferry owner to distinguish between a slaveowner and a hirer giving permission for a slave to board.[79]

Throughout the antebellum period, an escaped slave's appearance also mattered in determining the liability of common-carrier defendants. Because slaves came in different skin colors, Southern courts were reluctant to hold common carriers strictly liable for escapes of pale-skinned slaves. Ascertaining the status of each passenger would have cost substantial money and time, whereas the expected loss associated with slaves passing as white was comparatively low.[80] In an 1825 New Jersey case, a ship captain answered for the value of a slave who masqueraded as a free black, then escaped. In an 1856 South Carolina case, on the other hand, a railroad was not liable for the value of two escaped slaves who looked white, dressed as white gentlemen, and held tickets. Nor was the railroad liable in an 1861 Georgia case for the escape of a light-skinned slave who was employed by his owner as a salesman – a job typically reserved for free whites. Similarly, an Alabama carrier did not violate a statute in 1863 by transporting a slave without authority when the slave looked white. If someone other than an employee was responsible for such a slave being on board, North Carolina did not impose liability either, at least early on. Louisiana courts also refused to award damages for white-complected escaped slaves.[81] Missouri's 1845 Code was explicit: Common-carrier operators needed to be "prudent" but not to take the greatest possible diligence in determining passengers' status.[82]

In rejecting strict liability, the common law helped prevent slave escapes when common-carrier owners and operators could cheaply take precautions, but it also enabled masters to move slaves about freely when they wanted. Courts also recognized the nettlesome incentive effects a strict standard could have generated. As a New Jersey defense counsel pointedly put it in 1821: "[Strict liability for escapes] would be a very convenient doctrine for those who had worthless [N]egroes and wished to get rid of them."[83]

Southern courts logically discarded a strict-liability standard in other cases related to slave escapes. Common-carrier operators often faced a statutory duty to return stowaways. Tennessee's Act of 1833 required operators of boats and stagecoaches to put discovered slaves into the nearest county jail and publicize the act in the newspaper, for example. Yet people did not have to drop their own business to send back a slave, nor did they have to take extraordinary precautions, even in the late antebellum period. To illustrate: The owner of a boat in which a slave stowed away did not have to compensate a Louisiana slaveowner in 1849 for extra costs of retrieving the slave. A court ruled that the shipowner complied with a statute requiring him to put the slave ashore and notify the owner, even though the slave was found at night but not expelled until morning. Had the court decided otherwise, any reasonable shipowner simply would have released the slave rather than incur extra expenses to stop at night and locate the proper official after hours. In an 1867 Louisiana case that also involved returning a runaway, the slave prisoner had been heavily chained and guarded. When the slave was permitted to go to the privy alone – still chained and guarded – he apparently jumped overboard, leaving nothing but a handful of his jacket. The ship company was not held liable for the escape, as the court determined that it had taken sufficient care in protecting the slaveowner's property.[84]

Toward a Strict Liability Standard in Later Years

The possibility of slave escapes always concerned the South, but it loomed larger as the Civil War approached.[85] During the 1850s and '60s, Southern legislatures acted decisively to stem the flow of escaped slaves aboard common carriers. Under Virginia's Acts of 1855/56, nonresident shipowners had to pay a fee and have their vessels searched for slaves. (The Virginia Supreme Court decided that this practice was constitutional in *Baker v. Wise*.)[86] The fine for noncom-

pliance was double the value of any escaped slave plus the value of
the vessel itself. In other situations, those who carried slaves off faced
as much as five to ten years in prison, a penalty equal to double the
value of the slaves plus the costs of recapture, and public whipping.[87]
Virginia's desperation shows vividly in a law passed in March 1863.
To prevent slaves from escaping to the enemy, county courts in the
Tidewater area had the authority to remove all boats from the water
and destroy them, with a county levy established to compensate boat
owners. Maryland even prevented free blacks and slaves from using
boats on the Potomac in its act of 1858. Maryland's law of December
1861 granted slaveowners the right to recover the value of any slave
traveling on a common carrier without a white person. Missouri's Act
of 1855 imposed a fine of double the value of slaves who had boarded
trains without owners' permission – whether they escaped or not.
Escaped Missouri slaves therefore could generate triple their value in
compensation.[88]

Judicial rulings reflected the additional stringency of legislative
actions, the growing tensions between North and South, and the burgeoning costs of maintaining slavery when rivers, rails, and roads
increasingly linked slave lands to free soil. Kentucky's case law dis-
tinctly demonstrates the heightened control courts began to impose
on common carriers. The state claimed the entire Ohio River within
her borders under the cession agreement from Virginia. Early cases
did not penalize masters of vessels who received fugitive slaves from
the Indiana riverbank – because the boats themselves never left Kentucky – but later cases did.[89]

The Missouri courts were among the first to hold a common-
carrier defendant liable for a slave who gained entry with falsified
documents. Slave Charles closely resembled free Negro Pompey
Spence, whose papers he had taken. Charles even pretended to have
a stiff finger – Spence's papers indicated a broken right hand. Yet a
ship captain had to pay $900 when Charles escaped. In its opinion,
an appellate court stressed deterrence: "Our slaves would be very
much impaired in value, if injuries to our property in them could go
unredressed, under the plea that those who committed them were
ignorant of the fact that they were slaves. . . . It is true, slaves have volition; they may leave the service of their masters, and may impose
themselves on others for free men, but it is necessary for the security
of the owners of such property, that they who treat them as such
should do it at their own peril. . . . [Slaves'] ingenuity will be exerted
to invent means of eluding the vigilance of captains, and many ways
will be employed to get off unnoticed. One escape by such means,
will stimulate others to make the attempt." Other states followed Missouri's lead. A Delaware trial court found a ship captain criminally

liable and ordered him to pay a $500 fine for an undocumented slave, even though the slave had been traveling with her mistress (who was running away from her husband). In 1856, an Alabama slaveowner recovered a statutory $50 fine from the owners of a steamboat that had transported his slave without permission, although the slave later returned home safely.[90]

In cases heard after the peace of Appomattox, the courts seemed more concerned with salvaging the fortunes of former slaveowners than with evaluating the blame of common-carrier defendants. A postbellum Georgia court granted damages of $207 for pale-skinned slave Amanda after she escaped on a train, for example. The court's rationale was that, because of abolition, the railroad would never have to pay damages in another escape case, whereas slaveowners had suffered great losses. In an 1867 Kentucky case, one of plaintiff Young's two escaped slaves had returned to his hometown two months after departing on the train. Although the slaves may have had papers, the railroad owed damages for the full value of the vanished slave and two months' hire of the returned slave. In a Georgia case heard the same year, a railroad paid damages for an escaped slave not carrying written permission, even though the slave was traveling with a white companion presumed to be his owner. This case contrasts with an earlier, similar, South Carolina case, in which a jury had found for the defendant and an appellate court had denied a new trial. The South Carolina court had been reluctant to impose liability, saying: "If the rule urged upon us were adopted, it would seem to make the transportation of slaves by the rail road quite an impracticable business."[91] But as the Georgia justices well knew, their 1867 ruling could no longer affect the practicability of transporting slaves: War's end had robbed them of that power.

CONCLUSION

The cases focused on here demonstrate that, in the nineteenth century as today, law reflects the needs of the time. Slave-carrier cases show logical geographic patterns. More cases and more statutes concerning slave escapes appeared in border and coastal states, and in states located along an interstate waterway or containing interstate railroads (predominantly Kentucky, Delaware, Maryland, the District of Columbia, and Virginia). States with the most railroad miles or the most miles per slave (particularly Georgia, North Carolina, South Carolina, Virginia, Tennessee, and Florida) were the first to codify and clarify their laws regarding railroads and slaves. As railroads grew in importance, so did the specificity of the common law, especially in Tennessee. States with more slaves and more common carriers (for example, Virginia, Georgia, and South Carolina) naturally had more lawsuits because conflict was likelier. Virtually no railroad cases were heard in states like Arkansas, Texas, Missouri, and Mississippi, where tracks were scarce.[92]

But the law mirrored the needs of the time in a more subtle way as well. Common-carrier cases reveal that nineteenth-century carriers were responsible for injured slaves – more so than for injured free persons, but less so than for damaged livestock. Common carriers faced less liability for runaway slaves than for lost commodities. These verdicts recognized the market value of slaves, yet acknowledged slaves' ability to avoid danger and to carry out ingenious escapes. As a result, the judiciary helped conserve slave property values as well as protect the expansion of public transportation.

Even more significant, the doctrines developed in common-carrier cases to protect valuable slave property later served as an important foundation for modern personal-injury cases. Postbellum courts accommodated the changing attitudes toward injurers and victims, in part, by borrowing from laws that pertained to a vanished way of life.

5

The Law Regarding Governments, Government Officials, Slave Patrollers, and Overseers

Protecting Private Property versus Keeping Public Peace

To keep the peace of Southern society, slaveowners relinquished to others a certain amount of control over slaves. Sheriffs, constables, and jailors had some authority over others' slaves, just as they had over others' lives and possessions generally. But these public officials were not the only persons legally entitled to supervise slaves. In lieu of a standing police force, many Southern states established citizen patrols to keep order. Slave patrols might be thought of as a way of institutionalizing the "hue and cry," an old English practice that required bystanders to shout loudly when a felon escaped and to pursue the criminal until he was caught.[1] The object of pursuit differed, of course: Southern patrollers often hunted those whose only "crime" was attempting to escape a life of bondage. Besides providing for public control of slaves, Southerners also granted some power to private individuals, particularly overseers.

By comparison to present-day disputes, nineteenth-century plaintiffs (slaveowners and otherwise) were more likely to sue – and to recover damages from – public officials rather than the government itself. As the first section reveals, governments hid behind a shield of sovereign immunity, whereas local officials (particularly sheriffs) faced personal liability if they negligently caused injuries. The second and third sections show that slave patrollers and overseers faced duties of care similar to those of local officials. Although I cannot say for sure that these legal rules were efficient, I suggest that sovereign immunity coupled with private responsibility of public officials probably suited the antebellum system of law and order better than it would fit today's regime. And, by balancing the property interest of masters against society's interest in cheaply preserving peace in the slave quarters, the law governing patrollers and overseers generally kept small the joint costs of moral hazard and adverse selection.

Although the law for patrollers and overseers is cut from the same cloth as the rest of slave law, by its nature it did not often serve as a pattern for nonslave cases.[2] The law for governmental defendants did. Here, as elsewhere, slave cases appear far more often than similar contemporaneous nonslave cases – partly because fugitive slaves landed in county jails, partly because slaves often served as collateral easily seized by sheriffs on behalf of creditors, and partly because slaves represented large chunks of marketable property. Slave cases were also occasionally cited as precedents in postbellum disputes, as they were in other areas of law.

CASES INVOLVING GOVERNMENTAL DEFENDANTS

Sovereign Immunity versus Personal Liability of Public Officials

Government cannot be sued without its consent. In antebellum days, federal and state governments, officials, and employees were virtually immune from suit. Governments at these levels rarely acceded to suits for torts committed by their officers or employees. Federal tort immunity was so firmly entrenched at the time of the Civil War that, when Congress in 1863 established the Court of Claims to adjudicate claims against the United States, plaintiffs brought only contract claims.[3] Although states can waive the immunity granted them by the Eleventh Amendment to the U.S. Constitution, no Southern state did so before the Civil War.[4] What is more, although antebellum federal and state civil servants theoretically bore personal liability for professional acts, they seldom faced suit.

Sovereign immunity extends to local governments when they carry out services that state government might otherwise have to provide. Since 1842, courts have attempted to distinguish between these "governmental" services and so-called "proprietary" services that private businesses might furnish just as reasonably.[5] Little uniformity exists across jurisdictions even today. Edwin Borchard called for standardizing reform in 1924, but as yet none has transpired.[6] Indeed, the state of South Carolina grew so impatient at the imprecision of the law that it conferred blanket immunity upon local government in 1911.[7] Few people actually brought lawsuits against local governments before the late 1800s and even fewer won, particularly in the South. Instead, plaintiffs sued local officials – especially sheriffs – for injuries sustained when defendants did their jobs.[8] Cities and counties now face greatly expanded liability for the acts of their employees, particularly when plaintiffs allege deprivation of civil or constitutional rights.[9]

Is sovereign immunity efficient? Certainly, such a legal rule is cheap to administer, especially if coupled with immunity for government officials and employees. Moreover, shielding government from liability for injuries to private citizens guards against underprovision of public goods and services, particularly if juries are swayed by "deep-pocket" arguments.[10] Some people have argued that official immunity is equally important, because liability would discourage qualified individuals from seeking office and prevent public officials from exercising good judgment. Judge Learned Hand put it most eloquently in 1949: "[I]t is impossible to know whether the claim is well founded until the case has been tried. . . . [T]o submit all officials, the innocent as well as the guilty, to the burden of a trial and to the inevitable danger of its outcome, would dampen the ardor of all but the most resolute . . . in the unflinching discharge of their duties."[11] Yet sovereign immunity gives little incentive to governments to select employees wisely, monitor behavior adequately, and fire miscreants. Official immunity raises bothersome problems as well: Irresponsible individuals would more likely run for office if they could escape accountability for their own carelessness or bad judgment.

On balance, the antebellum practice of sovereign immunity plus personal liability for local officials likely suited the times well. The fears expressed by Judge Hand carry more importance in today's bureaucratic world than they did earlier. Before the Civil War, one could more easily trace the cause of an injury to the person responsible: Did a prisoner escape because the sheriff left the jail unlocked? Was an innocent person shot by a drunken deputy in a case of mistaken identity? Not only is officialdom now more bureaucratic, pay structures have also changed. Today's sheriffs and jailors earn salaries. Richard Posner has pointed out that contemporary law enforcement officers are unlikely to capture all the benefits of aggressive police work, so neither should they pay all the social costs of being too zealous.[12] In contrast, the pay of nineteenth-century officials was based on fees for services rendered and so more closely matched their performance.[13] The greater liability borne by those municipal employees encompassed the costs of their reckless and careless acts, then, just as the pay structure of the day internalized the benefits of their behavior. Moreover, because antebellum courts generally placed liability on officials only when the facts indicated negligent or vindictive behavior, they therefore gave government employees incentives to take reasonable care of others' belongings.

Cases Against Government Itself

In slave cases, as in most other antebellum Southern cases, lawsuits against local government almost never generated damages. Judges offered three principal reasons. First, judges decided that police actions intended to preserve public peace should not create public liability even if slaves, other property, or free persons were injured. Public-goods arguments provided underpinnings: If government

were responsible for injuries in such cases, lawlessness and chaos
would abound. The second reason had to do with causation. When
slaves were responsible for their own injuries, judges were reluctant
to make government (like any other defendant) pay. Finally, most
courts held that the public should not pay for injuries attributable to
the negligence of public officials, particularly sheriffs.

Police actions, even vicious ones, did not generate public liability.
Dicta in two slave cases illustrate this. In one, the officers of the
Second Municipality of New Orleans discovered a slave in a dram
shop. The slave tried to escape; the officers brutally clubbed him to
death. A district judge held the city liable, but an appellate court
reversed in 1854, saying that the officers had acted in a public capacity to preserve the order and tranquility of the city. I suspect, however,
that the ruling also aimed to deter slaves from frequenting bars. In a
similar case heard four years later, the city of Mobile did not pay
damages for slave Henry, shot down by the city guard. Henry was
meeting with three other slaves after midnight, thus violating assembly and curfew ordinances. Again, the court appealed to the need to
protect the common peace.[14]

Public-necessity arguments later protected municipalities in nonslave cases as well. These disputes took two forms: Bystanders sustained injuries as police chased animals, and plaintiffs lost property
through police actions. In one case, a policeman pursued a dog
running loose in the streets against city ordinance; the officer shot
the plaintiff instead of the dog. In another, police chased a renegade
cow into a house where it gored the plaintiff. In neither case did the
plaintiff recover damages from the city. Nor did plaintiffs who had
lost property. The Georgia city of Augusta was not liable to a plaintiff
whose dog was killed by an officer, even though the animal had worn
a collar as the law required. In a Civil War–era case, the city of Lynchburg, Virginia, paid nothing for the loss of 169 gallons of whisky
poured into the streets by public officials in mid-April 1865. Why?
Public necessity. Appomattox and hordes of soldiers were barely
twenty miles away – soldiers and liquor certainly would have made an
explosive combination.[15]

Not only did judges permit public-necessity defenses, they also lis-
tened sympathetically to government defendants who established that
slaves had caused their own injuries. As in hiring and transportation
cases, the slaveowner typically knew more about his slave's character
than the defendant. Placing the consequences of slaves' acts on their
owners therefore helped combat adverse selection problems by
encouraging masters to keep a tight rein on rebellious slaves.
Louisiana passed a statute in 1812 denying compensation for slaves
killed while running away or rioting and for slaves executed for rebel-

lious activities, for example. In a South Carolina dispute, slave Nicholas had beaten other slaves and guards at the Charleston workhouse where he was imprisoned for a three-year term. Nicholas then escaped with two other slaves. After he was recaptured, the city executed Nicholas for brutalizing whites. His master could not recover damages in 1851 because "it was no act of defendant that made Nicholas a pestilence and the other slaves susceptible of the infection." In an 1853 Kentucky case, a slave found guilty of a criminal offense committed suicide in jail before receiving his sentence; the commonwealth did not have to compensate his owner.[16]

Rather than charging the government with negligence when they suffered injuries through the acts of their own slaves, masters sometimes brought actions in eminent domain – again, unsuccessfully. Plaintiffs argued that, when the government convicted slaves of crimes, slaveowners were unjustly deprived of property. In one such case, the federal government refused to compensate Amy's owner in 1859 when Amy went to jail for stealing mail. Chief Justice Roger Taney stated: "A person, whether free or slave, is not taken for public use when he is punished for an offense against the law . . . and the loss which the master sustains in his property . . . necessarily arises from its twofold character, since the slave, as a person, may commit offenses which society has a right to punish for its own safety, although the punishment may render the property of the master of little or no value. But this hazard is invariably and inseparably associated with the description of property. . . ."[17] Three Kentucky cases examined a different but related question: Was emancipating slaves who enlisted – or their families – a lawful taking by the government? In a show of defiance, an 1865 Kentucky court said no, the practice was unconstitutional. The majority opinion bemoaned the death of slavery; Judge Rufus Williams instead accepted slavery's demise and suggested that courts might more fruitfully focus on minimizing slaveowners' losses. In his dissent, Williams pointed out that the U.S. Congress had proposed setting up a fund to compensate slaveowners up to $300 per enlisted slave. If the Kentucky court called unconstitutional the practice of denoting enlisted slaves as emancipated, then Kentucky slaveowners would never receive compensation because enlisted blacks would still have been slaves until the Thirteenth Amendment was passed. The proposed fund then would not apply.[18]

In addition to accepting public-necessity and causation defenses, most antebellum courts refused to find governments liable for the acts of their employees.[19] Judges often suggested that plaintiffs should have targeted the employees instead. Two slaveowners who sued cities discovered this, much to their chagrin. The city of New Orleans avoided liability in 1857 for the actions of its jailor. Slave Jesse, valued at $1,500, had been jailed by his owner. He languished, cold and wet, later dying in jail from exposure. Jesse's owner bore the loss. Ten years later, a Virginia plaintiff's slave suffered from smallpox and entered a public hospital; the slave escaped and died of exposure. The city of Richmond claimed immunity. An appellate court reversed the plaintiff's jury award of $516.60, saying that public liability for private negligence would cause government to stop functioning.[20] Only in Georgia did the courts depart from sovereign immunity in slave cases, without giving particular reasons. In the 1849 case of *Mayor v. Howard*, Justice Joseph Lumpkin allowed an $800 jury verdict for slave Braden to stand. Braden had been hired to work on the streets of Columbus, but instead went to work on the embankment at the mouth of a sewer. The embankment broke, killing Braden. Because the city had used the slave for an unauthorized job (and in a grossly negligent manner), Braden's owner won damages. Lumpkin revealed his opinion of slaves in this case: "The want of discretion in our slave population is notorious. They need a higher degree of intelligence than their own, not only to direct their labor, but likewise to protect them from the consequences of their own improvidence." Of course, these words also betray an inconsistency. If slaves were notoriously incapable, who knew this better than their owners? Slaveowners should therefore have specified adequate supervision and direction in hiring contracts. This case was a simple breach of contract that should perhaps have thrown blame on the defendant – or, more consistent with the rest of Southern law, on the defendant's agent. In his vehemence about the duties of others to watch out for careless slaves, Lumpkin instead inadvertently made an argument to place more responsibility on slaveowners. In a case heard the same year as *Howard*, slave Crawford died from smallpox after going without food or vaccine in a filthy, unventilated room of a house cordoned off by the city of Columbus, Georgia. (Crawford's wife lived in the house.) Crawford's master won the right to recover the slave's value from the city. The court's opinion rested partly on the fact that a doctor could have readily inoculated the slave: Edward Jenner developed the first smallpox vaccine in 1796. (This court also recognized incentives, honoring the plaintiff's objections to seating any citizens of Columbus on the jury "inasmuch as they were liable to be taxed for the payment of the verdict which might be recovered against the defendants.")[21]

Like slaveowners, other Southern plaintiffs virtually never recovered damages from nineteenth-century governments for losses caused by the acts of public officials – mayors, charity-hospital workers, or other employees.[22] *Dicta* in most cases indicate that the plaintiff should have sued the official, not the municipality. In many cases, free persons sued cities for false arrest or false imprisonment

– to no avail, even when innocent plaintiffs sickened after exposure to filthy jails. The city of Louisville even cited slave cases to support its position in an 1877 case. Here, Hattie Pollack had been arrested on a charge of infanticide and taken to jail just after giving birth; she died as a result of the harsh treatment. The city argued that it was not liable because Pollack had committed a crime against the commonwealth, not the city; furthermore, sovereign immunity barred any recovery of damages. The city won. The cities of Montgomery and Baltimore also avoided liability in cases heard just after the Civil War where police might have prevented plaintiffs' injuries but failed to do so. Albany, Georgia, was not liable for damages caused by the town's nightwatchman in 1880, who drunkenly assaulted the plaintiff and broke his leg. Nor was the city of Atlanta liable in an appalling case heard in 1896. In this case, the plaintiff's husband had been in the city stockade for violating some minor ordinance. While he was working on city streets, the prison-guard foreman forced him to lift a large rock. The rock fell on the man's hand, causing it to balloon enormously. He was compelled to work for nine more days without seeing a doctor; on the evening of the tenth day, he died of blood poisoning.[23]

Cases Against Government Officials

In contrast to antebellum governments, local officials – particularly sheriffs – frequently found themselves losing in court. The verdicts in these cases matched up the benefits and costs of activities undertaken by individuals: Just as officials received fees for services rendered, so too did they pay the costs of shoddy service. Negligence of sheriffs and jailors generated personal liability in several slave cases. In one 1847 dispute, a Louisiana sheriff and his deputies seized slaves on behalf of a creditor when the slaves returned from work. The sheriff allowed the slaves to stay in their cabins overnight without a guard. Next morning, the slaves were gone, apparently over the state line. The plaintiff lost at trial, but an appellate court set aside the verdict and allowed recovery of $600 and costs. In a similar case heard two years later, an Alabama sheriff seized two slaves and placed them under his overseer's care. One slave escaped; the sheriff was liable to the creditor for the slave's value. In a Missouri case, a jailor entrusted a prisoner slave with opening the gate for visitors. Although the slave-owner might have known of this practice (because his agent went to visit the jail), a court allowed the owner to complain of jailor negligence and recover damages in 1859 when the slave escaped. In 1860, a Georgia sheriff brought mortgaged slave Rhena home with him because the jail was cold and unsecured. Someone apparently stole

Rhena; the sheriff went to Alabama and various parts of Georgia to find her. He succeeded but could not reimburse himself for the costs of recapturing Rhena from the proceeds of her sale.[24]

Antebellum sheriffs also faced responsibility for the acts of underlings. This reflected the sheriffs' concomitant rights: They generally made hiring, firing, and pay decisions for their deputies. In fact, the first use of the principle of *respondeat superior* – when a person answers for the acts of his agent or subordinate – arose with sheriffs' deputies. For example, the owner of runaway slave Bartlett wanted compensation from Sheriff Dabney when Bartlett returned from jail frostbitten, crippled, and diseased. James Thornton, a tavernkeeper at the courthouse, had failed to provide food, fire, or blankets to Bartlett. Dabney argued that he was not responsible for the actions of jailor Thornton, but a jury disagreed and awarded the plaintiff $400. A Virginia appellate court affirmed the verdict in 1826.[25]

Slaveowners won damages from other public officials as well. An Alabama magistrate paid damages of $200 in 1860 for imprisoning slave Battiste. The man knew Battiste was a slave but sentenced him to four months for gambling as if Battiste were free. If the evidence had indicated that the magistrate had reasonably thought Battiste was free, he would have paid nothing. Here, however, the defendant had ample knowledge of Battiste's bondage. Even a constable who allowed a Kentucky mob to frighten a slave was potentially liable for damages when the slave committed suicide in 1860. And those who posed as public officials naturally faced liability for losses caused by their own negligence. One slave escaped from his Tennessee owner Taylor only to be thrown into a Kentucky jail. Taylor retrieved the slave; as they were returning home, Munford and a companion approached the two and accused the slave of stealing a trunk. Munford seized the slave, who subsequently escaped. Munford was found responsible in 1859 for the slave's value of $1,135 because the arrest had been without legal authority, because Munford had not adequately supervised the slave, and, notably, because the slave's alleged offense had been only a misdemeanor – costing society less than the value of the lost slave himself.[26]

Antebellum public officials had duties in cases involving animals and other property that resembled their duties in slave cases. As in slave cases, these duties placed the costs associated with poor service upon those who received fees for that service. When debtors escaped from jail, creditors could recover the amount of the debt from negligent sheriffs.[27] Negligent sheriffs were liable as well for losing other people's money or property.[28] An Alabama sheriff who sold property without advertising it as the law required paid damages in 1827 equal to the difference between the sale price and the price of similar goods that had been advertised. In an 1859 Georgia case, a sheriff was even responsible for losses when he deposited the plaintiff's money into a bank that failed.[29] Negligent sheriffs were also liable for damages if they hurt livestock taken into custody on behalf of creditors.[30] Unauthorized persons naturally also faced liability: A man who went into a house late at night with a deputy and who violently took property, without the deputy's command, was liable for damages in an 1848 South Carolina case.[31] Negligent nineteenth-century sheriffs faced tort liability in certain cases brought by prisoners or their estates as well. Two postbellum examples are *Head v. Martin* and *Kopplecam v. Hoffman*.[32] In *Head*, the sheriff killed a man being arrested for bastardy (which was not a felony). In *Kopplecam*, the sheriff arrested the wrong man, then shot him and fractured his leg when the man tried to run away. A court said the sheriff had a high duty of care to ascertain he was shooting the true felon.

As in cases with private parties as defendants, plaintiffs typically did not recover damages from public officials who had taken good care of the plaintiffs' belongings – slaves or anything else. Had these verdicts been otherwise, officials might have spent excessive funds to prevent losses. In an 1850 Louisiana case, the sheriff had imprisoned a slave; the slave died in jail. A court said the sheriff would have been liable for the slave's value if poor prison conditions caused the death. Because the jailed slave was well treated, however, the sheriff avoided paying damages. Similarly, when a mortgaged horse died suddenly after being pampered by the sheriff's agent, a Tennessee sheriff was not liable in an 1873 dispute.[33] Reasonably careful sheriffs were not liable for lost property, either. In a North Carolina case heard in 1855, runaway slave George disappeared from an upper-floor dungeon from which no escapes had ever succeeded. The slave later turned up in a well, dead. A court did not hold the sheriff liable because, as it said, the benefits of preventing escapes would have cost too much. The opinion noted that the jailor could have averted the escape only at exorbitant cost, by putting guards around the entire jail or by cruelly chaining all slaves. Five years later, a Louisiana sheriff was not responsible for slaves breaking out of jail as long as the entrances had been guarded.[34] In like fashion, sheriffs did not pay for property lost when left in a place agreed to by the plaintiff.[35] And sheriffs were not liable for escaped debtors if courts had not actually committed the debtors, or if the sheriffs had followed certain approved procedures in accepting bail bonds.[36] One vigilant public official actually turned the tables on a slaveowner. South Carolina deputy sheriff Robertson took charge of a mortgaged slave on behalf of the creditor. Determined to prevent the slave's escape, Robertson chained the slave to a bedpost and roped the slave to himself. The slave's owner violently wrested the slave away from Robertson; in 1833 the state convicted the owner of assault and battery on the deputy.[37]

Public officials could find themselves responsible for slaves in one additional circumstance. Southern jails often served as a warehouse for runaways, and even for slaves thought likely to try an escape. Many states provided procedures to imprison runaway slaves apprehended by sheriffs or private citizens. Compliance with procedure protected one from liability; noncompliance generated damage awards or fines. Mississippi, for instance, passed a law in 1846 outlining the duties of jailors in keeping runaways. If jailors did not keep fugitives closely confined, they faced fines of $75 to $150, with one-half going to the informant and one-half to the school fund. But the statute recognized the potential utility of incarcerated slaves: It permitted jailors to take slaves out to work on public projects. In Kentucky, justices of the peace could commit apparent runaways to jail in order to preserve the peace and safety of the neighborhood. In one 1855 case, a justice committed slaves to jail for twenty-four hours. Their owner later showed that the slaves were not runaways and sued the justice. He failed to recover damages.[38]

Besides permitting the jailing of fugitives, some states passed statutes allowing masters to commit slaves to jail for safekeeping. Negligence standards applied to jailors in these circumstances, giving them (like other potential defendants) incentives to guard slaves prudently. In an 1833 case, master Slemaker jailed his slave Bill Phelps under Maryland's Act of 1818, which allowed owners to imprison slaves if they paid for upkeep and did not use the facility as a halfway house for slaves being traded. The sheriff of the Anne Arundel County jail argued he should not be liable for Phelps's escape because the jail had been in disrepair at the time. An appellate court disagreed because the sheriff could have refused under the statute to accept the slave. In another such case, owner Griffith committed his slave William Lee to jail in 1836 under Virginia's Act of February 25, 1824. Here, the sheriff answered for the negligence of his jailor George Caruthers in letting Lee escape and for his own failure to pursue the slave. A jury awarded Griffith $300.[39]

Unlike Marylanders and Virginians, Kentucky slaveowners did not have the statutory right to incarcerate their own slaves. Rather, they made deals with jailors. As a result, Kentucky courts viewed the responsibility of public officials differently. When a Kentucky slave escaped from jail, the owner often could not recover damages from the jailor under one of these private arrangements. Why? The courts wanted to discourage people from giving jailors an incentive to "convert the public jail to private use for [their] own profit" or to jeopardize "the safety of lawful prisoners." One Kentucky court also took direct action in 1851 to curtail jailor profits from private deals. It reduced jailors' fees as excessive when a sheriff, at the behest of a creditor, put mortgaged slaves in jail for safekeeping. The court did not consider these slaves (a woman and five small children) as true prisoners. The usual fees for prisoners legally committed ($138.70 for a 100-day confinement) appeared unreasonable to the court.[40]

ESTABLISHMENT AND DUTIES OF SLAVE PATROLS

Every Southern state except Delaware passed legislation to establish and regulate county-wide slave patrols. In his collection of state slavery statutes, Paul Finkelman reported 249 statutes regarding slave patrols.[41] County courts usually had local administrative authority; court officials appointed three to five men per patrol from a pool of white male citizens to serve for a specified length of time. Typical patrol duty ranged from one night a week for a year-long term to twelve hours a month for three months. During much of the ante-bellum period, patrollers earned 75 cents to $1.50 per twelve-hour shift, with patrol captains earning a higher rate. County taxes on slaves provided funds for patrollers' pay.

Not all white men had to serve as patrollers: Judges, magistrates, ministers, and sometimes millers and blacksmiths enjoyed exemptions. So did those in the higher ranks of the state militia. In many states, courts could choose only from adult males under a certain age, usually 45, 50, or 60. Alabama even passed a statute in 1838 exempting those who owned only slaves older than forty-five years of age. (Because these slaves tended to be more settled and less troublesome than younger slaves, legislators perhaps thought that their owners merited relief from night patrol duty.) Some states allowed only slave-owners or householders to serve on patrols. Kentucky originally selected patrollers from "housekeepers," but soon opened eligibility to all "discreet and temperate" white males. Kentucky also allowed the counties bordering the Ohio River to call up extra patrollers during times of unrest. Candidates for patrol duty paid fines for refusal to serve or failure to show up on appointed nights. Most states allowed men to send substitutes for patrol duty.

Patrollers enjoyed certain "perks" as well as pay and power. In some states, patrol duty exempted one from road or militia duty. Florida patrollers passed free on toll bridges and ferries. Many states set fees for captured runaway slaves, collectible from the slaves' owners or the state treasury. Florida patrollers earned $5 per captured slave under the state's Act of 1834; Kentucky patrollers who were also "house-keepers" could earn $25 for local fugitives and $50 for out-of-county fugitives under Kentucky's 1840 Act. Under Louisiana's Act of 1848, patrollers obtained $6 for slaves found in the woods and $3 for slaves found on roads or plantations, plus 10 cents per mile traveled. Mississippi's 1859 statutes granted patrollers $10 to $20 for retrieving fugitives.

Keeping order among slaves was the patroller's primary duty. Effectiveness of patrollers varied from county to county; most patrols directed their efforts against alleged runaways and thieves.[42] Statutes set guidelines for appropriate treatment of slaves and often imposed fines for unlawful beatings. In North Carolina, for example, a single patroller could not inflict punishment nor enlist non-patrollers to help. To perform their duties, a majority of patrollers had to show up and a plurality had to sanction each act, unless a county court authorized otherwise.[43] South Carolina's Act of 1740 did not allow patrollers to discipline slaves who were accompanied by a white person; the Act of 1800 permitted patrollers to disperse assemblies only if slaves met at night or in private. Missouri's 1844 statutes barred patrollers from molesting slaves on their way to or from divine worship on the Sabbath. Sometimes states gave additional powers to patrollers: Mississippi's Act of 1825 permitted patrollers to kill any dogs owned by blacks, for instance.[44]

The importance of slave patrollers waned and waxed over the antebellum period. Alabama's 1843 statutes, for example, exempted men over the age of forty-five from patrol duty in certain counties. In 1853, the state exempted those over age fifty in some additional counties and disbanded patrols entirely in other counties. Georgia's Act of 1855 shortened the tour of duty from six to three months. The coming of the Civil War heightened the need for slave control, however. Maryland employed a special police force in 1856 to arrest absconding slaves and their helpers; Georgia substituted mounted police for patrollers in certain counties in 1860. Many states passed laws allowing any three freeholders, slaveholders, or justices of the peace to form ad hoc patrols at any time. The pool of candidates expanded to include older men and nonslaveowners. Patrollers' powers also increased: In some states, patrollers in the 1860s could arrest or punish white persons keeping company with slaves. Tellingly, Virginia's Act of 1863 escalated the ordinary-patroller pay to $4 per twelve-hour shift and the captain's pay to $5 per shift.[45] And although few patroller cases exist at all, none appears in appellate-court reporters after 1857.

Why did so few slave patrollers appear as defendants? Two reasons seem likely. Suppose patrollers killed or abused a slave. If the slave came from outside the county, his owner probably could not determine who to sue. If the slave lived in the county, patrollers could likely justify their actions to the slave's owner. Because most patrollers were local slaveowners, they shared a common interest in discharging duties responsibly. A patroller who gratuitously shot his neighbor's slave one night could well find his own dead the next night.[46] Patrollers therefore had incentives to act within statutory constraints.

Plaintiffs sometimes complained of excessive force by patrols, of course. But judges, like other Southern citizens, recognized the importance of slave patrols in preserving peace: Patrollers were meant to possess quasi-judicial or quasi-executive powers. In an 1856 case, when a Louisiana patrol from New Iberia shot and killed a slave riding by on horseback, the killers were not held liable. As the court stated: "Recent disorders among slaves . . . had made it a matter of importance that the laws relative to the police of slaves, should be strictly enforced." Yet judges recognized that abuse occurred. Fear, high spirits, or malice undoubtedly motivated some patrol actions. In states where most white men faced patrol duty, slaves were easy targets for those too poor to own them. An 1837 South Carolina court put it best: "Slaves are our most valuable property. For its preservation, too many guards cannot be interposed between it and violent unprincipled men. [This] produce[s] the corresponding consequence of deep and abiding grateful attachment for the slave to the master." An 1855 Mississippi opinion echoed these sentiments. According to this court, everyone had the right to capture fugitives, but defendants not in mortal danger were liable if they killed a runaway. The opinion stated: "The same law which protects the master, guards [slaves'] rights as persons." Consequently, if a slaveowner could show that a patroller had acted contrary to statutory guidelines, courts awarded damages for injuries. Patrollers in an 1818 South Carolina case shot one of Mrs. Witsell's slaves just outside her house. The slave, who was killed, naturally had gone the other way when he saw patrollers in the yard. A court called the murder unjustified and awarded Mrs. Witsell the value of her slave. In another South Carolina case heard nine years later, a slaveowner recovered damages from a defendant who went to search for a party of mischievous runaways. The defendant shot in the air to intimidate the slaves as they fled, killing the plaintiff's slave. In 1850, yet another South Carolina court even upheld indictments for patrollers who whipped law-abiding slaves at a quilting bee. And in an 1851 Louisiana case, slave Ned fled in terror from someone out "hunting runaways." The patroller killed Ned. A jury found for the defendant; an appellate court reversed the verdict and granted the plaintiff $350 plus costs and interest. The court said that those who pursued and shot slaves had to justify their actions or pay owners for losses.[47]

To obtain damages, a slaveowner had to prove an injury occurred. An Arkansas patroller lightly whipped a slave (who was returning from a religious meeting) for alleged insolence in the 1854 case of *Hervy v. Armstrong.*[48] A jury found for the plaintiff but an appellate court reversed and remanded the case, saying no lost services meant no damages. Why? Because, according to the court, damages awarded for superficial injuries would have stimulated slaves to hurl insults out of malice or because masters egged them on. The *Hervy* court's reasoning is odd: If slaves had won damages for slight injuries, impudence might have been rampant. But masters, not slaves, recovered damages. The court might more profitably have cast the issue another way. Patrollers played key roles in protecting free persons from slaves and in keeping slaves submissive. If they were answerable for damages when no real harm occurred, patrollers would have failed to administer cost-effective, on-the-spot discipline. This would have exposed the slave system to possible breakdowns. Had the South overdeterred patrollers from punishing renegade slaves, the patrols would have been superfluous, a waste of public money. Indeed, slaveowners had a stake in these verdicts – entrusting patrollers with some corrective control discouraged thefts and slave escapes and resulted in lower costs for masters.

Perhaps the best illustration of the balance courts maintained in slaveowner-patroller disputes appears in an Alabama case heard in the mid-1850s. Here, Morton sued Bradley for killing Morton's slave. Morton had hired someone to recapture the runaway slave; Bradley accompanied Morton's employee. A jury found for Bradley, but an appellate court reversed and remanded the case. In *dicta*, the court said damages would have been inappropriate if the killer had been the slaveowner's employee or an official patroller. In this case, however, the court advised that Morton should recover damages equaling the slave's value: "It is a delicate and difficult duty, to designate the point at which the law, reconciling the claims of humanity and the necessity of subordination and subjection, permits the killing of a runaway slave, who resists apprehension. . . . These rules are essential to the good government of the slave population, and necessary to the safety of the community."[49] Only one word seems inapt: The opinion might better have substituted "property" for "humanity."

THE RESPONSIBILITIES OF OVERSEERS

The Southern overseer was the linchpin of the slave plantation. In many ways, he resembled today's middle manager. Like a middle manager, the overseer was buffeted from below and above. The overseer had to rouse the slaves, cope with their natural reluctance to work for someone else's gain, and mete out punishment. He also had to explain poor yields to his employer, face questions on management techniques, and occupy a position of responsibility with little matching authority. As a result, working as an overseer was often a thankless job. Most overseers faced social isolation, disparagement, uncertain job tenure, little real job authority, and only the rare day off. Many resented having to vie with black drivers for the master's ear.

Yet overseers were important to the South: They ran the large plantations and served as a first line of defense in safeguarding whites. The vigorous protests against drafting overseers into military service during the Civil War reveal their significance to the South.[50] Judges acknowledged that an overseer's brutality could benefit society – and the slaveowner as well, in some circumstances. An 1846 Alabama court determined that an overseer had reasonably beaten a slave accused of stealing, because "[I]t is certainly for the interest of the master, that the slave be taught habits of industry . . . it may be a duty to inflict corporal punishment. . . . The good morals and quiet of the state are not concerned in the prosecution of every slave who may commit a larceny. So far as it concerns the public, it is quite as well, perhaps better, that his punishment should be admeasured by a domestic tribunal. Certainly this mode of procedure would be preferable for the master, as it would relieve him both from anxiety and the necessity of expending money."[51] By granting overseers some control, courts promoted private discipline of slaves and sustained submission without using public dollars.

But slaveowners were rightfully wary of extending too much power to overseers, just as they feared giving control to slave employers. Masters naturally worried that overseers would supplant owners as the voice of authority. Verdicts in disputes between masters and overseers worked to block this possibility. In the 1848 case of *Boone v. Lyde*, a South Carolina court determined that slaveowner Lyde had sufficient reason for firing his overseer Boone, who had assaulted Lyde. Boone was angry because Lyde had not consulted him before changing the tasks of the slaves. One year later, a Louisiana court similarly decided that abuse and threats by an overseer entitled his employer to discharge him. An 1859 North Carolina court found that, if an overseer controlled slaves against the known wishes and positive commands of their owner, the owner had good grounds for dismissing the man. Even good treatment of slaves could not override the wishes of the master. An 1839 Alabama court said, for example, that an overseer could provision slaves if the master was absent but could not choose a different supplier of pork.[52]

Slaveowners also feared excess brutality on the part of overseers. Abuse that went undetected for a time could depreciate slaves' value and contribute to slave unrest, which could spread to adjoining plantations as well as harm the slaves' master. Certainly, masters could dismiss overseers who breached contracts. In *Boone v. Lyde*, for example, the written contract stated that the overseer had to be kind to the slaves. The slaveowner therefore had a second good reason for firing Boone: The overseer had snapped his gun at a slave who ran to escape punishment. But overseers also had implicit duties toward the slaves in their charge, just as they did toward other types of property. As an 1852 North Carolina court put it, overseers should use "only such moderate and usual correction, as would have reduced the slave to subordination, and been of good example to other slaves."[53] A mutual understanding of duties helped reduce the costs of supervising the overseer himself.

A set of disputes from the 1840s and 1850s demonstrates these implicit duties. Cruelty to slaves and immoral conduct toward female slaves gave a Louisiana owner sufficient reason to fire his overseer without facing damages for breach of contract. Another Louisiana master was entitled to discharge an overseer who had shot at a slave fleeing punishment. An 1858 North Carolina court heard evidence that an overseer was often absent, rode the family horses at night on patrol duty, and held parties until midnight that disturbed the neighbors. The livestock and fields apparently looked neglected as well. A jury awarded wages for the remainder of the year, but an appellate court reversed the award. In *dicta* the court said that, if a new jury believed the offered evidence, the overseer could not recover damages for breach of contract. Overseers who hurt slaves often had to pay masters for the injuries; those who demanded back wages after being dismissed for mistreating slaves instead ended up paying net damages. A Texas overseer sued for $300 back pay after he was fired for shooting slave Miles in the back fifteen to twenty-five times. Miles survived but was worthless to his master; the overseer eventually paid $516.67 to the owner – Miles's original value less the $300. An abusive Louisiana overseer was liable in a case heard the same year. Here, the discharged overseer wanted $800 in back pay; a jury awarded him $344.15. But an appellate court granted the defendant the value of his slave (about $1200) less the $344.15. A different cruel Louisiana overseer sued for his salary after being fired, but ended up paying $100 to the slaveowner for net damages and medical bills. In an 1843 case, North Carolinian Martha Copeland sent her slave Gilbert to help build a road. When the overseer angrily shot and disabled

Gilbert for backing away from a whipping, Copeland recovered damages. The court said: "The act of shooting the slave betrayed passion in the overseer, rather than a desire to promote the true interest of his employers, or to keep up the subordination, which the state of our society demands."[54]

Yet slaveowners, by virtue of knowing their slaves' characters and dispositions, occasionally lost such lawsuits. A Louisiana overseer who had shot a slave was not liable for damages in an 1838 dispute, because the slave had acted strangely and come at the man with a knife. An Arkansas overseer retrieved wages in 1856 without paying for a slave's value even though he had killed slave Nathan, because the slaveowner knew that Nathan had by nature been rough and disobedient. In an 1860 Georgia case, an overseer killed slave Jim and was assessed $1,200. An appellate court reversed the judgment, however, concluding that evidence of Jim's insubordinate character should have been admitted to mitigate the damages.[55]

Overseers certainly faced civil proceedings in brutality cases; rarely, they confronted criminal charges as well. A Georgia jury convicted overseer Jordan of voluntary manslaughter after he whipped thirteen-year-old Mariah 400 to 1,000 times with a heavy strap. Members of an appellate court wanted to convict Jordan of murder in 1857 but did not have the authority to revise the charges. In 1843 Alabama, an overseer received a ten-year sentence for killing a slave; a murdering Mississippi overseer faced a seven-year term in a case heard one year later. Another Mississippi overseer was convicted in 1856 for cruelly punishing a slave. In a third Mississippi case, however, an appellate court granted a new trial to an overseer after he was convicted for murdering a slave and sentenced to five years in prison. And South Carolina allowed those in charge of slaves to exculpate themselves if they confessed to killing a slave with good reason. In *State v. Raines*, for example, the owner of a slave alleged to be a dangerous thief requested defendant Raines to bring the slave in chains to the city of Columbia. When the slave balked, Raines whipped him – ultimately, to death. A jury brought back a verdict of manslaughter, but an appellate court decided that Raines could acquit himself by confessing under oath.[56]

Brutality by overseers naturally generated responses by their victims in some cases. Here, courts had to resolve tensions between protecting property rights and sustaining subordination. North Carolina courts sometimes reduced murder charges to manslaughter for slaves who had killed their overseers, provided the decedents had been cruel or violent to the slaves. And although an Alabama jury found slave Abram guilty of mayhem for biting off part of overseer Kirkendall's ear, Abram appealed a death sentence and received a

new trial in 1847. Why? Kirkendall had whipped Abram and threatened him with a knife and a gun. In many cases, however, slaves who
turned on free persons – whether they were overseers, masters, or
anyone else – faced heavy punishment or execution.[57]

CONCLUSION

Although Southern courts assiduously protected property rights in
slaves, they also wanted to preserve public peace. Accordingly, they
granted some authority over slaves to sheriffs, jailors, and other local
officials. But exceeding this authority landed these individuals in
court. (Because antebellum Americans subscribed wholeheartedly to
the doctrine of sovereign immunity, people seldom sued municipalities and even more seldom won damages.) As in other types of slave
cases, these defendants typically faced liability when they had injured
slaveowners through their negligence.

Citizen patrols also wove into the protective blanket of measures
that insulated white Southerners from the slaves living among them.
Patroller cases were uncommon, perhaps partly because patrollers
typically owned slaves and therefore identified more with slaveowners than did other potential defendants. Still, a few disputes appear
in appellate records. They show that patrollers, like public employees, had duties to act as a buffer between slave and free society.
Nonetheless, patrollers could not overstep certain bounds in meting
out punishment to valuable property.

Nor could overseers. Southern judges, like other Southern citizens, regarded overseers as an essential element of slave control. But
they also kept a sharp eye out for evidence of brutality: Slaves were
too valuable to be left to the whims of frustrated, angry overseers.
Masters and overseers, like most parties to disputes, had different sets
of information – a master knew more about the personalities and dispositions of his own slaves (compared with a seasonally hired overseer, at least), but less about his overseer's day-to-day treatment of
them. The common law therefore balanced these potential adverse
selection and moral hazard problems, much as it did in other sorts
of slave cases. Overseers could protect themselves against slaves that
the master likely knew were dangerous, but overly controlling and
brutal overseers faced substantial legal penalties.

The law involving slave patrollers and overseers is largely self-
contained; the need for separate laws governing these individuals
disappeared with the demise of slavery. Legal rules concerning the
acts of governments and government officials remained necessary, of
course. In antebellum days, these rules were similar for slave and non-

slave cases. Public employees had like duties of care toward slaves, animals, and other private property, although here, as in other areas of law, slave cases sometimes served as precedents for postbellum disputes.

6

The Legal Rights and Responsibilities of Strangers Toward Slaves, Animals, and Free Persons

The threads of slavery ran seamlessly through the fabric of Southern society. Whether they liked it or not, many antebellum Southerners dealt with slaves on a near-daily basis. Many of these dealings triggered controversy. Public officials, slave patrollers, and common-carrier owners and operators constituted a number of the defendants in cases where strangers injured the interests of slaveowners. But disputes with ordinary citizens and business owners came up as well. As the following sections discuss, four major questions arose: (1) What duty of care did strangers have toward slaves, particularly when protecting other types of property? (2) What recourse did slaveowners have against those who kidnapped slaves and what did masters owe to slave catchers? (3) What penalties were appropriate for those who traded and gamed with slaves, sold liquor to slaves, or otherwise undercut the authority of masters? (4) When should defendants avoid liability (and perhaps recover fees) for treating another's slave well?

In these disputes where interested parties could not cheaply have transacted, people asked judges to allocate liability and damages. Here as elsewhere, slave law typically apportioned risks as people would have done themselves, had they been able to do so easily. Slave law accounted for relevant externalities as well. Because drunken, merchant, or fugitive slaves might have stirred up their compatriots or stolen from whites, slave law imposed stiff penalties on those who sold liquor to or bought goods from blacks, and on those who facilitated slave escapes. And slaveowners had to acquiesce to some discipline of slaves by outsiders and some reward for those who captured fugitives or treated slaves with special care. As legal historian Lawrence Friedman put it, slavery was too important to leave to the slaveholder.[1]

Here, as in other areas of antebellum law, judges worked to preserve the value of property (particularly slaves) but turned a blind eye to personal injuries. As previous chapters have shown, the law encouraged employers to take better care of slaves than of free employees and encouraged common-carrier owners and operators to watch out more for slaves than free persons, simply because slaves were valuable property. So too did the law shield slaves more than free persons from the brutality of strangers. People were more likely to recover civil damages for injuries to slaves than for injuries to other property – or to themselves. And criminal convictions occurred more often in slave-stealing cases than in other criminal cases. The law also recognized more offenses against owners of slaves than against other property owners because slaves, unlike other sorts of property, succumbed to influence.

GENERAL LEGAL RULES GOVERNING STRANGERS

General Standards of Care

Southern courts usually made negligent strangers, like other negligent defendants, pay damages for injuring slaves. This legal rule gave people incentives to look out for others' slaves as they would have their own. In an 1835 Louisiana dispute, defendant White had borrowed a slave to haul a load seven or eight miles. A storm came up but the defendant refused offers of shelter. The slave, who had been wearing thin clothing, froze to death. White paid damages equaling the slave's $600 value. Another Louisiana litigant illegally seized a slave to pay land rents. The slave died in a damp and unhealthy jail. In 1849, the slave's owner recovered the value of the slave less accounts due. An 1856 Missouri plaintiff likewise recovered damages in *Morgan v. Cox*. Here, the defendant had asked the plaintiff and the plaintiff's slave to help him drive a cow across the Osage River. The defendant punched the cow with a loaded gun, then placed the gun over his saddle. The gun discharged and killed the slave. Negligent defendants sometimes also paid for similar injuries to free persons. In a Kentucky case heard three years after *Morgan*, defendant Chiles was liable for civil damages of $1,000 to George Drake's grieving widow. Chiles had brandished a loaded gun in a crowded room; the pistol went off and killed Drake.[2]

To win damages, plaintiffs naturally had to meet certain standards of care as well. Otherwise, potential defendants would have been more cautious than was economically warranted. In one illustrative 1853 case, a Louisiana plaintiff asked the defendant's slave to pick up a "walking cane" in the plaintiff's yard. The "cane" was actually a gun; it went off and killed the plaintiff's slave. A court held that, because the gun had been lying in the plaintiff's yard for several months, she could not recover damages. In a Louisiana case heard three years later, plaintiff Sarah Hill had sent her slave Edmund with the defendant to be sold, without revealing that Edmund was a runaway. In fact, she claimed he was humble and obedient. Edmund asked to retrieve his clothes; the defendant sent him along with a trusted slave. When Edmund escaped, the defendant was not liable for his value. As in other cases, the humanness of slaves also helped set the responsibilities of litigants. In an 1852 South Carolina case, the administrator of an estate let slaves go home to visit; they drowned en route. The administrator did not answer for damages because "the property [consists of] chattels that have intelligence and will."[3] The slaves' failure to take care of themselves defeated the plaintiff's claim as well as caused their death.

For a standard of care to carry weight, a defendant's acts also had to relate directly to the plaintiff's injury. A Louisiana defendant was not accountable for faulty construction by a hired contractor, for example, although he might have been liable if he had directed a servant or overseer in building the structure. In this 1856 case, the building had fallen and killed the plaintiff's slave. And in a fascinating case involving the death of a free man, the plaintiff complained that the defendant had driven the plaintiff's husband away from his farm, forcing him to wander in the woods. The vagabond then joined the Union army, later dying as a prisoner of war in a Southern camp. A Tennessee court determined that the defendant's aggressive act was not the proximate cause of death and refused to award damages.[4]

Protection of Property Other Than Slaves

Trespassing Slaves and Animals: Civil Cases. As well as negligently injuring slaves, strangers hurt and killed slaves in efforts to protect other property. Many former slaves later recalled stealing food, for example, especially hens and hogs.[5] Sometimes they did so out of hunger, sometimes for spite, sometimes at their master's bidding. Some states even passed statutes to make slaveowners responsible for thefts from other plantations, as the next chapter discusses. Burglarized homeowners responded by shooting at intruders, finding at times they had injured valuable property. Courts awarded damages to slaveowners in many of these cases because the losses to slaveowners often far exceeded the value of the damaged property. As courts noted, these rulings would deter potential injurers from overreacting to petty crimes or minor property damage. In 1827, a South Carolina court even sent back one case in disgust for a recalculation of damages. The defendant had caught two slaves stealing potatoes; he shot and killed one of them. A jury had awarded damages – of one cent, far below the true value of the slave.[6]

In other such cases, masters recovered the market value of slaves hurt or killed while trespassing in a field or taking livestock. In 1851 cases from South Carolina and Louisiana, the defendants' teenaged sons killed slaves who had been crossing canefields. The Louisiana court reproached the defendant, saying that one could shoot just to scare, or simply refrain from shooting because return fire endangered others. The court also disapproved of the man's only comment, that his son should have tried to kill more slaves. Eight years later, a different Louisiana defendant killed slave Charles in the henhouse. Louisiana statutes allowed firing on runaways thought to be armed, but the court said chicken stealing was not a heinous offense and the defendant did not know that Charles was carrying a knife. The plaintiff claimed Charles's value was $1,800, the defendant claimed $500; the court split the difference and granted $1,150. A third Louisiana case established that seeing a slave rustle hogs did not justify shooting him. The plaintiff won at trial, although an appellate court had to remand the case on the question of damages. In 1857, a Texas plaintiff won damages of $1,300 from his neighbor Kirby. Here, the plaintiff's slave John had pulled down Kirby's fence to extricate a wagon loaded with cotton, which had broken down in a bog. Kirby's overseer threatened the slave, then John ran toward the river as the overseer called out his dogs and shot his rifle. The ferryman refused to put John across, so the slave apparently began to swim. He was never seen again.[7]

Some states gave citizens more power to protect their property from renegade slaves. Kentucky, a state outside the Cotton Belt with a lower proportion of slaves than many other Southern states, is an example. One defendant was not liable for damages in an 1832 dispute, for instance. In this case, a slave had been killed by a spring gun when burglarizing the defendant's warehouse at night. The court justified its verdict by saying that Kentucky was a place "where the rights of self defence are so dearly cherished and so well maintained by the sentiments of our population." In a case heard two decades later, *McClelland v. Kay*, a jury awarded damages for a slave killed in a poultry yard, but an appellate court reversed and remanded the case. This defendant claimed he had not intended to kill the slave: Someone had loaded his gun with large shot without his knowledge. *Dicta* indicated that shooting to wound without murderous intent did not create civil or criminal liability. Notably, the defense closely resembles that in the 1850 Louisiana case of *Arnandez v. Lawes*, but the two courts advocated opposite holdings. Still, like Kentucky, Louisiana allowed some residents – namely, freeholders – to shoot at trespassing slaves under certain circumstances. Why? Because in most areas the state had no standing salaried police force to keep the large population of slaves under control. Only freeholders had this privilege, however. In an 1849 case, a neighbor's overseer shot the plaintiff's slave, fracturing a knee, after he had asked the slave for a pass. The

slave had replied in French, which the overseer considered disre-
spectful (not to mention unintelligible to the ignorant defendant).
The overseer was not excused because he was not among freeholders, who were thought to have "prudence and discretion." He therefore paid $700 to the plaintiff for reduction in the value of property
plus medical bills. Defendant Angelo, a nonfreeholder, paid $1,500
in a case heard ten years later when he blinded McCutcheon's slave
John. John had been in Angelo's chickenhouse.[8]

The nineteenth-century law for animals yields interesting parallels
to slave law. People could not simply kill trespassing horses or other
livestock, especially in regions where stock customarily ran free.
Animal owners typically won damages in these cases unless the
animals had endangered the defendants' safety. These rules look like
many states' laws for slaves. In nineteenth-century Texas, for instance,
one could not injure stock to protect crops. But in some states, the
law logically weighted the interests of defendants more heavily, just
as Kentucky courts did in slave cases. In North Carolina, where
grazing rights were less treasured than in Texas, people could injure
animals that had broken into enclosed fields under cultivation. And
when a North Carolina sow with a "bad reputation for eating poultry"
was spotted with a duck in her mouth, the duck's owner was entitled
to shoot the pig.[9] Animals with slight market value, primarily dogs,
had little legal protection. An 1891 Connecticut case even advised
gardeners to kill dogs destroying garden plants, essentially because
dogs were worth less than the vegetation. At any time, people
could lawfully kill dogs suspected of being sheep worriers. A line of
Missouri cases warned against putting out poisoned meat for dogs,
however – Missouri ranchers naturally feared that other animals
might consume the tainted food.[10] Still, as in most states, Missouri
defendants did not have to take particular care of trespassing animals:
They were not liable for negligence when strays suffered harm on
their property.[11]

Trespassing Free Persons: Civil and Criminal Cases. How did slave law
compare with nineteenth-century law for free persons who tres-
passed? In some states, the two bodies of law seemed to have points
in common. *Dicta* in a few cases indicate that people could protect
themselves against burglars but could not kill intruders except in self-
defense – or sometimes to prevent large property losses.[12] Killing just
to prevent a trespass was considered homicide, at least in Delaware,
North Carolina, and Alabama.[13] Property-holders had a duty in some
states to warn off trespassers before using force.[14]

Yet the law regarding free trespassers in fact departed significantly from slave law in many parts of the South. As in other areas of law, the established property value of slaves seemed to carry greater weight than the ambiguous value of human life, especially that of a criminal. Owners of homes and businesses received gentler treatment from judges when they injured a nonslave intruder than when they harmed slaves. As late as 1883, a Mississippi court decided that a homeowner was justified in using force to eject a trespasser, even to the point of killing him. Breaking into a house to retrieve one's property still gave rise to justifiable homicide on the part of a homeowner, decided one Virginia court. In 1885, Texas even held that killing in defense of property of slight value was warranted.[15] The primary legal authority for antebellum citizens, William Blackstone, advised that actions taken to prevent a capital crime were justified, even if the criminal was killed.[16] What is more, people in many Southern states could legally set spring guns to protect their belongings. English and American common law held that a person injured by a spring gun had no civil complaint if he knew a gun was set, even if he did not know its exact location.[17] In much of the antebellum South, of course, rules providing compensation for thieving slaves (though not for other robbers) probably discouraged people from setting spring guns and firing on burglars in the dark: One could not be sure of one's target. Because South Carolinians assumed that slaves committed most thefts, for instance, slave law likely controlled the actions of Palmetto Staters looking out for thieves.[18]

Long after the Civil War, states began to institute official measures to protect petty thieves. Statutes outlaw spring guns in most states today; notices do not necessarily protect one under common law, either.[19] Louisiana and Iowa courts even used chicken-stealing slave cases as precedents in post–World War I cases to convict defendants of manslaughter or assault. In two cases, the Louisiana courts said that the slave cases, though civil in nature, established the principle that nonviolent larceny of goods of small value did not give a warrant to kill to prevent theft. (A dissent in a 1933 case hints at the trouble of those times, however: "Society is confronted today with the shocking and continuous depredations of organized, desperate, and merciless gangsters and racketeers. Property rights have lost entirely their legal sanction.") The Iowa defendant had shot at a thirteen-year-old playing in his pasture, alleging that he had seen someone earlier stealing chickens. The man was convicted of assault with intent to inflict great bodily harm. In a pointed aside, the court stated that Iowans could not justify killing someone thought to be committing a misdemeanor or a felony without force, although Texans probably could.[20]

Assaults by Strangers

Southern courts were quick to grant civil damages for wanton attacks
upon slaves and animals; they showed more reluctance to award
damages for assaults upon free persons. Because slaves were considered property and property crimes greatly concerned antebellum citizens, assaults upon slaves often generated criminal penalties as well.
Abuse of animals less often led to criminal punishment; assaults of
free persons rarely did. In sum, the Southern legal system worked
better in deterring strangers' abuse of slaves (and, less so, animals)
than preventing assaults of free persons.

Assaults of Slaves, Animals, and Free Persons: Civil Cases. Because slaves
could disrupt the peace of the surrounding community and inflict
harm on those other than their owners, outsiders could discipline
slaves and protect themselves physically from slaves, particularly as the
antebellum years came to a close.[21] Louisiana's code justified firing
on armed or recalcitrant slaves, for instance. People were to try to
wound rather than kill, but killing a slave did not necessarily impose
civil liability. For example, a Louisiana defendant killed a slave who
had no pass and was trying to steal a gun, but he did not have to compensate the slave's owner in 1821. In a Kentucky case heard about
the same time, Hancock's slave had been on Smith's Kentucky plantation at a covert meeting. The slave came at Smith with a club, so
Smith killed him with a pitchfork. Smith was cleared of liability. In an
Alabama case heard nearly four decades later, a man ran into a pack
of slaves. One slave approached the defendant with a stick; the defendant quickly fired his gun. The slave later died from bullet wounds.
A court granted judgment to the defendant.[22]

For those who wantonly inflicted damage on slaves, however, the
outcomes were different. These abusers had to pay slaveowners for
the loss, just as did those who maliciously killed animals. (In one
animal case, the defendant could not justify killing a dog for trivial
offenses like stealing an egg, snapping at a man's heel, barking at a
horse, and allegedly worrying a sheep years before.)[23] Courts used
civil liability to deter injuries to slaves and thus to their owners. In a
complicated 1792 Virginia case, Kuhn thought that Holmes's slave
had robbed his slave, so he whipped Holmes's slave. Holmes then
beat Kuhn. Kuhn brought assault and battery charges against Holmes
and prosecuted Holmes's slave. All parties were acquitted. Holmes
then brought an action against Kuhn for whipping Holmes's slave and
recovered £17. In another Virginia case heard not long after, a slave
was beaten in his own quarters by someone who had entered with the
master's permission. But because the defendant had no good reason

for the beating, it cost him $150. A North Carolina slaveowner in 1843 even recovered jail fees and the value of lost services when she established that the defendant had maliciously prosecuted her slaves. *Dicta* in an 1858 Tennessee case advocated a substantial damage award to the owner of slave Austin, who had been apprehended for rape and murder. A mob broke down the door to the jail and lynched Austin. A jury gave Austin's owner damages of 1 cent. An appellate court reversed and remanded the case, saying the jury should have determined Austin's value from his age, appearance, health, and other relevant characteristics. Moral traits determined value as well, said the court, but because the law presumed innocence the murder charge could not be taken into account. The court also said vindictive damages were appropriate because the act set an evil example for the community: "The courts and juries, public officers and citizens, should set their faces like flint against . . . mobs in all their forms."[24]

Slaves who were hurt when they fled from menacing strangers usually created liability for their injurers as well. In a case heard in 1827, a North Carolina court decided that evidence of a slave's submissive character could rebut the presumption that the slave, killed while running from his attacker, had committed a felony. The reward to the slave for his "good character," naturally, would have been damages paid to his owner. In the 1850 Louisiana case of *Arnandez v. Lawes*, slave William ran away from the defendant, who was attempting to tie up William and two other slaves, all of whom had legitimate passes from their masters. The defendant shot and killed William. At trial, he protested his innocence, claiming he had not intended to kill William: Someone else had loaded his rifle with buckshot instead of birdshot. A jury granted the plaintiff $1,000, the defendant appealed, and, in a highly unusual move, an appellate court raised the award to $1,200. One Tennessee court downplayed the violence of a slave's attackers, however, emphasizing instead that slaves had an affirmative duty to flee from danger. In this 1858 case, the owner of slave Isaac could not recover damages from another slaveowner who had hosted a corn husking at which an uninvited, drunken white man stabbed Isaac. Why? Because "as persons, [slaves] are considered by our law, as accountable moral agents, possessed of the power of volition and locomotion." The outcome likely would have differed, however, if Isaac's owner had sued the murderer instead of his slave-owning neighbor.[25]

Slaves who defended themselves against threatening strangers might themselves earn reprieves. An 1840 North Carolina court granted a slave a new trial after he had been sentenced to death for murdering a Mr. Chatham, who had hit the slave and accused him of stealing. Another North Carolina case, heard in 1849, gave slaves permission to protect their friends from the abuse of strangers (although the court came to the opposite conclusion a mere eight years later). When Alabama slave Dave used a pocketknife to cut Mr. Cunningham superficially, a trial court convicted Dave of assault with intent to kill. An 1853 appellate court reversed and remanded the case. Apparently, Dave's hirer had sent him to hunt for a mad dog; Cunningham encountered Dave, told him to drop his pants, and began to whip him. Dave's owner showed him to have a peaceful nature; the court determined that Cunningham's actions were unjustified.[26]

An 1849 Florida court in *McRaeny v. Johnson* expressed the pride judges took in these verdicts: "[I]n cases of injury to the peculiar species of property, the American courts, by a spirit of enlightened humanity ... have extended a more enlarged protection than prevails in the case of mere chattels." Here, the plaintiff recovered $435 for the beating and killing of her slave.[27] Despite the *McRaeny* court's rhetoric, the sheer wealth represented by slaves probably influenced courts as much as humanity did. Southerners well knew the value of slaves: In an unusual Alabama incident, a mob that had killed a slave even took financial responsibility without coercion by the courts. Farmer MacDonald had punished his slave for disobedience; the slave later clubbed MacDonald to death. The slave gave himself up to an angry crowd, which burned him alive. Afterward, people in the mob passed the hat until they raised enough money to match the slave's value, then handed the cash to the MacDonald family.[28] Oddly enough, the "spirit of enlightened humanity" touted by the *McRaeny* court did not extend to personal-injury cases, at least not before the Civil War. Theoretically, injured persons could bring civil suits for damages when others assaulted them. Injured servants could bring actions for personal damages; their masters could also request consequential damages resulting from lost services. But virtually all Southern appellate cases addressing these issues appear in postbellum years. Heirs, representatives, and employers of persons who died as the result of assaults also typically failed to recover damages in antebellum years.[29]

Assaults of Slaves and Animals: Criminal Cases. Strangers who abused or killed slaves in an assault might face criminal prosecution as well as civil liability. Context mattered, however: Antebellum Southerners considered slave assault a property crime rather than a crime against a person. Consequently, even though terms like "assault," "battery," and "manslaughter" appeared in slave cases, they referred to brutal acts committed on property – notwithstanding the paradoxical concept of "manslaughter of property." And property crime was a serious matter in the nineteenth century. Before that time, only malicious acts against property were criminal; this requirement loosened considerably in the 1800s.[30] Harming valuable slaves was considered a particularly heinous crime. Damaging other types of property, even livestock, created less concern. Only rarely did antebellum abuse of animals generate criminal suits, at least at the appellate level. Stabbing a horse was criminal in a single Tennessee case heard in 1808. Here, a horse had broken into a lawfully fenced cornfield several times. The owner of the field finally stabbed the horse, then faced a criminal charge under the Act of 1803. A North Carolina defendant was not convicted in 1816, however, for stabbing a horse that suddenly provoked him. And killing dogs did not result in criminal convictions.[31]

Strangers who abused slaves more likely faced criminal proceedings than employers, overseers, and sheriffs, who understandably had some coercive power over slaves entrusted to their care. An 1823 North Carolina court gave an economic rationale to indict strangers who assaulted slaves: "[This legislation] has rendered [slaves] of more value to their masters, and suppressed many outrages. . . . If [assaults] may be committed with impunity, the public peace will not only be rendered extremely insecure, but the value of slave property must be much impaired, for the offenders can seldom make any reparation in damages."[32] An 1860 Kentucky court explained likewise: "The preservation of the peace, and the repose of society, will be the more effectually secured, and this kind of property be rendered the more valuable to their masters, by thus protecting slaves from the wanton abuse and injury to which they might otherwise be exposed." A contemporaneous D.C. court also said that public punishment of a slave (or an animal) annoyed passersby and was therefore a public nuisance.[33]

Punishments in slave-assault cases ranged from hard labor, imprisonment, and fines to sentences of death. A North Carolina court sentenced defendant Roane for manslaughter in 1828, for example, when he killed slave Levin as Levin crept through Roane's gate in the middle of the night. Levin, a waiter in the tavern of Roane's employer, had apparently burglarized Roane's kitchen. The court said that one might justifiably kill to prevent a felony, but not to punish a felony already committed. (An 1847 Mississippi court similarly called it murder when the defendant killed a free man with a deadly weapon, because the victim had stolen the defendant's horse long before.) A Louisiana defendant killed slave Hardy Ellis and was sentenced to seven years at hard labor for manslaughter in 1843. A Louisiana trial court sustained a motion to quash the indictment of another defen-

dant for felonious shooting of a slave, but an appellate court reversed
and remanded the case in 1859.[34] North Carolina and Mississippi
courts actually pronounced the death sentence in three cases,
although Governor Miller later pardoned the Mississippi defendant.
In a North Carolina death-sentence case from 1817, the opinion
echoed Shylock's plaint: "Is not the slave a reasonable creature, is not
he a human being . . . ?"[35]

Of course, many murders of slaves went unpunished by criminal
courts, particularly in the last years before the Civil War. Some cases
never went to trial; others ended in acquittal or generated only light
punishment. Defendant Tackett was sentenced to death for murder,
for example, but a North Carolina appellate court granted a new trial
in 1820 to examine evidence that murdered slave Daniel had had a
violent temper and that Tackett should have been charged with
manslaughter. (Tackett had continually harassed Daniel's wife.) In
one miscarriage of justice, an 1857 South Carolina court released the
defendant on a technicality. Although defendant Winningham had
killed a slave who was trying to prevent him from stealing the slaveowner's oxen, Winningham claimed he had failed to receive a copy
of the indictment. Sometimes judges expressed dismay in such cases.
A North Carolina defendant was found guilty at trial of murdering a
slave, but an appellate court arrested the verdict in 1801. Judge Johnston regretted that the legislature would not let him sustain it: "It is
evidence of a most depraved and cruel disposition, to murder one,
so much in your power." As the previous chapter discussed, Georgia
judges in 1857 had similarly thought that a brutal overseer should be
charged with murder rather than manslaughter but could not order
a new trial on that basis.[36]

In some states, criminal actions and remedies took precedence
over civil ones – but retrieving money from jailed or fined defendants
proved difficult. Consequently, slaveowner plaintiffs sometimes tried
to block criminal charges. Alabama master Rhodes wanted $1,000 for
a slave killed by Morgan, for example, so he tried to prevent Morgan's
indictment. A jury granted his request, but an appellate court
reversed and remanded the case in 1827 because "public justice must
be answered before the owner . . . can obtain redress. . . . If an acquittal should be brought about by his collusion, he cannot afterwards
sustain an action for the trespass." A case heard nine years later in
the same state followed up by saying that criminal trials must be held
first; otherwise, people would pay civil damages if plaintiffs promised
not to complain of public wrongs. An 1851 Georgia case bears this
out. Here, Nancy Farmer brought a civil action against defendant
Neal for killing her slave and won a judgment of $825. Farmer under-
standably argued that killing a slave was not a felony: Georgia courts

suspended the civil remedies for felony murder until the criminal trial ended. Southern judges were looking to the large interests of the South when they ruled against slaveowners in such cases. No matter how understandable plaintiffs' motives, slaveholding society had a stake in thwarting these types of maneuvers to the extent criminal penalties achieved general deterrence.[37]

Assaults of Free Persons: Criminal Cases. Crimes against persons – if committed by whites – seemed to alarm antebellum Southerners much less than crimes against property.[38] Although criminal penalties could deter property crimes, people thought that many assaults and murders were crimes of passion or self-defense that society could not or should not deter.[39] As a result, assaulting a slave, like damaging any valuable property, tended to carry far more serious legal consequences than assaulting a free person. Many white criminals were never arrested or charged for nonproperty crimes: Sheriffs found tax collection more lucrative, and overworked prosecutors knew that the chances of conviction were slim.

Throughout much of the nineteenth century, those few Southerners indicted for assault and battery, manslaughter, or murder of a free person brought successful defenses under the notorious 1830 Tennessee case of *Grainger v. State*. The opinion in *Grainger* essentially excused the killing with a deadly weapon of an unarmed assailant. The 1856 Mississippi case of *Ex parte Wray* significantly expanded justifiable circumstances for self-defense.[40] In this case, Jacob Wray killed a schoolmaster simply for expelling Wray's younger brother. In most of the antebellum South, the rule was to "stand one's ground" against an assailant, rather than the customary Northern "duty to retreat." Texas retained the "stand one's ground" rule until 1973.[41]

Other factors ensured that antebellum Southern white criminals of all stripes evaded punishment, especially for nonproperty crimes. Southern states featured more capital crimes on the books than Northern ones; Southerners in turn were more reluctant to press charges initially and to convict those successfully charged. Daniel Flanigan reported that Virginia's criminal law was one of the most repressive, for example, yet the state's daily practice of law was the most humane in the South.[42] Prosecutors sometimes even encouraged people to bring charges of assault and battery so they could share in fees or fines, then either failed to pursue the charges or signed petitions of remission that enabled defendants to obtain pardons.[43] In several Southern states, juries determined sentences; in Georgia, juries that convicted a defendant of a capital crime could even recommend clemency. In at least one case, a jury acquitted a man who had pled guilty. The foreman reported that the members of the South Carolina jury thought the defendant had always been a liar and expected he always would be.[44] First offenders frequently avoided punishment by obtaining the benefit of clergy – essentially, an exemption from the death sentence for those who could read – or receiving a pardon. Kentucky and three other states even allowed pardons before trial. And minor technical errors caused frequent reversals of verdicts. Those few white Southerners who were convicted – of capital and noncapital crimes – often escaped poorly built jails. All in all, the punishments for white-on-white assaults were virtually nonexistent, especially compared with the consequences of assaulting slaves.

KIDNAPPING OF SLAVES, SERVANTS, AND FREE BLACKS
AND RECOVERY OF FUGITIVE SLAVES: LEGAL RULES

Kidnapping Cases

Kidnapping a slave, to free or to sell him, could yield civil damages for an owner or creditor. The Virginia owner of legal title to a slave retrieved $1,000 in 1845 from someone who had helped the slave escape, for example, even though the owner had probably obtained the title fraudulently. Such rules were established early on: A 1797 Maryland court allowed the plaintiff to prove consequential damages in the amount of lost profits when the defendant absconded with the plaintiff's slaves. Another Maryland court faced an interesting issue about the value of female slaves. An 1818 lawsuit determined that defendant Sewell had to pay for female slaves he had stolen in 1812. The damages awarded equaled the female slaves' value as of 1812, with interest accumulated to 1818. Between 1812 and 1818, the slaves bore children. The plaintiff brought a second lawsuit in 1821 for the value of the children; the court refused to award damages in this case. In effect, the court denied double compensation to the plaintiff: Because the 1812 price for the women presumably included the expected value of the children the slaves would bear, the plaintiff should not also have received the value of children actually borne.[45]

But taking a slave from his owner, like disciplining and abusing another's slaves, could generate criminal as well as civil penalties. Jack Williams noted, in fact, that kidnapping a slave was often considered worse than killing a fellow citizen.[46] The sheer property value inherent in slaves – along with their persuadability – required correspondingly stricter protection than for other forms of property. An 1819 South Carolina court explained why the state had the death penalty for taking a slave: "The object and policy of the act was to give the most ample protection to the most valuable species of personal property, owned in this country; and to effect that object, it became necessary to resort to terms suited to the nature of the property intended to be protected. Negroes, being intelligent creatures, possessing volition, as well as the power of locomotion, are capable of being deluded by art and persuasion, as well as of being compelled by fear or force to leave the service of their owners."[47] An 1807 Tennessee court likewise explained the necessity of fining those who stole slaves: "This species of property should be inviolably guarded from the control of others than their master. They differ from all other kinds of property; they have reason and volition." In an 1849 Tennessee case, defendant Cash was even indicted for stealing slave Wilson, a runaway. A court said that Wilson was still the subject of larceny, so Cash received an eleven-year prison sentence.[48]

Some states had the death penalty for those who took slaves with the intent to re-sell but only fined those who tried to help slaves escape to freedom. Distinguishing the two crimes made sense: Helping a slave to escape took the slave out of the marketplace, reducing supply and increasing slave prices, *ceteris paribus*. Selling slaves obtained fraudulently, on the other hand, created uncertainty about title and thus reduced slave prices. Although both acts injured the robbed slaveowner, the second bollixed up the inner workings of slave markets.[49] In an illustrative 1839 Alabama case, the defendant had not wanted to keep slave Jane or profit by concealing her, so a court decided that he had not violated a statute calling for the death penalty for larceny. Ten years later, a D.C. court determined that the defendant had not committed larceny if he had simply invited a slave onto a vessel bound for a free state.[50] Virginia's law was different: The state often added jail time, even for those merely aiding slaves to escape. In an 1850 case, the defendant received an additional two-year sentence for urging a slave to escape after he had already been sentenced to four years for advising the slave's compatriot at the same time. The owner of another Virginia slave taken by force faced no time bar to an action, even if someone had eventually emancipated the taken slave.[51] Why did Virginia have different laws? Because Virginia itself was different. The state's slave population was the country's largest, and Virginia bordered the North and the Atlantic Ocean, which offered slaves tempting escape routes. Accordingly, state law built in greater deterrence against helping slaves escape. Virginia even passed a law specifically directed against citizens of New York who carried away slaves. In the spirit of unity, South Carolina enacted a similar law.[52]

Penalties for stealing slaves or advising slaves to escape did not always apply, especially if discovering a slave's status was difficult. One defendant pretended that Frank (a white-complected slave with red hair and freckles) was his servant so Frank could ride a stagecoach at half-price, for example. Because the defendant did not know and could not reasonably have known Frank was a slave, strict application of statutes in cases like these would have overpenalized defendants. In fact, a South Carolina appellate court reversed a trial court's finding for the plaintiff and ordered a new trial in 1845.[53] In a case heard the same year, a Virginia court advised acquittal if an escapee was not clearly a slave. And Virginia did not convict a minister in 1850 under the state's Act of 1847–48, which made denying the right of owners to their property a criminal offense. The minister had merely preached that owning and selling slaves was immoral but had not named names or called for specific action. Jurisdictional issues mattered in a third Virginia case heard about the same time. Here, the defendants had stepped into the Ohio River to help escaped slaves ashore into Ohio. Because Virginia extended her borders across the river, the court had to settle whether Virginia's boundary was the high-water or low-water mark. The majority voted for the low-water mark, with five dissents. The court therefore determined that the defendants were beyond the court's jurisdiction, not having left Ohio.[54] An 1861 Maryland court recognized an interesting perversity that would have arisen from strict application of penalties for harboring slaves. Like many states, Maryland did not require written hiring contracts. In one dispute, the defendant could show no written proof that he had employed a slave working on his boat. The slave-owner plaintiff therefore asked to collect the $500 penalty imposed on boat owners who harbored slaves. But the court said that adopting the plaintiff's rule would encourage slaveowners to hire their slaves for a single day under an oral agreement, then to try collecting the statutory $500. The court ruled for the defendant as a result.[55]

Rarely, nineteenth-century courts heard other sorts of lawsuits concerning the taking of productive property. Only a smattering of civil suits appeared. For example, a few property owners sued those who took tame beasts or merchandise. And postbellum courts sometimes granted masters the right to recover damages from those who had enticed servants away or prevented servants from performing their duties. Most of these cases were directed toward unions or toward those who had attempted to hire away black sharecroppers. An 1872 Georgia case provides one example: Here, damages to the plaintiff equaled his average net profit lost through the defendant's act of enticing away a servant.[56] But the large property value of slaves made civil suits more likely when people kidnapped slaves rather than when they meddled with other factors of production. Kidnaps of slaves also generated more criminal suits than the theft of other property such as livestock. Protecting livestock mattered in the agrarian nineteenth century, of course, but usually less than protecting slaves. (Missouri imposed a uniform seven-year jail sentence on those who stole slaves, horses, mules, or asses, however.)[57] Juries seemed to dislike imposing penalties for stolen property other than slaves or livestock; they sometimes even attempted to reduce charges. In 1815, one South Carolina jury found the value of stolen property to be less than 12 pence (the threshold for petit larceny), even though all witnesses had testified the property was worth much more.[58] Such finagling would have been difficult when slaves or horses were stolen.

Kidnapping a slave was a major offense throughout the South; by comparison, kidnapping a free black to sell him into slavery carried almost no penalties. The former deprived whites of property, while the latter injured only black persons. Some jurisdictions, such as Maryland and the District of Columbia, did pass statutes imposing a fine, imprisonment, or public whipping upon those who took away free blacks. But other jurisdictions punished free blacks for petty crimes by enslaving them. Florida, for example, sold free persons of color into slavery if they did not pay debts within five days of being served with a writ of execution. Regardless of jurisdiction, free blacks were always subject to kidnapping and enslavement. Few recovered their freedom, much less vindication in a criminal courtroom or compensation for their tribulations.[59]

Fugitive Slave Cases

The counterpart to helping slaves escape was picking up fugitives to send back to their owners. The law surrounding this enterprise was prodigious and unique to slave property. Slave catching was a dangerous business: One life insurance company even denied a claim on this basis. The deceased, William Callender, had stated his occupation as "farmer." He was actually a slavecatcher. The company representative said: "We would not take a person at any price if it was known he had engaged in slave-catching. I consider it a much more perilous occupation than farming."[60]

Owners sometimes offered rewards to slave catchers. This led to an unusual Delaware case heard in 1840. Here, two men named Maberry and Chase captured a runaway slave. Chase wanted to jail the slave. Maberry, a constable, offered to keep the slave in his garret while Chase visited the slaveowner to persuade him to increase the reward for capture from $60 to $100. Chase succeeded. Unfortunately for him, the slave had escaped in the meantime. Chase sued Maberry and recovered the incremental $40. A court reasoned that

Maberry had owed Chase a duty to keep the slave in jail-like security rather than simply to take ordinary care to prevent an escape.[61]

Because fugitive slaves cost society as well as individual slaveowners – hungry runaways stole from farms and fields and set a dangerous example for other slaves – some states also offered rewards to defray the costs of capture.[62] An 1850 Kentucky court explained why the state passed a statute requiring owners to pay $100 to captors of fugitive slaves: "[I]t was necessary to offer a greater reward, and such as would probably be sufficient to induce men to consult their own interests, regardless of the public sentiment around them. . . . [N]ot only [are] fugitives . . . more frequently now than formerly returned to their owners, but [also] the difficulty of final escape has had some tendency to prevent others from attempting it."[63] For similar reasons, an 1858 Louisiana appellate court upheld the right of a sheriff to sell a runaway slave who had been advertised but left unclaimed for nearly a year: "The provisions of the law . . . on the subject of fugitive slaves [are] a matter of police essential to the protection of the citizens of the states against the depredations of this class of persons, who are often driven by hunger to commit acts of violence and are dangerous from their evil example and nightly meetings to others of their race and the peace of the community at large. . . ."[64] Texas even passed a law in 1857 that gave a reward for any slave captured outside of American slave territory; the reward equaled half the slave's value.

UNDERMINING THE SLAVEOWNER'S AUTHORITY AND ENDANGERING THE COMMUNITY: LEGAL PENALTIES

Slaveowners sued strangers who stole, beat, or accidentally hurt slaves, just as anyone would sue for damages to property. But people could injure slaveowners in indirect ways as well. Slaves were unique property: They were capable of conducting business, playing cards, plotting crimes, and getting into all-too-human scrapes. Paramount among the South's concerns were persons who weakened slaveowners' authority by offering liquor to slaves, allowing slaves to gather together, trading with slaves, and influencing slaves in other ways. Such acts endangered not only the master but also the community and the institution of slavery itself.[65] The law surrounding these acts accounted for their external effects, as well as for injuries to particular slaveowners.

Most states prohibited the sale of liquor to slaves.[66] In 1860, Georgia Chief Justice Joseph Lumpkin floridly explained why: "[It is] an offense which is more destructive to our slave population; and therefore, to the rights of property than any in the penal code. . . . [The] number of [N]egroes destroyed by liquor every year . . .

average one to each county; and generally they are the most valuable slaves. . . . The lives and property of their owners are frequently jeopardized in this way. . . . [Drink] engenders recklessness, and nerves the arm of the timid and hesitating to deeds of desperate daring and death."[67] The question in many lawsuits was whether violation of such statutes generated civil damages as well as criminal penalties when drunken slaves hurt themselves. Generally, the answer was yes. In an 1822 case, for example, a Louisiana defendant sold liquor to slave Jasmin, who got drunk and drowned. The plaintiff won the slave's value; the court noted that this "law . . . is founded alike in a regard for the interests of the master and slave." A South Carolina court gave its reasons for imposing civil liability in the 1847 case of *Harrison v. Berkley*: "[W]here the mischievous purpose of a slave is manifest, or should be foreseen by ordinary prudence, the injurious act embraces the will of the slave, as one of its ingredients. . . ." In 1850, Missouri slaveowner Hughes sued Skinner, whose clerk had sold spirits to slave Willis. Willis collapsed in a drunken stupor, froze, and died eight days later. Citing *Harrison* as authority, the court compared the sale to "placing noxious food within reach of domestic animals." (In comparison, saloon owner Johnson was not held criminally negligent in 1890 under a Georgia statute when one of his patrons, Whitlock, killed another, Belding. Here, widow Belding sued Johnson for continuing to serve liquor to the drunken Whitlock, then failing to prevent Whitlock from shooting Belding in a fight over a gambled watch.)[68] In some states, sellers were protected from liability if masters had given written permission for slaves to buy liquor for a particular person. An 1851 Kentucky case established that shopkeepers could not sell liquor to slaves without such permission, for example. But another case heard four years later indicated that an indictment must state that the defendant did not have custody of the slave – oddly enough, Kentucky jailors or sheriffs could give liquor to arrested slaves without fear of punishment.[69]

Many states passed statutes to outlaw slave assemblies. As in liquor cases, people who permitted unlawful meetings of slaves might face civil liability as well as fines if slaves were injured or killed. Common law sometimes prohibited assembly of slaves as well, punishing those who allowed it. Keeping a grocery at which slaves (and free persons of color) assembled and drank was a public nuisance in Kentucky, for example. In at least one case, however, Kentucky did not add civil liability to the statutory fine of $2 per slave at an illegal assembly. Bosworth owned a farm where several slaves had held a dance; Brand's slave had attended. A patroller fired his pistol into a dark room, killing Brand's slave. A jury awarded Brand the value of the slave; an appellate court reversed and remanded the case, saying that the jury should have been instructed to find for the defendant. In this case, the court reasoned that the "wanton malice of the patrol" was the causal factor; in drunkenness cases, on the other hand, no interposing factor was present.[70]

Trading with a slave was typically taboo, because it carried external costs as well as possibly injuring the master. As Georgia Justice Lumpkin put it: "While the actual owner is damaged by corrupting his slave, every inhabitant in the neighborhood is made to suffer, by the stimulation given by this traffic, to acts of pilfering and plunder." An 1827 Kentucky opinion similarly said that such license would "beget idle and dissolute habits in the particular slaves so indulged, as well as in others, and lead to depredations upon the property of others, and to crimes and insubordination." For this reason, an 1851 Alabama court convicted a shopkeeper for selling shoes to a slave who had permission to purchase only "dry goods." The court determined that the statute required more specificity from the slaveowner so that slaves would not be tempted to peddle. The court stated: "[T]he Legislature designed [the law] to suppress . . . a general evil in some parts of the country, growing out of a clandestine traffic between slaves and a particular class of white persons." The opinion in an 1860 North Carolina case echoed these sentiments. Slaves could not own jackasses, because this was "inconsistent with [a slave's] social position. He will be, himself, tempted to pilfer and steal . . . and make other slaves dissatisfied with their condition, and thereby excite in them a spirit of insubordination."[71]

Some states had quite specific statutes about transactions with slaves. Kentucky (1841), Florida (1843), and Virginia (1855) passed laws to forbid people from selling, giving, or delivering poison to slaves. In 1864, Virginia imposed fines of up to $500 for buying items from a slave or free black, carrying blacks as boat hands, or transporting the goods of a slave. A Kentucky statute permitted masters to recover quadruple the value of property bought from a slave. An 1847 Kentucky court would not let master Hays sue a public officer for laying claim on behalf of creditors to the possessions of slave Dick, however. Dick had obtained property by acting as an independent businessman – with Hays's blessing. In the lawsuit, Hays claimed that Dick's possessions actually belonged to him. Obligations arising from Dick's business dealings were unenforceable, said Hays, because Dick was a slave. But the court logically reasoned that, if Hays himself treated Dick as free, Hays could not penalize others for doing the same.[72]

Giving non-emergency medical care to a slave without his master's permission infringed upon slaveholders' rights and so was not reimbursable – and might even create civil liability. In an 1813 case, for example, the doctor plaintiff wanted fees of $7.98 for giving a slave medicine to treat an unnamed "foul disease." The slave healed. But because the plaintiff (at the slave's embarrassed request) had not talked to the slave's master beforehand – and he had had time to – he could not recover fees. In an 1836 D.C. case, a slave of Manning's visited his wife at Cox's house. When the slave contracted smallpox, Manning offered to take him home. Instead, Cox sent her own children away so she could devote herself to nursing the slave. The slave died. Cox could not recover her expenses. And in an 1852 Kentucky case, the defendant administered drugs to slave Bill without his owner's consent. Bill then fell sick and died. Although the defendant won at trial, an appellate court reversed and remanded the case, saying that the plaintiff should recover Bill's full value.[73]

Courts also proscribed other interactions with slaves. Inducing a South Carolina slave to race generated civil damages of $450 in 1802 when the slave died after a horse threw him headfirst into a tree. Here, the court baldly stated that one answered for all consequences, intentional or not, arising from using another's property without permission. Procuring slaves to commit crimes – which required acknowledging that slaves were persons – brought on criminal penalties in Georgia.[74] Slaves were also considered persons for purposes of defining a riot and convicting a white man for passing counterfeit bills.[75] Even a potential influence over slaves concerned the courts. North Carolina indicted publisher Daniel Worth in 1860 for circulating Hinton Rowan Helper's inflammatory book *The Impending Crisis of the South*, even though Worth had sold the book to a white person. The court feared that a slave might find the book and become discontented and insubordinate.[76] Helper's book generally caused an uproar: In 1859, Florida passed a resolution calling for the expulsion of U.S. Congressmen who may have circulated *The Impending Crisis*, saying that these people would have been put to death had they committed the act in Florida.

LAW CONCERNING THE TREATMENT OF SLAVES THAT BENEFITED THEIR OWNERS

Southern courts approved of good treatment of another's slave, even when property damage resulted, if the slaveowner typically would have benefited from the defendant's actions. As judges recognized, slaveowners would have agreed beforehand to beneficial treatment had they had the chance. (In some of the cases described, plaintiff and defendant were not exactly strangers, but nor did they have a contractual arrangement.)

In some cases, courts excused kindly defendants from paying

damages. A Louisiana plaintiff's neighbor (a doctor), who had removed the plaintiff's sick slave Joseph from jail and started to bring him home, was not held liable in 1813 when Joseph escaped: "[T]aking the slave, diseased as he was, from the confined and unwholesome air of a prison, was certainly an act well intended . . . for the benefit of the master. . . ." Nor did an 1836 Kentucky appellate court wish to hold defendant Bakewell liable when young slave Washington escaped from a gig while Bakewell went hunting. Bakewell employed Washington's mother and had taken the boy along with him frequently with the plaintiff's permission, for the "welfare and gratification of the boy."[77]

Other cases involved the payment of doctors' fees. If slaveowners should have expected doctors to take action, they had to pay fees. In an 1803 D.C. case, employer Nicholas Voss had engaged Dr. Rogers to care for Mrs. Fenwick's slaves. A court decided that, if the custom of the region was for owners to pay for medical care and Fenwick did not tell Voss that she had a family doctor, then Voss could employ Rogers on Fenwick's account. (Voss's need for a doctor is a trifle suspicious. On at least one occasion, Voss was sued for beating a hired slave, although he paid no damages because the loss in services allegedly was minimal.) After a slave's owner had abused her and left her in a public road, the doctor who treated her had a claim for fees, according to an 1807 South Carolina court. Doctors also frequently recovered fees for tending to slaves if parties had implicitly agreed to the treatment beforehand. The administrator of an Arkansas estate had seen Dr. Belfour treating slave Orange for winter fever many times, for example, but refused to pay him. Although a jury found for the administrator defendant, an 1848 appellate court said that the estate should pay Belfour's fees (provided that Belfour gave more evidence of the value of his services). Similarly, an 1860 Kentucky court granted fees because the slaveowner knew that the doctor had often attended the slaves.[78] In contrast to these cases, employers were not obliged to pay physicians' bills for their free servants, even if the employer had requested the service or if the servant had been hurt on the job.[79] Nor were employers of free persons responsible for negligence by their medical officers.[80]

Just as doctors could sometimes claim fees for treating slaves well, executors and administrators could spend money from estates on slaves under some circumstances. In an 1834 Maryland case, executors of a will could claim an allowance to maintain and clothe the decedent's slaves, because it benefited the estate: "[C]lothing was indispensable before they could be hired out, or . . . most profitably hired out. "A Louisiana executor could even spend $100 of the estate to purchase mourning dresses for slaves in 1852 – arguably creating some benefit to the deceased by honoring him.[81]

CONCLUSION

In deciding disputes between slaveowners and ordinary citizens, judges certainly protected valuable property: They rewarded people who intended to benefit slaveowners and punished those who inflicted harm. Slaveowners had to pay fees to strangers who had captured fugitives or doctored slaves in emergencies. They obtained damage awards from those who had negligently or deliberately injured slaves, helped slaves escape, or sold spirits to slaves.

Despite their evident concern for the rights of slaveowners, judges also looked to the larger interests of Southern society. Keeping the peace mattered, as did preserving other property interests. In some circumstances, then, Southerners could discipline others' slaves and protect their homes and farms. Such legal rules preserved the value of individual slaves by protecting them from gratuitous or careless abuse, but they also preserved slavery itself by allowing people to defend themselves against wayward or menacing slaves.

How does slave law compare with other areas of law? The legal rights and responsibilities of strangers, like those of other sorts of litigants, hinged upon economic concerns. Because slaves represented such a large chunk of marketable property, both civil and criminal law shielded slaves from ill-treatment by strangers more than it protected livestock or, in many instances, free persons. As in other types of disputes, the laws governing animals and free persons later grew to resemble slave law.

7

Treatment of One's Slaves, Servants, Animals, and Relatives

Legal Boundaries and the Problem of Social Cost

> I'll conquer ye, or kill ye! – one or t'other. I'll count every
> drop of blood there is in you, and take 'em, one by one,
> till ye give up!
> – Simon Legree[1]

Uncle Tom's Cabin paints for many people the quintessential picture
of relationships between masters and slaves: Harriet Beecher Stowe
portrayed in fiction what scholars have since documented in fact.[2]
According to court records, antebellum Southern judges helped
frame these relationships.[3] They granted masters generous leeway in
their discipline of slaves, tolerating even the viciousness of real Simon
Legrees as long as the abusive behavior did not affect the community.
This practice had economic as well as political and social roots: Privately administered "plantation law" cost less to carry out than public
law, at least to those other than slaves.[4] But court proceedings show
that many slaveowners also treated their human property compassionately – caring for slaves in old age, granting slaves small favors,
keeping slave families together, and protecting illegitimate slave children from wrathful wives. To a degree, Southern judges supported
benevolence toward slaves, even when such kindness apparently con-
tradicted statutes. Why? Certainly some judges must have been motivated by humanitarian instincts or a desire to protect the powerless.
But judges' opinions also indicate their beliefs that good treatment
of slaves could enhance labor productivity, increase plantation profits,
and reinforce the sentimental ties between master and slave. Courts
also accepted masters' use of slaves as agents when doing so lowered
overall costs of production and distribution.

When the treatment of one's slaves might have inflicted costs on
other parties with legal standing, however, judges stepped in to regulate the master's behavior. Put simply, antebellum law made masters
internalize these costs. This practice helped keep slavery economically viable. For instance, courts and legislatures proscribed some
cruel treatment by masters for fear that unchecked slave abuse could
have led to unpleasant scenes of public beatings, pilfering, and insur-

rection. But Southern judges also curbed excesses of kindness that potentially injured other Southerners. As one example, courts and legislators restricted slave manumissions, fearing subversion by freedmen and reductions in property tax revenues. Because trusted slaves might well have come to want more than a taste of freedom, the law of the South also banned slaves from carrying out certain responsibilities and typically prevented slaves from hiring themselves out. Some might view certain of these constraints as granting rights to slaves.[5] Yet the judiciary did not confer legal status upon slaves when it restricted masters. Rather, by protecting the rights and preserving the tranquility of other citizens, Southern judges enabled their peculiar economy to endure part-slave, part-free.

As in other areas of law, the law governing master–slave interactions reflected the dual character of slaves. Like cattle and horses, slaves were living chattel property. Yet slaves were also humans, often considered as much a part of the family circle as children, apprentices, and domestic help. Not only does this chapter examine the law of masters and slaves, it also compares slave law with the legal rights of man over beast, master over servant, husband over wife, parent over child. In the years following the American revolution, great changes transpired in the relationship between master and servant. Well before the Civil War, employers had largely lost the right to administer corporal punishment, although they retained considerable economic power over employees and remained responsible to third parties for many acts carried out by their servants. By comparison, masters had far more power over the bodies of their slaves, even though statutes and common law imposed certain constraints. Along with this greater power came enhanced responsibility: Slaveowners bore more accountability for slaves' actions than they did for the actions of servants, although compensation for executed slave criminals sometimes offset this civil liability. Interestingly enough, protective law for animals (similar to slave law) developed shortly after the Civil War, but domestic abuse laws lagged far behind. The analysis that follows first explains these differences. It then turns to discussions of anticruelty laws, the law concerning kindness to slaves, and the law regarding responsibility for one's subordinates.

EXPLAINING THE DIFFERENCES IN LAWS

The early-nineteenth-century transformation in the relation between employers and employees reflected a desire to distinguish "free" workers from slaves, according to Robert Steinfeld.[6] Allowing an adult to physically punish an unrelated person, especially another adult, came uncomfortably close to granting employers the rights of slaveowners. The ideals of liberty embodied in the Declaration of Independence and the U.S. Constitution clashed with ancient customs of corporal punishment. Barring physical chastisement was thus part of a larger movement to set apart slave from free labor; such bars served in part to strangle the expansion of virtual slavery into free states and territories. Still, equality at the polls did not translate into equality in the mills, as Christopher Tomlins has noted.[7] Employers had other arrows in their quivers: namely, the ability to hold back wages.

Unlike employers, slaveowners had little coercive economic power over slaves. Certainly masters might withhold food or rewards from wayward slaves. But withholding food could hurt the master just as it did the slave, through lost productivity and diminished property value.[8] And holding back small rewards from slaves who were nonetheless clothed, fed, and housed (however inadequately) fell far short of cutting off a free worker's entire means of livelihood, including pay for services rendered. The shift from direct physical control to indirect economic control over free laborers did not adapt well to the conditions of slavery. Small wonder that the laws erasing corporal punishment for servants and employees did not extend to slaves. Barring the discipline and punishment of slaves by their masters would have amounted to renouncing slavery itself.

Yet the law protected slaves, at least somewhat, relatively early in the nineteenth century. Protection of animals occurred next. By contrast, legal institutions failed to succor wives and children until much later. Proposed legislation against cruelty to women and children completely failed during the antebellum temperance movement, for example.[9] Elizabeth Pleck called the eighteenth century and the first half of the nineteenth century a legislative vacuum in this area.[10] Of course, legislation is only as strong as the courts that enforce it. Michael Hindus, for one, did not accept arguments that appellate courts protected blacks.[11] But although judges were not necessarily advocates for slaves, they nevertheless paid attention to the social and economic repercussions of unchecked slaveowner cruelty. Antebellum Southern judges used common law and legislation (albeit narrowly interpreted) to shield slaves from their owners but rarely did the same for family members and animals. The contrast in *dicta* for slave- and domestic-abuse cases especially indicates the different attitudes taken by nineteenth-century courts. Judges thought that they protected the family best by leaving it alone, but that they safeguarded slavery best by interfering under some circumstances.

Why did protection laws for slaves – though less comprehensive than similar laws for unrelated free employees – predate those for animals, wives, and children? Four interrelated considerations help explain this: the size of the externalities potentially generated by mistreatment, the likelihood of abuse, the presence (or absence) of informal control mechanisms, and the marketability of the victims.[12]

Mistreatment of one's slaves likely cost the rest of Southern society more than mistreatment of one's livestock or relatives. Being human, neglected slaves had a greater capacity to steal food and other necessities than did neglected animals, and cruelly treated slaves could foment widespread insurrection, whereas animals could not. Theodore Weld in 1839 captured well the seething emotions that could sometimes erupt in violence: "The idea of property having a will, and that in opposition to the will of its owner, is a stimulant of terrible power to the most relentless human passions."[13] Not only were local revolts a possibility, a slaveowner's cruelty could reverberate beyond his immediate neighbors. Masters frequently sold slaves. As Chapter 2 discussed, the quality of slaves was more difficult for buyers to discover than the quality of other commodities. Unbridled slaveowner abuse could have led to a disproportionate number of slaves on the auction block who seemed healthy but actually suffered from hidden physical or psychological wounds. What is more, badly treated slaves might also have tried to escape their bondage and encourage others to do likewise. Such contagion was unlikely among animals, women, and children of the antebellum period because they could not find a nearby haven to grant them legal status. Ill-using slaves generated relatively larger potential external costs, then, and Southern legislatures and courts made greater efforts to force slave-owners to internalize these costs: The South needed formal law to sustain slavery. These efforts grew more important as the slave population expanded, increased slave trading lent itself to possibilities of adverse selection, regional tensions escalated, and better transportation improved the means of escape for slaves.[14] To preserve the family, by contrast, citizens and policymakers alike advocated less law. Intruding upon household matters was considered costly. A North Carolina court summarized this view in 1868: "[H]owever great are the evils of ill temper, quarrels, and even personal conflicts . . . , they are not comparable with the evils which would result from raising the curtain, and exposing to public curiosity and criticism, the nursery and the bedchamber."[15]

Besides generating greater external costs, slave abuse may have been relatively more pervasive. Because slaves could verbally defy and deliberately misunderstand instructions, they likely provoked their owners more than animals did. Guilt or shame might have mattered as well. As Doris Lessing wrote in another context: "When the white man . . . by accident looks into the eyes of a [black] and sees the human being (which it is his chief preoccupation to avoid), his sense of guilt, which he denies, fumes up in resentment and he brings down the whip."[16] Masters could also punish slaves as examples. And the feelings of master for slave were probably less strong than the natural family affection of parent for child or husband for wife.[17] All of these factors would have tended to generate relatively more mistreatment of slaves. This higher incidence, coupled with the greater external effects, implied that the benefits of institutionalizing anti-abuse rules more likely outweighed the costs in slave cases relative to other cases.

Official sheltering of slaves (and later animals) also stood in the place of informal sanctions against domestic abuse. Free persons could petition blood relatives or friends for protection and sustenance, whereas slaves (and animals) could not. In other words, the dearth of protection laws for women in the antebellum United States did not necessarily mean a lack of protection: Fathers, brothers, and neighbors could come to the rescue when a husband abused or neglected his wife.[18] Slaves, in contrast, could count on family and friends for protection under the authority of a single case – and the abuser here was a stranger, not an owner. North Carolina Chief Justice Thomas Ruffin dissented in this 1849 case; the court picked up his dissent and came to the opposite result eight years later. In the later case, slave Fanny killed an overseer who was viciously beating her husband. An appellate court upheld her conviction for murder, saying that "unconditional submission on the part of slaves must be exacted."[19]

One other point seems relevant in explaining the divergence in nineteenth-century anti-abuse laws. As subjects of commercial transactions, slaves and livestock provided an easily ascertainable source of value, whereas children and wives did not (Michael Henchard to the contrary).[20] To the extent antebellum society had a driving interest in preserving the value of property – to ensure productive activity and economic growth – the marketability of slaves and animals made them more likely candidates for legal protection. But protecting slaves was even more justifiable than protecting animals: Slaves were much more valuable than most livestock, especially Southern livestock.[21]

Unlike cruelty cases, cases concerning benevolence toward slaves had no counterpart in other areas of law. Slaves were unique chattels in that showing them excessive kindness might have caused them to forget their inferior position, and manumitting them might have agitated the slaves left behind. Because wives, children, and animals had little hope of changing their subordinate status, kind treatment did not yield such external costs and no comparable lawsuits exist.

Cases concerning the responsibility of masters for their slaves do have parallels in servant and animal cases, however. In antebellum years as today, the doctrine of *respondeat superior* – the master answers for the actions of his subordinates – typically applied to those working on the master's behalf and not on a frolic or detour of their own.[22] Yet slaves differed from other workers. One might even argue that a slave never engaged in a frolic or detour of his own because he, unlike employees and servants, belonged completely to someone else. In line with this reasoning, slaveowners in some states faced statutory liability for injuries that their slaves committed willfully and without benefit to the masters. In contrast to slaves, servants, and employees, animals that damaged property might be thought of as perpetually on a frolic or detour – which may explain why nineteenth-century individuals rarely faced responsibility for the acts of their animals (except dogs).

ANTICRUELTY LAWS

Law Surrounding the Treatment of One's Servants, Apprentices, and Employees

In his comprehensive study of the relationships between employers and workers, Robert Steinfeld wrote of the sweeping changes in Anglo-American labor law early in the nineteenth century.[23] Before that time, British and American masters had considerable control over the lives of their apprentices, servants, and employees.[24] Corporal punishment, particularly of adult servants, began to wane in eighteenth-century England. By the early 1800s, adult servants in England and the United States had obtained the legal right to leave their masters if they were cruelly treated.[25] An 1821 Indiana case marked a turning point in American employment law. Here, the court determined that a master had had no right to restrain his unhappy employee (a free black named Mary Clark) from leaving him.[26] After this time, courts left the decision to depart up to the employee. In place of physical coercion, employers could "persuade" their adult servants to stay through economic means – any adult who left a job without fulfilling all agreed-upon duties was not entitled to wages, even for services rendered.[27] Steinfeld surmised that Mary Clark's case and others like it arose because slaveowners had tried to expand slavery into free states and territories by the use of indentures.

The Clark case left an open question: Did employers still have the right to correct minors physically? Two Northern cases from the 1830s established that factory employers did not. In an 1831 Pennsylvania case, a supervisor in a room of thirty boys had beaten one of them in an attempt to keep order. The boy's father, who worked in the same shop, sued for damages and won. The court recognized the convenience to employers of allowing bodily correction but nevertheless refused to sanction it legally. In a Connecticut case heard four years later, a court determined that a factory owner could not subject any employee, minor or otherwise, to horsewhipping.[28]

Antebellum masters retained more control over minor apprentices, domestics, and farm workers. Judges considered these persons more like family than like employees and, as discussed later, rarely interfered in domestic matters. In an 1833 Louisiana case, for example, an appellate court reversed a judgment for the plaintiff. The plaintiff's son, apprenticed to the defendant, had quarreled with the defendant's slave. Both boys were wounded. The defendant then severely flogged the apprentice, leaving him bloody and feverish. In his defense, the man argued that he wanted his charges to appeal to him for redress rather than fighting amongst themselves. Although a parish court found for the plaintiff, an appellate court agreed with the defendant's argument. *Dicta* in an earlier South Carolina case had also countenanced the right of masters to physically punish young apprentices and servants.[29] Not until after the Civil War did Southern courts finally withdraw this right.[30]

Abuse of One's Slaves and Animals: Legal Limits

Everything must be interdicted which is calculated to render the slave discontented with his condition, or which would tend to increase his capacity for mischief.

– *Bryan v. Walton*, 14 Ga. 185, 203 (1853)

Christian nations do not consider themselves at liberty to sport away the lives of captives.

– *Fields v. State*, 1 Yerg. 156, 163 (Tn. 1829)

North Carolina Chief Justice Thomas Ruffin expressed the opinion of many Southerners, judges and laypeople alike, when he wrote in 1829: "The power of the master must be absolute, to render the submission of the slave perfect." The relation between slave and master by its very nature could never undergo the kind of transformation that the employee–employer relationship did. An 1827 Virginia court would not punish an owner who had cruelly beaten his slaves, for instance. Nor would an 1842 Tennessee court reduce a murder charge to manslaughter in the case of a slave who had killed his abusive master. The court stated that "the law cannot recognize the violence of a master as a legitimate cause of provocation." An 1860 Mississippi court would not limit a slaveowner in viciously punishing his slave, even if the slave died. And in an intriguing 1831 dispute, a Louisiana court refused to allow a man to bring a civil action compelling his abusive neighbor to sell a slave. The court believed that the plaintiff was "actuated by feelings which we cannot but respect. But what in this instance was the suggestion of humanity, might, in the next, be the promptings of envy, malice, and all uncharitableness."[31]

In spite of the necessary subjugation entailed by slavery, courts – particularly in the last three decades of the antebellum period – limited owners in their mistreatment of slaves if doing so improved the economic well-being of the community.[32] Many states required masters to provide adequate food and clothing to slaves, for example, just as states later required livestock owners to tend to their animals.[33] An 1849 South Carolina court succinctly explained why: "It is due to public sentiment, and is necessary to protect property from the depredation of famishing slaves."[34] Antebellum writer George Stroud belittled the efficacy of these laws because slaves could not testify against their masters.[35] But free persons could and did testify if slaves stole from them or if a derelict master's profitability exceeded theirs.[36] Economic interests therefore guaranteed at least some enforcement of laws against neglecting slaves. A Delaware court even made clear in 1841 that, for economic reasons, a slave's master and no one else should be responsible for the slave's care. Here, blind slave Anthony was supported by the estate of his former master Howard. Howard had divided his estate into thirds; one heir sold off his third of the land to Hall. Anthony ended up in the poorhouse. The poorhouse trustees sued Hall to recover the money spent in supporting Anthony but failed to win a dime. The court, stating that "the policy of our law is to avoid secret liens upon land," recognized that entrammeling land or other real estate would have made transactions more cumbersome and costly.[37]

Courts sometimes restricted masters in order to protect the interests of people with claims to specific slaves but no current ownership. These restrictions helped preserve the value of slaves. In an 1836 case, for example, the owners of a life estate in slaves could not transport them from Tennessee to Mississippi: The court considered Mississippi to be a state with a "less favorable" climate where "the temptation would be to overwork" slaves. Allowing such a move could have injured the slave and, more important, the interests of the remainderman.[38] (Those with a "life estate" in property effectively own the property until they die, at which time the property reverts to the remainderman.) Kentucky's Act of 1850 stated that life tenants who removed slaves from the commonwealth forfeited title to the remaindermen. Virginia decided in 1857 that life tenants who moved slaves out of state without the consent of the remaindermen had committed felonies.[39] Slave Phil was the subject of a different sort of dispute heard in 1833. Phil died before the dispute was resolved, so the defendant obtained an injunction that released him from the obligation of delivering Phil or Phil's value to the plaintiff. An Alabama appellate court invalidated the injunction, saying that the defendant could deliver cash even if neither party wanted to transfer a corpse: "[The] high state of excitement and rancorous feelings which are often produced by a lengthy litigation, might induce defendants, when they found the results must be against them, to destroy property sued for . . . in so secret a manner that it would be difficult, if not impossible, for the plaintiff to prove that the destruction was intentional."[40]

But appellate courts also curbed other sorts of slaveowner cruelty. *Dicta* in various cases suggest why: Free persons might have suffered. Beating one's slave in public caused "terror and disturbance and annoyance [to] the good citizens of the United States."[41] Tormenting one's slave in private had external costs as well. Southerners certainly feared that cruelty by slaveowners could lead to widespread slave escapes and rebellions like those plotted by Denmark Vesey and Nat Turner. Justice Brockenbrough's dissent in a cruelty case heard four years before Turner's bloody uprising – coincidentally, with a Virginia defendant named Turner – anticipates the view that would later prevail: "[W]hilst kindness and humane treatment are calculated to render [slaves] contented and happy, is there no danger that oppression and tyranny, against which there is no redress, may drive them to despair?"[42]

Lawsuits heard after the turbulent 1820s and early '30s show that most states stopped short of permitting people to kill their slaves. North Carolina, Alabama, Mississippi, and Virginia courts were willing to convict masters who had murdered their own slaves, with an 1839 North Carolina court sentencing the master to death in *State v. Hoover*. The *Hoover* court was appalled at the defendant's barbaric behavior – he had beaten his slave with clubs and iron chains, scourged her, and forced her to work in bad weather and at tasks beyond her capacity, even while she was in the latter stages of pregnancy and immediately after she delivered her child. In an 1843 Alabama case, Isabel's master beat her to death with clubs and sticks; he received a ten-year sentence. In 1844, a Mississippi court sentenced a man and his overseer to seven years in prison for manslaughter when they killed the man's slave in a drunken rage. In an 1851 Virginia case, a slave came home tipsy, so his master Souther beat him, burned him, rubbed red pepper into the slave's burnt flesh, tortured him, then finally strangled him. Souther was found guilty of second-degree murder and received a five-year prison sentence.[43] Courts put sanctions on cruel treatment as well as on homicide. Louisiana courts convicted and substantially fined masters for cruelly punishing their slaves in some cases.[44] Public beatings constituted a nuisance in the District of Columbia and generated a fine. In an 1834 case, for example, a slaveowner was fined $100 for beating and exposing his slave to public view. In an Alabama case heard twenty years later, a trial court convicted a man for mayhem in shooting his slave Maria and causing her to lose a leg. Tennessee determined that the state's Act of 1829 forbidding malicious castration protected slaves as well as free men. Its court imposed a two-year sentence on one slaveowner defendant in 1850, saying: "The slave is to be regarded as a reasonable creature ... and as a person upon whom the offense before stated may be committed."[45]

Although masters probably seldom faced legal punishment for cruelty to their own slaves, then, such cases did appear.[46] Attention to animals came years later. The decades after the Civil War heralded a great surge of interest in animal protection. New York City started the first chapter of the American Society for Prevention of Cruelty to Animals in 1866; New York State passed the first comprehensive anticruelty legislation in 1875. Other states enacted anticruelty laws, mostly assessing fines against abusers, after the mid-1870s. Missouri (1879), Maryland (1880), Tennessee (1881), and North Carolina were among the earliest Southern states to pass such laws. Indiana (1881) and New Hampshire were among the earliest Northern states. England preceded the United States in protecting animals, passing the Martin Act for cattle in 1822 (which was rarely enforced) and establishing the Society for the Prevention of Cruelty to Animals in 1824. England passed the first national protection laws for animals in 1884.[47] Despite these measures, nineteenth-century judges rarely punished owners who beat their animals – sometimes even to death – during training or discipline. An 1852 Missouri court decided that tying sticks or brush to a horse's tail – which could cause the horse to run itself to death – was not necessarily cruel. In an 1858 New Jersey case, a court refused to indict someone for maliciously wounding a recalcitrant animal during training. Postbellum North Carolina courts agreed, refused to indict even in cases of fatal wounds.[48]

Protection Laws for Family Members: Lagging Behind Other Protection Laws

A woman, a dog, and a walnut-tree,
The more you beat 'em, the better they be.
–Thomas Fuller, *Gnomologia*, line 6404

By comparison to the law for adult servants, legislation and common law provided only a small measure of physical protection to slaves (and later animals) from the wrath of their masters. But the law did even less for nineteenth-century American wives and children. And married women and children, like slaves and animals, could do little to change their lot: They could not vote, write contracts, own property, or enjoy various other amenities that men had. Divorce was nearly impossible. Antebellum Mississippi did pass a law allowing married women to hold title to property that only men and single women formerly had rights to – not in an effort to protect women's rights, but rather to shield the assets of husbands bankrupted in the panic year of 1837.[49] The 1848 Seneca Falls convention led by Elizabeth Cady Stanton and Lucretia Mott was the first major attempt to secure rights for women. In large part, it failed. Ironically, the two women had met eight years earlier at the World Anti-Slavery convention in London when male participants voted to exclude women from the proceedings.[50] (The lone male at the gathering in favor of including women was former slave Frederick Douglass.) Wyoming finally granted the first full suffrage to women in 1869; national suffrage did not occur, of course, until 1920.[51]

Before the Civil War, the American legal system seldom penalized men who neglected their families. Under colonial and early state law, the town or county of legal settlement typically had to support paupers. As one might suppose, innumerable cases expose wrangling about which community the pauper had established as a legal settlement.[52] (Similar cases arose for indigent slaves.)[53] Courts of the period were actually more likely to remove children from the homes of neglectful parents rather than prosecute the parents.[54] Although eighteenth-century English legal authority William Blackstone had advised that parents should support their children, this duty was not usually enforced; neglectful parents were rarely liable (civilly or criminally) for nonsupport.[55]

Not until the close of the nineteenth century were men officially obliged to support their immediate families. As in slave cases, the obligations of male heads of household often arose only because the community would otherwise have had to pay the bills for destitute women and minors. Although New York passed laws against neglect in 1871 and 1875, for instance, its courts refused to convict a man for abandonment because his wife did not become a public burden. The opinion stated: "The statute . . . was not intended to furnish a civil remedy to deserted wives, but to protect the public against the expense of supporting paupers." An 1887 Alabama court similarly explained why the state prescribed support payments in cases of abandonment: Abandoned persons burdened the public treasury.[56]

The Northern states took the lead in passing antineglect laws, just as they did for animals. Antebellum Michigan law had actually made abandonment of children a felony but the law was only narrowly applied. Pennsylvania required support of children under the Act of June 13, 1836, and made nonprovision of food and clothing a misdemeanor under the Act of June 11, 1879. Yet in applying the law, circumstances mattered: In one 1893 case, a court determined that liability was not automatic but depended upon the children's need and the parent's ability to provide support. (But in another Pennsylvania case heard about the same time, a court explained that, if a wife repented within two years of leaving her husband, she was entitled to support even if he refused to take her back).[57] Wisconsin made the abandonment of destitute minor children a misdemeanor in the 1880s and Connecticut made the failure to support one's wife a crime. Postbellum Rhode Island imprisoned men who did not support their wives and children even if wives had unfairly withheld the company of the children.[58] For the most part, however, support laws were neither broadly applied nor particularly well enforced in the North throughout the nineteenth century.

The same was true in much of the South. Southern statutes of the 1880s and 1890s did outlaw nonsupport; the degree of enforcement varied. In prosecutions for bastardy, some Southern states went so far as to reserve the right to sell putative fathers into servitude for up to four years in order to provide support for children. South Carolina repealed these laws in 1847, but North Carolina kept its statutes on the books until 1939.[59] Abandonment gave rise to statutes as well. For example, the 1886 Alabama Code required husbands to support abandoned wives and offspring. The codes of Georgia and North Carolina made nonsupport a misdemeanor. Georgia courts applied the statute for children even if the husband had had sufficient cause to abandon the wife or if he had abandoned his wife before a child was born. In contrast to Georgia courts, Missouri courts applied support statutes very narrowly. And an 1885 Arkansas court decided that a husband did not commit a misdemeanor under common or statutory law for leaving his wife and child without support. In a burst of faith in family fidelity, the opinion stated this: "After all, the natural affections are the best reliance."[60]

Nineteenth-century American courts were even more reluctant to interfere in cases of family cruelty than they were in cases of neglect. Although the Puritans had passed laws against family violence, they rarely enforced them. (Domestic crimes surely occurred, often fueled by alcohol: Average annual alcohol consumption per American adult ranged from 6 to 10 gallons in the early nineteenth century. By comparison, today's average is about 2 gallons.)[61] Certainly, antebellum governments filed murder charges against people who killed nonslave human victims, regardless of familial ties. Yet crimes against persons – particularly "crimes of passion" – alarmed Southerners less than crimes against property, as Chapter 6 discussed. According to Elizabeth Pleck, murder charges often were reduced to manslaughter when the victim was a relative and frequently were dismissed altogether.[62]

Spousal abuse that did not end in fatality caused even less of a stir.[63] By 1860, only two states had prohibited wife-beating. Antebellum Southern judges in particular showed very little patience with lawsuits against abusive husbands. A Mississippi court stated in 1824 that husbands were entitled to "moderate chastisement [of their wives] . . . without being subjected to vexatious prosecutions resulting in the mutual discredit and shame of all parties concerned." (Although the husband was found guilty in this case, the court sent a clear message to potential litigants not to waste its time in such matters.) An 1852 Alabama trial court fined a man for assaulting his wife, but an appellate court determined that he could reduce his fine if "provoked to this unmanly act by the bad behavior and misconduct of his wife."[64] Similar attitudes prevailed after the Civil War in many Southern jurisdictions. Through the 1870s, North Carolina courts refused to consider convicting husbands for assault or battery of their wives unless the men inflicted permanent injury or acted with exceptional malice. In one case, a husband convicted of assault and battery received a new trial because "the law permits him to use towards his wife such a degree of force, as is necessary to . . . make her behave herself." In another, a court convicted a husband of assault and battery but stated: "[F]rom motives of public policy – in order to preserve the sanctity of the domestic circle, the courts will not listen to trivial complaints." It fined the defendant only $10. The notorious *State v. Rhodes* case advocated beating one's wife with a stick no bigger than one's thumb. Kentucky had similar standards for wife abuse.[65] In a very few instances, postbellum courts suggested that abusive husbands should pay a nontrivial fine or receive alternative punishments. In *dicta*, a Texas court gave mothers permission to fight off husbands who were abusing the children, at least under some circumstances. In this 1875 case the husband was convicted at trial but his conviction was reversed on a technicality – his wife's given name was wrongly recorded. In another Texas case heard four years later, a court fined an abusive husband $500 for assault. Other Southern courts stated that husbands who physically chastised their wives could be found guilty of assault. Few Northern cases exist. In two – heard in 1882 Nebraska and 1871 Massachusetts – husbands were found guilty of assault. The Massachusetts court determined that husbands could not beat their wives even if the women were drunk or violent.[66]

Official protection of children from the violence of their parents, like protection of young apprentices and household servants, occurred relatively late in the United States.[67] Most nineteenth-century judges simply refused to apply criminal sanctions in cases of parental cruelty. Just as they did in wife-abuse cases, North Carolina courts adhered to a no-interference rule in child-abuse cases unless the child's injury was permanent or maliciously inflicted. In practice, North Carolina appellate courts consistently set aside convictions for child abuse.[68] Texas and Tennessee determined that parents could not administer excessive punishment, with juries deciding what was excessive. Sadly enough, the two lone guilty verdicts in these states were overturned.[69] In the Tennessee case a father had hit his child with his fists, banged the child's head against the wall, tied the child to a bedpost for two hours, and switched her. A jury convicted him. But an appellate court reversed and remanded the case, saying that a jury had to decide explicitly if the father had imposed "excessive punishment." Only in a few cases did nineteenth-century courts punish abusive parents. An 1869 Illinois court fined a father $300 for imprisoning his blind son in a dark, damp cellar, then pouring kerosene over the child and setting him on fire to "get rid of the vermin." An 1875 Georgia court found a father guilty for whipping his young daughter with a saw. The reason for the whipping? He had left the child alone with her stepmother without food. The step-mother ordered the little girl to break open a chest in the pantry; her father lost his temper when he discovered the splintered chest and beat the girl unmercifully. A Mississippi man who fatally bludgeoned his son was himself sentenced to death in 1889. Notably, this father was black.[70]

Institutionalized protection of children and wives eventually appeared in the late nineteenth and early twentieth century. With the help of the founder of the ASPCA, New York established the first Society for the Prevention of Cruelty to Children in 1874.[71] After this, such societies took root. By 1900, there were 161 societies for children, animals, or both. Yet up through the early 1900s, child-protection laws were designed primarily to benefit adult laborers, reduce crime, or shield children from "immorality" and bizarre public display, rather than to prevent physical abuse. Child labor laws, compulsory education, and juvenile reformatories effectively preserved adults from the competition of cheaper workers and kept youths off the streets. A 1914 compendium of child protection laws explained that parents particularly feared the corruptive influence of a new menace: moving pictures. New Jersey and New York therefore passed laws forbidding children to enter theaters without their parents. Wyoming outlawed the hypnotizing of children in public and Arkansas prevented parents from making their children into actors or contortionists.[72] Wives fared little better: Only one protective agency (in Chicago) existed for women as of 1885. Despite legislation against wife-beating, wife-abusers were seldom punished.[73] In an era when women stayed at home, victims of beatings often refused to give evidence because fines, jail time for the husband or father, and divorce all deprived the family of its livelihood. Victims who did appear in court gained little sympathy.

Interestingly enough, the successful passage of early anticruelty laws resulted in part from the efforts of those who had formerly participated in the abolition movement.[74] But socioeconomic factors mattered as well. As population density grew and people saw more of each other, the costs to one's neighbors of domestic neglect and abuse multiplied. Elizabeth Pleck noted that postbellum support for criminal penalties increased as family violence threatened the social order.[75] In addition, as family ties loosened after the Civil War, less private policing of household violence took place. Extralegal methods of resolving disputes began to diminish in importance. And, as women increasingly worked outside the home, husbands who battered wives cost society in a relatively more obvious way: through lost market productivity. Concomitantly, financial independence made women more likely to press charges against brutal husbands. As the external costs of cruelty increased and the internal controls against it decreased, then, so did pressures to implement official sanctions against cruelty to family members. Economic considerations therefore helped lead to anti-abuse laws for family members that looked like antebellum rules protecting slaves from their masters.

Some argue, however, that modern-day wives and children continue to suffer. Women and children still find support payments hard to collect, in spite of large increases in government spending on enforcement efforts.[76] As late as the 1980s, only three states prohibited rape within marriage; five others recognized marital rape as a valid claim under limited circumstances. Not one was in the South. In fact, in the 1980s thirteen states extended to cohabitants the marital exemption from rape, including Alabama, Delaware, Kentucky, Tennessee, and West Virginia.[77] Other gender-related issues have persisted as well. Not until 1975 did the U.S. Supreme Court decide that support obligations were the same for sons and daughters.[78] Today's legislatures and courts remain generally reluctant to intrude upon the parent–child relationship. The Supreme Court did not grant states authority to intervene to protect children from abusive parents until 1944.[79] Parental immunity from lawsuits brought by their children, particularly for torts, has been an explicit part of American common law since 1891 and an implicit part for far longer.[80] Not even sexual abuse by parents will generate damages for children in many cases.[81] Some states have abrogated parental immunity, but only in the last two decades. Quite recently, Gregory Kingsley made history by suing his parents for "divorce."[82] Many courts still presume that a child is merely an extension of his or her parents.[83]

KINDNESS TOWARD ONE'S SLAVES: WHAT WAS LEGALLY ACCEPTABLE?

> As to the consequences of slavery, they are much more hurtful to the master than the slave. . . . When the condition of our slaves is contrasted with the state of their miserable race in Africa; . . . we are almost persuaded that the introduction of slavery amongst us was . . . a means of placing that unhappy race within the pale of civilized nations.
>
> – *Dred Scott v. Emerson*, 15 Mo. 576, 587 (1852)

> There was no such thing as being good to slaves. Many white people were better than others, but a slave belonged to his master, and there was no way to get out of it.
>
> – Former slave Thomas Lewis[84]

Lawful Benevolence: Rules to Reinforce the Bonds of Slavery

Southern courts allowed benevolence by slaveowners to the extent it supplemented the lash and the shackle. According to the Southern judiciary, a slavemaster could treat his slaves well as long as the community also benefited and slavery was thus reinforced. The Carolina courts demonstrated this in a series of cases. In 1816, a North Carolina court upheld a will that directed the executor to pay funds to the lowest bidder who promised to care for the testator's aged slave Sarah. As a result, Sarah received a new owner rather than being thrown on the mercy of the state. At the same time, the court removed these funds from the reach of the testator's creditors. Creditors – then as now – typically might have invoked fraudulent conveyance laws, which are designed to prevent debtors from hiding assets from their creditors. But the court determined that the creditors could not protest because the directive benefited the community, "which in case of a deficiency of assets, is entitled to a preference against the claims of individuals."[85] Nearly thirty years later, the North Carolina Supreme Court allowed the slaves of a testator to keep the profits from the cotton they had grown; the court refused to distribute the money as part of the estate. Chief Justice Thomas Ruffin explained the ruling in *Waddill v. Martin* by saying that, although slaves could not legally own property, "leaving to the [N]egro the spending of his money at his own pleasure, is then a pecuniary saving to the estate; and these slight indulgences are repaid by the attachment of the slave to the master and his family, by exerting his industry and honesty, and a spirit to make and save for the master as well as himself." A South Carolina court used reasoning parallel to that in *Waddill*, adding that "nothing will more assuredly defeat our institution of slavery, than harsh legislation rigidly enforced." And just before the Civil War, a North Carolina equity court allowed a representative of the deceased defendant to make small gratuities to slaves (Christmas gifts, 25 cent bonuses at the end of the week, and the like) to encourage their good conduct, just as their dead owner had done.[86]

Allowing slaves to control small amounts of property, such as tillable land, was an oft-sanctioned practice, then. South Carolina masters sometimes even borrowed corn from their slaves to feed the horses.[87] Although some South Carolina farmers wanted to prevent slaves from raising food and selling the surplus, saying that the habit encouraged theft, the state legislature would not pass laws against it.[88] Large plantation owners persuaded legislators that letting slaves work their own plots of land helped increase productivity by rewarding hard-working slaves. (Some have speculated that wealthy South Carolina planters blocked such bills, however, because they liked having slaves do the marketing.) One Alabama planter cleverly surmounted the theft problem: He let his slaves raise corn – but not cotton – and sell it to him. Why? Cotton was far more valuable per pound than corn, so stealing corn entailed more risk and work for less profit than stealing cotton. As a result, slaves who possessed corn for sale were less likely to have stolen it than slaves with cotton to sell.[89] Slaves could not always keep property, of course. Under an 1851 South Carolina case, a slave could acquire property for the benefit of his master but could not enforce his own contracts. And a Tennessee court said that allowing a slave to keep a tract of land given to him as a reward for fighting in the Revolutionary War would have been absurd. The court claimed that it did not wish to insult the intelligence of North Carolina legislators by saying that the men had intended to provide a home and fireside to someone incapable of enjoying them.[90]

Still, courts permitted slaves some small diversions. Justice Ruffin ruled in 1849 that Christmas parties did not violate a North Carolina statute that forbade keeping a disorderly house for Negroes because such parties occupied the slaves' idle hours and kept them from mischief. He concluded: "There was nothing contrary to morals or law in all that – adding, as it did, to human enjoyment, without hurt to anyone, unless it be that one feel aggrieved, that these poor people should for a short space be happy at finding the authority of the master give place to his benignity, and at being freed from care and filled with gladness." One year later, a South Carolina court saw eye to eye with Ruffin, upholding indictments for patrollers who whipped several slaves at a quilting bee. The slaves had licenses from their masters; the court saw their activities as "innocent . . . even meritorious" because they were occupied in a productive pursuit.[91]

Judges also allowed indulgence borne of sentimental attachments, provided no free person was harmed. To illustrate: An 1855 South Carolina equity court labeled master Henly Trussell as overfond of his slaves, imprudent, and a fool, but refused to equate these qualities with incapacity and permitted him to bequeath slaves as he wished. The court applauded Trussell's desire to keep his slaves content because "[h]is increasing age served but to render them more necessary to his happiness."[92] As Chapter 2 revealed, several courts also recognized the strength of family or sentimental ties even among slaves, upholding contractual covenants that required purchased slaves to remain in the neighborhood. These slaves – who usually sold for less than market value – could then stay near friends, parents, children, or partners. The discounted price often reflected the seller's willingness to forgo cash in order to keep his remaining slaves happy and productive. In an unusual holding, an 1856 Texas court acknowledged the dark side of family relationships as well: It allowed a white father, Spire Hagerty, to convey his slave children and their mother to Hagerty's sister when Hagerty's legal wife sued him for divorce. Hagerty died before the divorce suit commenced; his wife insisted that the slaves belonged to her as community property. But the court allowed the conveyance to stand "rather than leave [the slaves] to the injured and infuriated wife who would possibly, yea probably, inflict severity, cruelty, and hardship on them when the offender was beyond the reach of her angry passions." (The court did insist that the "conveyance . . . be done without injury to the community share of [the] wife." Apparently the widow received the slaves' cash-equivalent value.)[93]

Family disputes over slaves were common; some betray judicial attitudes about other areas of law as well as reveal courts' tolerance of kindness to slaves. In an 1847 Kentucky dispute, for instance, the court upheld a man's will that directed slaves to be freed and sent to Liberia even if the directive overrode the widow's right of dower.[94] Kentucky's Act of 1846 did prevent a husband from selling his wife's slaves if she owned the slaves before the marriage or acquired them herself after the marriage. Yet if the husband violated the Act, the wife could regain possession of the slave only if the suit was brought jointly by husband and wife. Married women in Kentucky, as elsewhere, had no legal standing.[95]

Restrictions on Manumission: Considering External Costs

Although the legal system countenanced kindness to slaves, it curtailed masters' indulgence of their slaves if such behavior infringed on the well-being of the community or another prospective owner. Judges might refer to the effects of verdicts on slaves but typically made decisions based only on how verdicts affected persons with legal standing. A Maryland court noted in 1849, for example, that the South allowed manumissions in order to enlarge the privileges of the master rather than to benefit slaves. In fact, the judges in this case – like many Southerners – thought slaves were better off than freedmen.[96] Restrictions on manumission provide the most obvious example of constraints masters faced; they also demonstrate the external economic considerations at issue. By setting one's slave free, one might release an agitator, weaken the profitable system of forced labor, dump a nonproductive individual on the state, or remove the value of slave property from the tax base or the reach of creditors.[97]

Legal documents, including court opinions, offer unusually savage remarks on the effects of emancipation. The preamble to Delaware's Act of 1767 gave one early, vitriolic justification for limiting manumissions: "[I]t is found by experience, that freed [N]egroes and mulattoes are idle and slothful, and often prove burdensome to the neighborhood wherein they live, and are of evil example to slaves."[98] Seventy years after these words were written, the Georgia Supreme Court further vilified freed blacks: "[We wish] to prevent a horde of free colored persons, from ravaging the morals, and corrupting the feelings of our slaves. Experience ha[s] taught our Legislators, that such a class, lazy, mischievous, and corrupt, without any master to urge them to exertion, and scarcely any motive to make it, was an extremely dangerous example to our naturally indolent slaves." In an opinion two decades later, Georgia's Chief Justice Joseph Lumpkin added: "To inculcate care and industry upon the descendants of Ham, is to preach to the idle winds. . . . Under the superior race and no where else, do they attain the higher degree of civilization. . . ."[99]

Postmortem manumissions especially caused consternation among Southern judges. South Carolina Chancellor Job Johnston displayed his frustration in 1844 when confronted with a will emancipating slaves: "This is another of those cases, multiplying of late with a fearful rapidity, in which the superstitious weakness of dying men, proceeding from an astonishing ignorance of the solid moral and scriptural foundations upon which the institution of slavery rests, and from a total inattention to the shock which their conduct is calculated to give to the whole frame of our social policy. . . ." A Missouri case echoed this sentiment three years later: "Neither sound policy nor enlight-

ened philanthropy should encourage, in a slaveholding state, the mul-
tiplication of a race whose condition could be neither that of freemen
nor of slaves, and whose existence . . . tend only to dissatisfy and
corrupt those of their own race and color remaining in a state of servitude." In 1855, Justice Lumpkin expostulated that "all post mortem
manumissions of slaves should be absolutely and entirely prohibited"
because "Are there not now in our midst large gangs of slaves who
expected emancipation by the will of their owners, and who believe
they have been unjustly deprived of the boon? . . . Are they not likely
to sow the seeds of insubordination, perhaps of revolt, amongst the
slaves in their neighborhood? [and] without them, a large portion of
our most productive lands would be worthless . . . [slaves] alone
render . . . cotton and rice lands valuable. . . ." A Louisiana court
agreed in 1856, saying: "Emancipation is considered to be a matter
which concerns the state, inasmuch as its tendency is to substitute a
free colored population for the system of compulsory labor, which
involves to such a vast extent the fortunes of our citizens and the production of our agricultural staples."[100]

In response to the urgings of judges and other citizens, many
Southern legislatures eventually enacted all sorts of restrictions on
manumission. As an 1838 Alabama case put it, "the state owes to its
citizens at large . . . [to put] suitable guards around the institution of
slavery . . . [because emancipation disturbed] the quiet of the
country."[101] One of the most fascinating constraints had to do with
bequests of freedom. States occasionally refused to permit owners to
manumit slaves by will if the testator had written the will during his
or her last illness. Such wills were thought to arise from "judgment-
day fear" rather than any reasoned consideration on the part of the
decedent.[102]

But reasoned consideration by slaveowners could also have led to
manumissions that injured society; in fact, most manumission laws
clearly aimed to deter masters from shifting costs onto the public after
previously enjoying the economic benefits of slavery. In efforts to
control the sorts of slaves who were emancipated, some states
required legislative approval of manumissions in the early part of the
nineteenth century.[103] Several states mandated that the former master
file an indemnifying bond with the state treasurer so the state or
county would not have to support indigent former slaves.[104] In other
states, former owners had to contribute to ex-slaves' upkeep if the
freedmen became paupers.[105] One 1852 Louisiana case even held
that a master might lose his right to claim services from slaves allowed
to go free for ten years, but his duty to care for them died only with
him.[106] Rather than instituting *ex post* remedies, some states limited
manumissions to slaves of a certain age who were capable of earning

a livelihood. Maryland law did not permit manumission of infants, even if freed mothers could provide financially for them. In one application of this rule, Sarah received a life interest in a slave from her sister Rachel Turner. The slave was to be freed after Sarah's death. The slave bore a child after Rachel's death; the child was two years old when Sarah died. A court in 1823 determined that, although the mother was free, the child was not. In another complicated Maryland dispute heard about the same time, slave Basil was set free at the death of his master Hall. Hall had sold Dolly (Basil's daughter) to Basil, who freed Dolly. Because Basil was over age forty-five, a court ruled that he could not be freed by Hall's will and could not own property (including Dolly). The interesting question in a separate case was this: Was Dolly free? Although she was not named in the will, Hall had provided that all his unnamed slaves were freed by default. A court therefore decided that Dolly was indeed free. In an 1829 case, a D.C. court interpreted Maryland law as forbidding emancipation of slaves older than forty-five years even if the master had provided funds for them. An 1836 case exemplifies a Kentucky court's use of economic principles in determining whether a slave was legally free under a Maryland manumission statute. In this case, Nancy claimed that she was free under a will written in 1801 even though Robert Boyce had held her as a slave for more than twenty years afterward. A court allowed the jury to infer that, when the will was executed, Nancy must have been capable of earning a living. Otherwise, Boyce would not have kept Nancy enslaved. Nancy therefore went free.[107]

Instead of requiring masters to provide in advance for former slaves or limiting manumissions to productive slaves, many states enacted residential limitations. Some made masters emancipate their slaves in another state or encouraged slaveowners to bequeath slaves to the Colonization Society, which would then send the freedmen to Liberia. The Kentucky legislature even passed a resolution in 1849 to send the laws of the state to the Governor of Liberia.[108] Rather than restricting masters' ability to free slaves within the state, some Southern states instead forced newly freed blacks to depart or pay a hefty price. In its 1851 constitution, for example, Virginia required ex-slaves to leave the state within a year or face being sold – with the proceeds going to the literary fund. North Carolina gave freed slaves only twenty days to leave the state or pay a $500 fine.[109] Freedmen sometimes paid on the other end, too. For example, Michigan in 1827 required incoming blacks to post a bond. In one interesting 1848 case, a Georgia court struck down a city ordinance requiring free colored persons to be jailed if they did not pay a fee of $100 upon arrival. The fee was lawful, according to the court, because it aimed to prevent the increase of the black population. It was the imprisonment that perturbed the court – why not hire out the offenders, instead of losing productive labor and costing the city extra jail fees?[110] Some states even required freed slaves (or their former owners) to forfeit a percentage of their value on their way out of the state – to compensate for the lost property tax caused by the manumission.[111] In some cases, the estate paid the bill if a will manumitted the slave. An 1855 Kentucky court allowed an executor to appropriate part of the legacy or to hire slaves out until enough money was raised to replace tax revenue, for example.[112]

States protected the interests of creditors as well as public treasuries. Naturally, masters could not free slaves if they simultaneously cheated creditors of payment. Courts either disallowed the manumission or put slaves to service until debts were repaid.[113] A Maryland court decided in 1827 that, even if real estate could cover a debt, creditors had a right to the slaves because selling real estate was relatively more costly and time-consuming.[114] (Courts also blocked gifts of slaves if creditors lost out; a North Carolina court in 1830 even invalidated a gift made to a child twenty years earlier.)[115]

Not only did states attempt to minimize the population of restless, poverty-stricken, and debt-laden freedmen within their borders, they also prohibited forms of manumission that smacked of giving choices to slaves. Slaves typically could not enter a contract with their masters to gain freedom.[116] Nor could they usually choose their next masters.[117] In an 1856 opinion, Justice Pearson explained why North Carolina slaves could not select their owners: "It may seem hard that one is not allowed to dispose of his own property as he pleases; but private right must yield to the public good . . . [we cannot] establish in our midst a set of privileged [N]egroes, causing the others to be dissatisfied and restless. . . ." And the South refused to tolerate half-slavery. One Kentucky defendant would not emancipate his elderly slaves, for instance, but he took $200 from them in exchange for letting them control their own lives. Despite the agreement, a court did not let the slaves act as if they were free – but neither did it let the master keep the money.[118]

As the Civil War approached, many Southern states banned all further manumission. Some states, including Alabama, Louisiana, Georgia, South Carolina, Texas, and Virginia, in fact enacted procedures by which free blacks could elect to reenslave themselves.[119]

Other Restrictions

In addition to constraints on manumission, other laws prevented slaveholders from burdening their fellow Southerners with the external costs arising from masters' largesse. Some states placed restrictions on masters who equipped their slaves with guns, for example, whereas others barred slaves from possessing musical instruments.[120] Firearms enabled slaves to hunt for game, but they also made slaves dangerous to neighbors and livestock. Drums and horns enlivened slaves' evenings and signaled mealtimes, but they also allowed slaves to communicate news and call secret meetings. Slaveowners themselves might be chary of treating slaves too well, of course: In her diary, Mary Boykin Chesnut referred to two examples of slaves murdering indulgent owners.[121]

Some legal constraints aimed to reduce the likelihood of slaves gathering to plot insurrections. Slaveowners sometimes tried to cut the costs of supervision by hiring fewer free overseers or by running plantations in absentia; many states passed laws to require white residents to live among slaves. Violators of these statutes paid fines, usually split between the informant and the government.[122] Statutes also curbed masters from exposing slaves to activities – such as reading and writing – that might have encouraged slaves to think for themselves. For example, North Carolina slaves could not learn to read or write although they could be schooled in the use of figures.[123] Along the same lines, most states refused to allow slaves to assemble and many states outlawed black preachers.[124] The fear of assembled slaves manifested itself in other ways, including tax policies. Although an Alabama court declared the state's Act of February 1846 unconstitutional because it taxed the slaves of nonresidents more heavily, Judge Collier forcefully dissented by noting that the policy addressed a police power issue, not a tax one. Partly for this reason, the state of Georgia did allow cities to tax only slaves of nonresidents.[125]

Under the law, owners also had to consider how cosseting slaves could cost others. For example, an 1858 Kentucky court castigated life tenant Colston Crabtree for allowing slaves to go about as if free, making contracts with them, and permitting them to trade with others. The court said that these indulgences would make slaves insubordinate, thus reducing their value to the remainderman. Other cases also refer to costs – and benefits – imposed by life-estate owners. If a life tenant sold a slave to avoid the consequences of a capital charge (homicide, for example), the remainderman received a share. If the holder of the life estate spent more than market value to retrieve a fugitive slave from a free state, the remainderman had to contribute toward expenses.[126] The latter seems odd: At some expense, the remainderman would rather have let the slave escape than pay for his return. Yet escaped slaves imposed external costs by stirring up slaves left behind. Retrieving slaves, even at a cost greater than their value, could benefit society. Their owners, present and future, had to bear these costs. Courts also chastised slaveowners who omitted to contribute expected benefits to the community.[127] In many Southern states, antebellum citizens (or their slaves) faced road duty – slaves were generally required to work on roads in the county where they lived. Consequently, an Alabama slaveowner who lived elsewhere paid damages in 1846 because his slaves resided in a county where a road was being built but did not help out.[128] In the same vein, Louisiana fined owners who did not send their slaves to work on levees.[129]

RESPONDEAT SUPERIOR: WHEN DID THE MASTER ANSWER FOR HIS SUBORDINATES?

> It is impossible for us to suppose these creatures [slaves] to be men, because, allowing them to be men, a suspicion would follow that we ourselves are not Christians.
> – Montesquieu, "On Slavery"

> The slave is adjudged to be a mere thing, except where the master's interest or convenience require that he should be regarded as a man.
> – Goodell, *American Slave Code*[130]

Southern courts acknowledged the useful role slaves could play in carrying out chores, including some that entailed decision-making and responsibility. For example, slaves acted as agents in such varied tasks as receiving and loading cotton, conducting transactions for tanning leather, selling a horse (although the slave could not compel payment), accepting a notice, delivering a boat, and keeping books. An 1838 Tennessee court determined that receiving goods from a slave with the slaveowner's consent was not larceny. Moreover, the defendant slaveowner in this case had a viable countersuit for malicious prosecution of his slave.[131]

But some responsibilities naturally could not fall to slaves. One Louisiana defendant ordered his slave to whip the plaintiff, who had used the defendant's canal without permission. The man sued in the 1847 case of *Stachlin v. Destrehan* and won $1,000, with the court commenting, "The outrage upon the plaintiff was not only without justification or excuse, but the chastisement inflicted was the most ignominious to which a free man can be subjected." An Alabama case heard one year later referred to a statute that forbade slaves from sampling cotton unless their employer was also their owner. The court explained that the statute aimed to protect cotton owners. (The court also decided that slaves under supervision or slaves merely carrying out manual labor could work with sampled cotton.)[132] Besides denying certain jobs to slaves, the legal system balked at permitting masters to let slaves hire themselves out. Slaveowners caught allowing this practice paid fines; their slaves often faced prison.[133] Judges and legislators feared that such practices would create unrest among slaves and rend the social fabric. Kentucky slaveowner Elizabeth Gilbert was indicted in 1831 for letting her slave hire herself out, for example. A trial court found for Gilbert but an appellate court reversed and remanded the case, saying that Gilbert had "endangered the security of the aggregate society" and should be fined. An Alabama court in 1856 rationalized the state's Act of 1805, which prevented slaves from making their own contracts: "[Its] purpose was, to prevent the demoralization and corruption of slaves, resulting from a withdrawal of discipline and restraint from them, and to prevent the pernicious effect upon the slave community of the anomalous condition of servitude, without a master's control."[134]

Entrusting one's slaves was a double-edged sword, then. Although using slaves as agents could profit their master, it could also cost him: Owners faced fines and (as *Stachlin* shows) possibly damage payments if their slaves caused injuries. The latter contrasts with liability rules for animals. Nineteenth-century citizens (except in Louisiana) usually were not liable for losses caused by their animals – other than dogs – unless they had known of the animals' ill temper, encouraged the animals' viciousness, or failed to keep animals responsibly when they had such a duty.[135] Whereas those who kept animals negligently might be responsible for damages caused by the beasts, people generally did not have the right to injure or kill trespassing animals – again, except for dogs.[136] The acts of dogs clearly raised the hackles of many Southern judges. In one case a defendant who had caused his dog to worry the plaintiff's animal was responsible for damages even though the *plaintiff's* animal had been trespassing.[137]

In making owners responsible for the acts of their slaves, slave law looked more like that for servants than for animals. Nineteenth-century commentator Horace Wood gave one reason why masters might face liability for the acts of their subordinates: "Servants generally are irresponsible, and unable to respond in damages for the injuries inflicted by them in the prosecution of their masters' business, so that it is regarded as no more than just, that he who has made it possible to injure another, should, so far as the injury results from the exercise of powers conferred upon him, be responsible in his stead."[138] But such a rule can be efficient as well as just. As Wood hinted, the action of the servant that had caused injury often profited his or her master. (Slave masters sometimes even helped out, as former slave Henry Johnson reported: "Our master would make us surround a herd of his neighbor's cattle, round them up at night, and make us slaves stay up all night long and kill and skin every one of them critters, salt the skins down in layers in the master's cellar, and put the cattle piled ceiling high in the smokehouse so nobody could identify skinned cattle.")[139] Making masters liable for certain damages caused by slaves and servants thus assigned costs to those who had expected to benefit.[140] Several slave disputes illustrate this pairing of costs and benefits; in fact, many served as precedents for nonslave cases. A Kentucky defendant was responsible in 1811 when his slave killed plaintiff Sacra's horse. The horse had frequently broken into Caldwell's wheatfields, so Caldwell's slave tied sticks to the horse's tail to make it run itself to death. Caldwell had to pay Sacra $100, the value of the horse. *Dicta* in the 1818 North Carolina case of *Campbell v. Staiert* held that a master should pay for timber his slave had cut on someone else's land if the slave had done so by the master's assent or command. Another North Carolina slaveowner was responsible for the value of trespassing hogs that his slave had helped kill. In an 1861 Arkansas case, the defendant paid damages because his slaves had pulled down a neighbor's fence and confiscated crops to feed the defendant's mules. *Campbell* was cited as a precedent in the 1907 case of *Stewart v. Cary Lumber Co.* (The question in *Stewart* was whether the employer was responsible for damages to a mule that was startled and hurt when an employee blew a whistle.) A 1927 Florida case also used a slave case as precedent. Here, the East Coast Lumber Company was held liable for the actions of its agent, who had shot and killed James Prevatt. Prevatt had been suspected of luring away laborers from the Company. By killing Prevatt, the Company's agent had eliminated a risk and therefore a cost for his employer.[141]

Cases involving slaves and fire damage provide especially intriguing illustrations of how verdicts could match economic benefits and costs. Many masters encouraged slaves to carry fire in the fields because their slaves worked better as a result – slaves enjoyed small comforts on breaks (warmth and pipe-smoking) and wasted no time returning to their quarters for meals. In one such instance, a North Carolina slaveowner was liable for accidental fire damage to his neighbor's crops caused by his slaves' cookfires. Although the weather had been calm in the morning when the fire was set, with the wind picking up later in the day, the master was still held liable for the damage. An 1857 court said that he should have instructed his slaves to wait to set a fire until after a rain, because the weather had been very dry and the master could have foreseen that an accident was likely. In an isolated early case, a South Carolina court came to the opposite result. A jury decided that a slaveowner had to pay for corn accidentally burned by his slaves, although the presiding trial court judge disagreed. An appellate court set aside the verdict and ordered a new trial. In *dicta*, the court stated that the master should not be liable because slaves, being a "headstrong, stubborn race of people," could not be trusted to act responsibly with fire – a puzzling statement, because exculpating the master would have done nothing to prevent slaveowners from allowing "irresponsible" slaves to handle fire.[142] Some fires were probably deliberate, of course. Actress Fanny Kemble, who married slaveowner Pierce Butler, recounted how slaves often "forgot" to put out cooking fires and thus burned down timber and buildings.[143] Slaves paid large penalties if a prosecutor proved they had set malicious fires. For instance, Tennessee passed a law in 1857 sentencing slaves to hang if they had committed arson or attempted arson.[144]

For other crimes as well as arson, slaves faced prison terms, whipping, and capital punishment.[145] But who paid for the damaged or destroyed property? In some states, owners bore no liability for certain willful, malicious, intentional acts of slaves, just as masters did not pay for such acts committed by servants. Mississippi did not make master Leggett liable in 1846 when his slave Moses killed the plaintiff's slave Solomon, for instance, although Leggett knew the two had been drinking and fighting. A trial court awarded the plaintiff $1,180 but an appellate court reversed and awarded a new trial, saying that the master's liability depended upon his knowledge of and involvement in the crime itself. A Texas defendant whose slave killed another slave could not be held responsible in 1849 under a statute concerning the actions of animals because slaves were considered moral agents. In an 1850 Missouri case, the defendant's slave had enticed another slave to escape. The latter drowned but his owner recovered nothing.[146] An 1828 Alabama case offers a compelling illustration of one court's view of the rights and responsibilities of slave masters. In this case, a slave had found a large amount of cash and given it to authorities. The court determined that the slaveowner was entitled to the cash if the true owner of the money did not come forward. But, interestingly enough, *dicta* indicate that the slaveowner would *not* have been liable to the owner of the money if his slave had destroyed the cash.[147] These cases prefigure the reasoning in an 1887 Kentucky case: Here, a streetcar company was not held liable for the death of a passenger, who had been thrown off the car by the angry driver and crushed under the wheels.[148]

Elsewhere, masters did face liability for deliberate acts of their slaves. Louisiana, with her civil-law tradition, was one state that placed more responsibility on masters. In an 1858 case, an overseer had directed twenty-nine slaves to eject the plaintiff from her shop, take her wares, and set fire to the structure. A mistrial occurred; a second jury held the master liable for $5,000. The appellate court cut down the award to actual damages of $1,000, saying that vindictive damages were inappropriate if the master had not directed the slaves' actions. Louisiana plaintiffs could retrieve the value of stolen property from a slaveowner – up to the value of the erring slave – even before the accused slave was criminally charged. For example, when a group of slave women stole $419.59 worth of fabric from the plaintiff's store, their master had to pay for the stolen goods. Louisiana hirers could also be accountable to a third party for injuries committed by a slave.[149] Not all Louisiana justices agreed that masters should answer for every volitional action of slaves, however. In *Maille v. Blas*, the defendant's slave had killed the plaintiff's slave in a knife fight. The plaintiff recovered damages in 1860 under a statute that made the owner of an animal responsible for the damage it caused. (As mentioned, this contrasts with the common law, under which owners typically faced no responsibility for the acts of their animals.) Chief Justice Merrick dissented, but not because he thought slaves differed from animals. Instead, Merrick noted that, when animals were penned together by consent of their owners, an owner might not have been responsible under the civil code for an injury because all parties were voluntarily exposed to accidents, each with an equal probability. Merrick's reasoning also reveals a perverse incentive created by the majority opinion in the case: an owner of an ill or obstreperous slave might deliberately have exposed his slave to the risk of injury or death at another slave's hands. The owner would have recovered more compensation than if he had tried to sell the slave because Louisiana statutes rescinded sales of slaves with certain "redhibitory" illnesses or character flaws.[150]

States other than Louisiana also placed some responsibility on masters for willful acts (mostly theft) by their slaves. (Slaves thieved as an understandable means of protest as well as to satisfy hunger caused by an owner's neglect.)[151] By 1844, Mississippi had made masters liable for the value of stolen property. Arkansas and Missouri passed theft statutes in the 1850s; Florida's Act of 1862 made slaveowners liable for the value of livestock stolen or killed by their slaves. A Tennessee plaintiff had argued for such measures in 1835, in fact, appealing to the court to provide appropriate incentives: "[I]t is better that he should run the risk than that his neighbor should, who had no concern in or control over the matter . . . it is surely a just policy to secure [nonslaveholders] from injury: as will secure the faithful watchfulness of the master in keeping clear of dissolute character in the selection of slaves; and also secure his fidelity in the exercise of that moral government over them . . . in which society is generally so deeply interested." Twenty years later, an Arkansas court urged that *all* slaves' actions be their masters' responsibility, explaining that this would "thus remov[e] many causes of jealousy and ill feeling against the owners of that species of property, and at the same time protect them by limiting their liability, as at the civil law, to the value of the offending slaves."[152]

Why did some states make masters responsible for willful acts by slaves? *Dicta* suggest that such laws may have served to appease certain nonslaveowners – like those living in the Ozarks – who otherwise might have opposed slavery. Nonslaveowners frequently suffered disadvantages in taxation, representation, and education.[153] Naturally, they would have clamored for laws that benefited them at the expense of slaveholders. Notably, the states that enacted these statutes sat on the fringes (apart from the Atlantic seaboard) of the slave South. Perhaps the presence of such statutes indicates that greater tensions existed between slaveowners and nonslaveowners residing along the border than between people living in interior states and in regions with more established slavery traditions, like the Virginia and Carolina territories. Another contributing factor no doubt was the composition of Southern state legislatures: Only Missouri and Arkansas had a majority of nonslaveholding legislators in the decade before the Civil War.[154] Curiously enough, today's employers – especially those with "deep pockets" – are increasingly responsible for the actions of their employees, much as masters were for slaves.

Masters sometimes faced civil liability for the crimes of their slaves, then, and more so than for crimes of servants. But civil damages in slave cases were in turn often offset by payment from state coffers when a criminal slave was executed.[155] Originally, many states had tried to transport criminal slaves out of state. For example, South Carolina at first granted compensation to owners of executed criminal slaves, then revised its laws in 1714 to provide for transportation of the slave to another state so South Carolina did not have to pay for small-time felons. Louisiana masters could abandon criminal slaves to the state within three days if the value of property damaged by slaves exceeded their value. The slaves would then be sold out of state and their victims compensated with the proceeds of the sale. But states quickly caught on to the external costs imposed by transportation policies. Accordingly, many states began to ban slave imports or to check for criminal backgrounds of imported slaves. Transportation soon gave way to capital punishment of slave criminals. (South Carolina abolished the transportation of criminal slaves in 1717 in part for another reason: Because lawmakers thought the policy gave slaves an incentive to commit crimes.[156]) Most states simultaneously implemented policies of compensating slaveowners – at least those who lived in the state – for part of the value of their executed criminal slaves.[157] Sometimes legislatures passed special acts to compensate for specific slaves. The executors of the will of Alabaman William Murrell successfully petitioned to receive half the market value of a slave who was killed while under sentence of death, for instance.

Compensating masters for executed slaves provided two incentives that helped the slave system function: It discouraged owners from concealing the crimes of their slaves and it gave owners an alternative to selling a criminal slave to an unsuspecting buyer. Yet the legal system did not want people to abuse the state's generosity. One way statutes accomplished this was to award only a portion of the slave's value. Another guard against such abuse came from the courts: Judges barred as evidence any coerced confession by a slave.[158] Owners who wanted easy cash for slaves could simply have said that the slave had confessed to a crime. Judge Pearson of North Carolina gave another reason for the bar in 1858: "If such evidence was received, crowds would always assemble when there was a charge of the commission of a horrid crime, in order to extort a confession."[159] By throwing out coerced confessions by slaves, then, Southern courts protected the fisc as well as prevented at least some lynchings. Other disputes, mostly heard in the 1850s, reveal related restrictions. Maryland refused to let a slaveowner appeal the value of a slave convicted of larceny. Louisiana did not allow a slaveowner to block the revision of a slave's sentence from execution by hanging to life imprisonment. (The slaveowner had argued that the state had expropriated property without adequate compensation, but the state maintained that the master's interest disappeared when he accepted the state's payment of $300 for the slave.) Missouri paid the cost of a criminal prosecution of a convicted slave if the slave was executed but not if he escaped or died at the hands of a mob. Kentucky would not reimburse an owner whose slave committed suicide in jail before sentencing because the court might have granted a new trial. Nor would South Carolina make the city of Charleston pay for a slave who was hanged after beating a white man in the workhouse, saying that the defendant could not be held as "an insurer against the mischief that may be designed and worked out by a creature endowed by moral and intellectual as well as physical attributes."[160] Perhaps the most unusual case in this area comes from 1821 Virginia. Apparently, Virginia had sometimes changed the status of jailed blacks from slave to free so that prisoners could go free. In *Comw. v. Tyree*, the court refused to do the reverse, saying that the "court . . . cannot convert a principle dictated by humanity into an instrument of cruelty."[161] But another motive may have been relevant: saving public funds. John Tyree had claimed to be a free black, but his purported owner

William Tompkins came into the jail in an attempt to change Tyree's status to a slave. If Tompkins had succeeded, the prisoner would have been hung rather than jailed because slaves received harsher punishment than free persons, including free blacks. Tompkins would then have been entitled to compensation from the state.

CONCLUSION

Southern judges played a part in establishing the slaveowner's control over his property: Even sadistic Simon Legree might have found himself in court. Nineteenth-century Southern law never granted slaves the physical protections enjoyed by adult servants and employees, but some restrictions did exist. Although the master wielded considerable power over his slaves, court records show that judges intervened when slaveowners' behavior generated social costs.

Cruelty cases certainly cast light on the awful conditions of bondage. But because the master controlled the life of the slave, slavery was evil in and of itself: Uncle Tom's kindly master Augustine St. Clare is only a shade less despicable than Simon Legree. Judges reinforced this control in ways other than allowing masters to have disciplinary rights. They generally approved of benevolence that bonded slave to master and sanctioned the use of slaves as highly effective agents. Still, even the benign St. Clare might have faced a Southern judge if his actions had adversely affected his neighbors. Southern courts thus tempered the authority of monstrous and munificent masters alike, making them internalize some costs they otherwise would have imposed on the outside world (excluding slaves, naturally). By placing such costs on the slaveholders who generated them, the judiciary in fact strengthened the shackles of slavery.

In crafting law regarding a master's treatment of his slaves, judges drew upon laws governing livestock and servants. Yet the peculiar characteristics of slaves – their human nature, their permanent bondage, and their marketability – gave rise to unique external effects. Neglect of and cruelty to slaves could have led to theft and rebellion that affected the neighbors; not so with abuse of animals. Indulgence of slaves, unlike indulgence of animals, could have generated all-too-human desires and behavior. And although using slaves as agents – like using servants as agents – could benefit Southern society, entrusting slaves carried extra costs. As a result, the law of slavery was unique. Livestock received some legal protection from cruel masters, but not as much as slaves, who represented much greater property value to the antebellum South. Masters bore some responsibility for the behavior of their servants, but not as much as they did for the acts of their slaves. Perhaps most intriguing, nineteenth-century courts considered interference with the family costlier than leaving it alone. Consequently, domestic abuse laws (especially in the South) appeared only decades after slavery disappeared.

8

The South's Law of Slavery
Reflecting the Felt Necessities of the Time

> The felt necessities of the time, the prevalent moral and
> political theories, intuitions of public policy, evolved or
> unconscious, even the prejudices which judges share with
> their fellow-men . . . [determine] the rules by which men
> should be governed. The law embodies the story of a
> nation's development through many centuries. . . . In
> order to know what it is, we must know what it has been,
> and what it tends to become.
>
> – Oliver W. Holmes, Jr.[1]

> [The slave] is made after the image of the Creator. He has
> mental capacities, and an immortal principle in his nature,
> that constitute him equal to his owner, but for the acci-
> dental position in which fortune has placed him.
>
> – *Ford v. Ford*, 7 Humph. 92, 95 (Tn. 1846)

To Southern judges, was a slave property or a human being made
after the image of the Creator? For many disputes, the judiciary considered the slave virtually the same as a valuable steed. But slaves,
unlike their equine counterparts, possessed reason and imagination.
Of all living property, the slave alone could mimic the master. Consequently, a slave often *was* equal to his owner in donning the mantle
of the reasonable person, even though fortune – or, more accurately,
misfortune – had cast him in the role of property. In recognizing the
twofold nature of the slave, antebellum judges balanced the property
interests of the master against the wider interests of Southern society.
The result was a set of legal rules that tended to be efficient, at least
within its peculiar context.

Efficient legal rules helped slavery survive. Although slaveowners
enjoyed substantial authority over their property, verdicts encouraged
masters to act humanely enough so that others would not suffer
depredations, violence, or economic ruin at the hands of slaves. At
the same time, judges granted outsiders some disciplinary power so
as to promote greater profits and public safety and to protect other
property, even as they discouraged people from mistreating or unduly

influencing another's slaves. The common law displayed awareness of the costs of preventing slave escapes, especially costs to owners of common carriers: Southern law preserved the property value of slaves without stopping public transportation in its tracks. Likewise, Southern judges were attuned to the costs of acquiring information about slaves put up for sale. They generally held the relatively knowledgeable slave seller accountable for representations about his stock-in-trade, but they refused to reward buyers who had known of slaves' defects or could cheaply have discovered them. Just as slave society fashioned laws to govern itself, therefore, so too did laws shape the behavior of those living among slaves – and in a way that promoted the economic viability of slavery.[2]

But above all, judges carefully sorted through the odd paradox presented by slaves themselves: Slaves combined the inert characteristics of mere chattels with the volitional attributes of human beings.[3] Slave law called for more complicated liability rules than the simple *caveat emptor* doctrine used for commodity sales and the strict liability placed by some states on railroads for damages to livestock. Despite the protests of slaveowners, and despite slaves' legal status as property, slaves therefore bore a legal burden to behave as reasonable persons. Hired slaves were expected to take precautions against danger, for example, and slaves generally were expected to watch for approaching trains. Still, injured slaveowners did not settle for the one-sided legal defenses granted to injurers and employers of free persons and the blanket immunity enjoyed in free-victim cases by municipalities, homeowners, husbands, and parents. By accounting for both property and personal characteristics of slaves, the law enhanced the operation of slave-sale and -hire markets, reduced the potential external costs of slavery to those with legal standing, circumvented asymmetries in information, and balanced the public's interest in extending mass transportation and protecting homesteads against its desire to maintain slavery. The common law of the South thus kept slavery alive, well, and palatable to Southerners with sundry interests.

I have chosen to treat this body of law as a single entity in order to highlight broad patterns and trends and to contrast it with the rest of the common law.[4] Where relevant, however, I point out and attempt to explain differences in slave law across states. For example, states varied in treating slaves as chattel or real property, considering mulattoes as *prima facie* slave or free, allowing masters to educate and emancipate slaves, permitting masters to work slaves on Sunday, holding masters responsible for the acts of their slaves, inferring warranties about the soundness of sold slaves, permitting common carriers to take side journeys, allowing masters to commit their recalcitrant slaves to the county jail, and assessing penalties for kidnapping or transporting slaves.[5] Variations in law corresponded to variations in the number or proportion of slaves in the population, the percentage of nonslaveowners in the jurisdiction, the navigability of northward waterways, the miles of railroad track, the importance of grazing rights, and the laws concerning husbands and wives. Economics helps explain divergence in law. For instance, developing nuanced rules regarding train accidents and slaves yielded greater benefits in states with a large slave population and many miles of track. Individual judges influenced law as well – Thomas Ruffin of North Carolina, John Belton O'Neall of South Carolina, and Joseph Lumpkin of Georgia, to name only a few.[6] Ruffin in particular handed down finely crafted decisions that preserved slave markets and displayed a clear understanding of incentives; Lumpkin, in contrast, often missed the critical economic implications of his verdicts. In spite of the variations across states and among judges, the law of slavery as a whole exhibits more similarities than differences.[7]

These similarities point to a common characteristic: efficiency. Let me stress again that the concept of "efficiency" used in this book excludes the effects of legal rules on those with no legal standing – namely, slaves. In this respect, my analysis of the common law of slavery resembles the economic analysis of slavery itself, a technique pioneered by Alfred Conrad and John Meyer, Robert Fogel and Stanley Engerman, and many other fine scholars.[8] By omitting costs to slaves from consideration, one can comprehend why slavery endured: It profited those whom it served. In the same fashion, one can understand why the common law helped perpetuate slavery: It efficiently accommodated the needs of a slave-holding society. Profitability and efficiency mean nothing good in this context. Even in these days of moral relativism, few would argue that slavery and the structures that supported it were anything but evil. To call slave law efficient is to condemn it. Had judges been less adept at tailoring the common law to protect this peculiar property, in fact, slaves would have been less valuable and slavery less profitable.

To consider slave law efficient, moreover, one need not assume that judges set out to create efficient law. As Karl Llewellyn admonished his first-year law students: "You will have to be distrustful of whether [judges] themselves know . . . the ways of their own doing, and of whether they describe it accurately, even if they know it."[9] Certainly, Southern judges must have felt many different impulses as they decided slave cases. For some, their pocketbooks were at stake.[10] For others, slave cases represented a test of their abilities to reconcile the marketable nature of slaves with the unmistakable human resemblance of slaves to the judges themselves.[11] For still others, the words of a distinguished twentieth-century judge seem most fitting: "The great tide and currents which engulf the rest of men do not turn aside in their course and pass the judges by. . . . The spirit of the age, as it is revealed to each of us, is too often only the spirit of the group in which the accidents of birth or education or occupation or fellowship have given us a place."[12]

Whatever the motivation of Southern judges, their verdicts in slave cases exhibit far greater sophistication in applying economic principles than the verdicts in contemporaneous commercial, employment, and tort cases. Why? In some instances, underlying conditions substantially differed. The *caveat emptor* doctrine was probably well suited to many antebellum commodity markets where buyers could easily ascertain the quality of their purchases. Wage premiums or injury-compensation funds may, in certain industries, have counterbalanced the legal defenses granted to employers of free persons. Even in family-violence disputes, abuse victims may have been able to resort to nonmarket protection other than that provided by courts. In these instances, the differences in law reflected the relative availability of alternatives to the courtroom for resolving disputes.

At times, however, slave cases led to efficient liability rules earlier than nonslave cases. I suggest that this occurred in part because slaves, unlike free persons, constituted valuable market property. The worth of property rights in slaves – to the master and to the South generally – gave rise to a multitude of disputes and generated detailed law designed to protect those property rights.[13] Yet because slaves were human beings as well as property, slave law also set precedents for the law surrounding free people. Slave law bred protection of property, but it necessarily sheltered the persons embodied by that property. Slave law therefore had unintended consequences: It created rules that judges could potentially apply to free persons as well as to those in bondage.

By dedicating their talents to deciding disputes over slaves, Southern judges like the brilliant Ruffin helped slavery flourish. As a result, their memory remains shackled to the evil institution they helped forge.[14] When Hinton Rowan Helper wrote in 1857 of the pernicious effect of slavery on Southern institutions, he might well have added the judicial system to his list: "The truth is, slavery destroys, or vitiates, or pollutes, whatever it touches. No interest of society escapes the influence of its clinging curse. It makes Southern religion a stench in the nostrils of Christendom – it makes Southern politics a libel upon all the principles of Republicanism – it makes Southern literature a travesty upon the honorable profession of letters."[15] But perhaps we can remember the unintended consequences of slave law as well. Many of the principles that we now consider standard, particularly in personal-injury disputes, had their origins in slave cases.

Put simply, the "felt necessities of the time" yielded a set of laws that have lasted long after the cause they supported was lost. By devoting considerable effort to preserving property rights in slaves, Southern judges in fact left a legacy of legal doctrines that eventually served the interests of ordinary Americans.

Notes

1. AMERICAN SLAVERY AND THE PATH OF THE LAW

1. Others have wrestled with the logic of slave law, concluding that judges could not consistently reconcile the characteristics of slaves as humans and as property, nor harmonize the master's property interests with society's security interests. See, for example, Reuel E. Schiller, "Conflicting Obligations: Slave Law and the Late Antebellum North Carolina Supreme Court," *Virginia Law Review* 78 (August 1992): 1243. A. Leon Higginbotham, Jr., and Barbara K. Kopytoff, "Property First, Humanity Second: The Recognition of Slaves' Human Nature in Virginia Common Law," *Ohio State Law Journal* 50 (June 1989), suggested that courts recognized the humanity of slaves only if doing so did not invade the right of property. I believe the evidence shows otherwise. Aside from the costs to slaves, slave law tended to be efficient.

2. Many scholars have expressed interest in the possible links between slave law and the general development of the common law. See, for example, Eugene D. Genovese and Elizabeth Fox-Genovese, "Slavery, Economic Development and the Law: The Dilemma of Southern Political Economists, 1800–1860," *Washington and Lee Law Review* 41 (Winter 1985), and Robert J. Cottrol, "Liberalism and Paternalism: Ideology, Economic Interests, and the Business Law of Slavery," *American Journal of Legal History* 31 (October 1987). For a discussion of slave law outside the United States, see Alan Watson, *Roman Slave Law* (Baltimore: Johns Hopkins University Press, 1987) and *Slave Law in the Americas* (Athens: University of Georgia Press, 1989).

3. For discussion of the use of precedents, see William M. Landes and Richard A. Posner, "Legal Precedent: A Theoretical and Empirical Analysis," *Journal of Law and Economics* 19 (August 1976). Some suggest that citations may serve as "historical window-dressing" rather than as precedents, that attorneys and judges cite any cases that may seem to support their views in the instant case. For any one lawsuit, this might be true. Yet the patterns of citations and of legal reasoning in postbellum cases suggest something beyond historical accident. Broad changes in contract, employment, tort, and other law occurred in the last four decades of the nineteenth century, and slave law prefigured these changes.

4. Most have analyzed a few laws pertinent to slaves as property or slaves

as persons but have only touched on the interaction of the two. One exception is Judith Schafer, who has examined all slave cases brought before the Louisiana Supreme Court. She emphasized the dual nature of slaves as property and persons; she also lucidly discussed Louisiana's civil-law tradition and contrasted it with the common-law heritage of other American states. Judith K. Schafer, *Slavery, the Civil Law, and the Supreme Court of Louisiana* (Baton Rouge: Louisiana State University Press, 1994). As part of a long-term research project on slaves, Professor Loren Schweninger of the University of North Carolina at Greensboro is currently collecting several thousand petitions that were made to various Southern legislatures and county courts. These data will also yield important information about the legal treatment of slaves as property and slaves as persons. In addition, Paul Finkelman has compiled all the state slavery statutes onto microfiche; no doubt researchers will use his work extensively to study the personal and property attributes of slaves. Paul Finkelman, *State Slavery Statutes* (Frederick, MD: University Publications of America, 1989). This indefatigable scholar has also collected and reproduced pamphlets on the statutes and common law of slavery. Paul Finkelman, *Slavery, Race, and the American Legal System, 1700–1872*, 16 vols. (New York: Garland Publishing, 1988).

The bulk of research on slave law has focused, however, on smaller concerns. Pure property issues surrounded many gifts, bequests, mortgages, and sales of slaves. William M. Wiecek, *The Sources of Antislavery Constitutionalism in America 1760–1848* (Ithaca: Cornell University Press, 1977), offered a history of property rights in slaves. Jacob D. Wheeler, *A Practical Treatise on the Law of Slavery* (New York: Pollack, 1837), discussed the laws of sale, hire, and dower, whereas James Oakes, *The Ruling Race: A History of American Slaveholders* (New York: Knopf, 1982), focused on bequests. Judith K. Schafer, "Guaranteed Against the Vices and Maladies Prescribed by Law: Consumer Protection, the Law of Slave Sales, and the Supreme Court in Antebellum Louisiana," *American Journal of Legal History* 31 (October 1987), and Andrew Fede, "Legal Protection for Slave Buyers in the U.S. South: A Caveat Concerning Caveat Emptor," *American Journal of Legal History* 31 (October 1987), analyzed the law of sales in specific states.

Slaves who committed crimes, on the other hand, generated law related to their personhood, although slaves often received harsher punishment than free persons. A slave was castrated after his conviction for rape in *State v. Anderson*, 19 Mo. 241 (1853), for example. Daniel J. Flanigan, *The Criminal Law of Slavery and Freedom, 1800–68* (New York: Garland Publishing, 1987); Don E. Fehrenbacher, *Slavery, Law, and Politics* (New York: Oxford University Press, 1981); and John Hope Franklin, *From Slavery to Freedom* (New York: Knopf, 1988), discussed the criminal law governing slaves. Robert McPherson collected the original documents pertaining to slave trials in Elbert County, Georgia, from 1837 to 1849. Robert G. McPherson, "Georgia Slave Trials, 1837–1849," *American Journal of Legal History* 4 (October 1960), "Georgia Slave Trials, 1837–1849," *American Journal of Legal History* 4

(July 1960). Philip J. Schwarz, *Twice Condemned: Slaves and the Criminal Laws of Virginia, 1705–1865* (Baton Rouge: Louisiana State University Press, 1988), wrote about Virginia's criminal law.

Slave law shared some attributes of the laws governing servants as well. William Goodell, *The American Slave Code* (New York: M.W. Dodd, 1853), and Thomas D. Morris, "'As If the Injury Was Effected by the Natural Elements of Air, or Fire': Slave Wrongs and the Liability of Masters," *Law and Society Review* 16, no. 4 (1981–82), discussed how masters used slaves as agents and when masters faced liability for their slaves' acts. Paul Finkelman, "Northern Labor Law and Southern Slave Law: The Application of the Fellow Servant Rule to Slaves," *National Black Law Journal* 11 (Summer 1989); Paul Finkelman, "Slaves as Fellow Servants: Ideology, Law, and Industrialization," *American Journal of Legal History* 31 (October 1987); and Mark V. Tushnet, *The American Law of Slavery, 1810–60: Considerations of Humanity and Interest* (Princeton: Princeton University Press, 1981), 183–87, considered the application of the fellow-servant rule in slave cases. The fellow-servant rule defended an employer from liability if an employee's injury stemmed from the negligence of a fellow worker, as Chapter 3 discusses.

Certain unique statutes also pertained to slaves as human beings: manumission laws, fugitive slave laws, and laws surrounding slaves' rights. Wheeler, *A Practical Treatise*; Paul Finkelman, *An Imperfect Union* (Chapel Hill: University of North Carolina Press, 1981); William E. Nelson, "The Impact of the Antislavery Movement upon Styles of Judicial Reasoning in Nineteenth-Century America," *Harvard Law Review* 87 (January 1974); James Turner, "The Use of Courts in the Movement to Abolish American Slavery," *Ohio State Law Journal* 31 (Winter 1970); and Thomas D. Morris, *Free Men All* (Baltimore: Johns Hopkins University Press, 1974), described manumission laws. Stanley W. Campbell, *The Slave Catchers* (Chapel Hill: University of North Carolina Press, 1968); Paul Finkelman, *Slavery in the Courtroom* (Washington, DC: Library of Congress, 1985); Fehrenbacher, *Slavery, Law, and Politics*; Harold M. Hyman and William M. Wiecek, *Equal Justice under Law 1835–75* (New York: Harper and Row, 1982); and Merrill D. Peterson, *The Great Triumvirate* (New York: Oxford University Press, 1987), analyzed fugitive slave laws. Goodell, *The American Slave Code*; Fehrenbacher, *Slavery, Law, and Politics*; and Stanley M. Elkins, *Slavery: A Problem in American Institutional and Intellectual Life* (Chicago: University of Chicago Press, 1976), focused on civil rights. Margaret A. Burnham, "An Impossible Marriage: Slave Law and Family Law," *Law and Inequality* 5 (July 1987), looked particularly at the interaction of slave law and family law.

5. Federal and state appellate-court reporters for the fifteen American slave states and the District of Columbia contain 10,989 cases concerning slaves that were heard in the period after statehood up to 1875. I focus strictly on the region commonly grouped as slave-holding; certainly, other American states had slave histories as well. For an interesting example, see Paul Finkelman, "The Law of Slavery and Freedom

in California, 1848–1860," *California Western Law Review* 17 (Spring 1981). I refer to important colonial and territorial cases as well, but these are not included in the count of 10,989. One note: I use the term "common law" to refer to court cases generally, although Louisiana actually had a civil-law rather than a common-law tradition.

6. By analyzing appellate slave cases, this work covers some of the same material as Thomas Morris's recently published *Southern Slavery and the Law, 1619–1860* (Chapel Hill: University of North Carolina Press, 1996). (Although I had heard of Dr. Morris's work shortly before I completed my manuscript, I did not see it until after my research was accepted for publication.) Yet the focus is far different. Dr. Morris systematically catalogued slave cases, investigated links between slave law and the law governing property generally, and compared legal doctrine with local practice. His research is a masterpiece of detail. My work instead uses cases as data to test the hypothesis that the common law is efficient. Rather than competing with Dr. Morris's research, mine complements his.

7. Oliver W. Holmes, Jr., "The Path of the Law," *Harvard Law Review* 10 (March 1897).

8. Robert D. Cooter and Daniel L. Rubinfeld, "Economic Analysis of Legal Disputes and Their Resolution," *Journal of Economic Literature* 27 (September 1989): 1070. This type of analysis stems from the work of Ronald Coase. Ronald H. Coase, "The Problem of Social Cost," *Journal of Law and Economics* 3 (October 1960). Also see Richard A. Posner, *Economic Analysis of Law* (Boston: Little, Brown, 1986), 21–24, 229–33; Richard A. Posner, *Tort Law: Cases and Economic Analysis* (Boston: Little, Brown, 1982), 1–6; Guido Calabresi, *The Costs of Accidents* (New Haven: Yale University Press, 1971); Richard A. Posner and Andrew M. Rosenfield, "Impossibility and Related Doctrines in Contract Law: An Economic Analysis," *Journal of Legal Studies* 6 (January 1977); Steven Shavell, *Economic Analysis of Accident Law* (Cambridge: Harvard University Press, 1987); Robert D. Cooter, "Economic Theories of Legal Liability," *Journal of Economic Perspectives* 5 (Summer 1991); Robert D. Cooter and Thomas S. Ulen, *Law and Economics* (Glenview, IL: Scott, Foresman, 1988), chap. 1; Stephen G. Gilles, "Negligence, Strict Liability, and the Cheapest Cost-Avoider," *Virginia Law Review* 78 (September 1992); Donald Wittman, "The Price of Negligence under Differing Liability Rules," *Journal of Law and Economics* 29 (April 1986); and Guido Calabresi and A. Douglas Melamed, "Property Rules, Liability Rules, and Inalienability: One View of the Cathedral," *Harvard Law Review* 85 (April 1972). A concise recent analysis is Roy J. Ruffin, "Externalities, Markets, and Government Policy," in *Economic Review, Federal Reserve Bank of Dallas* (Third Quarter 1996). These works focus primarily upon current law. Richard A. Posner, "A Theory of Negligence," *Journal of Legal Studies* 1 (January 1972), argued that economic efficiency provides the best explanation of nineteenth-century law as well. Posner's study begins, however, with appellate cases heard in 1875, whereas the slave cases I examine end there. In another application of

economic analysis to early law, Mark F. Grady, "Toward a Positive Theory of Antitrust," *Economic Inquiry* 30 (April 1992), found that the pre–Sherman Act common law of antitrust is efficient.

9. I do not consider controversies over slave ownership per se, because such disputes typically hinged on pure property issues and I am interested in laws that addressed both property and human aspects of slaves. Consequently, to investigate the allocation of legal entitlements, I look only at the restrictions that courts placed on the master–slave relationship. Put simply, masters were entitled to most of the benefits of property ownership, but they could not treat slaves however they wished because certain types of treatment interfered with free society's entitlement to peace and quiet.

10. Women held slaves as well. I use the term "masters" to include male and female slaveowners.

11. Morton J. Horwitz, *The Transformation of American Law 1780–1860* (New York: Oxford University Press, 1992), 160, claimed that focusing on the convergence of the wills of the parties became important only in the nineteenth century; before then, judges looked more to inherent justness or fairness. A.W.B. Simpson, "The Horwitz Thesis and the History of Contract," *University of Chicago Law Review* 46 (Spring 1979), disagreed. Instead, he argued that the real change in the nineteenth century was the wresting of power away from fickle juries. Regardless of the explanation adopted, nineteenth-century courts enforced most private agreements. Lawrence M. Friedman, *Contract Law in America* (Madison: University of Wisconsin Press, 1965), 206, noted that the law recognizes many substitutes for itself as sources of authority – churches, parents, teachers, corporations, unions, and private contracts. He also wrote that the nineteenth century was the heyday of contract law: Contract law emerged as a series of rules culled from appellate-court cases. The creeds developed in slave cases are an important manifestation of these rules.

12. *Watson v. Boatwright*, 1 Rich. 402, 403 (S.C. 1845).

13. This was true in both contract and tort cases. In contract cases, Posner and Rosenfield, "Impossibility," 122–25, noted that one can determine the least-cost risk bearer by answering three questions: Who can foresee the risk of loss most cheaply? Who can predict the size of loss most cheaply? Who can insure against the risk of loss most cheaply? Often, the answers to at least the first and third questions point to the same party. Their paper discusses several useful examples. In tort cases, negligence rules typically allot losses to the least-cost risk bearer. A negligence rule places blame on the injurer only if he fails to meet a certain standard of care or fails to act as a prudent person would have under similar circumstances. The injurer may defend himself by arguing the victim was contributorily negligent – the victim did not meet a certain standard of care – or assumed the risk of the injury. See William L. Prosser, *Handbook of the Law of Torts* (St. Paul: West Publishing, 1971), chaps. 5, 13; *American Jurisprudence 2d* (Rochester, NY: Lawyers' Cooperative, 1980), vol. 57, secs. 6–10. In the archetypal acci-

dent case where both injurer and victim can take precautions, negligence rules setting a reasonable standard of care for each party are allocatively efficient, provided that legal standards for reasonable care match efficient levels of precaution. See, for example, Cooter and Ulen, *Law and Economics*, chap. 8. For a formal exposition, see William M. Landes and Richard A. Posner, *The Economic Structure of Tort Law* (Cambridge, MA: Harvard University Press, 1987), chaps. 3–5. Guido Calabresi succinctly explained that the rules of tort liability are efficient if structured to minimize the sum of precaution, accident, and administrative costs. Calabresi, *Costs*. Twentieth-century judge Learned Hand expressed the negligence standard in clearly economic terms: An injurer is negligent only if the cost of avoiding an accident is less than the expected cost of the accident itself. *U.S. v. Carroll Towing*, 159 F.2d 169 (2d Cir. 1947).

14. Moral hazard and adverse selection are problems caused by information asymmetries. A moral hazard problem occurs when one person bears the cost of a risk but another person can influence the probability of that risk occurring without being detected. Suppose, for example, Mr. Smith carries insurance that will pay for any damage to his vehicles. He has incentives to park his vehicles carelessly to save time and effort, because someone else (who cannot observe Mr. Smith's behavior) will pay for dents and scratches. Deductibles and copayments are devices designed to reduce moral hazard problems. "Adverse selection" refers to the incentive a person has to falsely represent something as high-quality when other persons cannot discern quality immediately. The classic example of adverse selection occurs in the used-car market – owners of "lemons" want to sell but naturally do not want to reveal flaws that buyers cannot easily discover at the time of sale. Warranties provide one way to circumvent adverse selection problems.

15. These rules were grounded in standard bailment rules, which require persons (bailees) entrusted with another's property to take care of the property as if it were their own. And if one entrusts his property to someone else for a given purpose and the property is used for a different purpose, the bailee is liable for any loss that occurs even if he had taken appropriate care of the property. Examples of bailments include hiring, lending, and pawning property. Matthew Bacon, *Abridgment of the Law* (Philadelphia: T. and J.W. Johnson, 1852), vol. 1, p. 624; *American Jurisprudence 2d*, vol. 8, pp. 725ff. Also see Thomas Morris, *Southern Slavery*, 133ff.

16. Because presumably neither master nor slave wanted the slave to suffer or die, this merging of legal duties in injury cases matched the merged interests of masters and slaves. (Sometimes slaves committed suicide contrary to their masters' financial interests, of course, as Chapter 2 shows.) Naturally, no such merging of duties occurred in escape cases: Any reasonable slave would have wanted to run away.

17. *R.R. v. Yandell*, 17 B. Mon. 586, 589 (Ky. 1856). Soon-to-be U.S. Attorney General James Speed, brother of Abraham Lincoln's good friend Joshua, made this statement.

18. George Akerlof, "The Market for Lemons: Qualitative Uncertainty and the Market Mechanism," *Quarterly Journal of Economics* 84 (August 1970), developed the general theory of lemons.

19. *State v. B. & S. Steam Co.*, 13 Md. 181, 188 (1859).

20. For additional criticism of the law-and-economics approach, see Thrainn Eggertsson, *Economic Behavior and Institutions* (Cambridge, UK: Cambridge University Press, 1990), 112–16.

21. Richard B. Morris, *Studies in the History of American Law* (New York: Octagon Books, 1974), 249–50.

22. 1 Comp. 493 (1808).

23. 1 Cush. 475 (Mass. 1848). A few Northern courts allowed civil actions for wrongful death before *Carey*. In *Cross v. Guthery*, 2 Root 90 (Cn. 1794), for example, the plaintiff sued a surgeon for unskillfully performing an operation on the plaintiff's wife, who died. The defendant argued that, by common law, the public offense subsumed the private injury. The court disagreed and allowed the husband to maintain his civil action.

24. Quoted in Oakes, *The Ruling Race*, 190.

25. *Transformation*, chap. 2.

26. For discussion of these transformations, see Horwitz, *Transformation*, chap. 6; Joel Mokyr, *The Lever of Riches* (Oxford: Oxford University Press, 1990); and Nathan Rosenberg, "Technological Change in the Machine Tool Industry 1840–1910," *Journal of Economic History* 23 (December 1963).

27. Holmes, "Path," 467.

28. For an interesting general discussion of the common law, see Theodore F. T. Plucknett, *A Concise History of the Common Law* (Rochester, NY: Lawyers' Cooperative, 1936). For discussions of property law, see J. Willard Hurst, *Law and the Conditions of Freedom in the Nineteenth-Century United States* (Madison: University of Wisconsin Press, 1956); Horwitz, *Transformation*, esp. chap. 2; Herbert Hovenkamp, *Enterprise and American Law, 1836–1937* (Cambridge, MA: Harvard University Press, 1991), 11, 28, 183–87; and Lawrence M. Friedman, *History of American Law* (New York: Simon and Schuster, 1985), 235. The history of contract law appears in Kevin M. Teeven, *A History of the Anglo-American Common Law of Contract* (New York: Greenwood, 1990), 140, 187; Walton H. Hamilton, "The Ancient Maxim of Caveat Emptor," *Yale Law Journal* 40 (June 1931); Friedman, *Contract Law*, 17; Jamil S. Zainaldin, *Law in Antebellum Society* (New York: Knopf, 1983), 58; and Hurst, *Law and the Conditions*, 98. Although the *caveat emptor* doctrine reigned supreme through most of the nineteenth century, Northern courts created certain narrow exceptions. See Horwitz, *Transformation*, 199; Friedman, *Contract Law*, 103. Useful references for tort law include Landes and Posner, *Economic Structure*; Friedman, *History*; Prosser, *Law of Torts*; and Wex S. Malone, "The Genesis of Wrongful Death," *Stanford Law Review* 17 (July 1965).

29. Horace G. Wood, *A Treatise on the Law of Master and Servant Covering the Relation, Duties, and Liabilities of Employers and Employees* (Albany, NY:

John D. Parsons, Jr., 1877), 280. Accounts of the transformation in the Anglo-American employment relation appeared in Robert J. Steinfeld, *The Invention of Free Labor: The Employment Relation in English and American Law and Culture, 1350–1870* (Chapel Hill: University of North Carolina Press, 1991), and Christopher L. Tomlins, *Law, Labor, and Ideology in the Early American Republic* (New York: Cambridge University Press, 1993).

30. For estimates of nineteenth-century American growth, see Jeremy Atack and Peter Passell, *A New Economic View of American History From Colonial Times to 1940*, 2d ed. (New York: Norton, 1994), 8–12; Stanley L. Engerman and Robert E. Gallman, "U.S. Economic Growth, 1783–1960," in *Research in Economic History*, vol. 8, ed. Paul Uselding (Greenwich, CT: JAI Press, 1982); and readings in Robert E. Gallman and John J. Wallis, eds., *American Economic Growth and Standards of Living Before the Civil War* (Chicago: University of Chicago Press, 1992), particularly Robert E. Gallman, "American Economic Growth Before the Civil War: The Testimony of the Capital Stock Estimate," 79–120, and Thomas Weiss, "U.S. Labor Force Estimates and Economic Growth, 1800–1860," 19–78.

31. The leading proponent of the thesis is Horwitz, *Transformation*. According to Horwitz, Northern courts and other Northern institutions focused on growth and development, throwing their weight behind "new" property to the detriment of "old." *Transformation*, 63–64. See also Hurst, *Law and the Conditions*. Horwitz also pointed out that assigning the burdens of economic development through the legal system hit the weakest and least active elements of the population. If economic growth had been financed through the property taxes then in place, the burdens would have fallen more on the wealthy. *Transformation*, 101–2. In a related point, Joel Mokyr, "Technological Inertia in Economic History," *Journal of Economic History* 52 (June 1992), noted that governments could affect the path of development by their championing – or discouraging – of technological change. Some might characterize the bureaucrats of the antebellum period as exhibiting an excess of enthusiasm about technology. Gary Schwartz strongly disagreed with the subsidy thesis. He maintained, instead, that nineteenth-century tort law (at least in New Hampshire, California, South Carolina, Maryland, and Delaware) was much more balanced and contained a variety of doctrines. Gary Schwartz, "Tort Law and the Economy in Nineteenth Century America: A Reinterpretation," *Yale Law Journal* 90 (July 1981), and "The Character of Early American Tort Law," *UCLA Law Review* 36 (April 1989). Also see Christopher L. Tomlins, *Law, Liberty, and Ideology in the Early American Republic* (Cambridge: Cambridge University Press, 1993), 334ff.

32. See readings in Gallman and Wallis, *American Economic Growth*, particularly Richard H. Steckel, "Stature and Living Standards in the United States."

33. *Structure and Change in Economic History* (New York: Norton, 1981), 190. More generally, North has argued that the legal system (like other insti-

tutions) reflects the desires of those in power, as well as people's efforts to reduce transactions costs and to influence the governing authorities. North's writings also include "Institutions and Economic Performance," in *Rationality, Institutions, and Economic Methodology*, ed. Uskali Maki, Bo Gustafsson, and Christian Knudson (London: Routledge, 1993); "Economic Performance Through Time," *American Economic Review* 84 (June 1994); "Institutions," *Journal of Economic Perspectives* 5 (Winter 1991); *Institutions, Institutional Change, and Economic Performance* (New York: Norton, 1990); and North et al., *Growth and Welfare in the American Past: A New Economic History* (Englewood Cliffs, NJ: Prentice-Hall, 1983). For a brief lucid comparison of the neo-institutionalist approach and a neoclassical view, see Richard B. Du Boff, "Toward a New Macroeconomic History," in *The Megacorp and Macrodynamics: Essays in Memory of Alfred Eichner*, ed. William S. Milberg (Armonk, NY: M.E. Sharpe, 1992). Eggertsson, *Economic Behavior*, provided an excellent text-length treatise on the neo-institutionalist approach, along with several useful references. Coase influenced the neo-institutionalists as well as economics-and-law researchers. See especially Ronald H. Coase, "The Nature of the Firm," *Economica N.S.* 4 (November 1937). Yoram Barzel, *Economic Analysis of Property Rights* (Cambridge: Cambridge University Press, 1989), nicely combined elements of both sets of literature.

34. Paul Finkelman, "Exploring Southern Legal History," *North Carolina Law Review* 64, no. 1 (1985): n. 272. See also James W. Ely and David J. Bodenhamer, "Regionalism and the Legal History of the South," in *Ambivalent Legacy: A Legal History of the South*, ed. David J. Bodenhamer and James W. Ely (Jackson: University of Mississippi Press, 1984), 7. In a telling legal example, Virginia had no law requiring compensation for land taken by the government for roads until 1785, although the colony regularly paid for slaves killed as a result of unlawful or rebellious activities. Horwitz, *Transformation*, 63–64.

35. Few cases on chattels other than slaves appear in the pages of antebellum Southern appellate reporters. These cases consist of disputes over horses, mules, cotton and other commodities, and bank notes. Some cases also considered the duties of common carriers and warehousemen. The value of slaves relative to other chattels – and perhaps relatively more active markets as well – helps explain their owners' propensity to sue. Slaves cost more than livestock, especially Southern livestock. According to Eugene D. Genovese, *The Political Economy of Slavery: Studies in the Economy and Society of the Slave South* (Middletown, CT: Wesleyan, 1989), chap. 5, the South held vast numbers of the country's animals, but the quality (and thus the price) of animals was much lower in the South than in the North. Roger L. Ransom and Richard Sutch, *One Kind of Freedom* (Cambridge: Cambridge University Press, 1977), 52–53, estimated that slaves constituted 60 percent of agricultural wealth in five Southern cotton states and that the average slaveholder held two-thirds of his wealth in slaves. They conservatively estimated that the 1860 market value of the two million slaves in the five states was $1.6 billion. Ransom and Sutch later calculated that the

total value of slaves on the eve of the Civil War was about $3 billion. "Capitalists Without Capital: The Burden of Slavery and the Impact of Emancipation," *Agricultural History* 62 (Summer 1988): 151. Gavin Wright, *The Political Economy of the Cotton South: Households, Markets, and Wealth in the Nineteenth Century* (New York: Norton, 1978), also noted that even a few slaves would comprise the major part of most slaveholders' portfolios. Lee Soltow, *Men and Wealth in the United States, 1850–1870* (New Haven: Yale University Press, 1975), 65, 138–39, and Claudia D. Goldin, "The Economics of Emancipation," *Journal of Economic History* 33 (March 1973), also estimated the value of slaveholdings.

36. The importance of slave buying to a state seemed to influence verdicts. Most interstate sales involved transfers of slaves from the Old South to the cotton-producing states. Robert W. Fogel and Stanley L. Engerman, *Time on the Cross*, part 1 (Boston: Little, Brown, 1974), 47–55; Fede, "Legal Protection," n. 37; Michael Tadman, *Speculators and Slaves* (Madison: University of Wisconsin Press, 1989). South Carolina and the cotton states tended to protect slave buyers more than the other slaveholding states. Chapter 2 develops this point.

37. *Smith v. McCall,* 1 McC. 220, 228 (S.C. 1821); *Jarman v. Patterson,* 7 T. B. Mon. 644, 647 (Ky. 1825).

38. Friedman, *History*, 553–60. Friedman, among others, argued that certain policies (like maximum-hours standards) arose first for women and children because these workers competed with men for jobs. England implemented industrial policies earlier than America, in part because that country feared labor unrest. Hovenkamp, *Enterprise,* 67, 207ff.

39. For discussion, see Matthew W. Finkin, Alvin L. Goldman, and Clyde W. Summers, *Legal Protection for the Individual Employee* (St. Paul: West Publishing, 1989), 554–667, 709–12.

40. See the discussion in J. Willard Hurst, *Law and Markets in U.S. History: Different Modes of Bargaining Among Interests* (Madison: University of Wisconsin, 1982), 75–105. Hurst observed that the concentration of capital that took place in the nineteenth century left market society highly vulnerable at key points, so tort law of the late 1800s began to protect entrepreneurs' access to markets. Friedman, *History,* 476, noted that the rage of victims counted for very little in 1840 and not much in 1860, but became a roaring force by 1890.

41. Reported in Jonathan Lurie, *Law and the Nation* (New York: Knopf, 1983), 2.

42. One slave-train accident case, *R.R. v. Jones,* 2 Head 517 (Tn. 1859), is also a leading case in contracts. *Jones* established the rule that people cannot contract out of gross negligence.

43. Some American states passed statutes awarding damages in death cases – similar to Great Britain's "Lord Campbell's" Act – around the middle of the nineteenth century, but they placed low ceilings on the total dollar recovery. In addition, these laws typically made the defendant liable only if he was willfully neglectful. In practice, civil recoveries in

death cases have been minimal in America until recently. Well into the twentieth century, free Americans who died in accidents were unlikely to generate damage payments from manufacturers, employers, or common carriers. See Landes and Posner, *Economic Structure,* 187; Friedman, *History,* 473–76, 480–81; Prosser, *Handbook,* 402 n. 42; Malone, "Genesis," nn. 134, 143; and Hyman and Wiecek, *Equal Justice,* 41.

44. For a discussion of current law regarding the value of life, see Erin A. O'Hara, "Hedonic Damages for Wrongful Death: Are Tortfeasors Getting Away with Murder?," *Georgetown Law Journal* 78 (June 1990). A landmark twentieth-century case is *Sherrod v. Berry,* 629 F. Supp. 159 (N.D. Ill. 1985), aff'd 827 F.2d 195 (7th Cir. 1987), vacated 835 F.2d 1222 (7th Cir.), reversed on other grounds, 856 F.2d 802 (7th Cir. 1988). The caps on legal liability proposed by the current U.S. Congress may change the direction of the discussion.

45. Judges often declare their beliefs about general legal tenets in *dicta,* however.

46. Edward H. Levi, *An Introduction to Legal Reasoning* (Chicago: University of Chicago Press, 1949), 3. For an excellent discussion of what judges do, see Karl N. Llewellyn, *The Bramble Bush: On Our Law and Its Study* (New York: Oceana Press, 1960), 42–49.

47. I initially used 1875 as a cutoff date for all cases. After I decided to focus on the development of nineteenth-century law generally, I used the *American Digest, Century Edition* (St. Paul: West Publishing, 1899), and *Shepard's Digests* to locate additional nonslave cases heard after 1875.

48. Helen T. Catterall, *Judicial Cases Concerning American Slavery and the Negro* (1926; rpt., New York: Negro Universities Press, 1968); *American Digest.* Paul Finkelman's *State Slavery Statutes* helped place some of these cases into context.

49. For each state, I compiled slave cases beginning with the year statehood was established and ending with the year 1875. Few slave cases were heard after this date. The count of 10,989 refers to the number of cases heard, not the number of controversies. If a particular dispute came before a court twice, I counted it twice. The larger figure represented by the number of cases gives one a better idea of the amount of court time taken up by slave cases. Cases sometimes appeared in more than one reporter; if so, I counted the case only once. Published slave cases also appeared in the colonial and territorial periods; because these records were relatively less organized and standardized, I decided to concentrate my efforts on the volumes of state reporters. I refer to important earlier cases where appropriate.

Although the verdicts in some slave cases are reported in postbellum years, the disputes themselves arose before slavery was abolished. Judges typically tried to decide these cases by reference to laws in force at the time of the dispute. One complicated issue concerned defendants who were slaves at the time they allegedly committed a crime, but were freedmen when the lawsuit came to trial. Some states simply dismissed the charges; others tried to cobble together various criminal codes.

50. Over the entire time period, slave cases constituted roughly 5 to 10 percent of all appellate cases heard in Southern state courts. A greater proportion of slave cases occupied the dockets of the states lying along the lower Atlantic seaboard: South Carolina, North Carolina, and Florida. Other states with somewhat higher proportions of slave cases include Arkansas, Alabama, and Georgia. Missouri had the lowest percentage of cases that involved slaves; this state also had the lowest ratio of blacks to whites among the Southern states.

51. For a history of the precursors of modern tort actions, see Prosser, *Handbook*, 76–79; G. Edward White, *Tort Law in America: An Intellectual History* (New York: Oxford University Press, 1980), 15; Morris, *Studies*, 48ff; and Posner, *Tort Law*, 13–15.

52. Chapter 2 discusses law and equity (chancery) courts.

53. Fewer than 1 percent of the cases filed in state trial courts today will eventually appear on appellate-court dockets. State courts continue to be important (relative to federal courts) in terms of numbers of cases – 31.4 million civil and criminal cases were filed in state trial courts in 1990, as compared with 280,000 in federal district courts. State appellate courts faced 238,000 cases in 1990. Brian J. Ostrom, "Changing Caseloads: The View from the State Courts," *State Court Journal* 16 (Spring 1992).

54. This is especially true for slave cases. The sheer property value at stake made many slave cases worth appealing and worth recording. The breadth of the slave cases appearing in printed appellate-court records exceeds that of other types of contemporaneous cases – and of many types of modern-day disputes. Today, for better or for worse, legal costs may keep many conflicts out of court (especially appellate court), perhaps even to the extent that basic principles cannot be resolved. What is more, the lawsuits that do get filed may not reflect disputes over principles at all. Some are fueled by a desire for a capricious jury verdict, others are a response to proliferating regulations, and still others are an outgrowth of the increasing number of crimes on the books. In comparison with the number of appellate cases reported in state courts just before the Civil War, more than twenty times that number were filed in 1991. The 1991 U.S. population was only about eight times the size of the 1860 population. The biggest litigation explosion has occurred in Florida and Texas, states with significant population growth and drug trafficking. Steven E. Hairston, Roger A. Hanson, and Brian J. Ostrom, "The Work of State Appellate Courts," *State Court Journal* 17 (Spring 1993); Victor E. Flango and Mary E. Eisner, "Advance Report: The Latest State Court Caseload Data," *State Court Journal* 7 (Winter 1983).

55. G. Edward White, "The Appellate Opinion as Historical Source Material," *Journal of Interdisciplinary History* 1 (Spring 1971).

56. Dwight L. Dumond, *Antislavery Origins of the Civil War* (Ann Arbor: University of Michigan Press), 13, discussed the inadequacy of statutes in describing everyday law and society. Tushnet, *The American Law*, 11, 18, said that judicial opinions give better insights into the workings of the

law, whereas statutes represent what society thinks behavior should be. Zainaldin, *Law*, noted that the common law is a means of coping with constant change, whereas statutes arise only periodically. Nineteenth-century courts were especially influential. Horwitz, *Transformation*, argued that nineteenth-century law can be distinguished from that of the eighteenth century in the extent to which common-law judges began playing a central role in directing social policy. Hurst, *Law and Markets*, 127, and *Growth*, 86ff, stated further that meager legislative resources before the 1880s gave legislators a limited role in the antebellum era. Until the Civil War, according to Grant Gilmore, *The Ages of American Law* (New Haven: Yale University Press, 1977), 15, legislators – at least in the North – left most key questions for judges to answer. Bernard Schwartz, *The Law in America* (New York: McGraw-Hill, 1974), 54–58, noted that judicial opinions were extremely influential in the nineteenth century, particularly because the movement led by David Dudley Field largely failed to codify the common law. Admittedly, slave law was more codified than other types of law. As Finkelman noted, antebellum Southern legislators passed more acts about slavery than about anything else. *State Slavery Statutes* (introduction to the collection). He referred to manumission laws to argue that legislation (rather than lawsuits) reflected how Southern citizens viewed the world. Statutes certainly influenced the number and types of cases that appeared in court as well. Yet court cases offer much more insight as to what happened in specific fact situations. The frequency with which a particular type of dispute appeared in court also influenced the types of legislation introduced and enacted. Although I focus principally upon the common law, where possible I refer to the statutes that pertained to particular cases. Certainly, an extended study of the interactions between the statutes and the common law of slavery would be fascinating.

57. *Memoirs*, trans. Robert Baldick (London: Hamish Hamilton, 1961).
58. Not only might the law have acknowledged a slave's humanity as well as his property value, so might his master. By doing so, some argue, slaveowners could have influenced productivity and therefore profit. See Robert W. Fogel, *Without Consent or Contract: The Rise and Fall of American Slavery* (New York: Norton, 1989); James L. Roark, *Masters Without Slaves* (New York: Norton, 1977); and Yoram Barzel, "An Economic Analysis of Slavery," *Journal of Law and Economics* 20 (April 1977). For a set of contrasting views on slaveholders' behavior, see Fogel and Engerman, *Time*; Gavin Wright, *Old South, New South: Revolutions in the Southern Economy Since the Civil War* (New York: Basic Books, 1986) and *Political Economy*; and Genovese, *Political Economy*. Earlier influential studies include Alfred H. Conrad and John R. Meyer, *Economics of Slavery in the Ante-bellum South* (Chicago: Aldine, 1964), and Hugh Aitken, ed., *Did Slavery Pay? Readings in the Economics of Black Slavery in the United States* (Boston: Houghton-Mifflin, 1971). Paul A. David et al., *Reckoning with Slavery* (New York: Oxford University Press, 1976), offered a scathing critique of *Time on the Cross*.

59. Others have written extensively about the factors leading to secession and the causes of the Civil War. Many have focused on slavery. See, for instance, Kenneth M. Stampp, ed., *The Causes of the Civil War* (New York: Simon and Schuster, 1991); Michael F. Holt, *The Political Crisis of the 1850s* (New York: Norton, 1978); Gerald Gunderson, "The Origin of the American Civil War," *Journal of Economic History* 34 (December 1974); Avery O. Craven, "Why the Southern States Seceded," in *The Crisis of the Union, 1860–1861*, ed. George H. Knoles (Baton Rouge: Louisiana State University Press, 1965); Edwin C. Rozwenc, ed., *Slavery as a Cause of the Civil War* (Lexington, MA: D.C. Heath and Co., 1963); Avery O. Craven, *Civil War in the Making* (Baton Rouge: Louisiana State University Press, 1959); Dumond, *Antislavery Origins*; and C. Vann Woodward, *The Burden of Southern History* (Baton Rouge: Louisiana State University Press, 1970), 197.

60. Oliver W. Holmes, Jr., "The Gas Stokers' Strike," *American Law Review* 7 (1873).

2. THE LAW OF SALES

1. Because the U.S. banned the international slave trade in 1808, new U.S. slaveowners had to make domestic purchases or inherit their freshly acquired property after that time. Gary M. Anderson, Charles K. Rowley, and Robert D. Tollison, "Rent Seeking and the Restriction of Human Exchange," *Journal of Legal Studies* 17 (January 1988), surmised that interest groups seeking to close the slave trade in order to inflate slave prices may in fact have helped put a stop to the evils of international sales. Most states tried to prevent the introduction of merchandise slaves – similarly fearing downward pressures on slave prices and importation of criminal slaves – but found such policies hard to enforce and later withdrew them. *Groves v. Slaughter*, 15 Pet. 449 (U.S. 1841), challenged Mississippi's constitutional bar to the purchase of slaves in other states for resale within Mississippi. And Tadman, *Speculators*, 76, 85, recounted numerous ways that slave traders flouted such bans. In the Act of May 3, 1847, Louisiana tried another approach, imposing a $5 tax on each slave sold by a trader. For more discussion, see Tadman, *Speculators*, 84, and Frederic Bancroft, *Slave Trading in the Old South* (1931; rpt., New York: Ungar, 1959), 170–71.

   Domestic slave sales were common. Many transactions took place at the hands of slave traders like future Confederate Lieutenant-General Nathan Bedford Forrest, whereas others resulted from estate and bankruptcy sales. (Traders rarely purchased slaves at estate or judicial sales, according to Tadman, *Speculators*, 52, 113.) The reuniting of slave families motivated some sales. Fogel and Engerman, *Time*, 52–55. Fogel and Engerman also claimed that the rental market in slaves was much more active than the sale market. Using a study of Maryland from 1830 to 1840, they calculated total sales of only 1.92 percent of the slave population. But the *Virginia Times* in 1830 estimated that 40,000 slaves sold that year at an average price per slave of $600. Goodell, *American Slave*

Code, 56. Oakes, *Ruling Race*, 67, noted a large growth in the number of slaveholders in the period 1830–60 – to at least 170,000 masters. And Tadman, in his monumental study of slave trading, estimated that, from 1820 to 1860, an average of 200,000 slaves per decade moved from the upper South to the lower South. Most of the movement took place through trades rather than migration. Tadman asserted, in fact, that slaves who lived in the upper South faced a very real chance of being sold by their owners for speculative profit. Itinerant traders who operated in a few counties bought most slaves directly from slaveowners for cash, then moved slaves overland in coffles to the lower South. Big slave traders included Franklin and Armfield (Virginia) and Woolfolk, Saunders, and Overly (Maryland). The centers of the slave trade were Baltimore, Richmond, Washington, Norfolk, Charleston, Montgomery, Memphis, and New Orleans. Tadman, *Speculators*, esp. 5–8, 47, 113, 129; Franklin, *From Slavery*, 104. Forrest based his operations primarily in Memphis. For an account of Forrest's life as a trader and the profitability of trading, see Jack Hurst, *Nathan Bedford Forrest* (New York: Knopf, 1993), 31–68. Edmund L. Drago, ed., *Broke by the War: Letters of a Slave Trader* (Columbia: University of South Carolina Press, 1991), provided a fascinating set of letters written by a South Carolina slave trader to his employer that illustrate how slave trafficking seemed as impersonal as trading in any other commodity.

Roark, *Masters*, 88, referred to the brisk trade in slaves that went on until the last year of the Civil War. Delaware allowed slave sales to continue after the war; free blacks were sold in the state even after the passage of the Thirteenth Amendment. What is more, both houses of the Delaware state legislature rejected a proposal for a constitutional amendment prohibiting slavery or involuntary servitude on February 8, 1868. Richard B. Morris, *The Forging of the Union, 1781–1789* (New York: Harper and Row, 1987), 182. The Mississippi Senate finally ratified the Thirteenth Amendment in February 1995.

2. Fede, "Legal Protection," went so far as to argue that the law of slave sales foreshadows elements of the modern Uniform Commercial Code. Slave states typically inferred a warranty of title and effectively inferred a warranty of soundness, for example, unless buyer and seller obviously knew a slave was not sound. Similarly, the Code contains implied warranties of title and soundness in its implied warranty of merchantability (section 2-314). The Uniform Commercial Code, drafted (primarily by Karl Llewellyn) by 1952, has been adopted (at least in part) in all states of the union. Teeven, *History*, 222.

Fede also claimed that Southern judges leaned away from the *caveat emptor* doctrine in disputes concerning sales of items other than slaves. Southern judges may well have desired consistency in state commercial law for different items of personal property more than they wanted consistency across states – Northern and Southern – in commercial law for nonslave items. That is, slavery itself likely influenced the path of Southern law. Yet my research shows that the common law of slave sales differed from that of its closest relative, livestock sales. So while Fede may be right to contend that Southern commercial law diverged from Northern law, the common law of slave sales still stands alone. Morris, *Southern Slavery*, chap. 5, offered details on the law of slave sales and mortgages.

3. Kenneth M. Stampp, *The Peculiar Institution* (New York: Vintage Books, 1956), 240; Fede, "Legal Protection," 330; Tadman, *Speculators*. Not until the latter half of the nineteenth century did intermediaries spring up in other commodity transactions, along with new methods of financing and marketing. Teeven, *History*, 220; Alfred D. Chandler, *The Visible Hand: The Managerial Revolution in American Business* (Cambridge: The Belknap Press of Harvard University Press, 1977), 209–15, 236–37. For a discussion of the development of management techniques in England, see Sidney Pollard, *The Genesis of Modern Management* (London: Edward Arnold, 1965).

4. Fede, "Legal Protection," 330, also asserted that slaves were a high-risk investment and that slave buyers were at an informational disadvantage. This disadvantage (particularly for buyers who were not traders) persisted regardless of whether the seller had owned and employed the slave or the seller merely traded slaves as merchandise. Why? Long-time property owners had had the advantage of close companionship with the property they sold. Although professional traders may not have had this advantage, they had others. Because traders were in the business of assessing quality, they should have known more about their wares than the typical individual who bought from them. In the text at note 38, I take up the case of slave buyers who were also traders.

5. That slaves could talk might lead one to believe that slave buyers could also cheaply assess the slaves' health. As discussed later, however, slaves on the auction block had incentives to lie. Although they might have lied to their owners as well, owners at least had had the ability to observe the behavior and well-being of slaves over a longer period of time. And slaves who had frequently lied also gave information to their owners, albeit indirectly.

6. See Akerlof, "Market," for a general analysis of the lemon problem.

7. *Patton v. Porter*, 3 Jones 539 (N.C. 1856), noted that warranties shifted risk rather than necessarily indicating that slaves were sound. Of course, slave traders had market incentives to warrant only their sound slaves because a reputation for fraud or misrepresentation would have hurt their ability to trade later on. Sellers typically had better information about their wares than buyers. Consequently, if sellers were risk-neutral and buyers risk-averse, sellers might have found it particularly profitable to offer warranties.

8. For example, the court in *Aven v. Beckom*, 11 Ga. 1 (1852), awarded damages for breach of warranty even though the purchaser – who owned the bought slave's wife – probably knew more about the slave than the seller's agent, who was the administrator of the seller's estate. Rarely, courts rescinded slave sale contracts instead of awarding damages, at times with a setoff for use. For example, see *Scott v. Clarkson*, 1 Bibb 277 (Ky. 1808). Rescission of a sale is essentially a court-

ordered "undoing" of the transaction. If a court rescinded the sale of a slave, the seller took back the slave and the buyer took back the purchase money. Defendants who paid damages also sometimes requested an offset for the value of services rendered by the sold slave. In *Harvey v. Kendall*, 2 La. An. 748 (1847), the court refused such a request, saying that the defendant's use of the purchase money compensated for the slave's lost services.

9. *Bell v. Jeffereys*, 13 Ired. 356, 360 (N.C. 1852); *Dean v. Traylor*, 8 Ga. 169 (1850). *Chilton v. Jones*, 4 H. & J. 62 (Md. 1815), resembles *Dean*.

10. *Ayres v. Parks*, 3 Hawks 59, 60 (N.C. 1824).

11. *White v. Slatter*, 5 La. An. 29 (1850). For simple no-warranty cases, liability rules might not appear to matter because buyers and sellers could adjust prices. As discussed later, however, liability rules indeed could affect resource allocation because buyers and sellers had different costs of acquiring information.

12. *Pyeatt v. Spencer*, 4 Ark. 563 (1842); *Fry v. Throckmorton*, 2 B. Mon. 450 (Ky. 1842); *Lyons v. Kenner*, 2 Rob. 50 (La. 1842); *Stackhouse v. Kendall*, 7 La. An. 670 (1851). Tadman, *Speculators*, 107, reported that traders sometimes inoculated or insured their wares during times of epidemics. Louisiana buyers who abused or neglected slaves were quite likely to bear the loss if the slaves died. See, for example, *Roca v. Slawson*, 5 La. An. 708 (1850); *Williams v. Moore*, 3 Munf. 310 (Va. 1811) (in *dicta*). To sustain a statutory action, a Louisiana buyer had to care for newly bought slaves like a "prudent father." (See text at note 35 for reference to redhibition statutes.) *Sargent v. Slatter*, 6 La. An. 72 (1851); *Soubie v. Sougeron*, 5 Rob. 148 (La. 1843); *Kiper v. Nuttall*, 1 Rob. 46 (La. 1841). (The *Sargent* court sustained the buyer's action.) Neglecting to summon a doctor threw the loss of a dead slave on buyers in *Williams v. Talbot*, 12 La. An. 407 (1857); *Stoppenhagen v. Verdelet*, 10 La. An. 263 (1855); and *Hooper v. Owens*, 7 La. An. 206 (1852).

13. The phrases quoted are from slave cases *Ditto v. Helm*, 2 J.J. Marsh. 129 (Ky. 1829) (overturning *Smith v. Miller*, 2 Bibb 616 (Ky. 1812)); *Steel v. Brown*, 19 Mo. 312 (1854); and *Baum v. Stevens*, 2 Ired. 411 (N.C. 1842). Unlike warranties in land, a warranty did not run with the slave. *Offutt v. Twyman*, 9 Dana 43 (Ky. 1839).

14. Southern cases include *Lindsay v. Davis*, 30 Mo. 406 (1860); and *Erwin v. Maxwell*, 3 Murph. 241 (N.C. 1819). The words "sound to the best of my knowledge," "considered sound," "he is sound and will make a good horse," and "safe and kind and gentle" did not necessarily create warranties of soundness in the North. *Myers v. Conway*, 62 In. 474 (1878); *Wason v. Rowe*, 16 Vt. 525 (1844); *Duffee v. Mason*, 8 Cow. 25 (N.Y. 1827); *Jackson v. Wetherill*, 7 Serg. & R. 480 (Pa. 1822). By midcentury, some Northern states were more likely to discover a warranty for livestock and hold sellers liable. See, for example, *Morgan v. Powers*, 66 Barb. 35 (N.Y. 1866); *Smith v. Justice*, 13 Wis. 600 (1861); *Tuttle v. Brown*, 4 Gray 457 (Mass. 1856); and *Cook v. Moseley*, 13 Wend. 277 (N.Y. 1835).

15. *Dennis v. Ashley*, 15 Mo. 453 (1852); *Sipple v. Breen*, 1 Har. 16 (Del. 1832).

16. *Roberts v. Jenkins*, 1 Fost. 116 (N.H. 1850); *Smith v. Rice*, 1 Bail. 648 (S.C. 1830); *Thompson v. Bertrand*, 23 Ark. 730 (1861).
17. *Caldwell v. Wallace*, 4 Stew. & P. 282 (Ala. 1833); *Sloan v. Williford*, 3 Ired. 307, 309 (N.C. 1843) (also stated in *Simpson v. McKay*, 12 Ired. 141, 143 (N.C. 1851)); *Nelson v. Biggers*, 6 Ga. 205 (1849); *Smith v. McCall*, 1 McC. 220, 223 (S.C. 1821). The *Sloan* trial-court verdict for the plaintiff was reversed because a deposition taken on Sunday was erroneously admitted into evidence. Warranties of soundness naturally did not encompass casualties of parturition subsequent to the sale. *Hambright v. Stover*, 31 Ga. 300 (1860).
18. See, for example, *Eaves v. Twitty*, 13 Ired. 468 (N.C. 1852). (In this case, the plaintiff lost partly because he had not proved that the slave was a drunkard before the sale.) Nor was drunkenness a redhibitory vice giving rise to the rescission of a sale under Louisiana statutes. *Behan v. Faures*, 12 La. 211 (1838); *Xenes v. Taquino*, 7 Mart. N.S. 678 (La. 1829). For a discussion of redhibition, see text at note 35. Drunkenness in slaves could knock down their prices by as much as 55 percent. Fogel, *Without Consent*, 70, fig. 12.
19. *Wyatt v. Greer*, 4 S. & P. 318 (Ala. 1833), had a special warranty for character. *Creswell v. Walker*, 37 Ala. 229 (1861), addressed moral qualities and prices. Two livestock cases refer to character and resulted in verdicts similar to those in slave cases. A Missouri court held that a sale of a steer included no implied warranty of character. *McCurdy v. McFarland*, 10 Mo. 377 (1847). And a New York plaintiff could not recover damages by showing that the cattle he purchased were of "disorderly character." *Strevel v. Hempstead*, 44 Barb. 518 (N.Y. 1864).
20. In *Ayres v. Parks*, 3 Hawks 59 (N.C. 1824), and *Broughton v. Badgett*, 1 Ga. 77 (1846), damages equaled the difference between the price paid and the value of an unsound slave. In other cases, courts specified damages as the difference between values of sound and unsound slaves. See *Graham v. Bardin*, 1 Patt. & H. 206 (Va. 1855); *Stearns v. McCullough*, 18 Mo. 411 (1853); *Williamson v. Canaday*, 3 Ired. 513 (N.C. 1843); and *Adkinson v. Stevens*, 7 J.J. Marsh. 237 (Ky. 1832) (reversed for insufficient evidence). Although warranties were more difficult to prove in cases involving sales of animals, general damage rules – North and South – were similar to those for slaves. *Thornton v. Thompson*, 4 Gratt. 121 (Va. 1847), provides an example involving a jackass. Other cases refer to horses. *Wallace v. Wren*, 32 Ill. 146 (1863); *Moulton v. Scruton*, 39 Me. 287 (1855); *Comstock v. Hutchinson*, 10 Barb. 211 (N.Y. 1850); *Cary v. Gruman*, 4 Hill 625 (N.Y. 1843).
21. *Williams' Case*, 3 Bland 186 (Md. 1831). For another useful calculation, see *Thompson v. Bertrand*, 23 Ark. 730 (1871).
22. *Soper v. Breckinridge*, 4 Mo. 14 (1835); *Marshall v. Gantt*, 15 Ala. 682 (1849). These verdicts bear some resemblance to the "second-injury" rules in workers' compensation. If a preexisting injury or condition exacerbates an employee's injury on the job, the employer is responsible under such rules only for losses ascribable to the job-related injury. Such rules were designed to promote – or at least not discourage – the

employment of the disabled. The Americans with Disabilities Act may
alter the effect of these rules.

23. *Sessions v. Hartsook*, 23 Ark. 519 (1861). The verdict may have worked
to the interest of customers as well. If the traders were reasonably
scrupulous and accepted trade-ins without much fuss, the policy benefited buyers provided that, on average, the costs of litigation exceeded
the costs of exchanging slaves.

24. *Miller v. McDonald*, 13 Wi. 673 (1861).

25. *McKee v. Jones*, 67 Miss. 405 (1889); *Brown v. Bigelow*, 10 Allen 242 (Mass.
1865). I found one antebellum example in which Southern and Northern courts came to different rules. An Arkansan who proclaimed that
his horse had an eye "as good as any horse's" gave a warranty, but a
Hoosier – saying the same words – did not. *Buckman v. Haney*, 6 Eng.
339 (Ark. 1850); *House v. Fort*, 4 Blackf. 293 (In. 1837). The Southern
rule resembles that determined in the earlier-mentioned slave case of
Bell v. Jeffereys (note 9).

26. *Smith v. Swarthout*, 15 Wis. 550 (1862).

27. William Calderhead, "How Extensive Was the Border State Slave Trade?
A New Look," in *Articles on American Slavery*, vol. 8: *Slave Trade and Migration: Domestic and Foreign*, ed. Paul Finkelman (New York: Garland Publishing, 1989), 53, found that one-quarter of advertisements in the
Maryland *Gazette* of sales for the period 1809–39 – other than judicial
or estate sales – requested that the slaves remain in the state.

28. *Turner v. Johnson*, 7 Dana 435, 440 (Ky. 1838) (see quote at outset of
Chapter 1). Also see *Oldham v. Bentley*, 6 B. Mon. 428 (Ky. 1846); *Fenwick
v. Grimes*, 8 F.C. 1142 (D.C. 1838); *Price v. Read*, 2 H. & G. 291 (Md.
1828); *Young v. Palmer*, 30 F.C. 863 (D.C. 1825); and *Adams v. Anderson*,
4 H. & J. 558 (Md. 1819).

29. *Ross v. Carpenter*, 9 B. Mon. 367 (Ky. 1849). Equity courts arose in
England in the fifteenth century, primarily as a response to the anti-
quated practices of common-law courts that dealt mostly with land
matters. Ecclesiastics staffed equity courts at first. Plucknett, *A Concise
History*, 160, 603–35. Many American states had separate law and equity
(chancery) courts through the nineteenth century. Most states gradually merged the two, although Delaware is a present-day exception. A
plaintiff who seeks an equitable remedy must show that his remedy at
law – usually damages – is inadequate. An equity court could compel a
creditor to return a fine gem that was unlawfully or mistakenly seized
or sold, for example, instead of ordering a plaintiff to seek money
damages in a court of law. The plaintiff in such a case could argue that,
because no other gem could substitute for his, money damages could
not "make him whole" – only the restoration of his gem could.

Equitable remedies, particularly in contract cases, generally might
offer greater deterrence and lower administrative costs than damage
remedies. Cooter and Ulen, *Law and Economics*, 320–24, pointed out
that specific performance of contracts should perhaps be the routine
remedy for breach, because contractual partners by nature face low
transactions costs. But Cooter and Ulen also noted that, when contracts

are impossible to perform (as in the restricted-locality cases) or when behavior is hard to monitor, damages are the efficient remedy.

30. *Brent v. Richards*, 2 Gratt. 539 (Va. 1846).

31. *Hanks v. McKee*, 2 Litt. 227, 229 (Ky. 1822). The burden of proof fell on the plaintiff, as in warranty cases. In the case of *Stewart v. Dugin*, 4 Mo. 245 (1835), for instance, the buyer had to prove that he did not know of the slave's disease, but that the slave had had the disease at the time of the sale and died from it.

32. The South Carolina courts generally relied on the early case of *Timrod v. Shoolbred*, 1 Bay 324 (S.C. 1793). Fede, "Legal Protection," 331–32, surmised that South Carolina subscribed to the sound-price doctrine to protect buyers because, of all the slave-holding states, South Carolina had the highest proportion of its population enslaved and had numerous slave buyers.

33. *Venning v. Gantt*, Cheves 87 (S.C. 1840). Judge O'Neall dissented, saying the court should not use the doctrine because the seller had expressly refused to warrant the slave. The majority opinion countered that, to cover himself, the seller also should not have accepted a full price.

34. *Lightner v. Martin*, 2 McC. 214 (S.C. 1822); *Watson v. Boatwright*, 1 Rich. 402 (S.C. 1845).

35. For slaves, such flaws included illness, impairment, and the habit of running away. The buyer bore the burden of proof and had to offer to return the slave to be entitled to a rescission. *Bach v. Barrett*, 2 La. An. 955 (1847); *Barrett v. Bullard*, 19 La. 281 (1841). Buyers could not recover transportation costs. *Coulter v. Cresswell*, 7 La. An. 367 (1852). The bulk of Louisiana slave cases involved redhibitory actions. For further discussion, see Schafer, "Guaranteed" and *Slavery*.

36. *Fazande v. Hagan*, 9 Rob. 306 (La. 1844); *Nott v. Botts*, 13 La. 202 (1839). Also see *Rist v. Hagan*, 8 Rob. 106 (La. 1844); *Icar v. Suares*, 7 La. 517 (1835); and *Macarty v. Bagnieres*, 1 Mart. 149 (La. 1810).

37. The favorable rules toward South Carolina and Louisiana slave buyers resemble the legal rules that favored expanding industries like railroads. Slave sellers naturally had more sway in states where they figured more prominently. See Fede, "Legal Protection," and Schafer, "Guaranteed."

38. *Wilson v. Shackleford*, 4 Rand. 5 (Va. 1826). Also see *Smith v. Miller*, 2 Bibb 616 (Ky. 1821); and *Brooks v. Cannon*, 2 A.K. Marsh 526 (Ky. 1820).

39. *Turner v. Huggins*, 14 Ark. 21, 25 (1853).

40. One might expect that liability rules holding sellers to their representations would have stopped sellers from claiming anything about their wares. Yet sellers commonly made some sort of representation about their stock-in-trade. Goodell, *American Slave Code*, 43, referred to advertisements attesting to slaves' piety, intelligence, honesty, and sobriety. But theory as well as empirical evidence suggests that sellers would have described slaves' attributes. Suppose sellers had claimed nothing. Then "good" and "bad" slaves would have sold for the same price if buyers could not ascertain the difference. Any seller with a "good" slave would therefore have found it worthwhile to pass along that information to a

potential buyer in exchange for a higher price, provided sellers could distinguish "good" from "bad" slaves. As long as the price differential exceeded the expected costs of litigation and damages, sellers would have provided such information even when responsible for their representations.

41. The domestic case is *Pilie v. Lalande*, 7 Mart. N.S. 648 (La. 1829). Sickly-slave cases include *Hancock v. Tucker*, 8 Fl. 435 (1859); *Overstreet v. Phillips*, 1 Litt. 120 (Ky. 1822); *Smith v. Rowzee*, 3 A.K. Marsh. 527 (Ky. 1821); and *Burton v. Wellers*, Litt. Sel. Cas. 32 (Ky. 1808). Runaway cases include *Ward v. Reynolds*, 32 Ala. 384 (1858); and *Scott v. Perrin*, 4 Bibb 360 (Ky. 1816). Fogel, *Without Consent*, 70, fig. 12, delineated premiums and discounts for various characteristics.

42. *Hardin v. Brown*, 27 Ga. 314 (1859); *Sherwood v. Walker*, 66 Mich. 568, 33 N.W. 919 (1887); *Scott v. Renick*, 1 B. Mon. 63 (Ky. 1840). Fogel and Engerman, *Time*, 81–82, measured the effect of reproductive capacity on the price of female slaves.

43. The typical "foal-getter" case is *Roberts v. Applegate*, 48 Ill. App. 176, aff'd 153 Ill. 210 (1894). Kentucky cases include *Lamme v. Gregg*, 1 Metc. 444 (Ky. 1858); and *Dickens v. Williams*, 2 B. Mon. 274 (Ky. 1842).

44. Fogel, *Without Consent*, 68, fig. 11, showed that slave prices were affected by age, gender, health, skills, and reliability, with age being most important. Also see Drago, *Broke*, on the importance of age, sex, weight, and height of slaves to one trader. Interestingly, names figured into some slave sale contracts. A Louisiana court held that "Slaves, being men, are to be identified by their proper names, which distinguish them from one another; and where there are two or more of the same name, by some other; which distinguishes them in relation to physical, or, perhaps, moral qualities." *Johnson v. Field*, 5 Mart. N.S. 635, 636 (La. 1827).

45. *Walker v. Cuculla*, 18 La. An. 246 (1866); *Lobdell v. Burke*, 5 Rob. 93 (La. 1843); *Roberts v. Yates*, 20 F.C. 937 (S.C. 1853).

46. Julius Lester, *To Be a Slave* (New York: Laurel Leaf Library, 1970), 30. Tadman, *Speculators*, 98–101, and Stampp, *Peculiar Institution*, 259, cited evidence that slaves being readied for market had gray whiskers shaved off and gray hairs plucked or blackened. Stampp also said that slaves were taught that their ages were some ten to fifteen years younger than their true ages.

47. *Whitson v. Gray*, 3 Head 441 (Tn. 1859); *Banfield v. Bruton*, 7 B. Mon. 108 (Ky. 1846); *Thomas v. McCann*, 4 B. Mon. 601 (Ky. 1844) (reversed and remanded for an error in the proceedings, but with *dicta* supporting the outcome of the trial); *Scott v. Clarkson*, 1 Bibb 277 (Ky. 1808); *Hogan v. Carland*, 5 Yerg. 283 (Tn. 1833).

48. *Burge v. Strogert*, 42 Ga. 89 (1871); *Martin v. Edwards*, 11 Humph. 374 (Tn. 1850); *Willard v. Stevens*, 4 Fost. 271 (N.H. 1851). See also *Ferguson v. Oliver*, 8 S. & M. 332 (Miss. 1847).

49. *Miller v. Gaither*, 3 Bush 152 (Ky. 1867). Allan Nevins, *The War for the Union: War Becomes Revolution, 1862–1863* (New York: Scribner's, 1960), 463–66, discussed the Draft Act. Other evidence of a buyer wanting

slaves for a particular purpose appeared in the Charleston *Mercury* on October 12, 1838. Dr. T. Stillman advertised for fifty Negroes who were affected by certain incurable diseases so that he could perform experiments on them. Goodell, *American Slave Code*, 87.

50. *Brown v. Hawkins*, 3 Bush 558 (Ky. 1868).

51. See, for example, *Morton v. Scull*, 23 Ark. 289 (1861).

52. *Cozzins v. Whitaker*, 4 S. & P. 282 (Ala. 1833); *Johnson v. Wideman*, Rice 325, 342 (S.C. 1839). Theodore Rosengarten, *Tombee* (New York: McGraw-Hill, 1987), 162, described a typical slaveowner who tolerated pilfering – especially of food – to buy tranquility and avoid open discussions of human needs. *Eaves v. Twitty*, 13 Ired. 468 (N.C. 1852), exemplifies the verdicts in drunkenness cases.

53. *Brownston v. Cropper*, 1 Litt. 173, 176 (Ky. 1822); *Eckles v. Bates*, 26 Ala. 655, 660 (1855). Also see *Allen v. Vancleave*, 15 B. Mon. 236 (Ky. 1855); *Rowland v. Walker*, 18 Ala. 749 (1850); and *Tumey v. Knox*, 7 T.B. Mon. 88 (Ky. 1828). Raymond A. Bauer and Alice H. Bauer, "Day to Day Resistance to Slavery," in *Articles on American Slavery*, vol. 13: *Rebellions, Resistance, and Runaways Within the Slave South*, ed. Finkelman, 95–102, 108, discussed instances of slaves who pretended to be sick or disabled, particularly on the auction block.

54. Posner, *Economic Analysis*, 99.

55. Such defects included peritonitis and pleuritis (*Wade v. Dewitt*, 20 Tx. 398 (1857)); scrofula (*Thompson v. Botts*, 8 Mo. 710 (1845)); venereal disease (*Samuel v. Minter*, 3 A.K. Marsh. 480 (Ky. 1821)); and leg ailments (*Burton v. Willis*, Litt. Sel. Cs. 32 (Ky. 1808)). *Brugh v. Shanks*, 5 Leigh 598 (Va. 1833); *Reading v. Price*, 3 J.J. Marsh. 62 (Ky. 1830); and *Hardwick v. Hardwick*, 4 Bibb 569 (Ky. 1817), also discuss this rule. The slave seller had an affirmative duty to inform the buyer about defects, according to Fede, "Legal Protection," n. 150. Yet the seller had to say only what he believed was true, even if other people said otherwise. *McIntire v. McIntire*, 8 Ired. Eq. 297 (N.C. 1852).

56. See, for example, *Hanks v. McKee*, 2 Litt. 227 (Ky. 1822). The Northern states eventually adopted a similar rule for commodities – the doctrine of *caveat emptor* began to apply more for spot sales of present goods than for goods the buyer could not have inspected before sale. Northern courts also cautiously began to infer warranties of quality and fitness for a particular purpose if the buyer had had no opportunity to inspect the goods. Fede, "Legal Protection," 326–27; Teeven, *History*, 187.

57. *Williams v. Vance*, Dud. 97, 100 (S.C. 1837). Plaintiff Williams purchased slave Robin, knowing of the exposure. When the slave died from measles, Williams recovered nothing.

58. *Clopton v. Martin*, 11 Ala. 187 (1847); *Scarborough v. Reynolds*, 13 Rich. 98, 99 (S.C. 1860); *Jordan v. Foster*, 11 Ark. 139 (1850). The *Ayres* case discussed in the text at note 10 is much the same – Peggy's nosebleeds were obvious, but their eventual effect on Peggy's ability to function was not. See also *Williams v. Ingram*, 21 Tx. 300 (1858).

59. See, for instance, *Vates v. Cornelius*, 59 Wis. 615 (1884), and *Burton v. Young*, 5 Har. 233 (Del. 1849).

60. *Limehouse v. Gray,* 3 Brev. 230 (S.C. 1812); *Hart v. Edwards,* 2 Bail. 306 (S.C. 1831); *Lyles v. Bass,* 1 Cheves 85 (S.C. 1840); *Otts v. Alderson,* 10 S. & M. 476, 481 (Miss. 1848); *Farr v. Gist,* 1 Rich. 68, 74 (S.C. 1844). People who eat dirt are now thought to be trying to satisfy some nutritional deficiency.

61. *Miller v. Yarborough,* 1 Rich. 48 (S.C. 1844); *Long v. Hicks,* 2 Humph. 305 (Tn. 1841); *White v. Hill,* 10 La. An. 189 (1855); *Fulenwider v. Poston,* 3 Jones 528 (N.C. 1856); *Parker v. Partlow,* 12 Rich. 679 (S.C. 1860).

62. Lester, *To Be a Slave,* 52.

63. *Bunch v. Smith,* 4 Rich. 581 (S.C. 1851); *Walker v. Hays,* 15 La. An. 640 (1860). The opinions in *Merrick v. Bradley,* 19 Md. 50 (1862), and *Thomason v. Dill,* 30 Ala. 444 (1857), also support the view that buyers had to pay when sold slaves committed suicide. In *Thomason,* the slave cried and begged the buyer to rescind the sale, as did the seller and the seller's wife. When the buyer refused, the slave hung himself. (The appellate court sent the case back for a new trial because the trial judge had given incorrect instructions.) Franklin, *From Slavery,* 131, noted the incidence of slave suicides. William Pierson, "White Cannibals, Black Martyrs: Fear, Depression and Religious Faith as Causes of Suicide Among New Slaves," in *Articles on American Slavery,* vol. 8, ed. Finkelman, 329, discussed the prevalence of slaves who committed suicide by drowning themselves. He speculated that slaves viewed death by water as a reversal of their original water passage from Africa to America.

64. Certainly, separations of mothers and children stirred up strong emotions. Former slave Lou Smith explained vividly why one slave mother killed her child: "[W]hen her babies would get about a year or two of age, (her master would) sell them and it would break her heart. . . . When her fourth baby was born and was about two months old, . . . she said, 'I just decided I'm not going to let ol' master sell this baby; he just ain't going to do it.' She got up and give it something out of a bottle and pretty soon it was dead." Lester, *To Be a Slave,* 40. Many scholars have examined the seeming prevalence of slave mothers who killed their own children; Todd L. Savitt, "Smothering and Overlaying of Virginia Slave Children: A Suggested Explanation," in *Articles on American Slavery,* vol. 11: *Women and the Family in a Slave Society,* ed. Finkelman, conjectured that most apparent murders were actually cases of sudden infant death syndrome.

65. *McCay v. Chambliss,* 12 La. An. 412 (1857); *Grant v. Bontz,* 10 F.C. 977 (D.C. 1819); *Stinson v. Piper,* 3 McC. 251, 253 (S.C. 1825); *Briant v. Marsh,* 19 La. 391, 392 (1840).

66. Samuel A. Cartwright, "Report of the Diseases and Physical Peculiarities of the Negro Race," *New Orleans Medical and Surgical Journal* 7 (1851).

67. Emancipation did not cause a breach of warranty for slaves warranted as "slaves for life." *Anderson v. Mills,* 28 Ark. 175 (1873); *Fitzpatrick v. Hearne,* 44 Ala. 171 (1870); *Porter v. Ralston,* 6 Bush 665 (Ky. 1869); *Thomas v. Porter,* 3 Bush 177 (Ky. 1868); *Bradford v. Jenkins,* 41 Ms. 328 (1867); *Walker v. Gatlin,* 12 Fla. 1 (1867); *Haslett v. Harris,* 36 Ga. 632

(1867). Nor did emancipation destroy an action against a slave vendor or vendee. *McNealy v. Gregory*, 13 Fl. 417 (1869-70–71); *Matthews v. Dunbar*, 3 W. Va. 138 (1869); *Riley v. Martin*, 35 Ga. 136 (1866); *Calhoun v. Burnett*, 40 Ms. 599 (1866). The emancipation at war's end did not penalize administrators of estates. Generally, administrators were not liable for refusing to sell slaves for Confederate currency or for failing to sell slaves before war's end. *Mickle v. Brown*, 4 Bax. 468 (Tn. 1874); *Womble v. George*, 64 N.C. 759 (1870); *State v. Hanner*, 64 N.C. 668 (1870); *Finger v. Finger*, 64 N.C. 183 (1870).

68. *Henderlite v. Thurman*, 22 Gratt. 466, 482 (Va. 1872); *McElvain v. Mudd*, 44 Ala. 48 (1870); *Dorris v. Grace*, 24 Ark. 326 (1866). *Blease v. Pratt*, 4 S.C. 513 (1872); *Kaufman v. Barb*, 26 Ark. 24 (1870); and *Fitzpatrick v. Hearne*, 44 Ala. 17 (1870), are similar cases. Only the relatively more protected Louisiana purchasers routinely avoided paying for slaves subsequently emancipated. Louisiana cases include *Satterfield v. Spurlock*, 21 La. An. 771 (1869), and *Sandidge v. Sanderson*, 21 La. An. 757 (1869). In a single Missouri case, the court refused to enforce a note given for slaves taken into Confederate states, saying: "Many slaves were taken to the states in insurrection . . . [to] enable the enemy to keep the field. To hold such intercourse as lawful, and enforce contracts made in prosecuting it, would suppose that government could sanction its own destruction. . . . The law tolerates no such absurdity." *Carson v. Hunter*, 46 Mo. 467, 472 (1870). Arkansas's 1868 constitution annulled slave sales retroactively, but an 1871 case made this provision unconstitutional. *Osborn v. Nicholas*, 13 Wall. 654 (U.S. 1871).

   The Emancipation Proclamation stated that all slaves in the states rebelling against the Union were to be free as of January 1, 1863. It did not apply to areas controlled by the Union army, nor to the border states. The proclamation was unenforceable in areas not controlled by the Union and, in fact, did not free the slaves in those areas, according to Southern courts. The end of the war or a clause in a revised state constitution typically conferred freedom in the Confederate states. Abolition in Texas did not occur officially until 1868. Catterall, *Judicial Cases*, various volumes.

69. *Haskill v. Sevier*, 25 Ark. 152, 157 (1867).

70. *Tidyman v. Rose*, Rich. Eq. 294, 301 (S.C. 1832); *Gayle v. Cunningham*, Harper Eq. 124, 129 (S.C. 1819). Louisiana, Georgia, and Alabama had statutes requiring joint sale of mothers and minor children. Hurst, *Forrest*, 41; Thomas D. Morris, "'Society Is Not Marked by Punctuality in the Payment of Debts': The Chattel Mortgages of Slaves," in *Ambivalent Legacy: A Legal History of the South*, ed. David J. Bodenhamer and James W. Ely (Jackson: University of Mississippi Press, 1984), esp. n. 59; Schafer, "Guaranteed."

71. Tadman, *Speculators*, esp. 144ff, noted that preserving slave families rarely concerned those who transacted in slaves – least of all, their sellers. In *Bertrand v. Arceuil*, 4 La. An. 430 (1849), Judge Slidell declared that related slaves would probably work more harmoniously together and therefore be more useful than unrelated ones. As a result,

buyers may have been willing to pay higher prices for a family of slaves. On the other hand, if a seller wished to keep a family of slaves together, he might have accepted a lower price than for unrelated slaves. *Pope v. Toombs*, 20 Ga. 762 (1856).

72. *Lawrence v. Speed*, 2 Bibb 401, 404 (Ky. 1811); *Cannon v. Jenkins*, 1 Dev. Eq. 426 (N.C. 1830). Also see *Fitzhugh v. Foote*, 3 Call 13 (Va. 1801).

73. *Clark v. Henry*, 9 Mo. 336, 344 (1845); *Williams v. Howard*, 3 Murph. 74, 80 (N.C. 1819).

74. I have already alluded to certain equitable remedies, such as rescission. In rescission cases, the plaintiff was put in the position he would have been in had no sale occurred. If the plaintiff had instead recovered appropriately calibrated damages, his position would have been the same as if the contract had been performed. As previously discussed, choosing between these two remedies entailed a tradeoff: deterrence on the one hand, flexibility plus compensation on the other. In the cases contained in this section, the motivating factor was to make the plaintiff whole by restoring his slave to his possession, rather than awarding inadequate money damages. As in rescission cases, an equitable remedy placed the plaintiff where he would have been had no sale (or seizure) occurred. Unlike rescission cases, however, a damage remedy corresponded to no alternative outcome because the plaintiff had not participated in the controversial transaction.

75. *Hinde v. Pendleton*, Wythe 354 (Va. 1791); *Heiligmann v. Rose*, 81 Tex. 222 (1891).

76. *Sarter v. Gordon*, 2 Hill Ch. 121 (S.C. 1835); *Horry v. Glover*, 2 Hill Ch. 515 (S.C. 1837); *Young v. Burton*, 1 McMul. Eq. 255 (S.C. 1841).

77. *Summers v. Bean*, 13 Gratt. 404 (Va. 1856). In an earlier Virginia case, the court decided that the plaintiff could obtain an injunction to stop the sale of a slave unlawfully executed on, even if the slave had no particular value. *Sims v. Harrison*, 4 Leigh 346 (Va. 1833). And under *Kelly v. Scott*, 5 Gratt. 479 (Va. 1848), the plaintiffs could seek a remedy in equity as long as the slave was not a complete stranger to the interested parties. Other Virginia cases considering equitable remedies in slave sale or debt cases include *Marshall v. Colvert*, 5 Leigh 146 (Va. 1834); *Allen v. Freeland*, 3 Rand. 170 (Va. 1825); *Bowyer v. Creigh*, 3 Rand. 25 (Va. 1825); *Scott v. Halliday*, 5 Munf. 103 (Va. 1816); and *Wilson v. Butler*, 3 Munf. 559 (Va. 1811). (The *Bowyer* court denied the use of equity because the plaintiff merely held a mortgage on, not title to, the slave.)

78. Mississippi courts were open to the use of equitable remedies. In *Farrar v. Gaillard*, Walk. 269 (Ms. 1827), the court allowed the defendant to refuse the delivery of substitute slaves of equivalent market value. Other cases include *Hill v. Clark*, 4 S. & M. 187 (Ms. 1850); *Sevier v. Ross*, Fr. Ch. 519 (Ms. 1843); *Murphy v. Clark*, 1 S. & M. 221 (Ms. 1843); and *McRea v. Walker*, 4 How. 455 (Ms. 1840). The Alabama court at first said that the plaintiff had to prove that a slave had particular value. *Baker v. Rowan*, 2 S. & P. 361 (Ala. 1830). Later, the state's courts tentatively accepted a wider use of equity, although they geared most equitable

remedies to family slaves. *Childress v. McCullough*, 5 Port. 54 (Ala. 1837); *Hardeman v. Sims*, 3 Ala. 747 (1842). North Carolina, Tennessee, and Missouri courts advocated equitable remedies in some slave sale cases as well. *Williams v. Howard*, 3 Murph. 74 (N.C. 1819); *Spendlove v. Spendlove*, Cam. & N. 36 (N.C. 1800); *Martin v. Fancher*, 2 Humph. 510 (Tn. 1841); *Loftin v. Espy*, 4 Yerg. 84 (Tn. 1833); *Mulford v. Anon.*, 2 Hayw. 431 (Tn. 1801); *Beaupied v. Jennings*, 28 Mo. 254 (1859).

79. A Kentucky plaintiff had to show that a slave had a particular nonpecuniary value under the ruling in *Caldwell v. Myers*, Hardin 560 (Ky. 1808). Equitable remedies were not allowed in *Watts v. Hunn*, 4 Litt. 267 (Ky. 1823), and *Williams v. Dorsey*, 4 Litt. 265 (Ky. 1823). The court in *Jones v. Bennet*, 9 Dana 333 (Ky. 1840), refused to consider equitable remedies if damages were feasible. Arkansas courts said that equity was not necessary for slaves sold as merchandise. *Sanders v. Sanders*, 20 Ark. 610 (1859). (But *Sanders* did overturn *Lovette v. Longmire*, 14 Ark. 339 (1854). *Lovette* had required a wife to seek damages in a court of law rather than relief at equity when a creditor seized the wife's slaves to satisfy her husband's debts.) Georgia courts expected slaves to have some peculiar value before allowing equity to prevail. *Hannahan v. Nichols*, 17 Ga. 77 (1855); *Dudley v. Mallery*, 4 Ga. 52 (1848).

80. *Dudley v. Mallery*, 4 Ga. 52, 65 (1848).

3. THE LAW OF HIRING AND EMPLOYMENT

1. For example, Robert Carter, one of the largest American slaveowners, rented out over two-thirds of his 509 slaves in 1791. Sarah S. Hughes, "Slaves for Hire: The Allocation of Black Labor in Elizabeth City County, Virginia, 1782 to 1810," in *Articles on American Slavery*, vol. 10: *Economics, Industrialization, Urbanization, and Slavery*, ed. Finkelman, 260, 265. Wright, *Old South*, 30, claimed that slave rental markets were well developed in manufacturing, construction, and mining, but not in agriculture. On the contrary, Randolph B. Campbell, "Slave Hiring in Texas," *American Historical Review* 93 (February 1988), said that farmers, like merchants and professionals, commonly hired slaves; he listed several sources. Clement Eaton, "Slave Hiring in the Upper South: A Step Toward Freedom," in *Articles on American Slavery*, vol. 7: *Southern Slavery at the State and Local Level*, ed. Finkelman, showed that slave hiring increased substantially in the last decade of the antebellum era, mostly in industry and domestic service, but also in agriculture in Virginia. Charles B. Dew, *Slavery in the Antebellum South Industries* (Bethesda: University Publications of America, 1991), and *Bond of Iron: Master and Slave at Buffalo Forge* (New York: Norton, 1994), noted that slaves frequently were hired on an annual basis. Using hired slaves gave nonslaveowners a stake in preserving slavery. Campbell found that 41 percent of slave employers in a Texas sample did not own slaves. Eaton (29) cited examples showing that owners sometimes hired slaves out to discipline or reform them and that employers often did not want the responsibility of owning slaves. For other discussions of slave hiring, see Robert S.

Starobin, *Industrial Slavery in the Old South* (New York: Oxford University Press, 1970), 128–37; Claudia D. Goldin, *Urban Slavery in the American South, 1820–1860* (Chicago: University of Chicago Press, 1976), 35–42; Conrad and Meyer, *Economics of Slavery*, 80; selections in Ira Berlin and Philip D. Morgan, eds., *The Slave's Economy: Independent Production by Slaves in the Americas* (London: Frank Cass, 1991); Larry E. Hudson, Jr., *Working Toward Freedom: Slave Society and Domestic Economy in the American South* (Rochester: University of Rochester Press, 1994); Steven F. Miller, "Plantation Labor Organization and Slave Life in the Cotton Frontier: The Alabama-Mississippi Black Belt, 1815–1840," in *Cultivation and Culture: Labor and Shaping of Slave Life in the Americas*, ed. Ira Berlin and Philip D. Morgan (Charlottesville: University Press of Virginia, 1993), 161; and John Campbell, "As a 'Kind of Freeman?': Slaves' Market-Related Activities in the South Carolina Up-Country, 1800–1860," in ibid.

2. Of the 10,989 cases, 535 involved disputes over hired slaves. Morris, *Southern Slavery*, chap. 6, reviewed some of these cases as well.

3. Peter Way, *Common Labour: Workers and the Digging of North American Canals, 1780–1860* (New York: Cambridge University Press, 1993), 110–12.

4. Stanley Lebergott, *Manpower in Economic Growth: The American Record since 1800* (New York: McGraw-Hill, 1964), tables A20, A23, A25–A29.

5. Price V. Fishback and Shawn E. Kantor, "'Square Deal' or Raw Deal? Market Compensation for Workplace Disamenities, 1884–1903," *Journal of Economic History* 52 (December 1992). Fishback's and Kantor's sample was drawn from Northern states.

6. Slave hiring was so prevalent at Richmond's Tredegar Iron Works, for example, that workers went out on their first strike in 1847 to protest the use of slave labor. Richard B. Morris, "The Measurement of Bondage in the Slave States," in *Articles on American Slavery*, vol. 7, ed. Finkelman, 145, 152; Patricia A. Schechter, "Free and Slave Labor in the Old South: The Tredegar Iron Workers Strike of 1847," *Labor History* 35 (Spring 1994).

7. See Ira Berlin and Herbert Gutman, "Natives and Immigrants, Free Men and Slaves: Urban Workingmen in the Antebellum American South," *American Historical Review* 88 (December 1983), for a review of findings. Also see Goldin, *Urban Slavery*, 37.

8. Dew, *Bond of Iron*, 109, and *Slavery*, found that the hourly rate for slave overwork was identical to that earned by free workers for the same job. Slaves typically had to supply a given weekly or daily output before they were eligible for overwork pay, however, so the daily wage taken home by slaves was relatively lower. But the employer also paid the slaveowner, so the total "wages" paid were the sum of the rent paid to masters and the overwork paid to slaves. Walter Licht, *Working on the Railroad: The Organization of Work in the Nineteenth Century* (Princeton: Princeton University Press, 1983), 67, indicated no difference in wages for slaves working on the railroad. Licht speculated that slaves may even have commanded higher wages because they were more reliable. Note that

these data correspond to industrial jobs; slaves and free workers likely did not have comparable jobs in agriculture because slaves could be forced to work in gangs.

9. Other types of slave disputes at times suggest slaves' and masters' interests did not coincide – slaves sometimes committed suicide to avoid being sold, for example, as Chapter 2 discussed. In theory, slaves faced with a distasteful employer or onerous tasks may similarly have chosen deliberate injury. Yet these situations did not seem to have occurred very often: Dew, *Bond of Iron* and *Slavery*, suggested that slaves often had considerable say over who employed them and what they did.

10. This was especially true for factory workers (as opposed to artisans), particularly during the unstable financial periods around 1837, the mid-1850s, 1873, and 1893. See Bruce Laurie, *Artisans into Workers: Labor in Nineteenth Century America* (New York: The Noonday Press, 1989); Thomas R. Brooks, *Toil and Trouble: A History of American Labor* (New York: Dell Publishing, 1971).

11. *Gunter v. Graniteville Mfg. Co.*, 15 S.C. 443 (1881). J. Willard Hurst and Morton Horwitz were instrumental in developing this theme of the pre-eminence of capital in the nineteenth century, as Chapter 1 discussed.

12. Richard A. Epstein, "The Historical Origins and Economic Structure of Workers' Compensation Law," *Georgia Law Review* 16 (Summer 1982); Posner, "A Theory of Negligence."

13. See Chapter 7.

14. Canal building is an example. See Way, *Common Labour*, 118.

15. Tomlins, *Law, Labor*, 320–82.

16. Shawn E. Kantor and Price V. Fishback, "Precautionary Saving, Insurance, and the Origins of Workers' Compensation," *Journal of Political Economy* 104 (April 1996): 427, found that the personal accident insurance business was very limited even in the early twentieth century.

17. I am indebted to Farley Grubb for this insight.

18. Slaveowners often brought actions charging employers with negligence in addition to contract breach. The next section discusses most of these cases.

19. *Hay v. Conner*, 2 Har. & J. 347 (Md. 1808); *Tyson v. Ewing*, 3 J.J. Marsh. 185 (Ky. 1830); *Alston v. Balls*, 12 Ark. 664, 669 (1852); *Knox v. R.R*, 6 Jones 415 (N.C. 1859); *Green v. Dibble*, 1 Jones 332 (N.C. 1854); *Bell v. Walker*, 5 Jones 43, 46 (S.C. 1857).

20. *Taylor v. Andrus*, 16 La. 14 (1840); *Deens v. Dunklin*, 33 Ala. 47 (1858); *Western v. Pollard*, 16 B. Mon. 315 (Ky. 1855); *Willis v. Harris*, 26 Tex. 141 (1861).

21. Oakes, *Ruling Race*, 174. Slave-hiring brokers' correspondence indicates that slavemasters frequently asked that their slaves not work in dangerous or laborious jobs. Eaton, *Slave Hiring*, 27.

22. *Mullen v. Ensley*, 8 Humph. 428 (Tn. 1847); *Harvey v. Skipwith*, 16 Gratt. 393 (Va. 1863). The *Harvey* court admitted evidence that slaves had complained about being used in blasting the year before. The defendant actually faced two lawsuits and paid two sets of damages: approximately half of Jefferson's value as reversionary interest to the

remainderman and the rest to the holder of the life estate. As discussed
later, free employees of the nineteenth century who routinely handled
dynamite typically recovered no damages for injuries.

23. *Wise v. Freshly*, 3 McC. 547 (S.C. 1826); *Seay v. Marks*, 23 Al. 532 (1853)
(sent back for more evaluation of the terms of the hiring contract);
Gorman v. Campbell, 14 Ga. 137 (1853); *Kelly v. Wallace*, 6 Fl. 690 (1856).
Kelly was later cited in *Peacock Motor Company v. Eubanks*, 145 So. 2d 498
(1962), as support for excusing a non-negligent garageman from liability for a burnt automobile.

24. *Clark v. R.R.*, 27 Tx. 100 (1863); *Dement v. Scott*, 2 Head 367 (Tn. 1859);
Kelly v. White, 17 B. Mon. 124 (Ky. 1856) (sent back for reevaluation of
the facts); *Rountree v. Steamboat Co.*, 8 La. An. 289 (1853); *Porée v.
Cannon*, 14 La. An. 501 (1859). Also see *Pridgen v. Buchannon*, 24 Tx.
655 (1860); and *Angus v. Dickerson*, Meigs 459 (Tn. 1839).

25. *Bell v. Bowen*, 1 Jones 316 (N.C. 1854); *Daughtry v. Boothe*, 4 Jones 87
(N.C. 1856); *Harvey v. Epes*, 12 Grat. 153 (Va. 1855) (an erroneous
instruction led to a new trial); *White v. Harmond*, 3 Sneed 322 (Tn.
1855). *Wallace v. Seales*, 36 Ms. 53 (1858), resembles *Harvey*.

26. Franklin, *From Slavery*, 109–10, noted that wage rates corresponded to
the type of work described in the hiring contract and reflected the skills
of the hired slave. Sale prices similarly reflected slaves' training and
capabilities. See Fogel, *Without Consent*, 70, and Chapter 2 of this book.

27. *Spencer v. Pilcher*, 8 Leigh 565, 574, 581 (Va. 1837).

28. *Murphy v. Kaufman*, 20 La. An. 559 (1868); *Fox v. Young*, 22 Mo. App.
386 (1886); *Kellar v. Garth*, 45 Mo. App. 332 (1891); *Cartlidge v. Sloan*,
124 Al. 596 (1899); *Evans v. Nail*, 1 Ga. App. 42 (1907) (citing slave
case *Columbus v. Howard*, 6 Ga. 213 (1849)); *Raines v. Rice*, 65 Ga. App.
68 (1941) (citing slave cases *Columbus v. Howard* and *Gorman v. Campbell*, 14 Ga. 137 (1853)); *De Voin v. Mich. Lumber Co.* 25 N.W. 552 (Wi.
1885). *Telephone Co. v. Potts*, 24 Ga. App. 178 (1920), is another Georgia
hiring case that relied upon a slave case as precedent. Also see *Har-
rington v. Snyder*, 3 Barb. 381 (N.Y. 1848).

29. *Farkas v. Powell*, 86 Ga. 800 (1891) (citing slave cases *Columbus v.
Howard*, 6 Ga. 213 (1849); *Gorman v. Campbell*, 14 Ga. 137 (1853); *Lewis
v. McAfee*, 32 Ga. 465 (1861); *Collins v. Hutchins*, 21 Ga. 270 (1857);
and *Kennedy v. Ashcraft*, 4 Bush 530 (Ky. 1868)). Also see *Carney v. Reese*,
60 W. Va. 676 (1906) (citing several slave cases); *Evertson v. Frier*, 45
S.W. 201 (1898) (citing slave case *Sims v. Chance*, 7 Tx. 561 (1852));
Malone v. Robinson, 77 Ga. 719 (1886) (citing slave case *Columbus v.
Howard*). See also the discussion of slave case *Duncan v. R.R.*, 2 Rich 613
(S.C. 1846) (at note 82). *Dicta* in *Farkas* suggested that, if the extra dis-
tance did not contribute to the animal's injury, the defendant should
not have to pay damages. This rule was cited approvingly in *Spencer v.
Shelburne*, 11 Tex. Civ. App. 521 (1895) (also citing slave cases *Sims v.
Chance* and *Mills v. Ashe*, 16 Tx. 295 (1856)). In an antebellum case, a
Louisiana defendant paid for a horse when he drove a hired gig beyond
the specified destination and killed the animal through exhaustion.
Guillot v. Armitage, 7 Mart. O.S. 710 (La. 1820).

30. *Austin v. Miller*, 74 N.C. 274 (1876). See also *Cochran v. Walker*, 49 S.W. 403 (1899) (citing slave case *Sims v. Chance*, 7 Tx. 561 (1852)); *Stewart v. Davis*, 31 Ark. 518 (1876); and Sir William Jones, *An Essay on the Law of Bailments* (London: C. Dilly, 1781), 120. Interestingly, the court in *Daugherty v. Reveal*, 54 Ind. App. 71 (1913), relied upon the slave case of *Spencer v. Pilcher*, 8 Leigh 565 (Va. 1837), to grant a directed verdict for the defendant. Here, a horse was not returned on time, but his injury occurred at a mutually agreed-upon place for safekeeping.

31. The fellow-servant rule excuses the employer from liability for injuries to a worker caused by the negligence of a fellow worker. It is based on two grounds: (1) employees know that fellow workers can be negligent and can request higher wages as compensation, and (2) employees have an incentive under the rule to be watchful of coworkers and careful of their own actions. *Corpus Juris Secundum* (St. Paul: West Publishing, 1994), vol. 56, sec. 321. The English case of *Priestley v. Fowler*, 3 Mees & W. 1 (1837), first suggested the rule; American courts soon followed in *Murray v. R.R.*, 1 McMul. 385 (S.C. 1841), and, in a better-known case, *Farwell v. Boston & W. R. Corp.*, 4 Metc. 49 (Mass. 1842). For discussion, see Finkin et al., *Legal Protection*, 364; Richard B. Morris, *Government and Labor in Early America* (New York: Columbia University Press, 1946). Epstein, "Historical Origins," 777, surmised that the dearth of employment cases before about 1840 in fact shows that the law of the early republic was even harsher than the law that followed. He argued that the appearance of defenses at least meant that nineteenth-century employees *could* sue under some circumstances.

32. Wood, *A Treatise*, 792.

33. See the discussion at note 13, Chapter 1.

34. *Clagett v. Speake*, 4 Har. & McH. 162 (Md. 1798); *Field v. Matson*, 8 Mo. 686 (1844) (described in *Cathcart v. Foulke*, 13 Mo. 561 (1850)); *Christy v. Price*, 7 Mo. 430 (1842) (reversed and remanded with a request for more information); *McDaniel v. Emanuel*, 2 Rich. 455, 457 (S.C. 1846).

35. *Cook v. Parham*, 24 Al. 21 (1853); *R.R. v. Jones*, 2 Head 517 (Tn. 1859); *R.R. v. Macon*, 8 Fla. 299 (1859); *Biles v. Holmes*, 11 Ired. 16, 21 (N.C. 1850); *Allison v. R.R.*, 64 N.C. 382 (1870). Ira Berlin and Philip D. Morgan, "Labor and the Shaping of Slave Life in the Americas," in *Cultivation and Culture*, ed. Berlin and Morgan, 4, reported that mining was one of the most dangerous jobs that hired slaves performed.

36. *Haden v. R.R.*, 8 Jones 362 (N.C. 1861); *R.R v. Kidd*, 7 Dana 245 (Ky. 1838). Philip may have been trying to escape. If so, his employer's refusal to oust him from the train had further benefited Philip's master – at least *ex ante* – by reducing the chances of escape. One might inquire, of course, whether the conductor had adequately supervised Philip on the return journey.

37. *Moran v. Davis*, 18 Ga. 722 (1855); *Nelson v. Bondurant*, 26 Ala. 341 (1855); *Lunsford v. Baynham*, 10 Humph. 267, 269 (Tn. 1849); *Sparkman v. Daughtry*, 13 Ired. 168 (N.C. 1851); *Hume v. Scott*, 3 A.K. Marsh. 260 (Ky. 1821). Employers also needed authority to direct slaves, as courts acknowledged. A Kentucky court decided that an employer, like

an owner, could grant a slave permission to take a ferry across the Ohio River. The employer paid the price, however – if the slave was lost, the employer (not the ferryman) was responsible to the slaveowner. *Moore v. Foster*, 10 B. Mon. 255 (Ky. 1850). Kentucky claimed the entire Ohio River within her borders under the cession agreement from Virginia; the Kentucky court therefore had jurisdiction in *Moore* because the slave was officially inside the state of Kentucky for the entire trip. Indiana acceded to this in the nineteenth century, although Ohio and Illinois did not until 1980 and 1991, respectively. *Indiana v. Kentucky*, 136 U.S. 479 (1889); *Ohio v. Kentucky*, 444 U.S. 335 (1980); and *Illinois v. Kentucky*, 500 U.S. 380 (1991). In each, the court determined that Kentucky's borders extended to the line of the 1792 low-water mark.

38. *Callihan v. Johnson*, 22 Tx. 596 (1858); *Hall v. Goodson*, 32 Al. 277 (1858); *James v. Carper*, 4 Sneed 397 (Tn. 1857); *Mann v. Trabue*, 1 Mo. 709 (1827). When an employer killed a slave, his surety was responsible for the slave's value in *Carney v. Walden*, 16 B. Mon. 388 (Ky. 1855). To complicate things, surety Carney had sold his property to Pettit to avoid paying for the slave. Because Pettit knew about the lawsuit, he lost out as well. See also *Helton v. Caston*, 2 Bail. 95 (S.C. 1831).

39. *Craig v. Lee*, 14 B. Mon. 119 (Ky. 1853); *Jones v. Glass*, 13 Ired. 305 (N.C. 1852); *Harris v. Nicholas*, 5 Munf. 483 (Va. 1817).

40. *Comw. v. Booth*, 2 Va. Ca. 394 (1824); *State v. Mann*, 2 Dev. 263, 266 (N.C. 1829). An earlier North Carolina case had found that killing a resisting slave was justifiable homicide on the part of the employer. *State v. Weaver*, 2 Hayw. 54 (N.C. 1798).

41. See *dicta* in *James v. Carper*, 4 Sneed 397 (Tn. 1857), for example. Also see *Hickerson v. U.S.*, 2 Hayw. and H. 228 (D.C. 1856), and *State v. Hale*, 2 Hawks 582 (N.C. 1823).

42. *Scott v. Bartleman*, 21 F.C. 813 (D.C. 1822); *Rasco v. Willis*, 5 Al. 38, 40 (1843) (an appellate court ordered a new trial because further proof was needed to connect the slave in question with the defendant's unlawful acts).

43. Courts referred to these practices in numerous cases (for example, *Gibson v. Andrews*, 3 Al. 66 (1841)). Employers paid the full hire rate for sick slaves, unless the slave was sick from causes clearly present at the time of hiring. *Corley v. Cleckly*, Dud. 35 (S.C. 1837); *Antonio v. Clissey*, 3 Rich. 201 (S.C. 1832). An employer paid full hire for a disabled slave in *Outlaw v. Cook*, Minor 257 (Ala. 1824). Employers also bore responsibility for doctor bills for a sick slave, according to *Foster v. Sykes*, 23 Al. 796 (1853); *dicta* in *Latimer v. Alexander*, 14 Ga. 259 (1853); *Magee v. Currie*, 4 Tx. 187 (1849); *Meeker v. Childress*, Minor 109 (Al. 1823); *Grundy v. Jackson*, 1 Litt. 64 (Ky. 1822); and *Redding v. Hall*, 1 Bibb 536 (Ky. 1809). One Virginia employer even had to pay full wages although the slave was emancipated partway through the term. As the court put it: "It was doubtless not contemplated by either party that property in slaves was in any immediate danger of the complete annihilation which afterwards happened to it; but still that was one of the risks which the [employer] encountered." *Scott v. Scott*, 18 Grat. 150, 181 (Va. 1868).

Employers paid wages for days worked but not the value of slaves who died (without the negligence of the employer) in *Collins v. Woodruff*, 9 Ark. 463 (1849); *Dudgeon v. Teass*, 9 Mo. 867 (1846); *Bacot v. Parnell*, 2 Bail. 424 (S.C. 1831); *Prewitt v. Singleton*, 3 J.J. Marsh. 707 (Ky. 1830); *Williams v. Holcombe*, 1 Car. L.R. 365 (1814); and *George v. Elliott*, 2 Hen. & M. 5 (Va. 1806). Franklin, *From Slavery*, 109, and Morris, *Southern Slavery*, 136ff, discussed the general rules on hiring, and Tushnet, *American Law*, 171, referred to the practice of employers paying medical bills. Goodell, *American Slave Code*, part 1, p. 149, noted that the common-law rule was to give medical aid if the interest of the owner demanded it. In all cases, of course, parties could expressly agree to other rules. Interestingly, numerous subsequent Arkansas cases have applied the apportionment rules described in *Collins v. Woodruff*, the latest being *Mullen v. Wafer*, 252 Ark. 541 (1972).

44. Like employers, mortgagees had duties to clothe and feed slaves and to prevent cruelties that might cause slaves to run away. *Overton v. Bigelow*, 1 Yerg. 48 (Tn. 1836). Mortgagees paid doctor bills for slaves in their possession. *Woodard v. Fitzpatrick*, 2 B. Mon. 61 (Ky. 1841). In *Shannon v. Speers*, 2 A.K. Marsh. 31 (Ky. 1820), an ill slave died while being used as collateral, but the mortgagee did not have to pay for the slave's value. The rule seems to have misapplied in *Hart v. Burton*, 7 J.J. Marsh. 322 (Ky. 1832). Here, Burton borrowed money from Hart, using his slave as collateral. The two agreed that Hart would keep the slave if Burton did not pay up by Feb. 20, 1827. Burton did not pay. The slave died in April. Hart wanted his money back and the jury awarded it. Justice Underwood logically dissented, saying that one should not be able to return a dead slave for cash when one had agreed not to return a live one for cash.

45. *Redding v. Hall*, 1 Bibb 536, 541 (Ky. 1809).

46. *Lennard v. Boynton*, 11 Ga. 109, 112 (1852); *Latimer v. Alexander*, 14 Ga. 259 (1853). For a discussion of *Lennard* and the Cobb statutes, see David J. Langum, "The Role of Intellect and Fortuity in Legal Change: An Incident from the Law of Slavery, "*American Journal of Legal History* 28 (January 1984).

47. *Harrison v. Murrell*, 5 T.B. Mon. 359 (Ky. 1827); *Ricks v. Dillahunty*, 8 Port. 133 (Al. 1838). For an analysis of slave sale cases, see Chapter 2.

48. The employer bore the hire rate plus the costs of recapture for an escaped white slave in *Ewing v. Gist*, 2 B. Mon. 465 (Ky. 1842). But an owner had to pay the county for slaves who were committed to the workhouse after running away from their employer. *White v. Arnold*, 6 Rich. 138 (S.C. 1853). Employers were not responsible for the value of runaways in *Woodhouse v. McRae*, 5 Jones 1 (N.C. 1857); *Ellett v. Bobb*, 6 Mo. 323 (1840); and *Graham v. Swearingen*, 9 Yerg. 276 (Tn. 1836). In *Woodhouse*, the employer had let the slave go visit his sick master, who had asked for the slave. The slave apparently escaped across the Albemarle Sound.

49. See, for example, *Alston v. Balls*, 12 Ark. 664 (1852). Wheeler, *Practical Treatise*, reported that the typical promise to return a slave at the end

of the hiring term was discharged if a slave died or ran away. Employers were therefore not responsible for returning runaway slaves in *Perkins v. Reed*, 8 Mo. 33 (1843), and *Singleton v. Carroll*, 6 J.J. Marsh. 527 (Ky. 1831).

50. *Singleton v. Carroll*, 6 J. J. Marsh. 527, 531 (Ky. 1831).

51. *M'Gowen v. Chapen*, 2 Murph. 61 (N.C. 1811); *Strawbridge v. Turner*, 8 La. 537 (1836), 9 La. 213 (1836); *Goldenbow v. Wright*, 13 La. 371 (1839); *Kings v. Shanks*, 12 B. Mon. 410 (Ky. 1851); *Collier v. Lyons*, 18 Ga. 648 (1855); *Johnson v. Steamboat Arabia*, 24 Mo. 86 (1856); *Jones v. Fort*, 36 Al. 449 (1860). For similar rulings, see *Barry v. Kimball*, 10 La. An. 787 (1855) (overturned in 1857 when formerly excluded witnesses were allowed to testify); *Knight v. Knotts*, 8 Rich. 35 (S.C. 1854); and *Garneau v. Herthel*, 15 Mo. 191 (1851). Not only were employers encouraged to make contracts, they also had to transact with the proper party or face the prospect of paying damages. In an 1852 Texas case, a drunken husband hired out his wife's slave against her wishes. When the slave died, the jury granted full hire to the wife. The appellate court indicated that she should also recover the slave's value if the husband had actually sold the slave. *Porter v. Miller*, 7 Tx. 468 (1852).

52. *Duncan v. Hawks*, 18 La. 548 (1841). Also see *Buel v. Steamer*, 17 La. 541 (1841), and *McMaster v. Beckwith*, 2 La. 329 (1830).

53. Jones, *Essay*, 88, 119–20, cited the rule that an employer needs to use the same degree of diligence that all prudent men use in keeping their own goods. He gave an example: If an employer leaves his stable door open and a horse is stolen, the employer must answer for the loss. Yet if the employer is robbed of the horse by highwaymen, he is not responsible unless he imprudently took an unusual route or traveled at an unusual time. The 1858 case of *Swann v. Brown*, 51 N.C. 150 (1858), relied on *dicta* in slave case *Heathcock v. Pennington*, 11 Ired. 640 (N.C. 1850), to hold a stable owner liable for the value of an escaped horse. The owner had let a client retrieve his own horses; the client had apparently let the plaintiff's horse loose as well.

54. See *Marshall v. Bingle*, 36 Mo. App. 122 (1889) (plaintiff received damages of $250 for a dead horse); *West v. Blackshear*, 20 Fl. 457 (1884) (plaintiff recovered value of runaway horse); *Hawkins v. Haynes*, 71 Ga. 40 (1883) (plaintiff recovered damages of $185.62 for a dead horse). No proof meant no damages. See *Fortune v. Harris*, 6 Jones 532 (N.C. 1859); *White v. Edgman*, 1 Overt. 19 (Tn. 1804).

55. *McNeills v. Brooks*, 1 Yerg. 73 (Tn. 1822).

56. *Rowland v. Jones*, 73 N.C. 52 (1875); *Johnson v. Ruth*, 34 Mo. App. 659 (1889).

57. *Buis v. Cook*, 60 Mo. 391 (1875); *Thompson v. Harlow*, 31 Ga. 348 (1860).

58. *Schroeder v. Faures*, 49 Mo. App. 470 (1892); *Cecil v. Preuch*, 4 Mart. N.S. 256 (La. 1826). For other cases, see *Reddick v. Newburn*, 76 Mo. 423 (1882); *McCarthy v. Wolfe*, 40 Mo. 520 (1867); *Goodfellow v. Meegan*, 32 Mo. 280 (1862); *Winston v. Taylor*, 28 Mo. 82 (1859); and *Rey v. Toney*, 24 Mo. 600 (1857). Chapter 4 discusses fencing laws in detail.

59. *Carrier v. Dorrance*, 19 S.C. 30 (1883).

60. Tomlins, *Law, Labor,* cited several Northern cases that illustrate this as well. Both Tomlins and Steinfeld, *Invention,* demonstrated that nineteenth-century workers had largely won the right to be free of corporal punishment administered by employers. See Chapter 7 of this book.

61. *Arkadelphia Lumber Co. v. Bethea,* 57 Ark. 76 (1892); *Steinhauser v. Spraul,* 127 Mo. 511 (1895) (citing *Blanton v. Dold,* 101 Mo. 64 (1891)); *R.R. v. Banks,* 104 Ala. 508 (1894); *Hendricks v. R.R.,* 52 Ga. 467 (1874); *R.R. v. Sampson,* 97 Ky. 65 (1895); *Reinder's Adm'r v. Coal Co.* 13 S.W. 719 (Ky. 1890). Tomlins, *Law, Labor,* 321, remarked on the commonness of brakemen's injuries because of insufficient clearance under railroad bridges. Even if raising bridges had been costly, railroad companies could have used other relatively cheap methods of helping workers avoid injury. In Minnesota, for example, railroads used devices known as "tell-tales" to warn brakemen of an upcoming bridge. Tell-tales were frames hung with long ropes that dangled above the tracks; they were designed to brush the brakeman without touching the train.

62. *McMillan v. Union Press Brick Works,* 6 Mo. App. 434 (1879); *R. Co. v. Kindred,* 57 Tx. 491 (1882); *Larson v. Berquist,* 34 Kan. 334 (1885). A defendant's demurrer essentially said that the plaintiff had no legal grounds or standing to bring a case.

63. *Deweese v. Meramec Iron Min. Co.,* 54 Mo. App. 476 (1893) (plaintiff recovered $2,500 for injured back and hip); *Durant v. Lex. Coal Min. Co.,* 97 Mo. 62 (1888) (plaintiff recovered damages for fractured leg). The statute appears in the Acts of 1881, 165. *Biles v. Holmes,* 11 Ired. 16 (N.C. 1850), is discussed in the text at note 35.

64. *Britt v. R.R.,* 144 N.C. 242 (1907) (citing *Allison v. R.R.,* 64 N.C. 382 (1870)); *Bush v. R.R.,* 63 P. 500 (Wash. 1900) (citing *Allison*). Also see *McGhee v. R.R.,* 147 N.C. 142 (1908).

65. *Brodeur v. Valley Falls Co.* 16 R.I. 448 (1889). Also see *Mire v. R.R.,* 42 La. An. 385 (1890); *R.R. v. McDaniel,* 12 Lea 386 (Tn. 1883); *Hanrathy v. R.R.,* 46 Md. 280 (1877); and *Evans v. R.R.,* 62 Mo. 49 (1876).

66. *Walker v. Spullock,* 23 Ga. 436 (1857). The Georgia legislature responded to the *Walker* case by passing the Act of 1863, which applied the statute to the W.& A. Railroad. The first case in which the court considered the W. & A. Railroad as potentially liable was *Cannon v. Rowland,* 34 Ga. 422 (1866). The cracks in sovereign immunity are mostly creatures of the twentieth century, as Chapter 5 discusses. Interestingly, the few antebellum Southern cases that made municipalities liable involved damages to slave property.

67. Slave cases rejecting the fellow-servant rule include *Howes v. Red Chief Steamer,* 15 La. An. 321 (1860); *White v. Smith,* 12 Rich. 595 (S.C. 1860); *R.R. v. Yandell,* 17 B. Mon. 586 (Ky. 1856); *Forsyth v. Perry,* 5 Fl. 337 (Fl. 1853); and *Scudder v. Woodbridge,* 1 Ga. 195 (1846). *Dicta* in *Murray v. R.R.,* 1 McMul. 385 (S.C. 1841), also rejected the rule for slaves. Finkelman, "Slaves as Fellow Servants," offered a detailed, state-by-state analysis of cases. Also see Tushnet, *American Law,* 45–50, and Morris, *Southern Slavery,* 148.

68. Ruffin's reasoning appears in *Ponton v. R.R.*, 6 Jones 245 (N.C. 1858).
69. Schwartz, "The Character," n. 362, surmised as well that the fellow-servant rule should probably have been rejected.
70. *Scudder v. Woodbridge*, 1 Ga. 195 (1846); *Shields v. Yonge*, 15 Ga. 349 (1854).
71. *Cannon v. Rowland*, 34 Ga. 422 (1866); *Cooper v. Mullins*, 30 Ga. 146 (1860). (Nonrailroad employers could still use the defense as late as 1881. *Crusselle v. Pugh*, 67 Ga. 430 (1881).) A Kentucky court later decided similarly in *R.R. v. Lowe*, 118 Ky. 260 (1904), following the slave case of *R.R. v. Yandell*, 17 B. Mon. 586 (1856). Under the Revised Code of 1855, Missouri sometimes allowed an action against an employer if a fellow servant caused an injury. *Schultz v. R.R.*, 36 Mo. 13 (1865). Civil War Kentucky and Tennessee appellate courts also entertained the possibility that the fellow-servant rule might not apply if the injuring employee had supervised the victim. *R.R. v. Collins*, 2 Duv. 114 (Ky. 1865); *Haynes v. R.R.*, 3 Colw. 222 (Tn. 1860); *Wasburn v. R.R.*, 3 Head 638 (Tn. 1859). Yet an 1869 Kentucky court decided that an injured engineer might not be able to recover damages for injuries caused when his train derailed after hitting a tree lying across the tracks. *R.R. v. Filburn*, 6 Bush 574 (Ky. 1869). Why? Because the man responsible for the fallen tree also worked for the railroad: He was a fellow servant. Despite the engineer's inability to influence his coworker, he probably was not entitled to damages.
72. *R. Co. v. Strong*, 52 Ga. 461 (1874). In another Georgia case, a court decided that the statute making a company liable for criminal or voluntary negligence did not apply in a situation where a fellow servant committed homicide. *McDonald v. Mfg. Co.*, 68 Ga. 839 (1882).
73. *R.R. v. Bishop*, 50 Ga. 465 (1874). A Missouri court decided the same. *Gibson v. R.R.*, 46 Mo. 163 (1870). See also *R.R. v. Sampson*, 97 Ky. 65 (1895).
74. *Augusta Factory v. Barnes*, 72 Ga. 217, 228 (1884). Also see *Southern Agricultural Works v. Franklin*, 111 Ga. 319 (1900).
75. *Walker v. Bolling*, 22 Al. 294 (1853).
76. See, for example, *R.R. v. Vail*, 142 Ala. 134 (1904).
77. See *Tyson v. R.R.*, 61 Ala. 554 (1878) (citing *Cook v. Parham*, 24 Ala. 21 (1853)); *Britt v. R.R.*, 144 N.C. 242 (1907) (citing *Allison v. R.R.*, 64 N.C. 382 (1870)); *Mason v. Ry. Co.*, 16 S.E. 703 (N.C. 1892) (citing *R.R. v. Jones*, 2 Head 517 (Tn. 1859)). See Tomlins, *Law, Labor*, for Northern cases.
78. The United States Supreme Court during this time was at its most active in invalidating state statutes that regulated the terms and conditions of employment. These statutes included minimum wage and maximum hours provisions, as well as laws prohibiting yellow-dog contracts (contracts that required workers to refrain from union membership as a condition of employment). The court viewed these statutes as interference with private economic transactions rather than measures designed to improve the lot of relatively powerless individual workers. See Laurence H. Tribe, *American Constitutional Law* (Mineola, NY: Foundation Press,

1978), 417–47; John E. Nowak, Ronald D. Rotunda, and J. Nelson Young, *Constitutional Law* (St. Paul: West Publishing, 1986), 323–58.

79. Insurance companies, like slaveowners, built in risk premiums. Companies charged higher life insurance premiums for slaves working in the deep South or in industries like transportation, mining, and construction. Both owners and employers took out policies; companies wrote only short-term policies, typically for less than the full value of the slave. Instead of escalating premiums for hazardous work, companies sometimes restricted the place or nature of employment. Most contracts limited the slave's movement outside the state. Todd L. Savitt, "Slave Life Insurance in Virginia and North Carolina," in *Articles on American Slavery*, vol. 11, ed. Finkelman, discussed life insurance policies for slaves. Slaveowner disputes with insurance companies, like disputes with employers, centered around the danger of slave jobs. Here, however, the moral hazard problem lay with the slaveowner. In one case, an insurance company tried to avoid paying out the proceeds of a life insurance policy on a slave who had drowned after falling off a plank that stretched from a steamboat to the shore. The slave had been working in a tobacco warehouse; the policy stated that the company would not cover more dangerous employment. Although the slave was being sent to work on a sugar plantation (which was considered more hazardous work), he had not yet changed jobs. The company therefore had to pay up. *Summers v. Ins. Co.*, 13 La. An. 504 (1858).

80. *Randolph v. Hill*, 7 Leigh 383 (Va. 1836); *Rice v. Cade*, 10 La. 288 (1836); *Mills v. Ashe*, 16 Tex. 295 (1856); *Pridgen v. Buchannon*, 24 Tx. 655 (1860). *Crutcher v. R.R.*, 38 Ala. 579 (1863), raised similar issues.

81. *Williams v. Taylor*, 4 Port. 234 (Ala. 1836); *Horsely v. Branch*, 1 Humph. 199 (Tn. 1839); *Dowty v. Templeton*, 9 La. An. 549 (1854); *Rice v. Cade*, 10 La. 288 (1836); *Morgan's Syndics v. Fiveash*, 7 Mart. N.S. 410 (La. 1829). Louisiana and Maryland courts tended to be more relaxed than others about self-hiring, as Chapter 7 discusses.

82. *Myers v. Gilbert*, 18 Al. 467 (1850); *Duncan v. R.R.*, 2 Rich. 613 (S.C. 1846); *Perry v. Beardslee*, 10 Mo. 568, 574 (1847) (although the plaintiff won at trial, an appellate court reversed the verdict, spelling out the plaintiff's duty in the opinion); *Meekin v. Thomas*, 17 B. Mon. 710, 713 (Ky. 1856); *Beverley v. Capt.*, 15 La. An. 432 (1860). *Duncan* differs from *R.R. v. Kidd* (discussed at note 36) because slave Wesley in *Duncan* had been visible to the conductor at all times, whereas slave Philip in *Kidd* had been discovered en route. *Beverley*, *Myers*, and *Duncan* contrast with *Jones v. Fort* (discussed at note 51): In *Jones*, customs were held to be unimportant in determining expectations. One could argue that these cases differ from *Jones* because they involved customs pertaining specifically to the contract itself. In more recent (and more famous) cases, courts have held that custom was not a viable defense for ophthalmologists and tugboat owners. *Helling v. Carey*, 84 Wash. 2d 514 (1974); *The T.J. Hooper*, 6 F. 2d 737 (2d Cir. 1932).

83. *Sims v. Chance*, 7 Tx. 561, 564, 571 (1852); *Collins v. Woodruff*, 9 Ark. 463 (1849); *R.R. v. Nash*, 12 Fl. 497, 515 (1868). The *Sims* jury never-

theless found for the plaintiff because it determined that the slave had been doing a job other than the one specified in the contract. Although the chief justice of the appellate court disagreed with the jury's finding, he did not find enough reason to overturn the verdict.

84. *Couch v. Jones,* 4 Jones 402, 408 (N.C. 1857); *George v. Smith,* 6 Jones 273 (N.C. 1859); *Slocumb v. Washington,* 6 Jones 357, 360 (N.C. 1859); *Madre v. Saunders,* 3 Jones 1, 3 (N.C. 1855); *Heathcock v. Pennington,* 11 Ired. 640, 643 (N.C. 1850). Although certain facts are similar, *Madre* differs from *Kings v. Shanks,* 12 B. Mon. 410 (Ky. 1851) (discussed at note 51). In *Kings,* the defendant had employed the slave without his master's consent. In *Madre,* defendant Saunders had explicitly hired Davy from his owner; Davy drowned while riding a Mr. Richardson's horse without Saunders's permission or knowledge. Under the reasoning in *Kings,* Madre might plausibly have had a case against Richardson.

85. *McLauchlin v. Lomas,* 3 Strob. 85, 89 (S.C. 1848). Justices Richardson and O'Neall dissented, saying that ordering the slave to work with the new saw was not part of the usual trade or usage of hired slave carpenters. This opinion raises interesting questions about Southern attitudes toward technological advances and their compatibility with slavery.

86. *Swigert v. Graham,* 7 B. Mon. 661 (Ky. 1847); *Horlbeck v. Erickson,* 6 Rich. 154 (S.C. 1853).

87. *Ry. Co. v. Eubanks,* 3 S.W. 808 (Ark. 1887); *R.R. v. McDade,* 59 Ga. 73 (1877); *R. Co. v. State,* 75 Md. 152 (1892); *Birm. Furnace v. Gross,* 97 Al. 220 (1893); *Sexton v. Turner,* 89 Va. 341 (1892); *Wilson v. R.R.,* 18 S.W. 638 (Ky. 1892). Also see *Ray v. Jeffries,* 86 Ky. 367 (1887).

88. Workers subsequently employed by these defendants may have requested higher wages; I have no data to confirm or deny this.

89. *Texas v. Denny,* 5 Tex. Civ. App. 359 (1893); *Ct. R. and Bkg. Co. v. Chapman,* 96 Ga. 769 (1895); *R.R. v. Huffman,* 83 Tx. 286 (1892); *Gunter v. Graniteville Manufacturing Company,* 15 S.C. 443 (1881); *Worheide v. Mo. Car and Foundry,* 32 Mo. App. 367 (1888).

90. *R.R. v. Lucado,* 86 Va. 390 (1889); *R.R. v. Morgart,* 8 S.W. 179 (Ark. 1888). Other cases include *Beard v. Am. Car Co.,* 63 Mo. App. 382 (1896); *R.R. v. Mara,* 16 S.W. 196 (Tx. 1891); *Muirhead v. R.R.,* 19 Mo. App. 634 (1885); *Bradley v. R.R.,* 14 Leas 374 (Tn. 1884); and *R.R. v. Thomas,* 51 Ms. 637 (1875).

91. *O'Brien v. Western Steel Co.,* 100 Mo. 182 (1889); *Daly v. Haller,* 48 La. An. 214 (1896).

92. *Haynie v. Power Co.,* 157 N.C. 503 (1911) (citing *Slocumb v. Washington,* 6 Jones 357 (N.C. 1859)).

93. See, for example, *Ry. Co. v. Piggott,* 116 S.W. 841 (Tx. 1909); *Johnston v. Fargo,* 77 N.E. 388 (Ct. App. N.Y. 1906); and *R.R. v. Carroll,* 53 Tn. 360 (1871). Many other conflicts also relied on *R.R. v. Jones,* 2 Head 517 (Tn. 1859), including those with such diverse plaintiffs as car owners, small-business owners, drag racers, cotton owners, and the parents of retarded children training for the Special Olympics.

94. *Price v. R. Co.* 33 S.C. 556 (1890).

95. People disagree as to whether workers' compensation actually improved the lot of laborers. See, for instance, Price V. Fishback and Shawn E. Kantor, "Did Workers Pay for the Passage of Workers' Compensation Laws?," *Quarterly Journal of Economics* 110 (August 1995). Employee plaintiffs have sometimes cited slave cases in efforts to invalidate workers' compensation statutes and to win legal damages for on-the-job injuries. See, for example, *Kaylor v. Magill*, 181 F.2d 181 (Tn. 1950) (citing *R.R. v. Jones*).

96. *Essay*, 2. I refer to the law of bailments in Chapter 1, note 15.

4. THE LAW REGARDING COMMON CARRIERS

1. *Historical Statistics of the United States, 1789–1945* (Washington, DC: Bureau of the Census, 1975), 220.

2. *England v. Gripon*, 15 La. An. 304 (1860). Also see *Lobdell v. Bullitt*, 13 La. 348 (1839).

3. *Hunter v. Ins. Co.*, 11 La. An. 139, 140 (1856). The general average contribution is the payment made by all parties to a sea adventure to make good a loss sustained by one of them on account of sacrifices made of part of the ship to save other people's lives from peril, or for extraordinary expenses incurred for the general benefit of all.

4. *Boyce v. Anderson*, 2 Pet. 150 (U.S. 1829). No explicit contract existed in this case, but the implicit contract can be analyzed in much the same way.

5. *Scruggs v. Davis*, 5 Sneed 262 (Tn. 1857), 3 Head 664 (Tn. 1859).

6. *Clark v. McDonald*, 4 McC. 223, 225 (S.C. 1827).

7. *McClenaghan v. Brock*, 5 Rich. 17 (S.C. 1851) (the court held that Richard's owner might have a case against the mulatto boat hand); *Grigsby v. Chappell*, 5 Rich. 219 (S.C. 1852) (the court held as well that a toll bridge was not a common carrier); *Pelham v. Messenger*, 16 La. An. 99 (1861). *Downey v. Stacy*, 1 La. An. 426 (1846), resembled *Pelham*.

8. *R.R. v. Holt*, 8 Ga. 157 (1850). Jacob was carrying a written pass, but it was intended only to protect him from being whipped. I discuss these sorts of passes later in the chapter.

9. *Brousseau v. Hudson*, 11 La. An. 427 (1856); *Purcell v. Southern Exp. Co.*, 34 Ga. 315 (1866). Also see *Jones v. Pitcher*, 3 S. & P. 135 (Al. 1832).

10. See, for example, *Fish v. Chapman*, 2 Kelly 349 (Ga. 1847); *Ewart v. Street*, 2 Bail. 157 (S.C. 1831); *Campbell v. Morse*, Harp. 468 (S.C. 1824); and *Craig v. Childress*, Peck 270 (Tn. 1823).

11. See *Fergusson v. Brent*, 12 Md. 9 (1857); and *Turney v. Wilson*, 7 Yerg. 340 (Tn. 1835).

12. *Chevallier v. Straham*, 2 Tex. 15 (1847); *Merchants Dispatch Co. v. Smith*, 76 Ill. 542 (1875).

13. *Goldey v. R. Co.*, 6 Casey 242 (Pa. 1858); *Charleston & C. Steamboat Co. v. Basin*, Harp. 262 (S.C. 1824).

14. *Southern Exp. Co. v. Womack*, 1 Heisk. 256 (Tn. 1870); *Sawyer v. R.R.*, 37 Mo. 240 (1866); *Bland v. Adams Exp. Co.*, 1 Duv. 232 (Ky. 1864); *Pat-*

terson v. R. Co., 64 N.C. 147 (1870); *R. Co. v. Estes*, 7 Heisk. 622 (Tn. 1872), 10 Lea 749 (Tn. 1882).

15. See, for example, *R.R. v. Scruggs*, 69 Miss. 418 (1891); *R.R. v. Bigger*, 66 Miss. 319 (1889); *Baker v. R. Co.*, 10 Lea 304 (Tn. 1882); and *Hall v. Renfro*, 3 Metc. 51 (Ky. 1860).

16. See, for instance, *Douglass v. R. Co.*, 53 Mo. App. 473 (1893), and *Peters v. R. Co.*, 16 La. An. 222 (1861).

17. *Porterfield v. Humphreys*, 8 Humph. 497 (Tn. 1847).

18. See, for example, *R.R. v. Beatie*, 66 Ga. 438 (1881), and *Singleton v. Hilliard*, 1 Strob. 203 (S.C. 1847).

19. *Flinn v. R.R.*, 1 Houst. 469 (Del. 1857).

20. *Wright v. R.R.*, 34 Ga. 330 (1866); *Sawyer v. R.R.*, 37 Mo. 240 (1866); *R. Co. v. Johnson*, 38 Ga. 409 (1869).

21. *R.R. v. Sucking*, 5 Bush 1 (Ky. 1868). No damages were awarded to passengers under similar facts in *R.R. v. Jacoby*, 14 Ky. L. Rep. 763 (1893); *R.R. v. Scott*, 88 Va. 958 (1892); *Faire v. R.R.*, 91 Ky. 541 (1891); *R.R. v. Underwood*, 90 Ala. 49 (1890); *Dun v. R.R.*, 78 Va. 645 (1884); *Blodgett v. Bartlett*, 50 Ga. 353 (1874); *R.R. v. Woodward*, 36 Md. 268 (1874); *R.R. v. Andrews*, 39 Md. 329 (1873); and *Huelsenkamp v. R.R.*, 34 Mo. 45 (1864), 37 Mo. 537 (1866). Passengers might obtain damages, however, under the reasoning in *R.R. v. Danshank*, 6 Tex. Civ. App. 385 (1894); *Summers v. R.R.*, 34 La. Ann. 139 (1882); *Miller v. R.R.*, 5 Mo. App. 471 (1878); and *Winters v. R. Co.*, 39 Mo. 468 (1867). A South Carolina court left the question to the jury. *Quinn v. R.R.*, 29 S.C. 381 (1888).

22. *R.R. v. Young*, 51 Ga. 489 (1874); *Damont v. R.R.*, 9 La. An. 441 (1854); *R.R. v. Stratham*, 42 Ms. 607 (1869).

23. *Zemp v. R.R.*, 9 Rich. 27 (S.C. 1855); *R.R. v. Sanger*, 15 Grat. 230 (Va. 1860); *R.R. v. Mitchell*, 11 Heisk. 400 (Tn. 1872); *Ry. v. Cooper*, 20 S.W. 990 (Tx. 1893) (citing slave case *Mitchell v. R.R.*, 30 Ga. 22 (1860)); *R.R. Landauer*, 54 N.W. 976 (Neb. 1893) (citing *Mitchell*).

24. See, for example, *Fordyce v. Jackson*, 56 Ark. 594 (1892); *Eames v. Ry. Co.*, 63 Tx. 660 (1885); and *R.R. v. Ritter*, 2 Ky. Law Rep. 385 (1881).

25. Some airline passengers have successfully sued for damages related to emotional distress suffered upon near-crashes or loss of altitude. Certain damages are fixed by statute or international accord, such as the Warsaw Convention on air travel. Until fairly recently, victims had to suffer physical impact before they could sue for emotional distress. For discussion, see Mary Donovan, "Is the Injury Requirement Obsolete in a Claim for Fear of Future Consequences?," *UCLA Law Review* 40 (January 1994).

26. Goodell, *American Slave Code*, 39.

27. Morris, *Studies*, 208–9; Stephen Botein, *Early American Law and Society* (New York: Knopf, 1983), 38.

28. *Wilson v. R.R.*, 10 Rich. 52 (S.C. 1856); *Leseman v. R.R. Co.*, 4 Rich. 414 (S.C. 1851); *R.R. v. Anderson*, 33 Ga. 110 (1861). For other cases involving railroads and livestock, see *McPheeters v. R.R.*, 45 Mo. 22 (1869); *Lester v. R.R.*, 30 Ga. 911 (1860); *R.R. v. Ballard*, 2 Metc. 177 (Ky. 1859);

R.R. v. Sineath, 9 Rich. 185 (S.C. 1855); *Smith v. Causey*, 22 Ala. 568 (1853); *R.R. v. Milton*, 14 B. Mon. 75 (Ky. 1853); *Danner v. R.R.*, 4 Rich. 339 (S.C. 1851); and *Burton v. R.R.* 4 Harr. 252 (Del. 1845). Mississippi required the plaintiff to show the railroad had been negligent, whereas Louisiana held the defendant liable only for gross negligence. *Knight v. R.R.*, 15 La. An. 105 (1860). Neither state required railroads to fence animals out. In some states, the defendant was presumed negligent unless he could prove otherwise, rather than facing strict liability. For discussion, see *Clark v. R.R.*, 1 W. 109 (N.C. 1863); *Horne v. R.R.*, 1 Coldw. 72 (Tn. 1860); *R.R. v. Patton*, 31 Ms. 156 (1856); *Wilson v. R.R.*, 10 Rich. 52 (S.C. 1856). The Dakota territory also had a fencing-out policy. Frank L. Owsley, *Plain Folk of the Old South* (Chicago: Quadrangle Books, 1965), and Grady McWhiney, *Cracker Culture: Celtic Ways in the Old South* (Birmingham: University of Alabama Press, 1988), contain fascinating discussions of grazing and fencing arrangements in the Old South.

29. *Scaggs v. R.R.*, 10 Md. 268, 278 (1856); *R.R. v. Davis*, 13 Ga. 68, 86 (1853) (overturned in 1859). *Jones v. R.R.*, 18 Ga. 247 (1855), resembles *Davis*. The *Scaggs* opinion also said that the legislature never would have meant to encompass such valuable property by the phrase "et cetera."

30. *Couch v. Jones*, 4 Jones 402, 408 (N.C. 1857).

31. Friedman, *History*, 471.

32. *Felder v. R.R.* 2 McMul. 403 (S.C. 1842); *Richardson v. R.R.*, Rich. 120 (S.C. 1854); *Herring v. R.R.*, 10 Ired. 402, 408 (N.C. 1849); *Fleytas v. R.R.*, 18 La. 339 (1841); *Lessups v. R.R.*, 17 La. 361 (1841). Lessups's slave apparently had been told to stop at the crossing but did not. No warning was given in *Scaggs v. R.R.*, 10 Md. 268 (1856), either.

33. Two recent Minnesota accidents bear this out. In one, a youth running cross-country stepped onto an unguarded track and was crushed by a train. He apparently was concentrating on his race and did not expect the train – which was off-schedule – to pass. In the other, a young woman was walking on tracks at night near a restaurant area. She was killed by a train approaching her from behind. *Minneapolis Star-Tribune* (July 26, 1991), 1B.

34. *R.R. v. Applegate*, 8 Dana 289 (Ky. 1839); *Hentz v. R.R.*, 13 Barb. 646 (S.C.N.Y., 1852) (both cases are quoted in Zainaldin, *Law*, 62, 165); *R.R. v. Winn*, 19 Ga. 440, 447 (1856). *Winn* – involving free victims – was later reheard; an injured child received $7,000 for disfigurement. In a second rehearing, the child's father was denied damages for the death of his wife in the same accident.

35. See Zainaldin, *Law*, 58–62; Charles W. McCurdy, "Justice Field and the Jurisprudence of Government and Business Relations," *Journal of American History* 61 (March 1975); Edward C. Kirkland, *Industry Comes of Age: Business, Labor, and Public Policy, 1860–1897* (Chicago: Quadrangle Books, 1967); and Schwartz, "Tort Law." Also see the court's interpretation in *Walker v. Spullock*, discussed in Chapter 3, note 66.

36. *Aycock v. R.R.*, 6 Jones 231 (N.C. 1858).

37. *R.R. v. McElmurry*, 24 Ga. 75 (1858); *Whidby v. Lewis*, 32 Ga. 472 (1862); *Mitchell v. R.R.*, 30 Ga. 22 (1860); *R.R. v. Jones*, 2 Head 517 (Tn. 1859); *R.R. v. St. John*, 5 Sneed 524, 527 (Tn. 1858). Also see *R.R. v. Davis*, 27 Ga. 113 (1859). See Chapter 1 for additional detail on the last-clear-chance doctrine.

38. Posner, *Economic Analysis*, 159–60, demonstrated the efficiency of the last-clear-chance doctrine.

39. Yet although a train can derail when it strikes a human, it does so more easily when it hits cattle, mules, or horses.

40. *Sims v. R.R.*, 28 Ga. 93 (1853); *Boland v. R.R.*, 12 Rich. 368 (S.C. 1859); *Holmes v. R.R.*, 37 Ga. 593 (1868); *Poole v. R.R.*, 8 Jones 340 (N.C. 1861); *Herring v. R.R.*, 10 Ired. 402, 408 (N.C. 1849).

41. *Herring v. R.R.*, 10 Ired. 402, 408 (N.C. 1849); *Felder v. R.R.*, 2 McMul. 403 (S.C. 1842).

42. Wex S. Malone, "The Formative Era of Contributory Negligence," in *Essays in Nineteenth Century American Legal History*, ed. Wythe Holt (Westport, CT: Greenwood Press, 1976); Friedman, *History*, 477. The first case adopting the last-clear-chance rule – for a free victim – was an English case, *Davies v. Mann*, 10 M. & W. 546 (1842). Although English courts used *Davies* as a precedent, American courts lagged behind, except in slave cases. In the North, Indiana eventually determined that the last-clear-chance rule should apply for children, helpless victims, and drunkards (*R. Co. v. Wahl*, 145 N.E. 523 (App. Ct. Ind. 1924); *R. Co. v. Pitzer*, 6 N.E. 310 (S.C. Ind. 1886)). Wisconsin courts looked askance at the notion of compensating trespassers, however (*Sheehan v. Ry. Co.*, 76 F. 201 (Wisc. 1896)).

43. One last-clear-chance slave case, *R.R. v. Jones*, 2 Head 517 (Tn. 1859), is also a leading case in contracts. Opinions in Tennessee, Arkansas, North Carolina, New York, Texas, Oregon, and Oklahoma cite *Jones* to support the view that people cannot contract out of gross negligence. The most recent of these cases is *Childress v. Madison Cty*, 777 S.W. 2d 1 (1989), involving a retarded child who was injured while training for the Special Olympics.

44. See, for example, *Patterson v. R.R.*, 4 Hurst 103 (De. 1870).

45. See *R.R. v. Dunnaway*, 24 S.E. 698 (Va. 1896); *Ex parte Stell*, 22 F. Cas. 1242 (Cir. Ct. E.D. Va. 1882); *Bannon v. R.R.*, 24 Md. 108 (1865); and *Coughlin v. R.R.*, 24 Md. 84 (1865).

46. *R.R. v. Price*, 29 Md. 420 (1868); *R. Co. v. Anderson*, 31 Gratt. 812 (Va. 1883).

47. *Smith v. R.R.*, 6 Coldw. 589 (Tn. 1869); *State v. Mayor*, 3 Head 263 (Tn. 1859).

48. *Ry. Co. v. Prince*, 2 Heisk. 580 (Tn. 1871); *R. Co. v. Burke*, 6 Coldw. 45 (Tn. 1868). A later case, *R.R. v. Binkley*, 127 Tn. 77 (1912), awarded $500 to a plaintiff who was injured while lying on the tracks, drunk. Here, the court said that the Code of 1858 made railroad companies liable even if the plaintiff had been grossly negligent.

49. *Graves v. R.R.*, 126 Tenn. 148 (1912); *R.R. v. Noah*, 180 Tn. 532 (1937).

50. See *R. Co. v. Miller*, 285 F.2d 202 (Tn. 1960); *R.R. v. Toombs*, 6 Tenn.

Civ. App. 615 (1914); *R. Co. v. Truett*, 111 F. 876 (1901); and *R. Co. v. Walton*, 105 Tn. 415 (1900). All cited *R.R. v. St. John*, 5 Sneed 524 (Tn. 1858).

51. *Ry. v. Wright*, 133 Tn. 74 (1915); *R. Co. v. Matthews*, 29 F.2d 52 (Tn. 1925).

52. See *R.R. v. McElmurry*, 24 Ga. 75 (1858).

53. See *Pressley v. R.R.*, 48 Ga. App. 382 (1934); and *R.R. v. Brinson*, 70 Ga. 207 (1883).

54. *R. Co. v. Denson*, 84 Ga. 774 (1897); *R. Co. v. Pelfrey*, 74 S.E. 854 (Ga. 1912). See also *Humphries v. R. Co.*, 51 Ga. App. 585 (1935); and *R.R. v. Williams*, 74 Ga. 723 (1885).

55. *R.R. v. Stewart*, 71 Ga. 427 (1883); *R.R. v. Dixon*, 42 Ga. 327 (1871).

56. *R.R. v. Blake*, 101 Ga. 217 (1897).

57. *Parish v. R.R.*, 102 Ga. 285 (1897); *Raden v. R.R.*, 78 Ga. 47 (1886); *R.R. v. Hankerson*, 61 Ga. 114 (1878).

58. *R.R. v. Wynn*, 42 Ga. 331 (1871). Mason W. Stephenson, "Plaintiff's Last Clear Chance and Comparative Negligence in Georgia," *Georgia State Bar Journal* 6 (August 1969), discussed this case in detail.

59. See *Kennayde v. R.R.*, 45 Mo. 255 (1869); *Hickey v. Dallmeyer*, 44 Mo. 237 (1869); and *Bowler v. Lane*, 3 Merc. 311 (Ky. 1860).

60. See *R.R. v. Lowe*, 118 Ky. 260 (1904); *R.R. v. Schuster*, 10 Ky. L. Rptr. 66 (1888); and *R.R. v. Mahony*, 70 Ky. 239 (1870). All cited *R.R. v. Yandell*, 17 B. Mon. 586 (Ky. 1856).

61. See *dicta* in *Hainlin v. Budge*, 47 So. 825 (Fl. 1908); *dicta* in *R. Co. v. Bryant*, 30 Tex. Civ. App. 4 (1902); *Jackson v. Ry. Co.*, 385 S.W. 745 (Tx. 1897); *dicta* in *R.R. v. Neff*, 28 S.W. 286 (Tx. 1894); and *Lincoln RTC v. Nichols*, 55 N.W. 872 (Neb. 1893). All cited *Cook v. Parham*, 24 Ala. 21 (1853).

62. *Owen v. Delano*, 194 S.W. 756 (Mo. App. 1917); *Hamilton v. R.Co.*, 42 La. Ann. 824 (1890); *R. Co. v. Modawell*, 151 F. 421 (5th Cir. 1907).

63. See *R.R. v. Trainer*, 32 Md. 542 (1870).

64. *R.R. v. Jones*, 95 U.S. 439 (1877); *R.R. v. Miller*, 29 Md. 252 (1868).

65. *Deans v. R. Co.*, 12 S.E. 77 (N.C. 1890); *Smith v. R. Co.*, 19 S.E. 863 (N.C. 1894); *Moore v. Ry. Co.*, 186 N.C. 256 (1923).

66. *Irish v. Wright*, 8 Rob. 428 (La. 1844). Stealing or conveying slaves often brought criminal penalties as well, as Chapter 6 discusses.

67. The bill, proposed in 1846 by Pennsylvania Democrat David Wilmot, would have barred slavery from all lands acquired in the Mexican War.

68. *Beverly v. Brooke*, 2 Wheat. 100 (U.S. 1817); *Burke v. Clarke*, 11 La. 206 (1837); *Lepper v. Chilton*, 7 Mo. 221 (1841). In another Missouri case, a court granted damages for the entire value of an escaped slave in a suit against the boat itself; the same court logically denied double compensation to this slaveowner when he later sued the ship's captain and master for the same loss. *Calvert v. Timolean*, 15 Mo. 595 (1852); *Calvert v. Rider*, 20 Mo. 146 (1854). A case similar to *Calvert* is *Owen v. Brown*, 12 La. An. 172 (1857).

69. For the language of various statutes, see Finkelman, *State Slavery Statutes;* Hurd, *The Law of Freedom;* and Goodell, *American Slave Code.* For exam-

ples of cases, see *Wilson v. State*, 21 Md. 1 (1864); *McClain v. Esham*, 17 B. Mon. 146 (Ky. 1856); *Johnson v. Bryan*, 1 B. Mon. 292 (Ky. 1841); *Slatter v. Holton*, 19 La. 39 (1841); and *Case v. Woolley*, 6 Dana 17 (Ky. 1837).

70. Under the 1822 Negro Seamen's Acts, free blacks who left ships could be jailed and enslaved. U.S. Supreme Court Justice William Johnson declared the Acts unconstitutional in *Elkison v. Deliesseline*, 8 F.C. 493 (C.C.D.S.C. 1823), because they interfered with treaty obligations and intruded upon the federal commerce clause. The verdict mattered, because half of seamen by the 1850s were black. President Jackson referred the matter to his attorneys general, John Berrien and (later) Roger Taney, who disagreed with Justice Johnson. In an unpublished draft opinion, Taney anticipated his Dred Scott decision by saying that blacks were not citizens. Hyman and Wiecek, *Equal Justice*, 79–80.

71. See *Feltus v. Andrus*, 5 Rob. 7 (La. 1843); and *Russell v. Taylor*, 4 Mo. 550 (1837).

72. Slaves carried passes partly for their own protection. People could whip slaves traveling without papers in Maryland, the District of Columbia, Georgia, Mississippi, Virginia, and Kentucky. See Goodell, *The American Slave Code*, part I.

73. I learned this through private correspondence with Judith Schafer.

74. *State v. B.& S. Steam Co.*, 13 Md. 181 (1859); Act of 1838, Ch. 375, sec. 1, 187. Slaveowners recovered statutory damages for escaped stowaway slaves in *Steam Navig. Co. v. Hungerford*, 6 Gill & J. 291 (Md. 1834), and *Gibbons v. Morse*, 2 Hal. 253 (N.J. 1821). See also *Page v. Vandegrift*, 5 Harr. 176 (Del. 1849). An Alabama court decided that a statute requiring slaves to carry written permission from masters included situations in which slaves had stowed away. *Mangham v. Cox*, 29 Al. 81 (1856).

75. Act 3 July 1838, 5 Stat. at Large 306.

76. See Hurd, *The Law of Freedom and Bondage*, vol. 2, 163. Delaware's statute of January 19, 1826, resembled Louisiana law: It stated that a captain was presumed to know everything about his boat.

77. *McCall v. Eve*, 15 F.C. 1232 (1804).

78. See *Robards v. McLean*, 8 Ired. 522 (N.C. 1848); and *Redden v. Spruance*, 4 Harr. 217 (Del. 1845). In *Redden*, slave Jerry had stolen papers of a free Negro he resembled.

79. *Hurst v. Wallace*, 5 La. 98 (1832); *Daret v. Gray*, 12 La. An. 394 (1857); *Lowe v. Stockton*, 15 F.C. 1017 (D.C. 1835); *Moore v. Foster*, 10 B. Mon. 255 (Ky. 1850).

80. The court in *Ewing v. Gist*, 2 B. Mon. 465 (Ky. 1842), noted that light-complected slaves were worth less. This makes intuitive sense. Light-skinned slaves required more monitoring; higher surveillance costs reduced a slave's value. Fogel and Engerman, *Time*, 130–37, discussed slaves' complexions and the degree of miscegenation in the South.

81. *Cutter v. Moore*, 3 Hal. 219 (N.J. 1825); *O'Neall v. R.R.*, 9 Rich. 465 (S.C. 1856); *Wallace v. Spullock*, 32 Ga. 488 (1861); *Bell v. Chambers*, 38 Ala. 660 (1863); *State v. Johnston*, 1 Dev. 360 (N.C. 1828); *Williamson v. Norton*, 7 La. An. 393 (1852), *Spalding v. Taylor*, 1 La. An. 195 (1846).

82. Page 1018, art. 1, sec. 32.
83. *Gibbons v. Morse*, 2 Hal. 253, 269 (N.J. 1821).
84. *Botts v. Cochrane*, 4 La. An. 35 (1849); *Folse v. Transp. Co.*, 19 La. An. 199 (1867).
85. Various scholars have estimated the amount of escaped slave property. Not all fugitives ran away aboard common carriers, of course; public conveyances simply provided an attractive means of vanishing quickly. Allan Nevins, *Ordeal of the Union: Fruits of Manifest Destiny, 1847–1852* (New York: Scribner's, 1947), 243, reported that North Carolina Senator Clingman had calculated a loss of $15 million worth of slaves between 1776 and 1849. Peterson, *The Great Triumvirate*, 455, added that this figure represented some 30,000 slaves. The number of escaped slaves reported in the federal census in 1850 (the year the Fugitive Slave Act was passed) was 1,011; the number in 1860 was 803. Campbell, *The Slave Catchers*, 168, put the loss of slaves in the decade before the Civil War at 8,000 to 15,000. Georgia Justice Joseph Lumpkin claimed that the South had lost 60,000 slaves equivalent to $30 million as of August 1855. *Moran v. Davis*, 18 Ga. 722 (1855).
86. *Baker v. Wise*, 16 Grat. 139 (Va. 1861).
87. By the nineteenth century, bodily punishment of whites was relatively unusual. Chapter 7 discusses this.
88. See *McClure v. R.R.*, 35 Mo. 189 (1864); *Rogers v. R.R.*, 35 Mo. 153 (1864); and *Welton v. R.R.*, 34 Mo. 358 (1864).
89. See *Edwards v. Vail*, 3 J.J. Marsh. 595 (Ky. 1830); *Church v. Chambers*, 3 Dana 274 (Ky. 1835); and *McFarland v. McKnight*, 6 B. Mon. 500 (Ky. 1846). A Missouri slaveowner could not recover for his escaped slave Ambrose under Kentucky law, however, even though Ambrose made his escape along the Ohio River from New Madrid to Cincinnati. *Bracken v. Gulnare*, 16 B. Mon. 444 (Ky. 1855). Why would slaves who had already escaped to the free state of Indiana board vessels? Because Ohio citizens – Cincinnati residents particularly – were more sympathetic and more helpful to fugitives than Hoosiers. I suspect that the runaways were attempting to go upriver as quickly as possible to Cincinnati. See Chapter 3, note 37, for a discussion of the cession agreement.
90. *Eaton v. Vaughan*, 9 Mo. 734, 738 (1846); *Collins v. Bilderback*, 5 Harr. 133 (Del. 1849) (the appellate court did not approve of the method of pleading and the case evidently ended in a settlement); *Massey v. Cole*, 29 Ala. 364 (1856). The *Eaton* court came to a similar holding in *Price v. Thornton*, 10 Mo. 135 (1846), in a case brought under the common law. Missouri was one of the earliest states to tighten the rules for boat-related defendants in escape cases. Given the state's proximity to Illinois, this is not surprising. But the Missouri court also lay down a rule that railroads needed only to be prudent in ensuring slaves did not escape, not to take the most diligent of care. *Withers v. El Paso*, 20 Mo. 204 (1857).
91. *R.R. v. Pickett*, 36 Ga. 85 (1867); *R.R. v. Young*, 1 Bush 401 (Ky. 1867); *Brown v. R.R.*, 36 Ga. 377 (1867); *Sill v. R.R.*, 4 Rich. 154 (S.C. 1850). Also see *Jossey v. R.R.*, 11 Rich 399 (S.C. 1858); *Ellis v. Welch*, 4 Rich.

468 (S.C. 1851); *R.R. v. Fulton*, 4 Sneed 589 (Tn. 1857). Some early cases foreshadow later holdings, including *Harriss v. Mabry*, 1 Ired. 240 (N.C. 1840), and *Russell v. Taylor*, 4 Mo. 530 (1837).

92. Railroad mileage by state is reported in George R. Taylor, "Comment," in *Trends in the American Economy in the Nineteenth Century, Studies in Income and Wealth*, vol. 24, ed. William N. Parker (Princeton: Princeton University Press, 1981). Antebellum railroad maps also appear in Don E. Fehrenbacher, *The Era of Expansion, 1800–1848* (New York: Wiley, 1969), 64; Fletcher W. Hewes, "Statistical Railway Studies," in *The American Railway*, ed. Thomas Cooley (New York: Scribner's, 1897), 430; John F. Stover, *American Railroads* (Chicago: University of Chicago Press, 1961); and Albert Fishlow, *American Railroads and the Transformation of the Antebellum Economy* (Cambridge: Harvard University Press, 1965), map 1. The decennial federal censuses report the number of slaves by state.

5. PROTECTING PROPERTY VERSUS KEEPING PEACE

1. Plucknett, *A Concise History*, 381–82. Police forces were uncommon until the late nineteenth century, particularly in the South. Lawrence M. Friedman, *Crime and Punishment in American History* (New York: Basic Books, 1993), 67. Two modern-day parallels to slave patrols are the practice of community policing and the Ku Klux Klan. In both, people see themselves as actively preserving the peace of their neighborhoods.

2. As I point out later in the chapter, overseers acted as agents, much like supervisors or managers in a factory. The law governing overseers therefore bears some resemblance to the law concerning the bodily punishment of employees. I take up this matter in Chapter 7. Still, overseeing slaves was unique because slaves could be forced to work in gangs.

3. Peter H. Schuck, *Suing Government* (New Haven: Yale University Press, 1983), 37. The 1946 Federal Tort Claims Act waived federal immunity for most torts.

4. Clyde E. Jacobs, *The Eleventh Amendment and Sovereign Immunity* (Westport, CT: Greenwood Press, 1972), 106.

5. Sometimes commentators distinguish instead between "ministerial" and "discretionary" functions. See, for example, John C. Pine and Robert D. Bickel, *Tort Liability Today* (Washington, DC: National League of Cities, 1986). *Mower v. Leicester*, 9 Mass. 247 (1812), generally discussed the extension of immunity to municipalities. In a landmark case distinguishing governmental from proprietary functions, the city of New York was found liable for damages caused by its waterworks. Why? Because, according to the court, the city ran the works for its advantage and profit. *Bailey v. N.Y.*, 3 Hill 531 (N.Y. 1842). Cities were and are typically liable under mob laws for injuries or damages caused by mobs. Martin, *Sovereign Immunity*, 27. (Two antebellum Southern cities successfully avoided liability for injuries that police could have prevented, however. See discussion in the text at note 23.) And a city could and

can bear responsibility for the consequences of actions undertaken by municipal officials in the course of their employment, if those actions are of a private nature (like renting out rooms). *Worden v. New Bedford,* 131 Mass. 23 (1881). See also Waterman L. Williams, *The Liability of Municipal Corporations for Tort* (Boston: Little, Brown, 1901).

6. Edwin M. Borchard, "Governmental Liability in Tort (Part 3)," *Yale Law Journal* 34 (January 1925); "Governmental Liability in Tort (Part 2)," *Yale Law Journal* 34 (December 1924); "Governmental Liability in Tort (Part 1)," *Yale Law Journal* 34 (November 1924).

7. *Irvine v. Town of Greenwood,* 89 S.C. 511 (1911).

8. Military officers were also defendants. *Bates v. Clark,* 95 U.S. 204 (1877); *Mitchell v. Harmony,* 13 How. 115 (U.S. 1851); *Little v. Barrame,* 2 Cr. 170 (U.S. 1804). Under the important case of *Miller v. Horton,* 15 Mass. 540 (1891), local health officers were held personally liable for destroying an apparently diseased horse that was later proven healthy. For discussion of the tort liability of government and government officials up to 1955, see Williams, *Liability of Municipal Corporations;* Edward G. Jennings, "Tort Liability of Administrative Officers," *University of Minnesota Law Review* 21 (February 1937); and Fleming James, "Tort Liability of Governmental Units and Their Officers," *University of Chicago Law Review* 22 (Winter 1955).

9. Modern-day public officials often face suit for these charges under 42 U.S.C. sec. 1983. This 1871 law was enacted to support the Fourteenth Amendment and to mitigate the potential misuse of power by public officials. See Pine and Bickel, *Tort Liability;* Schuck, *Suing Government;* and Paul T. Hardy and J. Devereaux Weeks, *Personal Liability of Public Officials under Federal Law* (Athens: University of Georgia Press, 1988). Early plaintiffs who brought suits under sec. 1983 soon discovered that individual police officers and other city officials could not afford to pay damages. As a result, people began to file suit against cities as well – and win them, after the cases of *Monell v. Dept. of Social Services of N.Y.,* 436 U.S. 658 (1978), and *Owen v. Independence,* 455 U.S. 622 (W.D. Mo. 1980). In response, municipalities sometimes attempt to avoid liability by hiring independent contractors rather than employees.

As one example of municipal liability, the city of Minneapolis recently paid more than a million dollars in damages and fees for superficial injuries inflicted on an allegedly disorderly youth by an off-duty police officer. Police lieutenant Mike Sauro was moonlighting, in uniform, at Jukebox Saturday Night on New Year's Eve 1990. A local college hockey player accused Sauro of beating him in a back room and filed suit against Sauro and the city of Minneapolis. The city refused a $415,000 settlement, opting instead for a jury trial. The jury awarded the youth $700,000 in compensatory and punitive damages, in spite of evidence that the plaintiff was back on the ice in a matter of days. Legal fees added half again as much to the city's bill. The city was found guilty of maintaining a custom of deliberate indifference to complaints about excessive force in the police department. One source of tension in the case was a previous settlement (of $250,000) made by the city to the family of a black youth killed by a policeman who mistakenly thought the youth had a gun. In the ongoing Sauro saga, an arbitrator reinstated the officer; the city immediately placed him off regular duty. A district court judge then denied Sauro's request for an injunction that would allow him to return to work. In April 1997, another judge sent Sauro back to his job.

10. Albert Martin cites two other related reasons for sovereign immunity: (1) Funds raised for public purposes should not go to compensate private injury; and (2) government is not run for profit and so is distinguishable from private business. Albert B. Martin, *Sovereign – Governmental Immunity* (Topeka: League of Kansas Municipalities, 1965), 12.

11. *Gregoire v. Biddle*, 177 F.2d 579, 581 (2d Cir. 1949).

12. Posner, *Economic Analysis*, 642. To encourage good work, Posner suggested that officials could enjoy partial immunity, or, alternatively, public employers could provide indemnity for their workers.

13. Samuel Walker, *Popular Justice* (New York: Oxford University Press, 1980), 19–23.

14. *Stewart v. New Orleans*, 9 La. An. 461 (1854); *Dargan v. Mayor*, 31 Al. 469 (1858). Providing public services other than police also conferred immunity upon local governments. In one case, officials put a runaway slave on a chain gang after capturing him. Six men closely guarded 58 prisoners; each prisoner wore a ball and chain. Amazingly, the slave escaped. A court determined that the city was not liable because capturing, chaining, and returning runaways in fact delivered a service to slaveowners without increasing city revenues. (This "service" no doubt aimed to protect the public as well.) If the city bore responsibility for the escape, said the court, it would stop providing the service. *Chase v. Mayor*, 9 La. 343 (1835). A city was required to give the owner timely notice of an escape, however, or it might face liability. *Claque v. New Orleans*, 13 La. An. 275 (1859). In *Claque*, the slave escaped from a chain gang after being jailed for safekeeping.

15. *Whitfield v. Paris*, 84 Tex. 431 (1892); *Givens v. Paris*, 5 Tex. Civ. App. 705 (1893); *Moss v. City of Augusta*, 93 Ga. 797 (1894); *Harman v. Lynchburg*, 33 Grat. 37 (Va. 1880). Also see *Doster v. Atlanta*, 72 Ga. 233 (1884), and *Detroit v. Laughna*, 34 Mi. 402 (1876). For a Northern case, see *Elliott v. Philadelphia*, 75 Pa. St. 347 (1847). Today, verdicts might well go the other way, as the Sauro case discussed in note 9 shows. The defendant in *Harman* successfully argued that the plaintiff did not present enough evidence that the city had ordered the police to undertake this action. Alternatively, the city might have justified the action as a matter of preserving public safety and peace. This case also recalls the circumstances surrounding the Great Fire of London in 1666. Richard Posner reported that the Lord Mayor of London, Thomas Bludworth, refused to order houses taken down in the path of the fire to form a firebreak – Bludworth worried about the financial consequences to the city. As a result, the four-day fire destroyed 13,000 houses and made 100,000 people homeless. If Bludworth could have counted on a

public-necessity defense, the outcome may have been far less tragic. Posner, *Tort Law*, 187.

16. *Kelly v. City Council of Charleston*, 4 Rich. 426, 434 (S.C. 1851); *Hamilton v. Auditor*, 14 B. Mon. 230 (Ky. 1853). In the latter case, the court reasoned that slave might have won an appeal.

17. *U.S. v. Amy*, 24 F.C. 792, 810 (1859). Eminent domain is the power to take private property (typically land) for public use. As Chapter 7 notes, many states forestalled similar suits by providing compensation for slaves convicted of capital crimes.

18. The cases are *Sims v. Pearce*, 2 Duv. 202 (Ky. 1865); *Corbin v. Marsh*, 2 Duv. 193 (Ky. 1865); and *Hughes v. Todd*, 2 Duv. 188 (Ky. 1865). Judge Williams noted as well that slaves would fight only if given something that mattered – freedom. The funding statutes Williams referred to are Supp. Act Feb. 24, 1864, attached to the Act of July 17, 1862. A third act – approved March 3, 1865 – freed wives and children of any persons who enlisted in the Union army. According to Williams, the official statistics indicated that the black population provided 178,735 soldiers, of which Kentucky gave 23,703. Another 75,000 Kentucky slaves were freed after the war. Williams seemed to think loyal owners might still have obtained compensation for the latter group of slaves (at least up to $300), because many of the slaves had built trenches and otherwise helped the Union army. Between 1861 and 1863, the federal government proposed plans offering $300 for each slave freed in certain states (including Delaware, Maryland, Virginia, Kentucky, Tennessee, and Missouri), financed by thirty-year bonds at 5 to 6 percent interest. For details, see Goldin, "Economics," 74, and Leonard P. Curry, *Blueprint for Modern America: Non-Military Legislation of the First Civil War Congress* (Nashville: Vanderbilt University Press, 1968), 47–53. The case of *Noland v. Golden*, 3 Bush 84 (Ky. 1868), determined that Kentucky slaves were not officially freed, even if they had enlisted, until December 20, 1865. The issue in *Noland* was whether a black man had been a slave or a freedman when he had negotiated a contract. In contrast to the Kentucky cases, a Florida court determined that the freeing of slaves was not a taking of private property for public use without just compensation. *City Commissioners v. King*, 13 Fl. 451 (1869–71).

19. Cases against public employees uniformly produced damage awards, as I discuss later. Damages cost the individuals, not governments. If courts had instead entered judgments to compel or restrain the behavior of public officials or to require some specific performance, governments would have felt the cost.

20. *Lewis v. New Orleans*, 12 La. An. 190 (La. 1857); *Richmond v. Long*, 17 Grat. 374 (Va. 1867). Justice Spofford dissented in *Lewis*. He argued that the city profited because Jesse's owner had paid for services not received. His reasoning followed *Bailey v. New York*, discussed in note 5. (The jailing of slaves by their owners is discussed later in this chapter.) Perhaps to forestall similar lawsuits, Louisiana passed an act in 1863 to appropriate $500,000 to help pay for slaves lost while at work on public projects. Finkelman, *State Slavery Statutes*.

21. *Mayor v. Howard*, 6 Ga. 213, 220 (1849); *Mayor v. Goetchius*, 7 Ga. 139, 141 (1849). In a Louisiana case similar to *Goetchius*, the city of New Orleans was liable when slave Ned died in jail lacking food and warmth. Here, the plaintiff wanted $900 in damages, but, because the slave was known to have run away at least once, the defendant said that damages should not exceed the value of a runaway, $300. The court split the difference and granted the plaintiff $600. This case was overturned a mere four years later. *Johnson v. Municipality #1*, 5 La. An. 100 (1850) (overturned by *Stewart v. New Orleans*, 9 La. An. 461 (1854)). In a postbellum smallpox case, a Kentucky court made clear that county justices had legal authority to employ medical aid for any smallpox victim, regardless of the victim's skin color. *Rodman v. Justices*, 3 Bush 144 (Ky. 1867).

22. See, for example, *Hollenbeck v. Winnebago Cty.*, 1 Ky. Law Rep. 198 (1880); *City of Cumberland v. Willison*, 50 Md. 138 (1878); *Murtaugh v. City of St. Louis*, 44 Mo. 479 (1869); and *Sutton v. Carroll County Police*, 41 Miss. 236 (1866). The *American Digest* reveals that most nineteenth-century suits against municipalities were brought in the North.

23. *Worley v. Columbia*, 88 Mo. 106 (1885); *Attaway v. Cartersville*, 68 Ga. 740 (1882); *Harris v. Atlanta*, 62 Ga. 290 (1879); *Cook v. Macon*, 54 Ga. 468 (1875); *Pollack v. Louisville*, 13 Bush 221 (Ky. 1877); *Campbell v. Montgomery*, 53 Ala. 527 (1877); *Altvater v. Baltimore*, 31 Md. 462 (1869); *McElroy v. Albany*, 65 Ga. 387 (1880); *Nisbet v. Atlanta*, 97 Ga. 650 (1896).

24. *Sandridge v. Jones*, 2 La. An. 933 (1847); *Eldridge v. Spence*, 16 Al. 682 (1849); *Russell v. Lynch*, 28 Mo. 312 (1859); *Gill v. Wilkinson*, 30 Ga. 760 (1860).

25. *Dabney v. Taliaferro*, 4 Rand. 256 (Va. 1826). Yet in a postbellum case where a deputy had shot the plaintiff's husband (who was trying to flee after being arrested for horse theft), the sheriff was not held responsible under a negligence statute. *Hendrick v. Walton*, 69 Tx. 192 (1887). For general background, see Bacon, *Abridgment*, vol. 8; Walker, *Popular Justice*; Plucknett, *A Concise History*, 420. Chapter 7 discusses the doctrine of *respondeat superior* more fully.

26. *Withers v. Coyles*, 36 Ala. 320 (1860); *Tudor v. Lewis*, 3 Metc. 378 (Ky. 1860); *Munford v. Taylor*, 2 Metc. 599 (Ky. 1859).

27. See, for example, *Abbott v. Holland*, 20 Ga. 598 (1856); *Cook v. Irving*, 4 Strob. 204 (S.C. 1850); *Mabry v. Turrentine*, 8 Ired. 201 (N.C. 1847); *Jackson v. Hampton*, 6 Ired. 34 (N.C. 1845); *Warberton v. Wood*, 6 Mo. 8 (1839); *Koones v. Maddox*, 2 Har. & G. 106 (Md. 1827); *Stephenson v. Hillhouse*, Harp. 23 (S.C. 1823); and *Love v. McAlister*, 4 Hayw. 65 (Tn. 1817).

28. Cases include *Gilmore v. Moore*, 30 Ga. 628 (1860); *Byrne v. Anderson*, 8 La. An. 139 (1853); *Green v. Garcia*, 3 La. An. 702 (1848); *McLean v. Douglass*, 28 N.C. 233 (1846); and *Conover v. Gatewood*, 2 A.K. Marsh. 566 (Ky. 1820).

29. *Wright v. Spencer*, 1 Stew. 576 (Al. 1827); *Phillips v. Lamar*, 27 Ga. 228 (1859). Chapters 4 and 6 discuss how runaways were advertised.

30. See *Vance v. Vanarsdale*, 1 Bush 504 (Ky. 1867); *Snell v. State*, 2 Swan 344 (Tn. 1852); and *Collins v. Terrall*, 2 S. & M. 383 (Ms. 1844).

31. *McElhenny v. Wylie*, 3 Strob. 284 (S.C. 1848).

32. *Head v. Martin*, 9 Ky. Law R. 45 (1887); *Koppelcam v. Hoffman*, 12 Neb. 95 (1881).

33. *McCarthy v. Lewis*, 5 La. An. 115 (1850); *Turney v. Carter*, 3 Baxt. 199 (Tn. 1873).

34. *Brock v. King*, 2 Jones 302 (N.C. 1855), 3 Jones 45 (N.C. 1855); *Brainard v. Head*, 15 La. An. 489 (1860). In *Brock*, the slave had escaped from a steamboat and was brought into jail by someone other than the sheriff. In *Brainard*, slave Alfred had been put in jail for safekeeping while a debt was being settled. *Dicta* in *Brainard* also stated, however, that the sheriff would have been liable if he had seen Alfred outside the jail after the escape and failed to recommit the slave.

35. See *Freiberg v. Johnson*, 71 Tx. 558 (1886); *Cook v. Potts*, 3 Baxt. 227 (Tn. 1873); and *Emory v. Davis*, 4 Rich. 23 (S.C. 1872).

36. See *Comw. v. Reed*, 3 Bush 516 (Ky. 1868); *Siler v. McKee*, 2 Jones 379 (N.C. 1855); and *Jones v. Dunn*, 1 Dev. 326 (N.C. 1827).

37. *State v. Davis*, 1 Hill 46 (S.C. 1833).

38. *Bullitt v. Clement*, 16 B. Mon. 193 (Ky. 1855).

39. *Slemaker v. Marriott*, 5 Gill. & J. 406 (Md. 1833); *Burley v. Griffith*, 8 Leigh 442 (Va. 1836). The underlying conditions in *Slemaker* differ from those in *Brainard v. Head* (discussed at note 34). The Maryland sheriff had more responsibility concerning the repair of the jail, but he also had more discretion as to whether the slave should be housed. In a telling move, Maryland in 1856 increased the allowance to sheriffs for keeping runaways.

40. *Miller v. Porter*, 8 B. Mon. 282, 284 (Ky. 1847); *Harris v. Hill*, 11 B. Mon. 199 (Ky. 1851). Kentucky also determined that owners, not municipalities, were responsible for jailors' fees when runaway slaves were interned, because "the statutory provisions for apprehending, keeping, and selling runaway slaves were enacted for the security of the owners." *Bullitt Cty. Ct. v. Troutman*, 5 Bush 573, 574 (Ky. 1869). In a Virginia dispute, a county did not have to pay fees for slaves jailed while awaiting a suit for freedom. The opinion does not clarify who the responsible party was. *Rixey v. Fauquier Cty.*, 3 Leigh 811 (Va. 1831).

41. Finkelman, *State Slavery Statutes*, various microfiches. Georgia had the most statutes, with 31. North and South Carolina followed close behind, with 28 and 27 statutes, respectively. States with the fewest number of statutes were Maryland, Texas, Tennessee, and, surprisingly, Virginia.

42. Vigilantes also enjoyed going after abolitionists. Friedman, *Crime and Punishment*, 87, 180; William C. Henderson, "The Slave Court System in Spartanburg County," in *Crime and Justice in American History: Courts and Criminal Procedure*, ed. Eric H. Monkkonen (Westport, CT: Meckler, 1991), 220–21; Michael S. Hindus, "Black Justice under White Law: Criminal Prosecution of Blacks in Antebellum South Carolina," in ibid., 247. Franklin, *From Slavery*, 115–16, 191, briefly described slave patrols.

43. See, for example, *Richardson v. Saltar*, N.C. Term. Rep. 68 (1817), and
    State v. Hailey, 6 Ired. 11 (N.C. 1845).

44. See John Campbell, " 'My Constant Companion': Slaves and Their Dogs
    in the Antebellum South," in *Working Toward Freedom, Slave Society and
    Domestic Economy in the American South*, ed. Larry E. Hudson, Jr.
    (Rochester: University of Rochester Press, 1994), for a discussion of
    slaves and their dogs.

45. Part of the increase may reflect depreciation in the value of Confeder-
    ate currency.

46. This might be considered an example of a repeated game. For discus-
    sion, see Robert Axelrod, *The Evolution of Cooperation* (New York: Basic
    Books, 1984).

47. *Duperrier v. Dautrive*, 12 La. An. 664, 665 (1856); *Tennent v. Dendy*, Dud.
    83, 86 (S.C. 1837); *Thompson v. Young*, 30 Ms. 17, 18 (1855); *Witsell v.
    Earnest*, 1 N. & McC. 182 (S.C. 1818); *Jennings v. Fundeberg*, 4 McC. 161
    (S.C. 1827); *State v. Boozer*, 5 Strob. 21 (S.C. 1850); *Benjamin v. Davis*,
    6 La. An. 472 (1851). Franklin, *From Slavery*, 119, and Flanigan, *The
    Criminal Law*, 78–79, noted the tendency of overseers and patrollers to
    overpunish another's property.

48. *Hervy v. Armstrong*, 15 Ark. 162 (1854).

49. *Morton v. Bradley*, 27 Al. 640 (1855), 30 Al. 683 (1857). These concerns
    bring to mind today's controversies over the responsibilities of police
    to apprehend alleged criminals without excess bloodshed.

50. William K. Scarborough, *The Overseer: Plantation Management in the Old
    South* (Baton Rouge: Louisiana State University Press, 1966), 235, 242.
    North Carolina owners and overseers were exempt from military duty
    if they had at least fifteen slaves in their charge, for example. The Con-
    federate states as a whole passed laws exempting certain overseers from
    the draft during the Civil War – someone had to mind the fields and
    the slaves, after all. See, for example, Alabama's Act of August 1863.
    Finkelman, *State Slavery Statutes*. For descriptions of the overseer's life,
    see Scarborough, *The Overseer*; John W. Blassingame, *The Slave Commu-
    nity* (New York: Oxford University Press, 1972), 173–77; Franklin,
    From Slavery, 119; and Fogel and Engerman, *Time*, 212–14. Fogel
    and Engerman suggested that white overseers more commonly worked
    on plantations with absentee owners, partly because certain states
    required a white presence. For a description of the statutes that gave
    white residency requirements on slave plantations, see Chapter 7, note
    122.

51. *Gillian v. Senter*, 9 Ala. 395, 396 (1846).

52. *Boone v. Lyde*, 3 Strob. 77 (S.C. 1848); *Darden v. Nolan*, 4 La. An. 374
    (1849); *Lane v. Phillips*, 6 Jones 455 (1859); *Fisher v. Campbell*, 9 Port.
    21 (Al. 1839). In *Lane*, the slaveowner had offered to pay the overseer's
    salary for the months he had worked; the overseer held out for the
    entire yearly amount and lost it all.

53. *Jones v. Glass*, 13 Ired. 305, 308 (N.C. 1852). Several cases illustrate the
    tradeoff of owners' rights and the rights of others to protect themselves
    or others from marauding or runaway slaves, including *Morton v.*

Bradley, 30 Al. 683 (1857); *Dupérrier v. Dautrive*, 12 La. An. 664 (La. 1856); *Thompson v. Young*, 30 Ms. 17 (1855); *Benjamin v. Davis*, 6 La. An. 472 (1851); *State v. Boozer*, 5 Strob. 21 (S.C. 1850); *Tennent v. Dendy*, Dud. 83 (S.C. 1837); *Witsell v. Earnest*, 1 N. & McC. 182 (S.C. 1818); *Smith v. Hancock*, 4 Bibb 222 (Ky. 1815); and *Brown v. May*, 1 Munf. 288 (Va. 1810). Many of these cases are discussed elsewhere in the book.

54. *Dwyer v. Cane*, 6 La. An. 707 (1851); *Wilson v. Bossier*, 11 La. An. 640 (1856); *Hendrickson v. Anderson*, 5 Jones 246 (N.C. 1858); *Brady v. Price*, 19 Tx. 285 (1857); *Miller v. Stewart*, 12 La. An. 170 (1857); *Hendricks v. Phillips*, 3 La. An. 618 (1848); *Copeland v. Parker*, 3 Ired. 513, 515 (N.C 1843). In these cases, back pay was awarded because the term of hiring had been completed.

55. *Hood v. McCorkle*, 12 La. 573 (1838); *Brunson v. Martin*, 17 Ark. 270 (1856) (*Martin v. Everett*, 11 Ala. 375 (1847), holds similarly); *Williams v. Fambro*, 30 Ga. 232 (1860).

56. *Jordan v. State*, 22 Ga. 545 (1857); *State v. Flanigan*, 5 Al. 477 (1843); *Kelly v. State*, 3 S. & M. 518 (Ms. 1844); *Scott v. State*, 31 Ms. 473 (1856); *Dowling v. State*, 5 S. & M. 664 (Ms. 1846); *State v. Raines*, 3 McC. 533 (S.C. 1826). Schafer, *Slavery*, 49–54, discussed unreported Louisiana cases involving extreme cruelty to slaves in which juries simply refused to convict overseers of crimes.

57. *State v. Brodnax*, Phil. 41 (N.C. 1866); *State v. Will*, 1 Dev. & B. 121 (N.C. 1834); *State v. Abram*, 10 Al. 928 (1847). In *State v. David*, 4 Jones 353 (N.C. 1857), however, a North Carolina court upheld a murder conviction, saying that slaves had to show unconditional submission to overseers. For other cases, see Flanigan, *The Criminal Law*.

6. RIGHTS AND RESPONSIBILITIES OF STRANGERS

1. Friedman, *Crime and Punishment*, 87.
2. *Niblett v. White*, 7 La. 253 (1835); *Cox v. Myers*, 4 La. An. 144 (1849); *Morgan v. Cox*, 22 Mo. 373 (1856); *Chiles v. Drake*, 2 Metc. 146 (Ky. 1859). Part of the issue in *Cox v. Myers* was that only movable property could be legally seized – slaves were classified as immovables in Louisiana. This case points up only one absurdity associated with calling humans immovable property. The parties were not strangers in these cases, strictly speaking, but no contractual arrangement pertained to the slaves.
3. *Audige v. Gaillard*, 8 La. An. 71 (1853); *Hill v. White*, 11 La. An. 170 (1856); *Mikell v. Mikell*, 5 Rich. Eq. 220, 226 (S.C. 1852). *Mikell* superficially resembles the case of *Clagett v. Speake*, discussed at note 34 in Chapter 3. The two differ, however. Employer Clagett ordinarily would have benefited directly from sending the slaves without supervision, because his costs were lower as a result. The administrator in *Mikell* received no such benefit: The estate would have borne supervision costs. In fact, the administrator may have had a fiduciary duty *not* to send anyone along, as that would have diminished the value of the estate.

4. *Payton v. Richards,* 11 La. An. 62 (1856); *Wagner v. Woolsey,* 1 Heisk. 235 (Tn. 1870).

5. See Alex Lichtenstein, "That Disposition to Theft with Which They Have Been Branded," in *Articles on American Slavery,* vol. 13, ed. Finkelman, 259–65, and Philip J. Schwarz, *Twice Condemned: Slaves and the Criminal Laws of Virginia, 1705–1865* (Baton Rouge: Louisiana State University Press, 1988), 119ff.

6. *Richardson v. Dukes,* 4 McC. 156 (S.C. 1827).

7. *Priester v. Augley,* 5 Rich. 44 (S.C. 1851); *Carmouche v. Bouis,* 6 La. An. 95 (1851); *Gardiner v. Thibodeau,* 14 La. An. 732 (1859); *Bibb v. Hebert,* 3 La. An. 132 (1848); *Hedgepeth v. Robertson,* 18 Tx. 858 (1857).

8. *Gray v. Combs,* 7 J.J. Marsh. 478, 480 (Ky. 1832); *McClelland v. Kay,* 14 B. Mon. 103 (Ky. 1853); *Blanchard v. Dixon,* 4 La. An. 57, 58 (La. 1849); *McCutcheon v. Angelo,* 14 La. An. 34 (1859). *Arnandez v. Lawes,* discussed in note 25, also involved a nonfreeholder. A freeholder was essentially a person who owned land. Note 17 further discusses spring-gun rules.

9. *Hoskins v. Huling,* 2 Wills., Civ. Cas. Ct. App. sec. 161 (Tex. 1884); *State v. Waters,* 6 Jones 276 (N.C. 1859); *Morse v. Nixon,* 8 Jones 35 (N.C. 1860). See also *Thompson v. State,* 67 Ala. 106 (1880); *Bost v. Mingues,* 64 N.C. 44 (1870); *Cannon v. Horsey,* 1 Houst. 440 (Del. 1857); and *Hobson v. Perry,* 1 Hill 277 (S.C. 1833).

10. The Connecticut case is *Simmonds v. Holmes,* 61 Conn. 1 (1891). For other cases about dogs, see *Milman v. Shockley,* 1 Houst. 444 (Del. 1857); *Parrott v. Hartsfield,* 4 Dev. & B. 110 (N.C. 1839); and *Carpenter v. Lippett,* 77 Mo. 242 (1833). Chapter 4 shows similar attitudes toward dogs in accident cases involving common carriers. For more information about grazing practices in the South, see Owsley, *Plain Folk,* and McWhiney, *Cracker Culture.*

11. See *Christy v. Hughes,* 24 Mo. App. 275 (1887); and *Turner v. Thomas,* 71 Mo. 596 (1880).

12. See, for example, *Chapman v. Comw.,* 12 Ky. Law Rep. 704 (1891); and *Carroll v. State,* 23 Ala. 28 (1853).

13. See *State v. Woodward,* 1 Houst. 455 (Del. 1874); *State v. Brandon,* 6 Jones 463 (N.C. 1862); *State v. McDonald,* 4 Jones 19 (N.C. 1856); and *Harrison v. State,* 24 Ala. 67 (1854).

14. For example, see *Price v. State,* 72 Ga. 441 (1884).

15. *Ayers v. State,* 60 Miss. 709 (1883); *Parrish v. Commonwealth,* 81 Va. 1 (1884); *Lilly v. State,* 20 Tex. App. 1 (1885). Also see Brown, "Southern Violence," 27–41.

16. Sir William Blackstone, *Commentaries on the Laws of England* (London: A. Strahan, 1787).

17. Landes and Posner, *The Economic Structure,* 176, called this rule economically efficient. Notices appropriately focus the defendant's objective on deterrence, not retribution. For the antebellum period, one questions whether prospective burglars could have read signs. Perhaps a drawing of a gun would have sufficed as notice in those days. Bacon, *Abridgment,* 126, cited the English case of *Hott v. Wilkes,* 3 Barn. & A. 304, as support for spring-gun owners. But the English owner of a tulip

garden who had not warned of a spring gun was liable in civil damages to an innocent intruder who was gallantly trying to retrieve a peahen for a distraught female servant. *Bird v. Holbrook*, 4 Bing. 628 (1828). Alabama cases show an interesting development of the law in one Southern state. Alabama at first did not allow spring guns except to protect dwelling houses. *Simpson v. State*, 59 Ala. 1 (1877). But in *Scheuermann v. Scharfenberg*, 163 Al. 337 (1909), a storeowner could keep a spring gun in his warehouse to protect his valuable merchandise at night without worrying about paying civil damages to intruders.

18. See Michael S. Hindus, *Prison and Plantation* (Chapel Hill: University of North Carolina Press, 1980), 78.

19. See, for example, *Katko v. Briney*, 183 N.W. 2d 657 (Ia. 1971).

20. *State v. Plumlee*, 177 La. 687 (1933); *State v. Turner*, 190 La. 198 (1938); *State v. Metcalfe*, 206 N.W. 620 (Ia. 1925). In *McKellar v. Mason*, 159 So. 2d 700 (La. 1964), the court used slave cases to excuse a sixty-four-year-old defendant who shot a boy in a dark raincoat at night. The boy had been trying to steal the defendant's homing pigeons; the man had yelled at the boy, then shot in fear for the safety of himself and his wife.

21. In some states, nearly anyone could discipline an "insubordinate" free black as well. See, for example, *State v. Jowers*, 11 Ired. 555 (N.C. 1850), and *Roser v. Marlow*, R.M.C. 542 (Ga. 1837). One reason for allowing private citizens to have some disciplinary power was the existence of hidden runaway-slave communities. Herbert Aptheker, "Maroons Within the Present Limits of the United States," in *Articles on American Slavery*, vol. 13, ed. Finkelman, reported that at least fifty camps of fugitives were scattered about various states, including South Carolina, North Carolina, Virginia, Louisiana, Florida, Georgia, Mississippi, and Alabama. The biggest concentration was in the Dismal Swamp area between Virginia and North Carolina.

One intriguing question was whether private discipline of slaves (and free blacks) for petty offenses was more efficacious – at least for white people – than public discipline. Louisiana and South Carolina came to similar views on the appropriate treatment of "insolence": Both decided that punishment should be up to the public sector. Louisiana punished free colored persons, but not whites, publicly. As a result, a defendant who had killed a free man of color for insulting him could not reduce a murder charge to manslaughter because the legal system had provided a remedy for his "injury." *State v. Fuentes*, 5 La. An. 427 (1850). A South Carolina court was divided on this point. The majority determined that females and weak persons could not rely on a slave master to punish his slave for insolence; instead, they needed the courts to protect them. Although the justices hesitated to intrude on the master's rights, they wanted to preserve social order. Judge O'Neall dissented, saying: "[N]o jurisdiction ever did exist, which is liable to more abuse than that exercised by Magistrates over slaves. Clothe them with the power to try slaves for insolence, and the result will be that passion, prejudice and ignorance will crowd abuses on this inferior jurisdiction to an extent not to be tolerated by slave owners." *Ex parte Boylston*, 2

Strob. 41, 47 (S.C. 1846). Courts debated as well the appropriate level of judicial intervention when slaves committed petty offenses. A Florida court advocated that: "It is much better for the master, the slave, and the community at large that provisions be made for the summary punishment of slaves for such offenses [card playing] before a justice of the peace, than the slave be dignified and brought into court with the same importance with the white man, and the master in consequence thereof be put to heavy expense in employing counsel and protecting his slave." *Murray v. State*, 9 Fl. 246, 254 (1860).

22. *Allain v. Young*, 9 Mart. 221 (La. 1821); *Smith v. Hancock*, Bibb 222 (Ky. 1815); *Dearing v. Moore*, 26 Ala. 586 (1855). See also *Laperouse v. Rice*, 13 La. An. 567 (La. 1858).

23. *Dodson v. Mock*, 4 Dev. & B. 146 (N.C. 1838). For other examples involving animals, see *Wheatley v. Harris*, 4 Sneed 468 (Tn. 1857), and *Parker v. Mise*, 27 Ala. 480 (1855). Bacon, *Abridgment*, further discusses the law of livestock, particularly in vol. 8, p. 472.

24. *Holmes v. Kuhn*, 4 Call 274 (Va. 1792); *Brown v. May*, 1 Munf. 288 (Va. 1810); *Locke v. Gibbs*, 4 Ired. 42 (N.C. 1843); *Polk v. Fancher*, 1 Head 336, 338 (Tn. 1858). Other such cases include *Fail v. Presley*, 50 Al. 342 (1874); *Wheat v. Croom*, 7 Al. 349 (1845); *Sublet v. Walker*, 6 J.J. Marsh. 212 (Ky. 1831); and *dicta* in *Bayon v. Mollere*, 4 Mart. 66 (La. 1815). Under *Fail*, the action stood even though slave Israel had been emancipated. If a slaveowner could not prove a loss, he generally received no damages. *Hervy v. Armstrong*, 15 Ark. 162 (1854); *Belmore v. Caldwell*, 2 Bibb 76 (Ky. 1810); *Voss v. Howard*, 28 F.C. 1301 (D.C. 1805); and *Cornfute v. Dale*, 1 Har. & J. 4 (Md. 1800). In contrast, under *Garey v. Johnson*, 2 Cr. C.C. 107 (D.C. 1814), the plaintiff could recover damages without proof of loss if the defendant without sufficient provocation had beaten the plaintiff's slaves.

25. *Pierce v. Myrick*, 1 Dev. 345 (N.C. 1827); *Arnandez v. Lawes*, 5 La. An. 127 (1850); *Jones v. Allen*, 1 Head 626, 636 (Tn. 1858). Note the contrast of *Arnandez* with the case of *McClelland v. Kay* discussed at note 8.

26. *State v. Jarrott*, 1 Ired. 76 (N.C. 1840); *State v. Caesar*, 9 Ired. 391 (N.C. 1849) (overturned by *State v. David*, 4 Jones 353 (N.C. 1857)); *Dave v. State*, 22 Ala. 23 (1853).

27. *McRaeny v. Johnson*, 2 Fl. 520, 527 (1849).

28. Richard H. Haunton, "Law and Order in Savannah, 1850–1860," in *Crime and Justice in American History: The South*, part 1, ed. Eric H. Monkkonen (New York: K.G. Saur, 1992), reported this incident.

29. See Landes and Posner, *The Economic Structure*, 186; Malone, "Genesis"; Bacon, *Abridgment*, vol. 6, p. 551, and vol. 8, pp. 452, 462; and Chapters 1 and 7 of this book. See *Fluker v. R. Co.*, 81 Ga. 461 (1889), for an injured-servant case.

30. In Delaware, Maryland, and Louisiana, perpetrators had to provide restitution to those who suffered property damage. Arson was a criminal act highly feared in many states: Wooden structures crammed cheek-by-jowl and ineffective fire-fighting capabilities understandably made people nervous. In 1841, New York abolished the death penalty

– except for crimes of treason, murder, and first-degree arson. Like many states, New York later abolished the death penalty completely. But New York Governor George Pataki restored the death penalty for several serious crimes on March 7, 1995. For details of early law, see Friedman, *Crime and Punishment*, 74, 109–10; Lawrence M. Friedman, "The Development of American Criminal Law," in *Law and Order in American History*, ed. Joseph M. Hawes (Port Washington, NY: Kennikat Press, 1979), 14, 23–24; Jack K. Williams, "Crime and Punishment in Alabama, 1819–1840," in *Crime and Justice in American History*, ed. Monkkonen, part 1, p. 467; James A. Webb, "Criminal Law and Procedure," in *Two Centuries' Growth of American Law, 1701–1901* (New York: Scribner's, 1901), 375.

31. *State v. Council*, 1 Overt. 305 (Tn. 1808); *State v. Landreth*, 2 Term. 446 (N.C. 1816). Dog cases include *Davis v. Comw.*, 17 Grat. 617 (Va. 1867); *State v. Marshall*, 13 Tex. 55 (1854); and *Maclin's Case*, 3 Leigh 809 (Va. 1831).

32. *State v. Hale*, 2 Hawks 582, 583, 585 (N.C. 1823). Tennessee adopted the same reasoning in *Nelson v. State*, 10 Humph. 518 (Tn. 1850); Tennessee's Act of 1813 stated that beating the slaves of another was an indictable offense. The reasoning in *Hale* foreshadows the scholarly work of Landes and Posner, *Economic Structure*, esp. 189. Economic theory suggests that one purpose of criminal law is to control harmful externalities in circumstances where damage remedies are insufficient, mostly because optimal damages exceed the defendant's wealth.

33. *Comw. v. Lee*, 3 Metc. 229, 232 (Ky. 1860); *Hickerson v. U.S.*, 2 Hayw. & H. (D.C. 1856). Under *U.S. v. Butler*, 1 Cr. C.C. 373 (D.C. 1806), assault and battery of a slave was indictable. Public abuse of animals was likewise punishable by the state, as Chapter 7 notes.

34. *State v. Roane*, 2 Dev. 58 (N.C. 1828); *McDaniel v. State*, 8 S. & M. 401 (Miss. 1847); *State v. Moore*, 8 Rob. 518 (La. 1843); *State v. Davis*, 14 La. An. 678 (1859). The defense in *Roane* unsuccessfully argued that people had been worried about runaways in the neighborhood.

35. *State v. Walker*, N.C. Term. Rep. 230 (1817). The other two cases are *State v. Scott*, 1 Hawks 24 (N.C. 1820), and *State v. Jones*, Walk. 83, 85 (Ms. 1820). See also *Nix v. State*, 13 Tx. 575 (1855); *State v. Motley*, 7 Rich. 327 (S.C. 1854); *Chandler v. State*, 2 Tx. 305 (1847); *State v. Moore*, 8 Rob. 518 (La. 1843); *State v. Flanigin*, 5 Al. 477 (1843); *Comw. v. Howard*, 11 Leigh 632 (Va. 1841); *State v. Wilson*, Cheves 163 (S.C. 1840); *Fields v. State*, 1 Yerg. 156 (Tn. 1829); *Comw. v. Cheny*, 2 Va. Ca. 158 (1819); and *Comw v. Chapple*, 1 Va. Ca. 184 (Va. 1811).

36. *State v. Tackett*, 1 Hawks 210 (N.C. 1820); *State v. Winningham*, 10 Rich. 257 (S.C. 1857); *State v. Boon*, Taylor 103, 110 (N.C. 1801); *Jordan v. State*, 22 Ga. 545 (1857). Hindus, "Black Justice," 242–43, argued that in a sample of South Carolina cases only atrocious murders of slaves by men of low standing brought convictions. The defendant in *State v. Cheatwood*, 2 Hill 459 (S.C. 1834), for instance, had shot the winner of a gambling game. Hindus thought the conviction stood because the defendant had offended society by gambling with slaves.

37. *Morgan v. Rhodes*, 1 Stew. 70, 71 (Al. 1827); *Middleton v. Holmes*, 3 Port. 424 (Al. 1836); *Neal v. Farmer*, 9 Ga. 555 (1851). In *Middleton*, a slave-owner attempted to recover damages from a constable who had killed a slave fleeing arrest. English law prohibited plaintiffs from pursuing civil remedies until felons were first convicted. Most American states do not have this timing rule – one can even win in a civil trial when the defendant is acquitted in a criminal trial. Webb, "Criminal Law," 345; Bacon, *Abridgment*, vol. 1, p. 145; *American Jurisprudence* 2d, "Assault and Battery," sec. 109, "Actions," sec. 45. Criminal actions sometimes barred civil ones when slaves were sold. In *Johnson v. Lemons*, 2 Bail. 392 (S.C. 1831), the plaintiff had brought about the defendant's indictment on the charge of harboring slaves, so he could not also bring an action for the slave's services. On the other hand, civil suits sometimes took the place of criminal suits in kidnapping cases. The court in *McBain v. Smith*, 13 Ga. 315 (1853), determined that, when slaves were stolen, their owner could bring an action to recover the slaves themselves (rather than money damages) without prosecuting the thief in a criminal trial. An Arkansas court reasoned similarly in a brutality case against an overseer. *Brunson v. Martin*, 17 Ark. 270 (1856).

38. Crimes committed by slaves (and often free blacks) were a different story – slaves tended to be whipped or executed for their crimes, as Chapter 7 briefly discusses. North Carolina's Act of 1823, among others, made assaulting a white a felony, if done by a person of color. See Flanigan, *Criminal Law*, for greater detail on criminal slave law. For more discussion of criminal laws in the South generally, see Hindus, *Prison*, 90–95, 110–11; Williams, "Crime and Punishment," 471; Robert M. Ireland, "Law and Disorder in Nineteenth-Century Kentucky," in *Crime and Justice in American History*, ed. Monkkonen, 246; Walker, *Popular Justice*, 109; Richard M. Brown, "Southern Violence – Regional Problem or National Nemesis? Legal Attitudes Toward Southern Homicide in Historical Perspective," in *Crime and Justice in American History*, ed. Monkkonen, 26; Edward L. Ayers, *Vengeance and Justice: Crime and Punishment in the Nineteenth Century American South* (New York: Oxford University Press, 1984); Webb, "Criminal Law," 377–81; and Friedman, "The Development."

39. See Hindus, *Prison*, xxvii, for example. As one might expect, the South was a violent place well into the twentieth century – and still is, in some parts. H.C. Brearley wryly referred to the South as "that part of the United States that lies below the Smith and Wesson line." H.C. Brearley, "The Pattern of Violence," in *Culture in the South*, ed. W.T. Couch (Chapel Hill: University of North Carolina Press, 1934), 678.

40. *Grainger v. State*, 5 Yerg. 459 (Tn. 1830); *Ex parte Wray*, 30 Ms. 673 (1856).

41. Brown, "Southern Violence." Some Texans continue to cherish their right of self-defense: A Fort Worth man recently started a hugely successful corporation called "Dead Serious" that will pay $5,000 "in the event you kill someone in accordance with Texas Penal Code 9.42 while they are in the process of committing a crime against you, your family,

or your property" – all for only $10 annual dues. (The corporation will pay only after authorities clear the killer of criminal charges.) Texas has also recently approved laws that permit the carrying of a concealed weapon.

42. Daniel J. Flanigan, "Criminal Procedure in Slave Trials in the Antebellum South," in *Crime and Justice in American History: Courts and Criminal Procedure*, ed. Eric H. Monkkonen (Westport, CT: Meckler, 1991), 101.

43. Hindus, *Prison and Plantation*, 29, 63; Ireland, "Law and Disorder."

44. Walker, *Popular Justice*, 111, reported this incident.

45. *Law v. Law*, 2 Grat. 366 (Va. 1845); *Johnson v. Courts*, 3 Har. & McH. 510 (Md. 1797); *Hepburn v. Sewell*, 5 H. & J. 211 (Md. 1821). Also see *Irish v. Wright*, 8 Rob. 428 (La. 1844). Fogel and Engerman calculated that female slaves' prices included the value of the children they were expected to bear. Fogel and Engerman, *Time*, 75ff.

46. Williams, "Crime and Punishment," 465.

47. *State v. Miles*, 2 Nott. & McC. 1, 3 (S.C. 1819). See also *State v. Clayton*. The court in *Spivey v. State*, 26 Al. 90, 99 (1855), echoed the sentiment in *Miles* word-for-word, adding that "it was proper . . . to resort to terms suited to the nature of the property intended to be protected." Another Alabama court sentenced a slavestealer to ten years in prison. *Murray v. State*, 18 Al. 727 (1851).

48. *State v. Thompson*, 2 Over. 96, 99 (Tn. 1807); *Cash v. State*, 10 Humph. 111 (Tn. 1849). *Morehead v. State*, 9 Humph. 635 (Tn. 1849), provides another example.

49. Helping slaves escape might have harmed third parties, however, because successful escapes might have encouraged other slaves to flee. This effect would have mitigated the potential price increase caused by lower supply of slaves. The likelier slaves were to try and escape, the greater the costs of monitoring and thus the less that buyers would have been willing to pay.

50. *State v. Hawkins*, 8 Port. 461 (Al. 1839); *Drayton v. U.S.*, 1 Hayw. & H. 369 (D.C. 1849). *Hawkins* noted that many states, including South Carolina, Kentucky, and North Carolina, distinguished cases in similar ways. Under Rev. Stat. 1852, Kentucky could put a slave stealer to death. But the state typically only imposed a $10 to $200 fine for unlawfully taking a slave without felonious intent. The defendant paid $200 in *Jones v. Comw.*, 1 Bush 34 (Ky. 1866), for example. North Carolina imposed a $100 statutory penalty on those who harbored slaves – to be paid to the slaves' owner. Louisiana distinguished three separate offenses: stealing, inveigling, and carrying away slaves. The state also treated the acts of harboring slaves and criminally concealing slaves as distinct offenses. Acts of 14 April 1807 and 20 March 1809, Stat. of 6 Mar. 1819, sec. 3. Tennessee's Act of 1835 did not make harboring a slave a felony unless the defendant had persuaded the slave to leave his or her master.

51. *Smith v. Comw.*, 6 Grat. 696 (1849), 7 Grat. 593 (1850); *Kitty v. Fitzhugh*, 4 Rand. 600 (Va. 1826). Virginia's statute of 1 Rev. Code, chap. 111, sec. 30, made carrying slaves out of state a felony. The defendant in *Thomas*

v. Comw., 2 Leigh 741 (Va. 1830), received a three-year sentence and a fine. In *House v. Comw.*, 8 Leigh 755 (Va. 1837), the defendant paid $200 and spent six months in jail. In *Cole v. Comw.*, 5 Grat. 696 (Va. 1848), the defendant was sentenced to two years for advising slaves to abscond. (He received a new trial because of errors in evidence.) The defendant in *Sherman v. Comw.*, 14 Grat. 677 (Va. 1858), received a six-year sentence. See also *Young v. Comw.*, 1 Rob. 805 (Va. 1842); *Tooll v. Comw.*, 11 Leigh 714 (Va. 1841); and *Comw. v. Peas*, 4 Leigh 679 (Va. 1833).

52. Finkelman, *State Slavery Statutes.*

53. *Nelson v. Whetmore*, 1 Rich. 318 (S.C. 1845). The defendant should reasonably have owed something to the stagecoach operators for his fraud; the case did not address this issue.

54. *Logan v. Comw.*, 2 Grat. 571 (Va. 1845); *Bacon v. Comw.* 7 Grat. 602 (Va. 1850); *Comw. v. Garner*, 3 Grat. 655 (Va. 1846).

55. *Wilson v. State*, 21 Md. 1 (1864).

56. *Lee v. West*, 47 Ga. 311 (1872). Also see Wood, *Treatise*, 436–37; Bacon, *Abridgment*, vol. 8, p. 649.

57. Act of 1855. Several other Southern – and Northern – states passed statutes to punish the theft of livestock. The 1880s Texas Code, for example, imprisoned horse thieves for five to fifteen years and cattle rustlers for two to five years. Stealers of sheep, hogs, and goats were fined and imprisoned for a few months to five years, depending on the value of the beast stolen. Horse theft in Alabama was punishable by a $500 fine, a year in jail, thirty-nine lashes, and a "T" branded on the face or hands. Louisiana's 1821 laws imposed a $200 fine or six months in jail plus civil damages for injuries to horses, mules, and jackasses. In North Carolina's Act of 1741 (chap. 8, sec. 10), the punishment for one's first offense of horse stealing was whipping and loss of ears; the second offense brought a death sentence. Wisconsin and Pennsylvania formed societies in the 1860s to protect against larcenies of livestock. Friedman, *Crime and Punishment*, 110; Williams, "Crime and Punishment," 465; Friedman, "The Development," 19; Schafer, *Slavery*, 29. Haunton, "Law and Order," 183, noted that stealing slaves or horses in antebellum Savannah earned one a prison term for several years, whereas most other property crimes were misdemeanors.

58. *State v. Bennet*, 3 Brev. 515 (S.C. 1815).

59. For accounts of the travails of free blacks, see Hyman and Wiecek, *Equal Justice*, 105–6; Wiecek, *The Sources*, 88; Morris, *Free Men All*, chap. 2. Kidnapped blacks received no compensation in *Jason v. Henderson*, 7 Md. 430 (1855), *Franklin v. Waters*, 8 Gill 322 (Md. 1848), or *Currannee v. McQueen*, 6 F.C. 984 (1827–40). Damages of one cent were awarded in *McMichen v. Amis*, 4 Rand. 134 (Va. 1826), and *Hook v. Pagee*, 2 Munf. 379 (Va. 1811). Rarely, back wages were awarded to kidnapped freedmen. See *Gordon v. Duncan*, 3 Mo. 385 (1834); *Matilda v. Crenshaw*, 4 Yerg. 299 (Tn. 1833); and *Jones v. Conoway*, 4 Yeates 109 (Pa. 1804).

60. *Hartman v. Insurance Co.*, 21 Pa. St. 466, 471 (Pa. 1853). The insurance company had a fall-back position: Callender had committed suicide by

swallowing arsenic. For a discussion of fugitive slaves and the federal laws surrounding their capture and return, see Campbell, *Slave Catchers*. Some Northern states, including Indiana (1824) and Pennsylvania (1826), also had fugitive slave laws.

61. *Chase v. Maberry*, 3 Harr. 266 (Del. 1840). The plaintiff might appropriately have received half of the original $60 reward as well.

62. The external costs associated with fugitive slaves may even have exceeded the lost value of particular runaways to their masters – runaway slaves were worth considerably less than their stay-at-home brothers. Fogel, *Without Consent*, 70, fig. 12.

63. *Elliott v. Gibson*, 10 B. Mon. 438, 442 (Ky. 1850). The court in *Nall v. Proctor*, 3 Metc. 447 (Ky. 1861), clarified that the Act of 1860 granted the reward only to those who delivered the fugitive to his owner or to the jail in the owner's county of residence, not to the jail in the county where the arrest had occurred.

64. *Landry v. Klopman*, 13 La. An. 345, 346 (1858). The defendant, who had bought the slave from the sheriff, therefore retained title. States frequently provided procedural guidelines for advertising runaways. For example, Alabama's Act of 1809 required that announcements of the commitment of fugitive slaves be posted at the courthouse and two other public places. Texas required sheriffs to advertise the capture of fugitives in any Austin newspaper for three months before selling them. Finkelman, *State Slavery Statutes*.

65. Interactions with free blacks were similarly restricted. Many states forbade interracial gaming, for example.

66. Some states outlawed the sale of liquor to American Indians as well. Friedman, *Crime and Punishment*, 97. The District of Columbia also passed an ordinance in 1837 to forbid the sale of spirits to free persons of color. And Virginia freedmen could not own taverns. *Mayo v. James*, 12 Grat. 17 (Va. 1855).

67. *O'Halloran v. State*, 31 Ga. 206, 210 (Ga. 1860). Also see *State v. Miller*, 7 Ired. 275 (N.C. 1847). Under *Foster v. State*, 38 Al. 425 (1862), and *Comw. v. Smith*, 1 Grat. 553 (Va. 1844), an indictment for selling liquor to slaves need not even name the slaveowner. *Calvert v. Stone*, 10 B. Mon. 152 (Ky. 1850), and *Comw. v. Kenner*, 11 B. Mon. 1 (Ky. 1850), refer to state statutes disallowing such sales to slaves. For specific laws, see Finkelman, *State Slavery Statutes*.

68. *Delery v. Mornet*, 11 Mart. O.S. 4, 8 (La. 1822); *Harrison v. Berkley*, 1 Strob. 525, 550 (S.C. 1847); *Skinner v. Hughes*, 13 Mo. 440, 443 (1850) (citing *Harrison*); *Belding v. Johnson*, 86 Ga. 177 (1890).

69. *Wilson v. Comw.*, 12 B. Mon. 2 (Ky. 1851); *Comw. v. Hatton*, 15 B. Mon. 537 (Ky. 1855). Also see *Johnson v. Comw.*, 12 Grat. 714 (1855), and Va. Code (chap. 104, sec. 1, 459).

70. *Smith v. Comw.*, 6 B. Mon. 21 (Ky. 1845); *Bosworth v. Brand*, 1 Dana 377, 380 (Ky. 1833). See Chapter 7 for other references to slave assemblies.

71. *Dunn v. State*, 15 Ga. 419, 421 (1854); *Jarrett v. Higbee*, 5 T.B. Mon. 546, 551 (Ky. 1827); *Hurt v. State*, 19 Ala. 19 (1851); *Love v. Brindle*, 7 Jones 560, 561 (N.C. 1860). Yet Clarence Mohr, in a study of Oglethorpe

County, Georgia, found little evidence of a reduction in slaves' trading activities when a $10 fine was imposed. A larger fine was perhaps more successful. Mohr also reported that South Carolina in 1817 imposed a $1,000 fine and a year in jail upon those who traded with slaves; by 1834, free persons could not transact with slaves even if the slaves had permission from their masters. Clarence L. Mohr, "Slavery in Oglethorpe County, Georgia, 1773–1865," in *Articles on American Slavery*, vol. 7, ed. Finkelman. North Carolina imposed a penalty on those who traded with slaves, with half of the fine going toward the plaintiff and half to the wardens of the poor. The court in *State v. Hart*, 4 Ired. 222 (N.C. 1844), reasoned that the fine was meant to keep slaves faithful to their owners and to protect the community from vagabond slaves. Similarly, Tennessee's Act of 1813 granted half its fine to the slaveowner and half to the plaintiff, although the court in *Kelly v. Davis*, 1 Head 71 (Tn. 1858), made clear that trading with slaves did not lead to a criminal proceeding. Florida imposed a $100 fine on defendants who had bought grain from a black – slave or free – without a permit. *Harris v. State*, 9 Fl. 156 (1860). But Higginbotham and Kopytoff, "Property First," 517–19, observed that Virginia slaves could trade with the consent of their masters; they speculated that this practice increased slave values and facilitated business transactions. And Peter H. Wood, *Black Majority* (New York: Norton, 1974), 209–10, recounted how South Carolina rejected proposed legislation that would have prevented Negroes from taking produce from the country to sell in the city. Wealthy planters blocked the bill because they liked having slaves do the marketing, as Chapter 7 notes.

72. *Naylor v. Hays*, 7 B. Mon. 478 (Ky. 1847). For discussion of statutes, see *Barnett v. Powell*, Litt. Sel. Cas. 409 (Ky. 1821); *Enderman v. Ashby*, Ky. Dec. 65 (Ky. 1801); and Schwarz, *Twice Condemned*, 92–113.

73. *Dunbar v. Williams*, 10 Johns. 249 (N.Y. 1813); *Manning v. Cox*, 4 Cr. C.C. 693 (D.C. 1836); *Hord v. Grimes*, 13 B. Mon. 188 (Ky. 1852).

74. *Wright v. Gray*, 2 Bay 464 (S.C. 1802); *Berry v. State*, 10 Ga. 511 (1851); *Grady v. State*, 11 Ga. 253 (1852).

75. *State v. Thackam*, 1 Bay 358 (S.C. 1794); *Brown v. Comw.*, 2 Leigh 769 (Va. 1830).

76. *State v. Worth*, 7 Jones 488 (N.C. 1860). North Carolina had passed an act in 1830 to prevent the circulation of seditious material. Virginia Sess. Act. 1835–6, chap. 66, p. 44, also sought to suppress circulation of incendiary abolitionary materials. But eleven people who had signed a petition to end slavery and the slave trade in the District of Columbia were not necessarily indictable for it, because they did not belong to an abolition society. *Comw. v. Barrett*, 9 Leigh 665 (Va. 1839). Mississippi (1830) and Missouri (1836) barred the publication and circulation of abolition pamphlets. Tennessee's Act of 1801 was quite general – it forbade anyone from inflaming a slave or person of color with words. Finkelman, *State Slavery Statutes*.

77. *Bayon v. Prevost*, 4 Mart. 58, 65 (La. 1813); *Bakewell v. Talbot*, 4 Dana 216, 219 (Ky. 1836). A jury had found the defendant liable in *Bakewell*,

but an appellate court reversed and remanded the case, saying that preventing an escape required only ordinary (not extraordinary) care.

78. *Rogers v. Fenwick,* 1 Cr. C.C. 136 (D.C. 1803); *Voss v. Howard,* 1 Cr. C.C. 251 (D.C. 1805); *Fairchild v. Bell,* 2 Brev. 129 (S.C. 1807); *Belfour v. Raney,* 8 Ark. 479 (1848); *Keller v. Bates,* 3 Metc. 130 (Ky. 1860). *Toomer v. Gadsden,* 4 Strob. 193 (S.C. 1850), came to a conclusion identical to that in Belfour under similar circumstances.

79. See, for example, *Jesserich v. Walruff,* 51 Mo. App. 270 (1892), and *Sweetwater Mfg. Co. v. Glover,* 29 Ga. 399 (1859). Masters had some obligation to aid apprentices injured on the job. Wood, *A Treatise,* 193.

80. See, for example, *Quinn v. R.R.,* 94 Tn. 713 (1895), and *R.R. v. Price,* 32 Fl. 46 (1893).

81. *Evans v. Iglehart,* 6 Gill. & J. 171, 187 (Md. 1834); *Badillo v. Tio,* 7 La. An. 487 (1852).

7. THE PROBLEM OF SOCIAL COST

1. Harriet Beecher Stowe, *Uncle Tom's Cabin* (New York: Random House, 1985), 508.

2. Several historians and economists have discussed master–slave interactions within social and legal constraints, including Tushnet, *The American Law;* Fogel and Engerman, *Time;* Franklin, *From Slavery;* Schafer, *Slavery;* James Oakes, *Slavery and Freedom* (New York: Vintage, 1990); Atack and Passell, *A New Economic View,* 338–39; Avery O. Craven, *The Coming of the Civil War* (Chicago: University of Chicago Press, 1966); and Ely and Bodenhamer, "Regionalism," 3, 5. Blassingame, *The Slave Community;* Rosengarten, *Tombee;* and Leslie H. Owens, *This Species of Property: Slave Life and Culture in the Old South* (New York: Oxford University Press, 1976), sketched portraits of plantation life. Others have portrayed the life of blacks in the American Civil War. Bell I. Wiley, *Southern Negroes, 1861–1865* (New Haven, Yale University Press, 1965); James M. McPherson, *The Negro's Civil War* (New York: Ballentine Books, 1991).

3. Disputes surrounding slaveowners' treatment of their own property constitute 207 of the cases involving slaves; several other cases contain *dicta* setting forth guidelines for slaveowners as well.

4. For discussions of plantation law, see Franklin, *From Slavery,* 116; Fogel and Engerman, *Time,* 128–29; and Craven, *The Coming,* 91. Also see Hindus, "Black Justice," 238, 245; Roark, *Masters Without Slaves,* 69; and Oakes, *Ruling Race.*

5. See, for example, Oakes, *Slavery,* 159.

6. *Invention of Free Labor,* 6–7, 178. For a comprehensive discussion of indentured servitude, see David W. Galenson, *White Servitude in Colonial America: An Economic Analysis* (Cambridge: Cambridge University Press, 1981).

7. *Law, Labor.*

8. Fogel and Engerman, *Time,* 147, noted that slaveowners tended to whip slaves rather than withhold food or commit slaves to jail.

9. Elizabeth H. Pleck, *Domestic Tyranny: The Making of Social Policy Against Family Violence from Colonial Times to the Present* (New York: Oxford University Press, 1987), chap. 5.

10. Elizabeth H. Pleck, "Criminal Approaches to Family Violence, 1640–1980," in *Family Violence*, ed. Lloyd E. Ohlin and Michael H. Tonry (Chicago: University of Chicago Press, 1989).

11. Hindus, "Black Justice," 243.

12. Much of what follows could pertain to adult servants vis-à-vis animals and family members. These considerations, coupled with what has already been discussed, help explain why adult servants were protected more than animals and family members.

13. Quoted in Dumond, *Antislavery Origins*, 42.

14. Many judges, north and south, argued that slavery needed positive law to preserve its existence. Some courts followed English common law in this matter: Slave Somerset went free in the famous case of *Somerset v. Stewart*, 20 How. Str. Tr. 1 (1772), because England had no law establishing slavery. Lemuel Shaw, chief justice of the Massachusetts Supreme Court, argued that slavery was contrary to natural law because it was founded on brute force. Others said that the mere existence of slavery made it legal or that slavery was acceptable if no law prohibited it. Regardless, most judges agreed that slaves, like other property, required a scaffolding of laws to protect them. For discussions, see John C. Hurd, *Law of Freedom and Bondage in the United States* (Boston: Little, Brown, 1858); Goodell, *American Slavery*, 268; and Leonard W. Levy, *The Law of the Commonwealth and Chief Justice Shaw* (Cambridge, MA: Harvard University Press, 1957), 65. Peter J. Riga, "The American Crisis over Slavery: An Example of the Relationship Between Legality and Morality," *American Journal of Jurisprudence* 26 (1981), and Robert M. Cover, *Justice Accused: Antislavery and the Judicial Process* (New Haven: Yale University Press, 1975), chaps. 1–3, contain discussions of slavery and natural law. Chapter 4 of this book discusses the increasing need for intervention in the later antebellum period, especially with regard to slave escapes from common carriers.

15. *State v. Rhodes*, Phil. 453, 457 (N.C. 1868). According to Pleck, *Domestic Tyranny*, 75, the privacy of the antebellum family was sacrosanct.

16. *The Grass Is Singing* (London: M. Joseph, 1950), chap. 8.

17. Goodell, *American Slavery*, 196, 223, discussed why other animals also received gentler treatment than slaves. The closeness among family members might cut the other way, of course. Those to whom we are more attached also have more ability to enrage us.

18. Elizabeth H. Pleck, "Wife Beating in Nineteenth-Century America," *Victimology* 4, no. 1 (1979).

19. *State v. Caesar*, 9 Ired. 391 (N.C. 1849); *State v. David*, 4 Jones 353, 358 (N.C. 1857).

20. Men were entitled to their wives' property and their children's wages, but the nonpecuniary value of life was hard to quantify, then as now. (Chapter 1 also discusses this point.) Apparently, however, men sometimes sold their children and wives. The famous literary example is

Michael Henchard in Thomas Hardy, *The Mayor of Casterbridge* (New York: Signet, 1962), 16–20.

21. See note 35, Chapter 1, for a comparison of values. By this argument, animals should have received legal protection earlier than free persons because one could measure the benefits of protecting marketable property. This did occur, as I show later.

22. For discussion of employer liability, see Wood, *A Treatise*, esp. 499ff.; Oliver W. Holmes, Jr., "The History of Agency," in *Select Essays in Anglo-American Legal History* (Little, Brown, 1909), vol. 3, p. 368, and *Corpus Juris Secundum* (St. Paul: West Publishing, 1994), vol. 57, secs. 555–75. As Chapter 5 noted, the first use of the doctrine was in cases involving public officials, primarily sheriffs' deputies.

23. Steinfeld, *Invention*.

24. Households were considered small polities, in effect. In seventeenth-century England and Virginia, the murder of one's master was treason, not homicide. Steinfeld, *Invention*, 58.

25. Steinfeld referred mostly to Northern cases. *Invention*, 118. I also found a Kentucky case: *McGrath v. Herndon*, 4 T.B. Mon. 480 (Ky. 1827). Other rights accruing to servants were long in coming. The first American treatise written on master–servant law (in 1877) focused almost exclusively on the rights of the master, with almost no mention of the rights of servants. Wood, *A Treatise*.

26. Steinfeld devoted considerable discussion to this case. *Invention*, 144–49.

27. Employers still had to pay back wages for fired employees, as the overseer cases in Chapter 5 show. Tomlins, *Law, Labor*, 273, found that appellate courts disallowed awards granted to employees by trial courts if the employees had not finished out their terms. Ibid., 334ff., viewed these actions by judges as a refusal to innovate: Despite the new order brought about by industrialization, judges still gave employers the upper hand.

28. *Comw. v. Baird*, 1 Ashm. 267 (Pa. 1831); *Matthews v. Terry*, 10 Cn. 455 (1835). Insofar as factory supervisors are agents of owners, this practice contrasts with laws for slave overseers, who did have some physical control over their charges. See Chapter 5.

29. *Mitchell v. Armitage*, 10 Mart. 38 (La. 1833); *McKnight v. Hogg*, 3 Brev. 44 (S.C. 1812).

30. See, for example, *State v. Dickerson*, 98 N.C. 708 (1887).

31. *State v. Mann*, 2 Dev. 263, 266 (N.C. 1829); *Comw. v. Turner*, 5 Rand. 678 (Va. 1827) (Justice Brockenbrough's dissent appears in the text at note 42); *Jacob v. State*, 3 Humph. 483, 521 (Tn. 1842); *Oliver v. State*, 39 Ms. 526 (1860); *Markham v. Close*, 2 La. 581, 587 (La. 1831). In *Oliver*, the slaveowner was indicted for murder and convicted of manslaughter but received a new trial because jury instructions did not clearly state that a slave had to show unconditional submission. An appellate court did not rule as to whether slaveowners' rights included beating a slave on the head with a stick; it left the question to a new jury.

32. Andrew Fede, "Legitimized Violent Slave Abuse in the American South, 1619–1865: A Case Study of Law and Social Change in Six Southern States," *American Journal of Legal History* 29 (April 1985), claimed that Southern society increasingly circumscribed masters' behavior in order to maintain property values and slave discipline. Stampp, *The Peculiar Institution*, 217–24, and Eugene D. Genovese, *Roll, Jordan, Roll* (New York: Pantheon, 1974), 49–70, also noted that cruel masters faced legal actions more often after 1830. See also Morris, "'As If the Injury,'" 594. States differed as to what actions affected the community. The laws regarding Sunday work illustrate this. North Carolina refused to indict a slaveowner who worked his slaves on Sunday, for example, but South Carolina explicitly exempted slaves from Sunday labor. *State v. Williams*, 4 Ired. 400 (N.C. 1844); *State v. Miles*, 2 N. & McC. 1 (S.C. 1819) (citing the Act of December 1817). Louisiana allowed slaves to keep the proceeds of their Sunday labor. Arkansas passed a law in 1858 forbidding persons from hiring slaves to work on the Sabbath without the consent of the owner or overseer. Finkelman, *State Slavery Statutes*; Morris, "The Measurement of Bondage," 143, 160.

    Because slaves had no legal standing to sue for civil damages, only criminal actions made sense when a slaveowner hurt his own slave. If others hurt one's slave property, the legal system tended to merge civil and criminal liability – compensating the slaveowner typically sufficed for punishment. A court noted this point in *State v. Hale*, 2 Hawks 582 (N.C. 1823). For a discussion of *Hale*, see note 32, Chapter 6. In *Chandler v. State*, 2 Tx. 306 (1847), and *Fields v. State*, 1 Yerg. 156 (Tn. 1829), for example, the courts decided that killing another's slave without malice was at most manslaughter. The penalty in *Fields* – aside from any civil liability – was a burned hand, thirty days in jail, and costs. Criminal penalties could certainly deter those who could not afford to pay civil damages, however. Defendants occasionally received prison terms or capital punishment for abusing another's slaves, as previous chapters have discussed.

33. Postbellum livestock owners had duties to feed and care for their animals, at least in the North. See, for example, *State v. Bosworth*, 54 Ct. 1 (1886); Mass. Pub. St., chap. 207, sec. 52. An antebellum Vermont case ruled that servants were entitled to decent food and lodging as well. *Griffin v. Tyson*, 17 Vt. 35 (1842).

34. *State v. Bowen*, 3 Strob. 573, 575 (S.C. 1849). Alabama passed a statute in 1852 regarding the culpability of masters who failed to feed their slaves. *Cheek v. State*, 38 Ala. 227 (1861), provides an enforcement example. Louisiana, North Carolina, Florida, and Georgia codes also required suitable food and clothing for slaves; although the degree of enforcement varied. North Carolina masters paid damages for food that slaves stole and ate. David C. Rankin, "The Tannenbaum Thesis Reconsidered: Slavery and Race Relations in Antebellum Louisiana," in *Articles on American Slavery*, vol. 7, ed. Finkelman, 207–8, noted that, in spite of Louisiana's statutory requirements, the condition of Louisiana slaves differed little from that of other slaves by the time of the Civil War. For

discussions of various laws, see Friedman, *A History*, 225; Goodell, *American Slave Code*, part 1, chaps. 10–11; and Hurd, *Law of Freedom*, vol. 2, chaps. 17–19.

35. George M. Stroud, *A Sketch of the Laws Relating to Slavery in the Several States of the U.S.A.* (Philadelphia: Henry Longstreth, 1856), 40. Many courts also looked askance at allowing free blacks to testify.

36. People also reported others' cruel treatment of slaves. Cecil Harper, Jr., "Slavery Without Cotton: Hunt County, Texas, 1846–1864," in *Articles on American Slavery*, vol. 7, ed. Finkelman, 82, 95, noted a cruelty case brought against Texan Elizabeth Slack, for example.

37. *Trustees v. Hall*, 3 Harr. 322, 328 (Del. 1841).

38. *Henderson v. Vaulx*, 10 Yer. 30, 39 (Tn. 1836).

39. Finkelman, *State Slavery Statutes*.

40. *White v. Ross*, 5 S. & P. 123, 128 (Ala. 1833).

41. *U.S. v. Cross*, 4 Cr. C.C. 603 (D.C. 1835). Public beatings by those other than owners could create similar externalities, as the courts recognized. Chapter 6 discussed another D.C. case that used parallel reasoning: In *Hickerson v. U.S.*, 2 Hayw. & H. 228 (D.C. 1856), a court determined that the manager of a hirer was indictable for assaulting and battering slave James in a public highway if his actions had offended others. Although not all assaults and batteries were indictable, some were "because the offence is injurious to the citizens at large by its breach of the peace, by the terror and alarm it excites, by the disturbance of that social order which it is the primary objective of the law to maintain, and by the contagious example of crimes." *State v. Hale*, 2 Hawks 582, 584 (N.C. 1823). Judge Caruthers of Tennessee disapproved of mob violence against slaves in *Polk v. Fancher* (discussed in the text at Chapter 6, note 24), mainly because it could harm innocent people.

42. *Comw. v. Turner*, 5 Rand. 678, 690 (Va. 1827). *U.S. v. Brockett*, 2 Cr. C.C. 441 (D.C. 1823), is another case in point. Although a jury found the defendant not guilty of beating his own slave, it wanted the court to express its "strong disapprobation of similar conduct." Many major uprisings (or reports of uprisings) coincided with national elections, military actions, or economic recessions. Vesey, an ex-slave, allegedly planned the most extensive slave revolt in U.S. history in Charleston in 1822. Turner's uprising took place in Southampton County, Virginia, on August 21, 1831. An earlier rebellion took place on September 9, 1739, near the west branch of the Stono River in South Carolina. Even New York suffered from insurrections in 1712 and 1749. Slave Gabriel Prosser supposedly wanted to overtake Richmond in 1800. A large revolt occurred in 1811 just outside New Orleans; another took place in Texas in 1835 during the state's revolution. Waves of rebellions swept over the nation in 1856 and 1860. See Harper, *Slavery Without Cotton*, 91; Mohr, *Slavery in Oglethorpe County*, 104; Rankin, *The Tannenbaum Thesis*, 231; Wendell G. Addington, "Slave Insurrections in Texas," in *Articles on American Slavery*, vol. 13, ed. Finkelman, 2, 8–12; Richard C. Wade, "The Vesey Plot: A Reconsideration," in ibid.; Harvey Wish, "American Slave Insurrections Before 1861," in ibid.; Franklin, *From*

Slavery, 132–35; Stephen B. Oates, *The Fires of Jubilee: Nat Turner's Fierce Rebellion* (New York: Harper and Row, 1975); and Herbert Aptheker, *Nat Turner's Slave Rebellion* (New York: Humanities Press, 1966), "American Negro Slave Revolts," and "More on American Negro Slave Revolts," in *Articles on American Slavery*, vol. 13, ed. Finkelman. Aptheker reported that slaves even planned a multistate revolt in 1810, spanning Virginia and the Carolinas. Franklin, *From Slavery*, 130, also pointed out that mistreated slaves might commit arson, wreak havoc on tools and animals, commit suicide or mutilate themselves, or poison others. At least some of these actions could have affected free people other than the slaves' owners.

43. *State v. Hoover*, 4 Dev. & B. 365 (N.C. 1839); *State v. Jones*, 5 Al. 666 (1843); *Kelly v. State*, 3 S. & M. 518 (Ms. 1844); *Souther v. Comw.*, 7 Gratt. 673 (Va. 1851). Another North Carolina case carrying a criminal conviction was *State v. Robbins*, 3 Jones 249 (N.C. 1855). Here, a slaveowner had brutally murdered his sixty-year-old slave for allegedly failing to feed a horse. (The slave had in fact fed the beast.) In earlier years, North Carolina (along with Virginia and South Carolina) had exonerated masters who killed slaves in the act of resistance or under moderate correction. See William M. Wiecek, "The Statutory Law of Slavery and Race in the Thirteen Mainland Colonies of British America," *William and Mary Quarterly* 34 (April 1977): 266.

44. Ten Southern codes made mistreatment of slaves a crime, although such statutes were not always enforced. Louisiana provided for indictment of brutal owners (1806, 1855, 1857) and fined them under Art. 173 of the civil code. Cases include *State v. White*, 13 La. An. 573 (1858), and *State v. Morris*, 4 La. An. 177 (La. 1849). Yet often such brutality may have gone unreported, according to Schafer, *Slavery*, 49–52. Missouri's Constitution and Revised Code of 1845 (406) outlawed inhumane beating. South Carolina passed a law in 1841 that provided for a $500 fine and up to six months in jail for unlawful whipping of a slave.

45. *U.S. v. Lloyd*, 4 Cr. C.C. 470 (D.C. 1834) (a similar result held in *U.S. v. Cross*, 4 Cr. C.C. 603 (D.C. 1835)); *Eskridge v. State*, 25 Ala. 30 (1854) (an appellate court reversed the conviction for an error in the proceedings but left the possibility open for a new trial on similar charges); *Worley v. State*, 11 Humph. 172, 176 (Tn. 1850).

46. Many have emphasized the inadequacy of the legal system in protecting slaves, including Franklin, *From Slavery*, 130, and Schafer, *Slavery*, 32, 52. Fede, "Legitimized," extensively analyzed legislation and court records concerning slave abuse for six Southern states: Virginia, North Carolina, South Carolina, Georgia, Mississippi, and Alabama. He claimed that the codes of the first four states essentially sanctioned slave killings by their owners if slaves had been committing offenses, resisting their masters, or being corrected. But the murder cases cited above indicate that Virginia and North Carolina punished masters in some circumstances, at least. Like Louisiana and Missouri, the last four states fined those who subjected slaves to cruel or unusual punishment.

Fede found only one case in these states in which an owner was indicted – in *Turnipseed v. State*, 6 Ala. 664 (1843), a court assessed a $50 fine which was later reversed. *Dicta* in another Alabama case (*Eskridge*, cited in note 45) supported a fine, however. Mohr, "Slavery in Oglethorpe County," 107, noted that the Georgia penal code amply protected slaves, although the provisions may have meant little in practice. Also see Friedman, *A History*, 198–99; Goodell, *American Slavery*, part 1, chap. 8; and Hurd, *Law*.

47. For discussion, see Williams, "Administration"; John H. Ingham, *The Law of Animals* (Philadelphia: T. and J.W. Johnson, 1900); and (generally) Samuel Lindsay, ed., *Legislation for the Protection of Animals and Children* (New York: Columbia University Press, 1914). A few states had antebellum laws forbidding malicious treatment of one's own animals or those of another, some based on public-nuisance arguments. The legal code of the Massachusetts Bay Colony (1641) contained provisions against abusing animals, for example. A New York court indicted a man for beating his balky horse. *People v. Stakes*, 1 Wheel. 111 (N.Y. 1822). In the South, antebellum cases appeared predominantly in the nation's capital. Maliciously killing an animal could bring on an indictment in federal court; beating a cow to death in or near a public road was indictable as a public nuisance in D.C. *Respublica v. Teischer*, 1 Dall. 335 (U.S. 1788); *U.S. v. Jackson*, 4 Cr. C.C. 483 (D.C. 1834). Public cruelty to horses was a misdemeanor in D.C. and carried a fine of $10 and 20 days in prison. *U.S. v. Logan*, 2 Cr. C.C. 259 (D.C. 1821). For other cases, see Chapter 6.

48. *State v. Pugh*, 15 Mo. 509 (1852); *State v. Beekman*, 3 Dutch. 124 (N.J. 1858); *State v. Manuel*, 72 N.C. 201 (1875); *State v. Newby*, 64 N.C. 23 (1870). An abusive owner of livestock also went free in *State v. Avery*, 44 N.H. 392 (1862). But a postbellum Missouri court determined that overdriving a horse might be indictable. *State v. Roche*, 37 Mo. App. 480 (1880). See also Ingham, *The Law*, 523–56.

49. See Catherine Clinton, *The Other Civil War* (New York: Hill and Wang, 1984), 75. For a general discussion of nineteenth-century family law, see Michael Grossberg, *Governing the Hearth: Law and the Family in Nineteenth-Century America* (Chapel Hill: University of North Carolina Press, 1985). Detailed accounts of nineteenth-century law regarding husbands and wives, and parents and children appear in Tapping Reeve, *Baron and Femme* (Burlington, VT: Chauncey Goodrich, 1846) and (Albany, NY: W. Gould, 1862); and James Schouler, *Law of Domestic Relations* (Boston: Little, Brown, 1905).

50. Carol Hymowitz and Michaele Weissman, *A History of Women in America* (New York: Bantam Books), 86, reported that Stanton and Mott vowed at that time to form a society for women's rights.

51. Annie W. Porritt, *Laws Affecting Women and Children in the Suffrage and Non-Suffrage States* (New York: National Woman Suffrage Publishing, 1917), discussed the correlation between suffrage and child guardianship rights; Jessie C. Saunders, *The Legal Status of Women* (New York: National-American Women Suffrage Association, 1897), outlined the

legal status of women as of 1897. Married British women could legally own property as of 1870 but could not vote until 1928. Pleck, *Domestic Tyranny*, chap. 2.

52. See Mason P. Thomas, Jr., "Child Abuse and Neglect Part I: Historical Overview, Legal Matrix, and Social Perspectives," *North Carolina Law Review* 50 (December 1971).

53. See, for example, *Exeter v. Warwick*, 1 R.I. 63 (1834); *E. Hartford v. Pitkin*, 8 Ct. 393 (1831); *S. Brunswick v. E. Windsor*, 3 Halst. 64 (N.J. 1824); *Hopkins v. Fleet*, 9 Johns. 225 (N.Y. 1812); and *Winchendon v. Hatfield*, 4 Mass. 123 (1808).

54. See Pleck, *Domestic Tyranny*, 34–35; Scott E. Friedman, *The Law of Parent–Child Relationships: A Handbook* (Chicago: American Bar Association Press, 1992), 133. The policy of placing neglected children into orphanages has enjoyed a recent resurgence in popularity among some of today's politicians.

55. Friedman, *The Law of Parent–Child Relationships*, 101ff.

56. *People v. Walsh*, 11 Hun 292, 294 (N.Y. 1877); *Carney v. State*, 84 Ala. 7 (1887).

57. *Shannon v. People*, 5 Mi. 71 (1858); *Overseers v. Wilcox*, 12 Pa. Co. Ct. R. 447 (1893); *Comw. v. Boetcher*, 8 Pa. Co. Ct. R. 544 (1890).

58. Laws 1882, chap. 200, and Laws 1885, chap. 422, sec. 2; Gen. Stat. sec. 3402; Pub. Stat. p. 688, sec. 22. See also *State v. Sutcliffe*, 18 R.I. 53 (1892).

59. See Morris, "The Measurement," 148.

60. *Bull v. State*, 80 Ga. 704 (1888); *Bennefield v. State*, 80 Ga. 107 (1888); *State v. Weber*, 48 Mo. App. 500 (1892); *State v. Broyer*, 44 Mo. App. 393 (1891); *State v. Brinkman*, 40 Mo. App. 284 (1890); *State v. Fuchs*, 17 Mo. App. 458 (1885); *Ex parte Jackson*, 45 Ark. 158, 163 (1885).

61. Clinton, *The Other Civil War*, 58–59. For a social history of America's alcoholic binge from 1790 to 1830, see W.J. Rorabaugh, *The Alcoholic Republic: An American Tradition* (New York: Oxford University Press, 1979).

62. Pleck, "Criminal Approaches," 21.

63. Pleck, *Domestic Tyranny*, reported only twenty-three cases of spousal abuse, incest, or assault of a servant for the period 1633 to 1802.

64. *Bradley v. State*, Walk. 156, 158 (Miss. 1824); *Robbins v. State*, 20 Ala. 36, 39 (1852).

65. *State v. Black*, 60 N.C. 262, 263 (1864); *State v. Oliver*, 70 N.C. 60, 61 (1874); *State v. Rhodes*, Phil. 453 (N.C. 1868); *Carpenter v. Comw.*, 92 Ky. 452 (1883). Other North Carolina cases include *State v. Mabrey*, 64 N.C. 503 (1870); and *State v. Hussey*, 44 N.C. 123 (1852). The *Mabrey* court reversed an acquittal, saying that husbands could not inflict permanent injury or threaten to use a weapon. In *Hussey*, a convicted husband was acquitted by the appellate court.

66. *Gorman v. State*, 42 Tx. 221 (1875); *Owens v. State*, 7 Tx. App. 329 (1879); *Richardson v. Lawhorn*, 4 Ky. Law R. 998 (1883); *Fulghum v. State*, 46 Ala. 143 (1871); *State v. Buckley*, 2 Har. 552 (Del. 1838); *Turner v. State*, 60 Neb. 351 (1882); *Comw. v. McAfee*, 18 Mass. 458 (1871).

67. Early forms of child abuse included exposure and infanticide, particularly for crippled or female children. Under the Massachusetts Stubborn Child Law of 1646, parents could seek a state reprimand and even capital punishment for their rebellious children. Medieval churches and cities established some sanctions against child abuse, particularly for lying on top of a child and suffocating it. Early legislation in England included the first Factory Act (1802), which protected only orphans. The 1872 English Infant Life Protection Acts were passed in response to the practice of buying life insurance for children, then starving them to death. Samuel X. Radbill, "Children in a World of Violence: A History of Child Abuse," in *The Battered Child*, ed. Ray E. Helfer and Ruth S. Kempe (Chicago: University of Chicago Press, 1987), 5, 17–18; Robert M. Horowitz and Howard A. Davidson, eds., *Legal Rights of Children* (Colorado Springs: Shepard's/McGraw-Hill, 1984), 3; Donald Ford, "The Emergence of the Child as a Legal Entity," in *The Maltreatment of Children*, ed. Selwyn Smith (Baltimore: University Park Press, 1977), 404–8. Ford speculated that the Industrial Revolution and the French Revolution opened people's eyes about the value – economic and military – of children to the state.

68. Guilty verdicts were set aside in *State v. Jones*, 95 N.C. 588 (1886); *State v. Alford*, 68 N.C. 322 (1873); and *State v. Pendergrass*, 2 Dev. & B. 365 (1837). In the last, the defendant was a teacher but *dicta* indicate the court considered the defendant the same as a parent. The defendant in *State v. Harris*, 63 N.C. 1 (1868), a black man who had beaten his stepson to death, was awarded a new trial.

69. *Stanfield v. State*, 43 Tx. 167 (1875); *Johnson v. State*, 21 Tn. 288 (1840). Pennsylvania and Iowa had similar punishment standards. *Comw. v. Blaker*, 1 Brews. 311 (Pa. 1867); *State v. Bitman*, 13 Ia. 485 (1862).

70. *Fletcher v. People*, 52 Ill. 395 (1869); *Neal v. State*, 54 Ga. 281 (1875); *Powell v. State*, 67 Ms. 119 (1889).

71. This was a response to the horrendous case of Mary Ellen. Mary Ellen's foster mother had beaten her black and blue each day and cut her with scissors. The child had slept on the floor and possessed almost no clothing. Not until Henry Bergh, founder of the American Society for the Prevention of Cruelty to Animals, involved himself on Mary Ellen's behalf did the court system take notice. The foster mother was found guilty of assault and battery and sentenced to one year of hard labor in the penitentiary. Thomas, "Child Abuse," 308–11, and Pleck, *Domestic Tyranny*, chap. 3, contain discussions of protective agencies.

72. Lindsay, *Legislation*, esp. 34–35. Horowitz and Davidson, *Legal Rights*, discussed labor laws, education, and reformatories. Radbill, "Children," 6, pointed out that medieval guilds established the indenture system so as to prevent competition from cheap child labor. The New York House of Refuge, founded in 1825, was the first American reformatory. Thomas, "Child Abuse," 306ff.

73. Massachusetts, Tennessee, Nebraska, Georgia, Maryland, New Mexico, Delaware, Oregon, and Arkansas passed statutes against wife-beating in the last half of the nineteenth century. Punishment could be severe –

Maryland, Delaware, and Oregon laws recommended lashing – but was extremely rare. Friedman, *Crime*, 65–74, noted that the nineteenth century heralded a move from bodily punishment – which was associated with slaves – to prisons. (Arkansas even passed a law in 1854 repealing all laws inflicting stripes on a white person.) Tellingly, of the convicted wife-beaters who were flogged in Delaware between 1901 and 1942, two-thirds were black. At the same time, the black population of Delaware comprised only 13 percent of the total population. Pleck, "Criminal Approaches," 40–41. For more discussion, see Pleck, "Wife-Beating"; Myra C. Glenn, *Campaigns Against Corporal Punishment* (Albany: State University of New York Press, 1984); Robert L. Griswold, "Law, Sex, Cruelty, and Divorce," in *History of Women in the United States 3: Domestic Relations and the Law*, ed. Nancy F. Cott (Munich: K.G. Saur, 1992); Pleck, *Domestic Tyranny*, chaps. 2, 5; and Friedman, *Crime and Punishment*, 222–23. England preceded the United States in protecting women, just as it did in defending animals. Fitzroy's legislation passed in 1853, assessing a fine and six months in prison for wife-beaters. The English Society for the Preservation of Women and Children was established in 1857.

74. Some (Hymowitz and Weissman, *A History*, 79, and Clinton, *The Other Civil War*, 72) have speculated that those who excelled at organizing and promoting causes simply adapted the skills they had acquired in the antislavery movement. Barbara J. Berg, *The Remembered Gate: Origins of American Feminism* (New York: Oxford University Press, 1978), refuted the notion that the feminist movement grew out of the abolition movement, however. Rather, she claimed that the genesis of feminism lay in the benevolent organizations of the early nineteenth century.

75. Some perceived threats apparently stemmed from general fears of crime and instability and from apprehension about the immigrants that had poured into the United States in the latter part of the nineteenth century. Pleck, "Criminal Approaches," 20.

76. See Harry B. O'Donnell IV, "Title I of the Family Support Act of 1988 – The Quest for Effective National Child Support Enforcement Continues," *Journal of Family Law* 29 (Winter 1990), and Andrea H. Beller and John W. Graham, *Small Change: The Economics of Child Support* (New Haven: Yale University Press, 1993).

77. See Diana E. H. Russell, *Rape in Marriage* (New York: MacMillan, 1982); Rene I. Augustine, "Marriage: The Safe Haven for Rapists," *Journal of Family Law* 29 (May 1991); Sandra L. Ryder and Sheryl A. Kuzmenka, "Legal Rape: The Marital Rape Exemption," *John Marshall Law Review* 24 (Winter 1991). The first American husband still living with his wife to be charged and prosecuted for marital rape was John Rideout of Oregon. He was acquitted in 1980.

78. *Stanton v. Stanton*, 421 U.S. 7 (1975). The court invalidated a Utah statute that had required support of male children to age twenty-one and female children only to age eighteen.

79. *Prince v. Massachusetts*, 321 U.S. 158 (1944).

80. *Hewellette v. George*, 9 So. 885 (Ms. 1891). Several reasonable justifications for parental immunity exist: Courts do not want to upset family harmony, interfere with parental autonomy, drain family savings, or promote fraud and collusion by family members against insurance companies. See, for example, *Kirchner v. Crystal*, 474 N.E. 2d 275 (Oh. 1984); and *Black v. Solmitz*, 409 A. 2d 634 (Me. 1979).

81. See, for example, *Richards v. Richards*, 599 So. 2d 135 (Fl. 5th D.C.A.), *rev'w dismissed*, 604 So. 2d 487 (Fl. 1992); *Roller v. Roller*, 79 P. 788 (Wa. 1905).

82. *Kingsley v. Kingsley*, 623 So. 2d 780 (Fl. App., 5 Dist., 1993). Also see Friedman, *The Law of Parent–Child Relationships*, 196ff, for a discussion of abrogation.

83. See Caroline E. Johnson, "A Cry for Help: An Argument for Abrogation of the Parent–Child Tort Immunity Doctrine in Child Abuse and Incest Cases," *Florida State University Law Review* 21 (Fall 1993): 634–38; and Bart L. Greenwald, "Irreconcilable Differences: When Children Sue Their Parents for 'Divorce,'" *Journal of Family Law* 32 (Winter 1994).

84. Quoted in James Mellon, ed., *Bullwhip Days* (New York: Avon, 1988), 453.

85. *Littlejohn v. Underhill*, 2 Car. L. R. 377, 381 (N.C. 1816). For a modern-day application of fraudulent conveyance laws, see Jenny B. Wahl and Edward T. Wahl, "Fraudulent Conveyance Law and Leveraged Buyouts: Remedy or Insurance Policy?," *William Mitchell Law Review* 16, no. 2 (1990). In another debt case, a household slave had been bequeathed by name to the widow, who wanted to manumit the slave by her last will. The heir at law could not use this slave to pay his debts in order to protect his inheritance. *Alexander v. Worthington*, 5 Md. 471 (1834).

86. *Waddill v. Martin*, 3 Ired. Eq. 562, 564 (N.C. 1845); *Carmille v. Carmille*, 2 McMul. 452, 470 (S.C. 1842); *Washington v. Emery*, 4 Jones Eq. 32 (N.C. 1858). Fogel, *Without Consent*, 189–93, discussed instances in which slaveowners allowed slaves to till their own fields as a reward for good behavior. For a discussion of law and equity courts, see Chapter 2.

87. *Davis v. Whitridge*, 2 Strob. 232 (S.C. 1848).

88. Other states were more successful. Mississippi passed a statute in 1817 to prevent slaves from raising cotton for their own benefit. Georgia's law of 1816 fined masters $15 if their slaves sold cotton, tobacco, or grain; the law of 1830 forbade slaves in the city of Twiggs from selling poultry. Statutes appear in Finkelman, *State Slavery Statutes*. Some scholars have reported that, despite such laws, slaves continued to produce foodstuffs, raise stock and poultry, and engage in such activities as wood-cutting and moss-gathering. See Lorena S. Walsh, "Slave Life, Slave Society, and Tobacco Production in the Tidewater Chesapeake, 1620–1820"; Roderick A. McDonald, "Independent Economic Production by Slaves in Antebellum Louisiana Sugar Plantations"; Campbell, "As 'A Kind of Freeman?'"; and Miller, "Plantation Labor Organization." All papers appear in *Cultivation and Culture: Labor and*

the Shaping of Slave Life in the Americas, ed. Ira Berlin and Philip D. Morgan (Charlottesville: University Press of Virginia, 1993).

89. Lichtenstein, "That Disposition," 255, 266, reported the Alabama incident. For more discussion, see Wood, *Black Majority*, 209–10, and Morris, "The Measurement," 161. Judith Schafer (private correspondence) kindly informed me that some planters allowed their slaves to grow brown cotton because it was easy to distinguish from the planters' white cotton.

90. *Skrine v. Walker*, 3 Rich Eq. 262 (S.C. 1851); *Univ. v. Cambreling*, 6 Yerg. 79 (Tn. 1834). These cases were fairly typical. For extended discussions of hiring and trading contracts, see previous chapters.

91. *State v. Boyce*, 10 Ired. 536 (N.C. 1849); *State v. Boozer*, 5 Strob. 21, 23 (S.C. 1850).

92. *Reeves v. Gantt*, 8 Rich. Eq. 13, 17 (S.C. 1855).

93. *Hagerty v. Harwell*, 16 Tx. 663, 668 (1856). Ordinarily, the court would have returned the slaves to the wife under fraudulent conveyance law (discussed in note 85), as the court did in *Tucker v. Tucker*, 29 Mo. 350 (1860). In *Tucker*, the testator could not defraud his widow of her slaves by giving them to his children. Other husband–wife disputes over slaves arose in Texas as well. Under *Cartwright v. Cartwright*, 18 Tx. 626 (1857), slaves owned separately before marriage remained the property of their original owner, and the children born to these slaves belonged to the owner of the slave mother. Yet in *De Blane v. Lynch*, 23 Tx. 26 (1859), the court decided that crops grown on a wife's land and worked by her slaves were community property, subject to the husband's debts.

94. *Graham v. Sam*, 7 B. Mon. 403 (Ky. 1847). (Kentucky did not put the right of dower above the rights of creditors, either, although Arkansas, Virginia, and Maryland did.) Up through the nineteenth century, a married woman was legally entitled to a portion of her husband's estate – typically one-third of the value of the real estate – to use throughout the rest of her life. This provision, intended for the support of the woman and her children, was called dower. Curtesy was the less-used, parallel entitlement of married men. Note 108 discusses slaves sent to Liberia.

95. Married women could not bring suit in their own names in most states through much of the nineteenth century. See Schouler, *Law of Domestic Relations*; Saunders, *The Legal Status*; and Reeve, *Baron and Femme*.

96. *Spencer v. Dennis*, 8 Gill. 314 (Md. 1849). Fogel, *Without Consent*, n. 118, claimed that most manumissions occurred as the result of free blacks purchasing their relatives, then freeing them. Evidence from court records and legislative proceedings show, however, that manumissions by will or acts of legislature were also common. See Finkelman, *State Slavery Statutes*. Fogel, *Without Consent*, 246, also gave details of emancipation in the Northern states; Schafer, *Slavery*, devoted an entire chapter to the manumissions of concubines. See also Morris, *Southern Slavery*, chaps. 18 and 19.

97. Dumond, *Antislavery Origins*, 13, contended that restrictions on manumissions were designed to maintain the *status quo*; Tushnet, *American*

Law, 128–41, noted that the legal system had to concern itself with manumission because of the social ramifications. The counterpart to manumission law was the law determining who was a slave. A number of cases dealt with this issue, as have many scholars. See, for example, A. Leon Higginbotham, Jr., *In the Matter of Color, Race, and the American Legal Process: The Colonial Period* (New York: Oxford University Press, 1978); Wiecek, "The Statutory Law"; Fehrenbacher, *Slavery, Law, and Politics*; Campbell, *The Slave Catchers*; and Finkelman, *Imperfect Union.*

98. Reported in Hurd, *Law,* 293.

99. *Roser v. Marlow,* R.M.C. 542, 548 (Ga. 1837); *Am. Col. Soc. v. Gartrell,* 23 Ga. 448, 464 (1857).

100. *Gordon v. Blackman,* 1 Rich. Eq. 61 (S.C. 1844); *Charlotte v. Chouteau,* 11 Mo. 193, 200 (1847); *Cleland v. Waters,* 19 Ga. 35, 43 (1855); *Henriette v. Barnes,* 11 La. An. 453, 454 (1856).

101. *Trotter v. Blocker,* 6 Port. 269, 291 (Al. 1838).

102. See, for example, Maryland's Act of 1752, chap. 1. This Act was repealed in 1796. Mississippi revived such a law in its Act of 1842, however, as did Georgia in 1859. See Catterall, *Judicial Cases,* vol. 4, p. 7; Finkelman, *State Slavery Statutes.* More generally, most manumissions had to be in writing, as shown in *Major v. Winn,* 13 B. Mon. 250 (Ky. 1852).

103. Georgia (1801), South Carolina (1820), and Florida (1829) required the legislature to approve further manumission. Colonial Virginia and North Carolina allowed emancipation only for meritorious service.

104. North Carolina (1801), Tennessee (1801), Kentucky (1811, 1842), and Florida (1829), among others, required masters to post bonds. See, for instance, *Black v. Meaux,* 4 Dana 188 (Ky. 1836). I referred to community-support laws for paupers earlier in this chapter.

105. Delaware's Act of 1819 provided for this, for example. See *Trustees v. Hall,* 3 Harr. 322 (Del. 1841).

106. *Baker v. Tabor,* 7 La. An. 556 (1852).

107. *Hamilton v. Cragg,* 6 Har. & J. 16 (Md. 1823); *Hall v. Mullin,* 5 Har. & J. 190 (Md. 1821); *Wigle v. Kirby,* 3 Cr. C.C. 597 (D.C. 1829); *Boyce v. Nancy,* 4 Dana 236 (Ky. 1836). The court used the laws of Maryland because Nancy was actually a Maryland slave.

108. For most of the antebellum period, Georgia, Virginia, Mississippi, Kentucky, and Maryland, among other states, permitted decedents to bequeath slaves to the Colonization Society, which would then send the slaves to Liberia. David J. Grindle, "Manumission: The Weak Link in Georgia's Law of Slavery," *Mercer Law Review* 41 (Winter 1990), discussed the case of Georgia.

109. Virginia (1805), Florida (1829), North Carolina (1830), Maryland (1831, 1839), Tennessee (1831), Texas (1845), and Kentucky (1850) required freed slaves to leave the state, pay a fine, or reenter slavery. See, for example, *Jackson v. Collins,* 16 B. Mon. 214 (Ky. 1855). Maryland at first required resident ex-slaves to pay a weekly charge, then changed it to a flat fee. But a Kentucky executor could complain about emancipating slaves only if the emancipation hurt the estate, not if the

freedmen lacked funds to leave the state. *Davis v. Reeves*, 1 Metc. 589 (Ky. 1859). Many states, including Georgia (1818), Florida (1832), Texas (1840), and Arkansas (1843), forbade free Negroes and mulattoes from entering the state. See *Shue v. Turk*, 15 Grat. 256 (Va. 1859), *Sanders v. Ward*, 25 Ga. 109 (1858), *Bryan v. Dennis*, 4 Fl. 445 (1852), and *Trotter v. Blocker*, 6 Port. 269 (Al. 1838), for discussion of various states' laws.

110. *Cooper v. Savannah*, 4 Ga. 68 (1848).

111. See Maryland's Act of 1844, chap. 237, for instance. *Spencer v. Dennis*, 8 Gill. 314 (Md. 1849), applied a similar law.

112. *Isaac v. Graves*, 16 B. Mon. 365 (Ky. 1855).

113. Slaves could not be freed to the detriment of creditors under *Allein v. Hutton*, 4 Md. Ch. 537 (1847); *Wilson v. Barnett*, 9 Gill. & J. (Md. 1837); and *Woodley v. Abby*, 5 Call 336 (Va. 1805), for example. (Slaves went free in *Wilson*.) Courts followed a rule of putting freed slaves to service in *Bob v. Powers*, 19 Ark. 424 (1858); *Jincey v. Winfield*, 9 Grat. 708 (Va. 1853); *Wood v. Wickliffe*, 5 B. Mon. 187 (Ky. 1844); *Allein v. Sharp*, 7 Gill & J. 96 (Md. 1835); *Dunn v. Amey*, 1 Leigh 465 (Va. 1829); and *Adam v. Leverton*, 2 Har. & McH. 382 (Md. 1792).

114. *George v. Corse*, 2 Har. & G. 1 (Md. 1827).

115. *Peterson v. Williamson*, 2 Dev. 325 (N.C. 1830). *Bogard v. Gardley*, 4 S. & M. 302 (Ms. 1845), provides another example.

116. Alabama's Statutes of 1834 forbade manumission by contract, for example. Promises of freedom to slaves were unenforceable under *Beall v. Joseph*, Hardin 51 (Ky. 1806). Southern courts invalidated contracts for freedom in many cases, including *Bland v. Dowling*, 9 G. & S. 19 (Md. 1837); *Stevenson v. Singleton*, 1 Leigh 72 (Va. 1829); *Richard v. Van Meter*, 3 Cr. C.C. 214 (D.C. 1827); *Letty v. Lowe*, 2 Cr. C.C. 634 (D.C. 1825); *Fanny v. Kell*, 2 Cr. C.C. 412 (D.C. 1823); *Brown v. Wingard*, 2 Cr. C.C. 300 (D.C. 1822); and *Contee v. Garner*, 2 Cr. C.C. 162 (D.C. 1818). The celebrated exception to this rule is *Sally v. Beaty*, 1 Bay 260 (S.C. 1792). Here, a female slave used her own savings to buy freedom for her friend. Louisiana and Tennessee (Act of 1833) also permitted slaves to contract for their freedom in some circumstances.

117. Virginians generally could not write wills that allowed slaves to choose masters, choose between emancipation and sale, or receive land or wages. *Williamson v. Coalter*, 14 Grat. 394 (Va. 1858); *Bailey v. Poindexter*, 14 Grat. 132 (Va. 1858); *Osborne v. Taylor*, 12 Grat. 117 (Va. 1855); *Wynn v. Carrell*, 2 Grat. 227 (Va. 1845); *Rucker v. Gilbert*, 3 Leigh 8 (Va. 1831). In one case, however, a Virginia court upheld a will that let slaves select their masters if slaves sold for Confederate currency at less than market value. *Fugate v. Honeker*, 22 Grat. 409 (Va. 1872). Kentucky and Missouri courts permitted slaves to choose masters under *Hopkins v. Morgan*, 3 Dana 17 (Ky. 1835); *Blakey v. Blakey*, 3 J.J. Marsh. 674 (Ky. 1830); and *Beaupied v. Jennings*, 28 Mo. 254 (1859).

118. *Lea v. Brown*, 3 Jones Eq. 141, 145 (N.C. 1856); *Carter v. Leeper*, 5 Dana 261 (Ky. 1837).

119. For reenslavement statutes, see Finkelman, *State Slavery Statutes*, and

Franklin, *From Slavery*, 142. Alabama (1834), South Carolina (1841), Mississippi (1842), Georgia (1859), and North Carolina (1860) forbade further manumission by will, although emancipation outside the state was sometimes approved. Louisiana (1857) and Arkansas (1859) disallowed further emancipation by any means. For further discussion of restrictions on emancipation, see Goodell, *American Slave Code*, part 1, chap. 20, part 2, chap. 8; Wheeler, *A Practical Treatise*; Stroud, *A Sketch*, chap. 3; Catterall, *Judicial Cases*, various vols.; Hurd, *Law of Freedom*, vol. 2, chaps. 17–19; Schafer, *Slavery, The Civil Law*.

120. South Carolina's Act of 1819 allowed slaves to carry guns only if they had a ticket from their owners; Florida's 1832 laws required slaves to have permission as well. Arkansas in 1854 forbade slaves from carrying guns in certain counties. North Carolina (Rev. Code chap. 107, sec. 26, Act of 1854) forbade arming a slave or the slave would receive thirty-nine lashes. (The owner apparently paid no other penalty.) See *State v. Hannibal*, 6 Jones 57 (N.C. 1859). Texas's Act of 1850 did not permit slaves to carry firearms off the plantation; it revised its laws in 1856 to prevent any possession of guns or other weapons by slaves. Betty Wood, "'Until He Shall Be Dead, Dead, Dead': The Judicial Treatment of Slaves in Eighteenth Century Georgia," in *Articles on American Slavery*, vol. 7, ed. Finkelman, 281, reported that the state of Georgia did not want slaves to own drums or horns, fearing that these instruments could be used to signal revolts. Many states also prohibited free blacks from owning and using guns, including Maryland (1831), Florida (1832), Delaware (1835, 1851), North Carolina (1840), Mississippi (1852), and Georgia (1860). Maryland (1806) also did not let blacks own dogs.

121. C. Vann Woodward and Elisabeth Muhlenfeld, *The Private Mary Chesnut* (New York: Oxford University Press, 1984), 162 and 181.

122. South Carolina's Act of 1800 required a white resident on plantations with more than ten slaves. The state revised the law in 1819 to fine masters fifty cents per month per working slave if they owned ten or more slaves but had no white person residing with the slaves. Half the fine went to the state, half to the informant. Louisiana (1806) assessed a penalty if a master did not employ a white or free colored person as an overseer. In 1823, Georgia required a white presence on farms with ten or more slaves; in 1857, the state revised the law, requiring a white male to be present if twenty or more blacks aged sixteen or older resided on the plantation. (It repealed this law in 1863.) North Carolina (1830) required whites to live on the plantation in some counties. Under 1 Rev. Code, chap. 111, sec. 13, p. 424 (cited in *Comw. v. Foster*, 5 Grat. 695 (Va. 1848), and *Comw. v. Connor*, 5 Leigh 718 (Va. 1834)), Virginia masters faced indictment if more than five slaves not their own were on the premises. Florida imposed a fine of $100 on any slaveowner who allowed slaves to live alone: $50 to the county, $50 to the informant. Alabama's Act of 1856 (amended in 1862) mandated that a white person reside on the plantation in order to "secure subordinates." Otherwise, the slaveowner paid $100 to the county. In

November 1861, Texas passed a law prohibiting slaves from being in charge of farms or stock ranches detached from residences: Slaveowners faced a fine of $50 to $100 for violating this statute.

123. Masters could not teach slaves to read or write, except in Maryland and Kentucky (and in Louisiana until 1830, according to Schafer, *Slavery*, 146). Free blacks, especially, could not educate slaves. *Chandler v. Ferris*, 1 Har. 454 (Del. 1834). In most states, in fact, blacks could not even own slaves. *Ewell v. Tidwell*, 20 Ark. 136 (1859); *Davis v. Evans*, 18 Mo. 249 (1853); *Tindal v. Hudson*, 2 Har. 441 (Del. 1838).

124. See, for example, *Comw v. Booth*, 6 Rand. 669 (Va. 1828). (The statutory penalty in Kentucky for illegal assembly was $2 per slave. *Bosworth v. Brand*, 1 Dana 377 (Ky. 1833).) South Carolina did not allow slaves to attend religious meetings unless a majority of whites was present, or the slaves would be lashed. Free blacks had little more freedom of assembly than slaves. Maryland prohibited free blacks from assembling in retail stores at night under its Act of 1817; it passed a law in 1842 to prevent the formation of secret societies of Negroes. Allegedly to avoid having groups of freedmen roaming the streets at night, the District of Columbia passed a 10 o'clock curfew for blacks in 1838. But Tennessee struck down a similar ordinance passed in Memphis, recognizing that "the lot of a free [N]egro is hard enough at the best . . . and it is both cruel and useless to add to his troubles by unnecessary and painful restraints in the use of such liberty as is allowed him. He must live, and in order to do so, he must work. Every one knows that in cities, very often, the most profitable employment is to be found during the night." *Mayor v. Winfield*, 8 Humph. 707, 709 (Tn. 1848). Chapter 6 also discussed slave assemblies.

125. *Wiley v. Parmer*, 14 Al. 627 (1848); *Jones v. Council*, 25 Ga. 610 (1858). Such policies were often, of course, merely revenue issues. A Virginia court, for example, allowed the state to levy a tax on slaves over age twelve who were worth $300 or more in order to provide free schools – to free children, of course. *Bull v. Read*, 13 Grat. 78 (Va. 1856). And Kentucky allowed taxation of slaves who were temporarily out of state. *Comw. v. Hays*, 8 B. Mon. 2 (Ky. 1848). For further discussion of various restrictions, see Goodell, *American Slavery*, part 1, chap. 22, part 2, chaps. 6 and 7; Stroud, *A Sketch*, chap. 3; Hurd, *Law*; Elkins, *Slavery*, 60; Finkelman, *State Slavery Statutes*; Franklin, *From Slavery*, 124.

126. *Worthington v. Crabtree*, 1 Metc. 478 (Ky. 1858); *McKeil v. Cutlar*, 4 Jones Eq. 38 (N.C. 1859); *Blount v. Hawkins*, 4 Jones Eq. 161 (N.C. 1858). See also *Henderson v. Vaulx*, 10 Yer. 30 (Tn. 1836) (discussed in the text at note 38).

127. Verdicts also recognized the economic importance of fulfilling the expectations of individuals. In one dispute, the defendant did not want to hire out his slaves to a cruel hirer but neglected to inform the auctioneer of his wishes. When his slaves were hired to the lowest bidder, a notoriously harsh master, the defendant refused to deliver his slaves. He had to pay nominal damages to the bidder. *Ricks v. Battle*, 7 Ired. 269 (N.C. 1846). This was not just a contractual matter between two

parties; it also helped set the rules for a smoothly functioning hiring market. For more discussion, see Chapter 3.

128. *Barney v. Bush*, 9 Al. 345 (1846). Free blacks often faced more road duty than whites. Finkelman, *State Slavery Statutes*, xi. Northerners typically paid a tax instead of physically constructing roads themselves. Morris, *The Measurement*, 148.

129. Act of 1852, sec. 23.

130. Page 95.

131. *Dodge v. Brittain*, Meigs 84 (Tn. 1838). Other cases include *Chastain v. Bowman*, 1 Hill 270 (S.C. 1833); *Gore v. Buzzard*, 4 Leigh 249 (Va. 1833); *Bryant v. Sheely*, 5 Dana 530 (Ky. 1837); *Banks v. Merle*, 2 Rob. 117 (La. 1842); *State v. Daily*, 14 Al. 469 (1848); *Bailey v. Barnelly*, 23 Ga. 448 (1857).

132. *Stachlin v. Destrehan*, 2 La. An. 1019, 1021 (1847); *Wragg v. State*, 14 Al. 492 (1848). Free blacks were barred from certain occupations as well. Georgia (1845) would not allow blacks to work on buildings or keep eating establishments (1859). Louisiana (1859) prevented free colored persons from entering numerous occupations or owning certain types of businesses. Maryland (1805) would not let free blacks sell wheat, corn, or tobacco without a license; as of 1842, nor could Virginia blacks sell agricultural products without a certificate.

133. Most states restricted self-hiring by slaves. North Carolina's act of 1794 provided for indictment of slaves, a fine of £20 on masters, and loss of the slave's services for a year. Under the Acts of 1802 and 1840, Kentucky did not let slaves hire themselves out. But although courts expressed the desire to let jailors apprehend slaves who were working for themselves, they reserved the right to masters to investigate whether the slave was really guilty. *Jarman v. Patterson*, 7 T.B. Mon. 644 (Ky. 1825). Virginia slaveowners who allowed slaves to hire themselves paid fines ($20 under 1 Rev. Code., chap. 111, sec. 81, p. 442), with penalties most frequently applied during the 1830s. See *Abrahams v. Comw.*, 11 Leigh 675 (Va. 1841). Tennessee fined owners $20 and imprisoned their slaves until the fine was paid. *Hoggatt v. Bigley*, 6 Humph. 236 (Tn. 1845). South Carolina and Alabama owners paid fines as well. Yet masters still allowed the practice, at least in some states and over some time periods. See Morris, *The Measurement*, 158–59; Campbell, "As 'A Kind'"; and Loren Schweninger, "Slave Independence and Enterprise in South Carolina, 1780–1865," *South Carolina Historical Magazine* 93 (1992), and "The Underside of Slavery: The Internal Economy, Self-Hire, and Quasi-Freedom in Virginia, 1780–1865," *Slavery and Abolition* 12 (1991). And Louisiana and Maryland were more relaxed about self-hiring. See Wood, *Black Majority*, 214–15; Frederick Douglass, *Life of an American Slave* (Cambridge, MA: Harvard University Press, 1960), 139; Catterall, *Judicial Cases*, vol. 3, p. 129; and Stroud, *A Sketch*, 76–79. Conrad and Meyer, *Economics of Slavery*, 102, also recounted several instances of slaves hiring themselves out.

More generally, slaves usually could not make contracts or own property, so owners were not typically responsible for the debts of their slaves. See, for instance, *Tilly v. Norris*, 4 Ired. 229 (N.C. 1844). Some states passed similar laws for free blacks, but others recognized how such laws could backfire. The court in *Ewell v. Tidwell*, 20 Ark. 136, 143 (1859), stated: "If . . . [the freedman] could not make and enforce contracts, it is difficult to understand how he could, with any certainty, supply his commonest necessities . . . every incentive to industry would be at once destroyed; and, sinking into idleness and depravity, he would become an intolerable nuisance." A Maryland court noted similarly: "[S]o long as free [N]egroes remain in our midst, a wholesome system induces incentives to thrift and respectability, and no more effective could be suggested than the protection of their earnings." *Hughes v. Jackson*, 12 Md. 450, 464 (1858).

134. *Comw. v. Gilbert*, 6 J.J. Marsh. 184, 185 (Ky. 1831); *Stanley v. Nelson*, 28 Al. 514, 518 (1856) (an appellate court sent the case back for a jury to determine whether the slave had hired himself out or merely acted as an agent). A Kentucky court chose similar language when reviewing a statute forbidding trade with slaves, saying such license would "beget idle and dissolute habits in the particular slaves so indulged, as well as in others, and lead to depredations upon the property of others, and to crimes and insubordination." *Jarrett v. Higbee*, 5 T.B. Mon. 546, 551 (Ky. 1827). See also *Jarman v. Patterson*, 7 T.B. Mon. 644 (Ky. 1825), and trading cases discussed in Chapter 6.

135. *Smith v. Causey*, 22 Ala. 568 (1853), is just one example of the many cases in which the plaintiff recovered nothing because he could not prove that the defendant had known of the animal's viciousness and had kept the animal negligently. Chapter 4 discussed the duties of landowners to fence in or fence out livestock.

136. For details, see Chapter 6.

137. *Richardson v. Carr*, 1 Har. 142 (Del. 1832).

138. Wood, *A Treatise*, 534.

139. Lester, *To Be a Slave*, 37.

140. Richard Posner has pointed out that master–servant rules are economically based. *Economic Analysis*, 170–71. Servants who act to further their masters' business create liability for their masters. In the case of *Garretzen v. Duenckel*, 50 Mo. 104 (1872), for example, a gun-store employee loaded a pistol and fired it at his customer's request, even though doing so was against store rules. (The man was afraid he would lose the sale.) The shot hit the plaintiff, who was sitting in the window across the street. The gun-store owner was liable. The classic case in this area is *Limpus v. General Omnibus*, 1 H. & C. (Exch.) 528. Here, a bus driver drove in front of a rival bus in order to pick up a fare waiting at the stop. The rival bus overturned; the employer of the aggressive driver was liable for damages. For an exposition of master–servant rules, see *American Jurisprudence 2d*, vol. 53, secs. 404–45.

141. *Caldwell v. Sacra*, Litt. Sel. Cas. 118 (Ky. 1811) (it was unclear whether the value of the destroyed crop figured into the damage calculation); *Campbell v. Staiert*, 2 Murph. 389 (N.C. 1818); *Mardree v. Sutton*, 2 Jones 146 (N.C. 1855); *Graham v. Roark*, 23 Ark. 19 (1861); *Stewart v. Cary*

Lumber Co., 59 S.E. 545 (1907); *Stinson & E. Coast Lumber Co. v. Prevatt*, 84 Fl. 416 (1927) (citing *Kelly v. Wallace*, 6 Fl. 690 (1856)). *Patterson v. Kates*, 152 F. 481 (1907), also cites a string of slave cases.

142. *Garrett v. Freeman*, 5 Jones 78 (N.C. 1857); *Snee v. Trice*, 2 Bay 345, 350 (S.C. 1802) (also reported in different form in 1 Brev. 178). For more recent cases involving fire damages, see *Cook v. M.S.P. & S.S.M. Ry. Co*, 98 Wi. 624 (1898), and *Anderson v. M.S.P. and S.S.M. Ry. Co.*, 146 Mn. 430 (1920), cited in Posner, *Tort Law*, 566. *Garrett* was cited as a precedent in a number of spreading-fire cases, most recently *Zurich Ins. Co. v. Multi-ply Co.*, 170 S.E. 2d 526 (N.C. 1969).

143. Hymowitz and Weissman, *A History*, 56.

144. Schwarz, *Twice Condemned*, 114–18, also discussed slaves and arson.

145. Flanigan, *The Criminal Law*, discussed these.

146. *Leggett v. Simmons*, 7 S. & M. 348 (Ms. 1846); *Ingram v. Linn*, 4 Tex. 266 (1849); *Ewing v. Thompson*, 13 Mo. 132 (1850). *Wright v. Weatherly*, 7 Yerg. 367 (Tn. 1835), resembled *Ingram*. The court wanted to preserve the verdict of damages but recognized that only the legislature could decide this issue. *Cawthorn v. Deas*, 2 Port. 276 (Ala. 1838); *dicta* in *Campbell v. Staiert*, 2 Murph. 389 (N.C. 1818); and *Barret v. Gibson*, Rand. Sir J. 70 (Va. 1731), provide other examples. In *Barret*, a slave woman burned down a tobacco warehouse. Most states exonerated masters from civil liability stemming from their slaves' crimes for much of the antebellum period. See Flanigan, *Criminal Law*, 10.

147. *Brandon v. Bank*, 1 Stew. 320 (Al. 1828). The case left an open question as to the criminality of a slave who destroyed property.

148. *Winnegar's Adm'r v. R.R.*, 85 Ky. 547 (1887). In *dicta*, the court in *Jackson v. Ry. Co.*, 87 Mo. 422 (1855), said that a railroad company would not be liable for injuries if the conductor had forced a victim to board the train. The main issue in *Jackson* was causation, however. The victim in this case was a fugitive from justice who had been mortally wounded in a gunfight. An officer had put him on the train where the man died from his wounds. The railroad company was not liable because the gunshots had caused the death, not the company. In addition, the court decided the conductor had acted reasonably in accepting the fugitive on board.

149. *Boulard v. Calhoun*, 13 La. An. 430 (1858); *Moffat v. Vion*, 5 La. 346 (1833); *Gaillardet v. Demaries*, 18 La. 490 (1841). In the last case, a hired slave had driven a dray into the plaintiff's gig, breaking it. The plaintiff maintained an action against the slaveowner and the hirer. Also see *Guerrier v. Lambeth*, 9 La. 339 (1835); and *Jourdan v. Patton*, 5 Mart. 615 (La. 1818).

150. *Maille v. Blas*, 15 La. An. 100 (1860). For a discussion of rescission and redhibition statutes, see Chapter 2 and Schafer, "Guaranteed Against the Vices."

151. See Mohr, "Slavery in Oglethorpe County," 102, 114.

152. *Leggett v. Simmons*, 7 S. & M. 348 (Ms. 1846); *Wright v. Weatherly*, 7 Yerg. 367 (Tn. 1835); *McConnell v. Hardeman*, 15 Ark. 151, 158 (1854). For applications of theft laws, see *Fackler v. Chapman*, 20 Mo. 249 (1855);

Ridge v. Featherston, 15 Ark. 159 (1854). For more discussion of these sorts of statutes, see Goodell, *American Slave Code*, part 1, chap. 6; Hurd, *Law*, Schafer, *Slavery*; and Morris, "'As If the Injury.'"

153. See Allan Nevins, *The Emergence of Lincoln: Douglas, Buchanan, and Party Chaos 1857–1859* (New York: Scribner's, 1950), 214.

154. See Chapter 8, note 10, for a discussion of legislator interests. Morris, "'As If the Injury,'" also pointed out that Arkansas, Missouri, and Tennessee were not generally dominated by slaveowning interests.

155. As Chapter 5 noted, the federal government refused to do this.

156. Wood, *Black Majority*, 280.

157. As Chapter 5 noted, these payments resemble the compensation granted to those whose land is taken by the government in an action of eminent domain. South Carolina (1712, 1843), Delaware (1721), Maryland (1802, 1809), North Carolina (1810), Alabama (1824, 1836, 1837), Virginia (1839 and various other years), Mississippi (1846, 1848, 1850), Texas (1852), Louisiana (1854, 1856), and Kentucky (Rev. Stat. 178, sec. 7, and 641, sec. 24) compensated owners. South Carolina's average compensation in 1843 was $122.45. In 1858, South Carolina law granted half the value of an executed slave. Delaware gave two-thirds of the slave's value. North Carolina in 1820 even passed a law paying costs to owners whose slaves were convicted of capital crimes; it repealed this law one year later. Alabama let juries decide whether a slaveowner received compensation, with the maximum amount being half of the slave's value. The jury was to consider the blame of the master in making its award, and the state taxed slave property to obtain funds. Interestingly, Alabama granted an inordinate number of new trials to slaves convicted as criminals. (Perhaps the property tax was unpopular. Along the same lines, Kentucky had numerous changes of venue for prosecuted slaves. See Finkelman, *State Slavery Statutes*.) In 1845, Alabama denied compensation to nonresidents in some cases. Mississippi also awarded half the slave's value, but only to state residents. Louisiana originally gave owners up to $750, but later revised the figure down to $300. For discussion of slave compensation laws, see Finkelman, *State Slavery Statutes*; Hurd, *Law*, Goodell, *American Slave Code*, part 1, chap. 5; Friedman, *History*, 228; Catterall, *Judicial Cases*, esp. vol. 3, p. 128; Schafer, *Slavery*, chap. 3.

158. Others were not so lucky. South Carolina, for example, did not require the exclusion of a coerced confession by a defendant in a state criminal proceeding under the Fourteenth Amendment until 1936. *Brown v. Moss*, 297 U.S. 278 (1936).

159. *State v. George*, 5 Jones 233 (N.C. 1858). According to Schafer, *Slavery*, 65–74, Louisiana treated criminal slaves more harshly, often allowing coerced confessions to stand. Morris, *Southern Slavery*, 244, also discussed coerced confessions.

160. *Robinson v. City Comrs.*, 12 Md. 132 (1858); *McDowell v. Couch*, 6 La. An. 365 (1851) (the Louisiana legislature had earlier passed acts authorizing payment for slaves sentenced to life in prison and slaves killed while running away); *Hamilton v. Auditor*, 14 B. Mon. 103 (1853); *Kelly v.*

Charleston, 4 Rich. 426, 435 (S.C. 1851) (Chapter 5 discussed governmental defendants in greater detail). The slaveowner's argument in *McDowell* resembles that used by Amy's owner in *U.S. v. Amy,* discussed in Chapter 5. In a case with facts similar to those of *Kelly* but with a private defendant, a third-party insurer did not have to pay for slaves who had starved themselves to death after an insurrection aboard ship failed. *McCargo v. New Orl. Ins. Co.,* 10 Rob. 202 (La. 1845). According to the policy, the company did not have to pay off if a mutiny occurred; the slaves died as a result of their reaction to the failed mutiny.

161. *Comw v. Tyree,* 2 Va. Ca. 262 (1821).

8. REFLECTING THE FELT NECESSITIES OF THE TIME

1. Oliver W. Holmes, Jr., *The Common Law* (Boston: Little, Brown, 1881), lecture 1.

2. Lawrence Friedman has emphasized that society creates its own laws; one of his critics cogently pointed out that laws mold society as well. Friedman, *History of American Law* and *Crime and Punishment;* "Mirror, Mirror, on the Wall," *Harvard Law Review* 107 (1994). Also see Mark V. Tushnet, "Perspectives on the Development of the American Law: A Critical Review of Friedman's 'A History of American Law,'" *Wisconsin Law Review* 1977 (1977).

3. Some states' laws treated slaves as real estate or immovables rather than as chattels, at least during part of the antebellum period. Because slaves often worked the land, classifying the two types of property in the same way could have kept plantations intact. This work focuses on property/person distinctions rather than on the subtleties of chattel and real estate law. Differences in treatment of chattel and realty mattered mostly for debt and inheritance purposes. For discussion, see Schafer, *Slavery,* 8 and 26; Elkins, *Slavery,* 50; Wiecek, "Statutory Law"; and Morris, *Southern Slavery.*

4. Extensions of my work could delve more deeply into the contrasts between Northern and Southern law, and the particular characteristics of trial-court cases and maritime cases.

5. More generally, Tennessee and Kentucky courts tended to adhere to the idea that kinder treatment led to more productive slaves, whereas courts in the lower South tended to the reverse. The Alabama courts seemed kinder to slaves than neighboring states' courts. Schiller, "Conflicting Obligations," 1241, claimed that the North Carolina courts "humanized" slaves and steered away from proslavery rhetoric. Craven, *The Coming,* 114, said that newer states tended to be harsher than older ones. Differences occurred even within states, especially South Carolina, which did not establish a Court of Appeals until 1859 or a Supreme Court until 1868. Louisiana of course differed in having a civil-law rather than a common-law tradition. But Schafer, *Slavery,* maintained that Louisiana law as practiced differed little from that in other states by the time of the Civil War.

6. For more background, see Patrick S. Brady, "Slavery, Race, and the Criminal Law in Antebellum North Carolina: A Reconsideration of the Thomas Ruffin Court," *North Carolina Central Law Journal* 10 (Spring 1979); A.E. Keir Nash, "Negro Rights, Unionism, and Greatness in the South Carolina Court of Appeals: The Extraordinary Chief Justice John Belton O'Neall," *South Carolina Law Review* 21 (1969); and Mason W. Stephenson and D. Grier Stephenson, "'To Protect and Defend': Joseph Henry Lumpkin, The Supreme Court of Georgia, and Slavery," *Emory Law Journal* 25 (1976). A.E. Keir Nash, "Reason of Slavery: Understanding the Judicial Role in the Peculiar Institution," *Vanderbilt Law Review* 32 (January 1979), also discussed various Southern judges.

7. In fact, regional differences between North and South are perhaps more marked than any variations across Southern states. North and South had distinct laws of sales; the North acted earlier than the South in establishing anticruelty laws and workers' compensation laws; and the South, particularly Texas, clung to arguments for acquittal by self-defense far longer than the North did.

8. See, for example, Conrad and Meyer, *Economics of Slavery*; Fogel and Engerman, *Time on the Cross*; Aitken, *Did Slavery Pay?*; David et al., *Reckoning with Slavery*; Barzel, "An Economic Analysis"; and Wright, *Old South, New South*.

9. Llewellyn, *The Bramble Bush*, 14.

10. Apart from acting as agents of the state, the judiciary had a personal stake in maintaining slavery. Ralph A. Wooster, *Politicians, Planters, and Plain Folk: Courthouse and Statehouse in the Upper South 1850–60* (Knoxville: University of Tennessee Press, 1975), esp. table 12 and supp. table 8, listed numerous influential judges and legislators as slaveholders. Fede, "Legal Protection," 356, noted that state courts and legislatures were populated with those sympathetic to slaveholders. Harper, "Slavery Without Cotton," 90, wrote that many city officers and justices were slaveowners. More specifically, Oakes, *Ruling Race*, 144, reported that, of magistrate-level judges in Kentucky, three-quarters were slaveholders, although only one-third of the population held slaves. All Southern governors between 1850 and 1860 were slaveholders; so was the majority of legislators (except in Missouri and Arkansas) and lawyers. From 1789 to 1861, twenty of the thirty-five Supreme Court justices were Southern; the antebellum Court always had a Southern majority. In addition, for forty-nine of those seventy-two years, the U.S. President was Southern – and a slaveholder. James M. McPherson, *Abraham Lincoln and the Second American Revolution* (New York: Oxford University Press, 1991).

11. Some undoubtedly tried to distance themselves from their brothers in chains: "[T]he distinguishing characteristics of the different species of the human race are so visibly marked, that those species may be readily discriminated from each other by inspection." *Hook v. Pagee*, 2 Munf. 379, 386 (Va. 1811). One only hopes that, some day, no one will subscribe to the *dicta* in *Pendleton v. State*, 6 Ark. 509, 512 (1846): "The two races differing as they do in complexion, habits, conformation and

intellectual endowments, could not nor ever will live together upon terms of social or political equality."

12. Benjamin N. Cardozo, *The Nature of the Judicial Process* (New Haven: Yale University Press, 1921), 168, 174. Many have pondered the motives of judges. Elkins, *Slavery*, 58, said that the courts' primary objective was to protect the pecuniary interest of the slaveowners. Fehrenbacher, *Slavery, Law, and Politics*, 177, in his discussion of the Dred Scott case, agreed that the right of property was barren if not sustained by the judiciary. Cover, *Justice Accused*, 171, on the other hand, viewed judges' decision-making more from a psychological viewpoint. Cover was criticized by Ronald M. Dworkin, "The Law of the Slave Catchers," *Times Literary Supplement* (Dec. 5, 1978), and Derrick A. Bell, Jr., "Book Review: Justice Accused," *Columbia Law Review* 76 (March 1976). See also Anthony J. Sebok, "Judging the Fugitive Slave Acts," *Yale Law Journal* 100 (April 1991). Tushnet, *American Law*, 28ff, suggested that judges, like other people, must make the world coherent. Morris, *Southern Slavery*, chap. 9, surmised that judges balance a formal rationality with the values present in their particular community.

13. Slave law may have indirectly worked to protect free persons, as previous chapters have noted. For example, slave law may have helped improve safety conditions for all workers, and the last-clear-chance rule may have promoted greater care on the part of railroad engineers.

14. Southerners certainly wrote opinions and treatises on various types of disputes, but they are remembered principally for their shaping of slave law, as Paul Finkelman has noted. Finkelman, "Exploring Southern Legal History." My research shows that Southern judges used sophisticated reasoning and economic concepts in thinking through slave law. This view contrasts with that of people who may consider the antebellum South a backward, essentially precapitalist society that recoiled at the idea of slavery as an economic institution. Yet it is true that, because Southern judges spent so much time on slave law, they left less time for other disputes. As a result, they figured less directly in resolving other major economic issues of the day.

15. Hinton R. Helper, *The Impending Crisis* (New York: Putnam's, 1960).

Index

Court cases described in the text appear in the index with a text page number; if the text omits the case name, endnote page and note numbers also appear in parentheses. Court cases mentioned only in the endnotes do not appear in the index.

abandonment: of criminal slaves to the state, 170; of wives and children, 152–3
abolition, *see* emancipation of slaves by federal government
abolitionists, 156, 239 n76
Adams, Charles Francis, 18
adverse selection, 6, 7, 16, 28, 39, 48, 58, 62, 71, 83, 101, 104, 118, 145; definition of, 184 n14
agents, duties of, 45; *see also* *respondeat superior*; slaves, agency of
Allain v. Young, 126 (233 n22)
Allen v. Freeland, 45
Allison v. R.R., 60, 66
Alston v. Balls, 53 (206 n19)
Altveter v. Baltimore, 107 (227 n23)
Am. Col. Soc. v. Gartrell, 160 (252 n99)
American Society for the Prevention of Cruelty to Animals, 151, 155
animals: accidents involving, 10, 15, 57–8, 83–4, 85–6; cruelty to, 17, 33, 64–5, 126, 129, 151, 167; fencing rules for, 85–6, 124; governmental immunity and injury to, 104, 108, 109; law of common carriers and, 83–4, 85–6; law of hiring and, 57–8, 64–5; law of sales and, 28, 31–3, 36, 38, 40–1, 46; responsibility for, 147, 149, 166–7; theft of, 65, 134, 237 n57; *see also* chattels, differences between slaves and other; dogs

appellate cases, usefulness of, 22–4
Arkadelphia Lumber Co. v. Bethea, 65 (212 n61)
Arnandez v. Lawes, 123, 127
assaults involving only unrelated free persons, 11, 107, 109–10, 115, 131–2
assumption of risk: by nonslave passengers, 84; by nonslave workers, 10, 58, 74–6; by slaveowners, 69–71
Audige v. Gaillard, 121 (230 n3)
Augusta Factory v. Barnes, 68 (213 n74)
Austin v. Miller, 58 (208 n30)
Aycock v. R.R., 88 (218 n36)
Ayres v. Parks, 30
Ayers v. State, 125 (231 n15)

Bacon v. Comw., 134 (237 n54)
Badillo v. Tio, 140–1 (240 n81)
bailment, 76, 184 n15
Baker v. Bolton, 11
Baker v. Tabor, 161 (252 n106)
Baker v. Wise, 97
Bakewell v. Talbot, 140 (239 n77)
Banfield v. Bruton, 38 (199 n47)
Barney v. Bush, 165 (256 n128)
Baum v. Stevens, 31 (195 n13)
Bayon v. Prevost, 140 (239 n77)
Belding v. Johnson, 137 (238 n68)
Belfour v. Raney, 140 (240 n78)
Bell v. Bowen, 56 (207 n25)
Bell v. Chambers, 96 (221 n81)

transactions costs, 14–5, 67; *see also* North, Douglass
trespassing: by animals, 15, 16, 86, 124, 166, 167; by free persons, 9, 11, 16, 18, 91–3, 124–5; by slaves, 16, 86–90, 95–6, 122–4
Trotter v. Blocker, 161 (252 n101)
Trustees v. Hall, 149 (244 n37)
Tudor v. Lewis, 108 (227 n26)
Turner, Nat, 150
Turner v. Huggins, 36 (198 n39)
Turner v. Johnson, 1, 33 (197 n28)
Turner v. State, 154 (247 n66)
Turner v. Carter, 109 (228 n33)
Tyson v. Ewing, 53 (206 n19)

Uniform Commercial Code, 17, 193 n2
Univ. v. Cambreling, 158 (251 n90)
U.S. v. Amy, 105 (226 n17)
U.S. v. Cross, 150 (244 n41)
U.S. v. Lloyd, 151 (245 n45)

value of life, 11, 15, 18, 51, 125, 131
Venning v. Gantt, 35 (198 n33)
Vesey, Denmark, 150
voluntary enslavement, statutes concerning, 163
Voss v. Howard, 140 (240 n78)

Waddill v. Martin, 157–8
wage premiums: for risk of injury, 7, 14, 49, 50–2, 54, 56–7, 69–71, 72; for risk of slave escape, 7, 53, 71
Wagner v. Woolsey, 122 (231 n4)
Walker v. Bolling, 69
Walker v. Cuculla, 38 (199 n45)
Walker v. Hays, 42
Walker v. Spullock, 67
Wallace v. Spullock, 96 (221 n81)
warranties, *see* sale of slaves, and warranties
Washington v. Emery, 158 (250 n86)
Watson v. Boatwright, 5 (183 n12)
Way, Peter, 50
Western v. Pollard, 54 (206 n20)
Whidby v. Lewis, 89 (219 n37)
White v. Harmond, 56 (207 n25)
White v. Hill, 41 (201 n61)
White v. Ross, 149–50 (244 n40)

White v. Slatter, 30 (195 n11)
Whitfield v. Paris, 104 (225 n15)
Whitson v. Gray, 38 (199 n47)
Wigle v. Kirby, 162 (252 n107)
Wiley v. Parmer, 164 (255 n125)
Willard v. Stevens, 38 (199 n48)
Williams, Jack, 132
Williams, Judge Rufus, 105
Williams' Case, 32 (196 n21)
Williams v. Fambro, 117 (230 n55)
Williams v. Howard, 45–6 (203 n73)
Williams v. Taylor, 70 (214 n81)
Williams v. Vance, 40 (200 n57)
Williamson v. Norton, 96 (221 n81)
Willis v. Harris, 54 (206 n20)
wills, *see* executors and administrators; inheritance; life estate; manumission, by will; remaindermen
Wilmot Proviso, 94
Wilson v. Bossier, 116 (230 n54)
Wilson v. Comw., 137 (238 n69)
Wilson v. R.R. (Ky.), 74 (215 n87)
Wilson v. R.R. (S.C.), 86 (217 n28)
Wilson v. Shackleford, 36 (198 n38)
Wilson v. State, 134 (237 n55)
Winnegar's Adm'r v. R.R., 168 (258 n148)
Wise v. Freshly, 54–5 (207 n23)
Withers v. Coyles, 108 (227 n26)
Witsell v. Earnest, 113 (229 n47)
women: and cruelty by husbands, 17, 144, 152–4; protection of, 18, 144, 155–7; rights of, 99, 151–2, 159; *see also* dower; fraudulent conveyance; rape, marital
Wood, Horace, 166
Worheide v. Mo. Car and Foundry, 75 (215 n89)
workers: accidents involving nonslave, 14, 18, 51–2, 65–9, 74–6, 92; *see also* assumption of risk, by nonslave workers; assumption of risk, by slaveowners; contributory negligence, of nonslave workers; contributory negligence, of slaves; fellow-servant rule; hirers of free persons; hirers of slaves; hiring of slaves; labor movement; servants; wage premiums; workers' compensation

DATE DUE